THE HORROR HITS OF RICHARD GORDON

TOM WEAVER

The Horror Hits of Richard Gordon
© 2011 Tom Weaver. All Rights Reserved.

No part of this book may be reproduced in any form or by any means, electronic, mechanical, digital, photocopying or recording, except for the inclusion in a review, without permission in writing from the publisher.

Published in the USA by:
BearManor Media
PO Box 1129
Duncan, Oklahoma 73534-1129
www.bearmanormedia.com

ISBN 978-1-59393-641-9

Printed in the United States of America.
Cover design by Marty Baumann. *Marty's credits include work for Pixar Animation Studios, Walt Disney Pictures, Hasbro and Universal Studios. Please visit his website at* www.martybaumann.com.
Book design by Brian Pearce | Red Jacket Press.

TABLE OF CONTENTS

A Foreword from the Publisher 7

Introduction by Robin Askwith 11

The "Forgotten" Films of Richard Gordon 14

The Haunted Strangler (1958) 22

Fiend Without a Face (1958) 42

First Man Into Space (1959) 64

Corridors of Blood (1962) 80

Devil Doll (1964) and *Curse of the Voodoo* (1965) 96

Island of Terror, *The Projected Man* and *Naked Evil* (1966) 120

Secrets of Sex (1970) 144

Tower of Evil (1972) 158

Horror Hospital (1973) 174

The Cat and the Canary (1978) 190

Inseminoid (1981) 212

Index 229

THANK YOU!: Robin Askwith, Marty Baumann, Robert J. Kiss, Tim and Donna Lucas, Greg Mank, Mark Martucci, Dave McDonnell, Sam Sherman, Frederick E. Smith, Tony Timpone and Norman J. Warren.

A FOREWORD FROM THE PUBLISHER

In a perfect world there would be a Mount Rushmore of Horror, with the faces of all the principal architects of the horror movie genre. It would be dominated by the great pioneers of the silent era and the Golden Age, but there should also be room for at least one relative latecomer, Richard Gordon, who has been devoted to the genre since boyhood. In the 1940s, when still in his early 20s, he moved from fan to pro, establishing himself in the movie distribution business; and by the '50s he was working as a movie producer. He began with crime pictures but in 1957, with the Boris Karloff vehicle *The Haunted Strangler*, he segued into horror. He's produced quite a few pictures in the following quarter-century, but in all that time and all those subsequent movies, there has been only *one* brief detour outside the horror genre (a 1958 spy drama called *The Secret Man*). All of the other 13 (yes, 13!) films have been fright flicks, bringing to the screen brain-sucking Fiends and bone-sucking Silicates, cats and canaries, aliens, a mummy, a devil doll and other outlandish horrors. A movie-crazy boy with a dream had become a producer with a formidable legacy.

As Tim Lucas of *Video Watchdog* magazine once pointed out, people like Francois Truffaut, Martin Scorsese and Quentin Tarantino often get the credit, but Richard and his older brother Alex Gordon (1922-2003) were possibly the very first movie buffs to rise to the occupation of producer. As boys, they lived in the Hampstead suburb of London, supported by a father who imported plastics. The family would go to the movies every Saturday or Sunday; as soon as they were old enough, Richard and Alex also began going on their own.

Richard and Alex always had ambitions that were always directed towards the film industry. While still at school, Richard wrote articles on the cinema, edited fan club magazines and organized a film society; he continued some of these activities on a limited basis even during his World War II service in the British

Richard and Alex Gordon.

Royal Navy (1944-46). Following the war's end, the Brothers Gordon both landed jobs in the film industry, on the distribution side, in London. But conditions in England at that time were still so harsh (rationing, power cuts, etc.) that they began to feel that, career-wise, they would be better off shifting their talents to the American scene. With the encouragement of their father, they emigrated to New York at the end of 1947; and in 1949, at the amazing age of 23, Richard hung out his **Gordon Films Inc.** shingle and began representing British and other foreign film producers in securing distribution for the product in the U.S., and exporting independent American products overseas.

In 1956, in association with New Yorker Charles Vetter Jr., Richard formed Amalgamated Productions and embarked on a program of crime dramas made in England with Hollywood stars, among them Pat O'Brien, Richard Denning, Wayne Morris, Zachary Scott and Keefe Brasselle. Richard himself writes about these early credits on the following pages in the essay "The 'Forgotten' Films of Richard Gordon"; and then we are treated to a series of interviews (conducted by Tom Weaver) in which Richard discusses the details of every one of his subsequent, highly successful horror productions.

BearManor is privileged to bring you, in his own words, the story of the monster-mad career of living legend Richard Gordon. We think it will thrill you. It *may* shock you. So if any of you feel that you do not care to subject your nerves to such a strain, now is your chance to…

Well…we *warned* you…

INTRODUCTION BY ROBIN ASKWITH

Producers on a film set mean one of the following:

i. Everyone is fired.

ii. They've run out of money.

iii. To complete the film, everyone must take a 50 percent cut.

iv. They've come to sack the director.

v. Urgent business on set coinciding with a sex/nudity scene.

vi. Attractive actress/actor on set.

vii. Lost his way to restaurant.

viii. Free kipper rolls and a cup of polystyrene coffee.

None of the above apply to Richard Gordon. I was lucky enough to work with Dick on two feature films, *Tower of Evil* [1972] and *Horror Hospital* [1973]. We have, to this day, remained friends, which spans some 40 years now; and, very much like me, he is aging backwards! The curious case of Richard Gordon indeed!

In fact, Dick was always on the set. Somehow he made himself an integral part of the crew. Paradoxically, you might say, "Isn't a film producer part of the crew?" Well, no, not really. He is more like a chairman or owner of a football or baseball team, with the coach being the director. The wrong type of an opinionated producer's interference can cause havoc and the ultimate demise of a film.

I have made more than 40 feature films and it has not been unusual for the producer and director to be at loggerheads. If you know that I have worked with the likes of Pasolini, Zeffirelli and Lindsay Anderson, you'll know what I mean! To be honest, I would have been deeply worried if Dick hadn't been on the set. A

Listen up, mate! Robin Askwith wants you to know a thing or two about his friend Richard Gordon.

Dick Gordon film was just that — an axiom — it was a Dick Gordon film.

This is not to say he was dictatorial in any way. He just seemed to create a healthy, happy "calm" on set, which was a major plus.

Horror Hospital was a great example of this. Antony Balch, now sadly deceased, was the inspiration and director. Dick encouraged Antony in every way, without being too artistically involved. I'm not sure how he does this but it is a gift and I'm only sorry that Dick didn't make many more feature films. Perhaps therein lies the answer: They wouldn't have been special to him and he might have lost that effortless work ethic.

Dick chooses his friends equally carefully and he unconditionally stands by them. We met recently at a film festival in England where we both had to speak. Always our meetings are incident-prone! To save any expensive legal fees, you'll have to use your imagination; or, if you want further insight, read on in this excellent book. Or purchase the new, digitally remastered DVD of *Horror Hospital* and listen to Dick's outrageous commentary, encouraged by one Tom Weaver!

What a pleasure it has all been and will continue to be…

Robin Askwith
March 2011

THE "FORGOTTEN" FILMS OF RICHARD GORDON

In this essay by Richard Gordon, he recalls the seven crime films he co-produced in the mid-1950s, before horror and science fiction moviemaking became his specialty.

I have often been asked how I was able to start a production company of my own (Producers Associates Ltd.) in England in 1957 and make *The Haunted Strangler* (known in the U.K. as *Grip of the Strangler*) starring Boris Karloff as its first film. The answer is that my brother Alex and I had met Karloff shortly after our arrival from England when he was starring on the New York stage in J.B. Priestley's *The Linden Tree* and, soon after, again when he returned to the stage in Edward Percy's *The Shop at Sly Corner*. At that time, Alex and I interviewed him for several English fan magazines to which we were sending articles from the United States.

Boris and his wife Evie maintained a New York apartment because of his frequent trips to New York for stage and television work and we struck up a friendship and met from time to time. He knew of my ambition to get into film production, and one day he handed me a story called *Strangle Hold* which had been written as a vehicle for him by an English writer, Jan Read. He suggested that I read it and, if I liked it and would be interested to try and set it up as a production in England, he would be willing to come over to London to star in it.

When he offered me *Strangle Hold* in 1957, I had already been involved for a year in setting up a series of British co-productions with several different independent production companies in order to learn the business more thoroughly. The mid-1950s was a busy period for film production in England after years of wartime restrictions which the government finally withdrew. In fact, the government became directly involved in the industry not only with financing but also with new legislation in favor of the production of domestic (British) films. In addition to a quota system requiring every cinema in England to show a certain

Young Richard Gordon (right) not only helped to arrange American financing and distribution for *A Christmas Carol* (1951), he also attended a Museum of Modern Art charity performance along with Basil Rathbone (left) and two British Embassy representatives.

percentage of domestic product each year, it introduced a levy on box office receipts which was distributed to, and shared by, the makers of British films. This was known as the Eady Plan, so named after the minister who devised it. The Eady Plan money constituted a particular boon to second features which generally played on the circuits in support of major Hollywood product. It resulted in many of the American studios transferring production of their second features to England in order to participate in the benefits and created a highly competitive market.

To take advantage of all this activity, I formed a New York company called Amalgamated Productions Inc. in partnership with Charles F. "Chuck" Vetter Jr. Chuck owned and operated a New York City studio called Motion Picture Stages at 3 East 57th Street, between Madison and Fifth; mainly it was commercials that were shot there. We had met when he negotiated the American distribution rights for a British film that I was representing, and we got on well together. We both agreed to travel back and forth between New York and London as needed, and I was able to arrange a modest line of financing with Chemical Bank in New York, and also with Pathe Laboratories, to whom we guaranteed the American lab work for the films we intended to produce.

Amalgamated produced seven feature films during a period of 12 months as co-productions with different British independent companies. My brother Alex, who had meanwhile established himself as a producer in Hollywood at American International Pictures, agreed to help us obtain the Hollywood actors that we wanted to bring to England to play leading roles, and sometimes he was also able to offer us properties that had been submitted to AIP but were turned down by Jim Nicholson and Sam Arkoff, and which Alex thought might be suitable to be rewritten for production overseas.

Amalgamated's first British co-production was with Butcher's Film Distributors, an independent company that I was already representing in the U.S. Butcher's had a releasing arrangement with the Rank Organisation in the U.K. that guaranteed us good results there.

Gordon cooked up the idea to make *Mother Riley Meets the Vampire* (1952), which starred his friend Bela Lugosi and cross-dressing comic Arthur Lucan (right).

We bought the film rights to the Lindsay Hardy novel *Requiem for a Redhead*, a crime story set against the background of the Cold War, and in April 1956 we produced it under the title *Assignment Redhead*. With Alex's help I had signed Richard Denning and Carole Mathews to come to England to play the leads. Denning had been a star at Paramount, where his films included *Beyond the Blue Horizon* (1942) with Dorothy Lamour. He played the leading role in three of Alex's films, including *Day the World Ended* (1956) which Roger Corman directed. Carole Mathews had also made many films in Hollywood. We produced our feature as a British Quota film for under £15,000 plus the salaries and expenses of the American participants. I decided to call it *Million Dollar Manhunt* for its American release.

Our second picture was *The Crooked Sky* (1957), from an original screenplay on which Chuck Vetter collaborated. For this thriller about international smugglers, we teamed with independent English producer Bill Luckwell. To play the hero, I signed up Wayne Morris in Hollywood, who had already made a film in England [*The Gelignite Gang*, aka *The Dynamiters*, 1956] and enjoyed it. I had always liked him for his tough-guy roles at Warner Brothers, where he started with the boxing melodrama *Kid Galahad* (1937) with Bette Davis, Humphrey Bogart and Edward G. Robinson. He was very cooperative, his happy-go-lucky approach to his work making him a favorite with our production unit. For the feminine lead, Alex put me in touch with Karin Booth, who was doing well in Hollywood and liked the idea of a trip to England, which she regarded as a sort of holiday. Through Luckwell, we signed Anton Diffring to play the villain.

With two films in the can, I looked for a more ambitious project as our third production. George Minter of Renown Pictures was getting ready to do *Kill Me Tomorrow* (1957), a gangster story with a newspaper background, and Terence Fisher had agreed to direct it. The film needed a bigger American star, and Alex told me that he could persuade Pat O'Brien to come over to play the leading part. To me, this was exciting news: The newspaper reporter in *Kill Me Tomorrow* was just the

As a producer, Gordon's first film was *Assignment Redhead* (1956), a collaboration with Butcher's Film Distributors. In this shot, Butcher's bosses Jack Phillips (left) and William G. Chalmers (right) flank Gordon and the movie's stars Carole Mathews and Richard Denning.

kind of character he had frequently played in Hollywood. His salary was going to be considerably higher than we had paid previously, so I compensated by hiring as the female lead a Canadian actress who was already living in London, Lois Maxwell; that saved us the expenses of round-trip airfare and so on. Lois later became famous as the James Bond series' first Miss Moneypenny. George Coulouris, who was also living in England, accepted the role of the chief villain. George Minter arranged for a cameo appearance by a young English rock'n'roll singer who was beginning to make a name for himself in London's coffee bars and nightclubs. His name was Tommy Steele. Not long after *Kill Me Tomorrow* he became an overnight sensation on the London stage and then was signed by a major studio in Hollywood. Pat O'Brien was happy to play the crime reporter hero and gave us no problems. I had been warned about his drinking but there was no sign of it during our production.

It was now time to arrange for American distribution of our first three productions, and I made a deal with Tudor Pictures, an independent distributor of long standing with good theater circuit connections. Meanwhile, Bill Luckwell proposed we do another film together, *West of Suez* (1957). The story revolved around an American explosives expert who is recruited by smugglers to assassinate an Arab leader during a visit to London. It was an ideal role for Keefe Brasselle, with whom I had become friends in New York. Keefe had grown up in Hollywood where he started in show business as a singer, drummer and comedian with a touring orchestra. During World War II he served in the Army Air Corps and directed several stage shows. He returned to Hollywood and played supporting roles until he was discovered by Ida Lupino; he then starred in many different films including *The Eddie Cantor Story* (1953) in which he played the title role. Keefe was now looking for a deal to star in a film and also direct. He gladly accepted my proposal to do *West of Suez* but unfortunately, when we arrived in London, the British trade union would not give him a

Gordon's early crime flicks had a good bit of the history of Warner Brothers passing through their sets: Zachary Scott, Wayne Morris and, seen here, Pat O'Brien inking his contract for *Kill Me Tomorrow*. Left-right, Charles Vetter Jr., O'Brien, Gordon.

permit to direct. I had to bring in an English standby director, Arthur Crabtree. Some time later, Keefe was able to get his permit and made a second film of his own choosing that he also directed, *Death Over My Shoulder* (1958).

In the opening sequence of *West of Suez*, Keefe's character is seen fighting an out-of-control fire on a Middle Eastern oil field. There was no way that we could film such a stunt on our budget, so I made a deal with Paramount in Hollywood for stock footage from their Richard Arlen picture *Wildcat* (1942). When you see Keefe's character fighting the fire in our film, it's actually Richard Arlen. Or *his* double!

West of Suez, which I retitled *The Fighting Wildcats*, turned out so well that I wanted major distribution in America. Republic Pictures of Hollywood at that time maintained a London office to oversee its international activities; that office was managed by Gerald A. Fernback, a seasoned film executive. I invited him to screen our finished film, and he liked it. He recommended it for his studio to distribute in the United States, and I closed the deal with Republic in Hollywood. Keefe Brasselle often referred to *The Fighting Wildcats* as one of his favorite experiences.

I next made a deal to do three pictures in partnership with Nat Cohen's company Anglo Amalgamated Film Distributors, which was already making films in collaboration with AIP as well as producing its own more prestigious pictures. Our first joint venture was *The Counterfeit Plan* (1957), an exciting thriller by James Eastwood about a convict in a French prison who escapes to England and sets up a criminal operation. Intended for top-of-the-bill release, *The Counterfeit Plan* needed an important American star. I was introduced in Hollywood to Zachary Scott, who by then had left Warner Brothers after a long-term agreement that started with *The Mask of Dimitrios* (1944) and included a co-starring role with Joan Crawford in *Mildred Pierce* (1945). Scott's wife Ruth Ford had also been a Warners actress and had stage experience. They liked the idea of coming to England where they hoped to co-star in a play on the London stage.

Nat Cohen was delighted to have Scott in *The Counterfeit Plan*. I also brought over Peggie Castle for the feminine lead. Anglo assembled a very strong British supporting cast including Mervyn Johns (one of the stars of the English classic horror film *Dead of Night* [1945]) and Lee Patterson. The production was based at Merton Park Studios, which was in a suburb of London, and Montgomery Tully was the director.

The film turned out so well that we decided to offer it to Warner Brothers for U.S. distribution. I ran it in New York for Ben Kalmenson, Warners' sales manager, and they bought the rights. Anglo released it in the U.K. where it played as top feature on a major circuit, so it was very successful for us all.

We decided with Zachary Scott to do another picture together and Anglo suggested a screenplay called *Man in the Shadow* that had been written for them by a woman named Maisie Sharman using the pseudonym "Stratford Davis." I brought Faith Domergue from Hollywood to co-star with Scott. She had been discovered by Howard Hughes who starred her in a big film called *Vendetta* (1950). *Man in the Shadow* (1957) was an unusual thriller that required some location shooting in Italy. In the U.S., its title was changed to *Violent Stranger* as Universal had just released a film called *Man in the Shadow* with Orson Welles.

Unfortunately, *Man in the Shadow* did not turn out as well as *The Counterfeit Plan* although it was also directed by Montgomery Tully. The original story was quite complex but something was lost in its transfer to the screen. It also went over budget. I could not get the kind of distribution it needed in America so eventually I sold it directly to television. Meanwhile, Scott and his wife Ruth did appear on the stage at the Royal Court Theatre in London in the William Faulkner play *Requiem for a Nun*.

Our third picture in partnership with Anglo was *Escapement* (1958), based on the Charles Eric Maine novel of the same name. It was a thriller with science fiction overtones, set entirely on the French Riviera. This time I brought over Rod Cameron and Mary Murphy, who had been Marlon Brando's leading lady in *The Wild One* (1953). I would also have preferred an American director but it was too costly and Anglo wanted Montgomery Tully again. We had a good supporting cast including Meredith Edwards, Peter Illing and Carl Jaffe. There were major problems with the special effects. Also, Anglo did not want it to get an X Certificate in England, and I wanted more horror for the United States. The compromise was unsatisfactory and I could not afford any re-shooting in America.

Rod Cameron was a veteran of Hollywood action pictures including Westerns, serials and every kind of melodrama. In 1965, Alex starred him in two Technicolor Westerns that he produced, *Requiem for a Gunfighter* and *The Bounty Killer*, and a year later I was able to get him a leading role in a Western that Columbia made in Yugoslavia, *Thunder at the Border*.

I retitled the film *The Electronic Monster* and Columbia agreed to release it provided I could supply a second feature for the double bill. I found a 1958 British horror film called *Womaneater* with George Coulouris and Vera Day that had not yet been sold in America and I was able to buy it for Columbia. The program did well enough when it played in theaters like those where AIP was releasing its double bills but it did not pay off until Columbia's license expired and I was able to take back the two pictures for independent reissue and the sale of television rights.

While supervising our co-productions, Chuck and I also bought a number of independently made British Quota second features which we re-licensed in the United States. At that time, there was still a shortage of feature films for the TV market as the major studios had not yet made their libraries available. We licensed one package of 13 British films to the actor Eddie Bracken, who had started a company called Bracken Productions, Inc., to produce TV series.

With seven pictures completed during 12 months, Chuck and I decided it was time to go on our own and we formed Producers Associates in London to make *The Haunted Strangler*. This was followed by *Fiend Without a Face* (1958) starring Marshall Thompson and a second Karloff film, *Corridors of Blood* (made in 1958, released in 1962). We also made two more films with Marshall, *The Secret Man* (1958) and *First Man Into Space* (1959). At that point, Chuck and I went our separate ways; he subsequently produced two films for MGM in England, *The Green Helmet* (1961), a racing melodrama starring Bill Travers, and *Battle Beneath the Earth* (1967), a Technicolor science fiction thriller starring Kerwin Mathews.

I continued in production with films including *Devil Doll* (1964), *Island of Terror*, *The Projected Man* (both 1966), *Tower of Evil* (1972) and *Horror Hospital* (1973). In 1977 I produced a new version of *The Cat and the Canary* and in 1980 I entered into a co-production deal with Shaw Brothers of Hong Kong to produce *Inseminoid*. These movies, and others, are extensively discussed in this volume.

Alex Gordon, his wife Ruth and Richard Gordon on the set of one of the Rod Cameron Westerns that Alex made at Paramount in 1965.

THE HAUNTED STRANGLER
1958

CREDITS

Executive Producers	*Richard Gordon* & *Charles Vetter Jr.*
Produced by	*John Croydon*
Directed by	*Robert Day*
Screenplay	*Jan Read* & *"John C. Cooper"* [*John Croydon*]
Original Story	*Jan Read*
Lighting Cameraman	*Lionel Banes*
Music Composed by	*Buxton Orr*
Music Conducted by	*Frederic Lewis*
Editor	*Peter Mayhew*
Set Designer	*John Elphick*
Special Effects	*Les Bowie*
Dress Supervisor	*Anna Duse*
Camera Operator	*Leo Rogers*
Assistant Director	*Douglas Hickox*
Sound Recordist	*H.C. Pearson*
Dubbing Editor	*Terry Poulton*
Makeup	*Jim Hydes*
Hairdresser	*Barbara Barnard*
Continuity	*Hazel Swift*

78 minutes

CAST

Boris Karloff	*James Rankin*
Jean Kent	*Cora Seth*
Elizabeth Allan	*Barbara Rankin*
Anthony Dawson	*Superintendent Burk*
Vera Day	*Pearl*
Tim Turner	*Dr. Kenneth McColl*
Diane Aubrey	*Lily Rankin*
Max Brimmell	*Turnkey*
Leslie Perrins	*Prison Governor*
Jessica Cairns	*Asylum Maid*
Dorothy Gordon	*Hannah*
Desmond Roberts	*Dr. Johnson*
Roy Russell	*Medical Superintendent*
Derek Birch	*Hospital Superintendent*
Peggy Ann Clifford	*Kate*
John Fabian	*Young Blood*
Joan Elvin	*Can-Can Girl*

Uncredited

Michael Atkinson	*Edward Styles*
George Hirste	*Lost Property Man*
John G. Heller, Arthur Mason	*Male Nurses*
George Spence	*Hangman*
Robert Day	*Cab Driver*
Paul Frees	*Narrator of U.S. Trailer*

SYNOPSIS

Newgate Prison, 1860: Hysterically proclaiming his innocence, one-armed Edward Styles is led past a jeering crowd to the gallows and hanged for the murder of Martha Stuart, just one of *five* girls he allegedly half-strangled and then slashed to death. Later, as the coffin of "The Haymarket Strangler" is being closed, autopsy surgeon Dr. Tenant slips his scalpel into the wooden box. That night, Tenant passes out at Styles' burial and is taken to a hospital.

Twenty years later, novelist James Rankin is a crusader on behalf of criminally accused men unable to afford an adequate legal defense; determined to force a change in the system, he intends to write a pamphlet proving that Styles was wrongly hanged for want of a lawyer. The social reformer's inquiries lead him to suspect that Dr. Tenant was actually responsible for the Haymarket Strangler murders. Rankin and his assistant Dr. McColl visit a notorious dive, The Judas Hole, and interview singer Cora, who had testified against Styles. What Cora tells Rankin makes him even more certain that Tenant was actually the Strangler. Rankin continues to fail in his attempts to learn the current whereabouts of Tenant, who went missing from the hospital not long after his graveside collapse.

Rankin becomes convinced that Tenant tried to rid himself of the compulsion to kill by discarding the knife that had become the symbol of the murders; and he feels that the only place it can be is in the coffin of Styles. Bribing a Newgate turnkey to let him into the cemetery by night, Rankin unearths the coffin and, amidst Styles' bones, finds the knife. But holding it triggers a fantastic transformation: His face contorts and his left side becomes paralyzed as Rankin changes into the beast-like Haymarket Strangler. A man with no memory of more than half his life, Rankin *is* the very man he has been seeking! Driven by a lust to kill, the Strangler makes his way to The Judas Hole. As Cora belts out a bawdy song on-stage, he sneaks into

Do-gooder Rankin (Boris Karloff), invading the prison cemetery to prove the innocence of Styles, eyeballs a four-footed friend.

the dressing room of Cora's protégé Pearl, choking and slashing her to death.

At his home, and "himself" again, Rankin gets his wife Barbara to admit the truth about his past (20 years earlier, she was a widow with a young baby, working as a hospital nurse; she fell in love with her patient Tenant and smuggled him away when she learned that he was going to be placed in an asylum). Rankin again becomes the Strangler and savagely murders Barbara.

Despite his confession, no one believes Rankin that he was the Haymarket Strangler or that he committed the new killings; but officials *do* think he's gone mad, and he ends up a straitjacketed inmate in a Coldbath Fields padded cell. Again he transforms, mutilating a guard and killing a maid as he makes his escape. At the Rankin home, he wrestles with McColl and then menaces Barbara's daughter Lily before the spell of madness passes. Rankin becomes consumed with the thought that he must return the knife to Styles' grave; but Newgate guards are lying in wait. At the command of the crooked turnkey, Rankin is shot and killed.

RICHARD GORDON ON *THE HAUNTED STRANGLER*

Q: In the mid-1950s, after co-producing a number of low-budget crime pictures, you segued to a much bigger production, *The Haunted Strangler*. But the story really begins almost 25 years earlier, when you first became a Boris Karloff fan as a kid.

RICHARD GORDON: My brother Alex and I became aware of Boris Karloff as a screen presence at a very young age, in the early 1930s. We used to read the British film magazines, the weeklies like *Film Weekly* and *Film Pictorial*, and they often had spreads on the horror films. We could read about Karloff but we could *not* see his films, because in England all the horror pictures he had made were rated "For Adults Only." Alex and I would have to wait until we were 16; until then, we would not be able to go into the theaters that showed them.

After reading and hearing about Karloff for a few years, the first time I actually got to see him on the screen was in the George Arliss film *The House of Rothschild* [1934], in which he played a non-horror role — although he *did* play what was tantamount to a villain. I thought he gave a mesmerizing performance which seemed to justify everything I had heard about him but hadn't yet seen on the screen. Certainly I never dreamed that I would one day meet him in person, let alone work with him, but these things don't telegraph themselves in advance.

Of his horror films, *The Invisible Ray* [1936] was the first I saw, because it was rated for general audiences; kids under 16 could see it if they were accompanied by an adult. Most of Karloff's early horror films I did *not* see until they were reissued in later years.

As a kid in 1930s England, Gordon wasn't allowed to see horror movies, so the first time he saw Boris Karloff on the screen, it was as the virulent anti-Semite Count Ledrantz in the George Arliss historical drama *The House of Rothschild*.

Q: When did you and Alex see his breakthrough picture *Frankenstein* [1931] for the first time?

GORDON: Alex saw it ahead of me: In the late 1930s, the reissue double-bill of *Frankenstein* and *Dracula* [1931] came to London and my parents took us to see it, but I couldn't get into the theater because I wasn't yet 16 years old. My parents and Alex went in to see the program, and I was sent to another theater nearby to see the film *Bringing Up Baby* [1938]. I first got to see *Frankenstein* a little later, when the program went out on re-release on the circuit. A school friend and

I saw it in an outlying theater where we were able to be sneaked in by a friend of his who was an usherette.

Q: When Alex told me what his three favorite Karloff films were, all three surprised me a little: *The Raven* [1935], *The Invisible Ray* and *The Old Dark House* [1932]. What are *your* three favorites?

GORDON: I would have to say the original *Frankenstein*. Second, *The Black Cat* [1934], in which he co-starred with Bela Lugosi; I thought that was a wonderfully entertaining and brilliantly made film. The third film, because of his very moving performance, and something so different from what he was usually doing at the time, is the film he made for Warner Brothers called *The Walking Dead* [1936], in which I think he gave an absolutely marvelous and heart-rending performance.

Q: Once you and Alex moved to New York in 1947, Karloff was one of the first actors you got to meet.

GORDON: One of the things that Alex and I began doing once we arrived here was writing articles for British fan magazines. We were interviewing whatever actors we could get a-hold of, people like Bela Lugosi, Chester Morris, Kay Francis, Richard Arlen and William Boyd who were in the New York area to appear in summer stock or promote a new movie or whatever. English fan magazines had offered us a deal: If we would interview some interesting Hollywood actors and send them the interviews, they would pay us a fee. Obviously at that point, Alex and I couldn't afford to go to Hollywood (or anywhere *else*); we could only interview people who were in New York or available in and around the local area. Karloff at the time was appearing in the Broadway play by J.B. Priestley called *The Linden Tree*. Priestley, incidentally, was also the author of *Benighted*, a novel which James Whale filmed in Hollywood many years earlier as *The Old Dark House*, with Boris Karloff.

Q: How did you arrange to get the Karloff interview?

GORDON: At this late date, I don't recall exactly how Alex and I went about it, whether we contacted Karloff's agent or perhaps even went backstage after *The Linden Tree* to congratulate him on his performance and ask Karloff himself. But the answer was yes, and arrangements were made for Alex and me to meet with him at the Meurice Hotel, the small hotel on 58th Street where he was then staying. He gave us a very good interview, and he also asked *us* about our backgrounds and why we were in New York. He showed an interest in what *we* were doing, so there was immediately more than just a reporter-interviewee atmosphere.

The Linden Tree was not a success [it ran from March 2 to March 6, 1948], but then some time later Karloff appeared again on the New York stage in another play, a British crime melodrama called *The Shop at Sly Corner* [January 18-22, 1949], which had already been made into a movie in England with Oscar Homolka. We contacted Karloff again at that time — he remembered us from the first encounter — and that's when we really established a sort of relationship that went beyond just getting an interview. In the early 1950s, Alex went on to Hollywood and I remained in New York, and I more or less tried to stay in touch with Karloff whenever I knew he was coming to New York, and we maintained a friendly relationship. Whenever he was here, we would get together once in a while for a drink or for coffee.

Q: Did you see him on Broadway in *Peter Pan* [1950-51]?

GORDON: No, unfortunately not, but I did see him some years later when he played the bishop in Jean Anouilh's play *The Lark* [1955-56], which was based on the trial of Joan of Arc, in which Julie Harris was the star. Karloff was *absolutely* mesmerizing as the bishop, and *so* different from anything that I had ever seen him do on the screen. He was really an extraordinarily versatile person, able to play almost *any* kind of a role for which his physique, his age and his background made him a contender.

So that was our situation: I used to see Karloff socially, we always managed to get together at odd times, and so the relationship continued until the *Haunted Strangler* opportunity came along.

Q: Now, one *more* tangent before we get into *Haunted Strangler*: In 1949 you formed Gordon Films Inc., a company you've maintained ever since, above and beyond your movie*making* activities. What did — and *does* — Gordon Films do?

GORDON: From the beginning, Gordon Films Inc. imported a number of British and other European films for theatrical and TV distribution in North

America. These were divided into two categories: prestige productions for major-studio distribution, and exploitation pictures in the horror and science fiction categories which were being made in Italy, France, Germany and elsewhere. Among the titles in the latter category, there was the Italian-French co-production *The Playgirls and the Vampire* [1960], the West German-Yugoslavian *Cave of the Living Dead* [1964] and the Italian *Tomb of Torture* [1963]. I supervised the making of the English-language-dubbed soundtracks and the means by which they were assigned to American distributors. Most of them had a considerable success.

Additionally, from time to time I was asked to collaborate with filmmakers, mostly in England, on prestigious films that required American participation, whether only financially or in order to include international casting. I was able to arrange for Hildegarde Neff to go on loan to England from 20th Century-Fox for a starring role in producer George Minter's *Svengali* [1954], which was subsequently distributed by MGM in America. [*Editor's note: Gordon extensively discusses his role in the making of* Svengali *in the book* I Talked with a Zombie *(McFarland, 2009) by Tom Weaver.*] I brought William Bendix to London to co-star in [director] Robert Siodmak's film version of Robin Maugham's novel *The Rough and the Smooth*; we released it in America as *Portrait of a Sinner* through AIP. I also arranged American financing and distribution for such British prestige pictures as *Scrooge* [U.S. title: *A Christmas Carol*, 1951] with Alastair Sim, *Tom Brown's Schooldays* [1951] with Robert Newton, *Our Girl Friday* [U.S. title: *The Adventures of Sadie*, 1953] with Joan Collins and other interesting titles.

A venture for which I had great hopes, that unfortunately did not materialize, was a film version of a hugely successful German play called *Des Teufels General* [The Devil's General]. The play was written by Carl Zuckmayer, whose career stretched back to Marlene Dietrich's *The Blue Angel* [1930], among other properties. Together with John Sutro, the British producer of films like *49th Parallel* [U.S. title: *The Invaders*, 1941], I brought an English translation to the London stage; it opened at the Savoy Theatre with Trevor Howard in the title role. It failed to generate an interested audience and, as a result, never made it to the United States although Van Heflin had shown an interest to play in it on Broadway. Sutro and I had also optioned the film rights and eventually we sold them to a German company that was very keen to make the film with Curt Jurgens. When their film [1955] was shown at the Venice Film Festival, Jurgens was awarded the prize of Best Actor of the Year, resulting in his being offered a contract by Universal in Hollywood which he accepted. I released *Des Teufels General* to art houses in North America.

Since the Hollywood picture *The Desert Fox* [1951] with James Mason as Rommel had been a success, I hoped to do an American remake of *Des Teufels General*.

Boris Karloff at home in his New York apartment building "The Dakota," where Gordon occasionally visited with him.

It never came to pass although various directors like Otto Preminger, Billy Wilder and Charles Vidor were all interested in becoming involved.

Q: Why wouldn't Hollywood bite?

GORDON: 20th Century-Fox had gotten a lot of unfavorable publicity over *The Desert Fox* and its sympathetic portrayal of Rommel; there were protests here and in other countries, some theaters cancelled their bookings and so on. So they didn't want to make another picture that might show someone connected with the Nazi party in any kind of heroic light. The story of *Des Teufels General*, incidentally, was based on a real-life figure, Ernst Udet, one of the most famous

German flying aces in the first World War. As you may remember, he appeared as himself in *S.O.S. Eisberg* [1933].

Q: Okay, now it's 1956 and, movie*making*-wise, you've only done the low-budget crime genre co-productions and you're getting restless.

GORDON: Yes, I felt it was time that I should start doing pictures on my own and forming my own British production company. Therefore I began looking for a vehicle and an opportunity with which to do it. Karloff knew of my ambitions to become a producer and to make my own films. One day during one of our get-togethers in Karloff's New York apartment, he told me that he had received a story titled *Strangle Hold* which was written especially for him by a writer-friend of his in England by the name of Jan Read. Aware of my interest in getting into production for myself, he suggested that I read the story, and he made me the proposal that if I could set it up for production in England, he would be willing to star in it. He also said I could use his name in trying to set it up.

Well, to use a clichéd phrase, that was an offer I couldn't refuse! I went into the thing whole-heartedly and immediately made plans to go to England. I negotiated a deal with Jan Read's literary agent, a very charming and interesting lady named Margery Vosper, to acquire an option on the story, and then set about making the arrangements to produce the film. Just as an aside, although perhaps his name won't mean much to many people today, Margery Vosper was the sister of Frank Vosper, who was in the '30s a leading British stage and screen actor. I knew of him from his films. He mysteriously disappeared from a French ocean liner crossing the Atlantic [in March 1937], and to this day, it has never been established whether he fell overboard or he was murdered or had an accident. He just disappeared, the body was never recovered, and it's one of the great unsolved mysteries of British theatrical history. Prior to my meeting with Margery, I had been alerted not to bring up the subject of Frank Vosper.

Industry veteran John Croydon worked as line producer and sometimes writer on the four Producers Associates thrillers (and later produced, co-wrote and partially directed Gordon's *The Projected Man*).

Even at that time, 20 years after his disappearance, it was still something she could not talk about.

Q: How difficult was it to mount your first solo production?

GORDON: It wasn't as difficult as I thought it might be because, first of all, we all agreed that it should be a medium-budget movie, and secondly, Boris Karloff's name was such that every English distributor that I approached showed an interest in doing the film. So fairly rapidly, I was able to set up a production. I formed Producers Associates Ltd. as my British company. Charles F. Vetter Jr., who had been my American partner in the earlier co-productions, joined me and we invited John Croydon to become a member of the board and to function as line producer for *The Haunted Strangler*. I then negotiated a deal with Eros Films Ltd., a very important English independent distributor, to participate in the financing in return for which they would receive the distribution rights for the United Kingdom. Eros Films, which was owned and operated by brothers Phil and Syd Hyams, also owned a number of cinemas in England; Phil and Syd suggested that we simultaneously produce a second film so that they would have a double-feature program to release. The second film we made was *Fiend Without a Face* [1958].

Q: According to *Haunted Strangler*'s on-screen credits, "Screenplay by Jan Read and John C. Cooper."

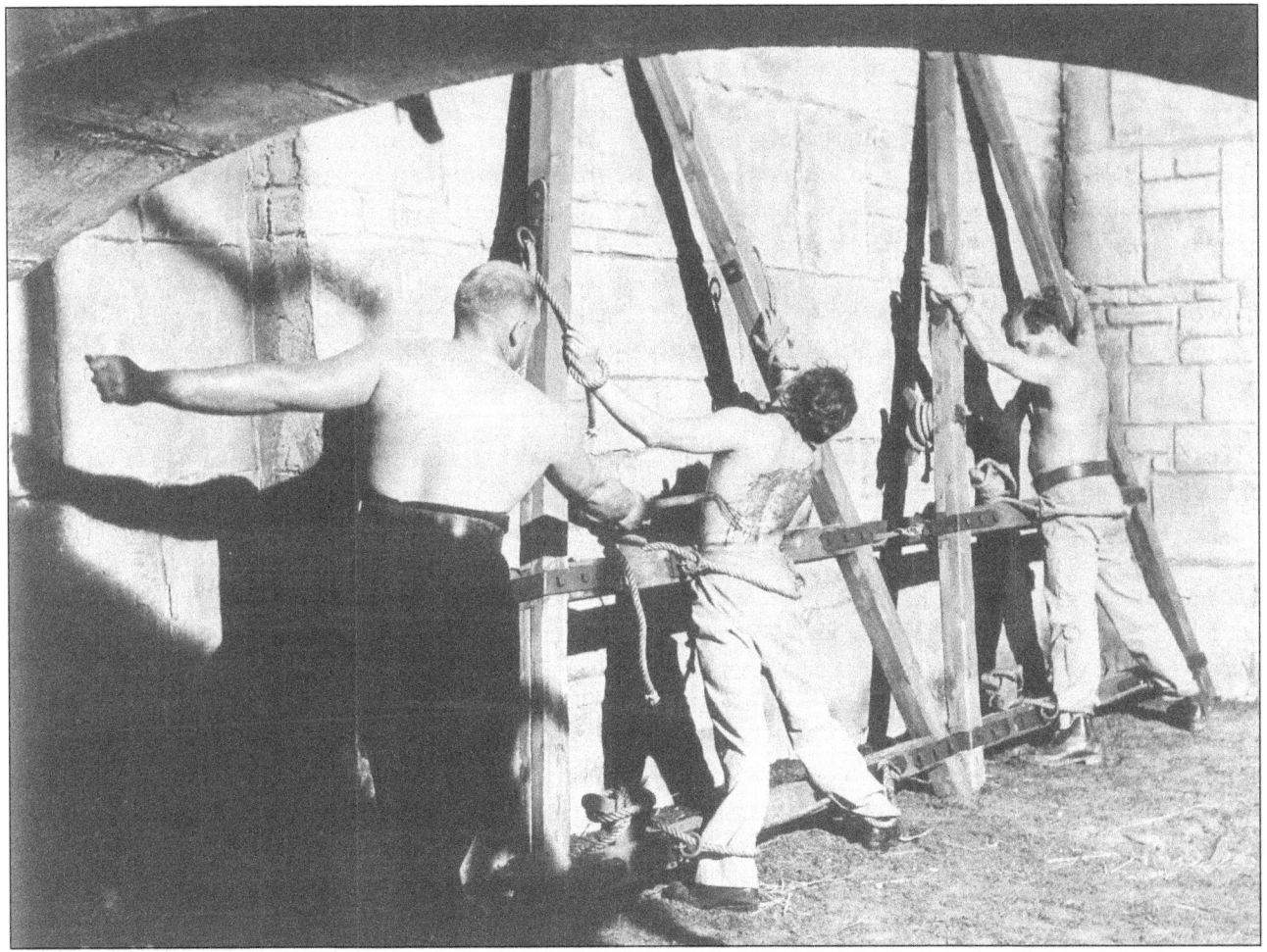

Boris Karloff once wrote that horror films fulfill "a desire in people to experience something which is beyond the range of everyday human emotion." He drew this conclusion from two facts: "First, from the tremendous success financially and otherwise of the early Frankenstein films and subsequent pictures of a similar type. Secondly, because of an incident on the set of [The Haunted Strangler]...We were about to shoot a sequence in which a man is flogged. Suddenly the set was crowded by studio workmen and office girls all eager to have a look! There is a violent streak in all of us: and if it can be exploded in the cinema instead of in some antisocial manner in real life, so much the better."

GORDON: John C. Cooper was the writing pseudonym of John Croydon. We were fortunate to be able to get the services of Croydon to join us in this venture and to become the line producer. John had been in the business for years; in fact, he worked on a picture that Boris Karloff made in England in 1933, called *The Ghoul*, and remembered meeting Karloff at the time. He also had a career as a novelist, a writer of detective stories; he used to write his novels under the name of John C. Cooper. So when it was agreed that he would work *with* Jan Read on transferring *Strangle Hold* from a story into a screenplay, he would use that pseudonym.

Q: Where was Karloff living in 1957?

GORDON: Karloff was living in Hollywood, but he had an apartment in New York, in the famous building "The Dakota," and he used it as a place to stay on occasions when he was in New York. But he was getting ready to move back to England, and in fact it suited him very well that we were planning the production of *Haunted Strangler* at that particular time, because he was going to England to acquire property where he would live. To the best of my recollection, I did not have to pay his airfare from the States to England because he was going over anyway.

Q: Where did he stay while you made *Haunted Strangler*?

GORDON: He had rented a flat in London — or perhaps purchased it, I don't remember now — and he stayed there with his wife Evie while he was making the movie. Evie was a very, very lovely person. They had been married for several years by that time. They had no children of their own, although he had a daughter, Sara, by a previous marriage. I got along very well with Evie. She was terribly protective of Boris, she insisted on being present at all times when he was filming, she insisted on looking after him and taking care of him, and she and I had a very good relationship.

Q: What kind of deal did you make with Karloff, and how much did you pay him?

GORDON: Karloff at the time was represented by MCA, which in those days was only a talent agency; this was before they metamorphosed into Universal Pictures and into producers of movies and television series. I negotiated a deal with Boris' agent at MCA for $27,500 for a period of four weeks, and if we went over the four weeks, then proportionately he would receive additional money. In addition to that, and this was customary in deals for American-based actors, it was part of the deal always that the producer would also pay his living expenses while he was making the film. And so the contract also included £100 per week for those expenses. Of course you have to remember that we're now talking about something that happened over 50 years ago, because £100 a week wouldn't even pay his expenses for one *day* in the London of today [*laughs*]. But that was the deal; and at the same time that I negotiated that deal, I also agreed with MCA that we could have an option on Boris' services for a second film, provided we made it within a given time period that allowed for his commitments in Hollywood and elsewhere. That was the film that eventually became *Corridors of Blood* [shot in 1958, released in 1962], which was made on a much bigger scale than *The Haunted Strangler*. Of course we paid him more money for *Corridors*; he got $37,500. That was for a minimum period of six weeks, a longer shooting schedule. In the tradition of Hollywood deals, it was customary that if you signed an actor for a picture with options, that the options were always for more money than the original deal.

Q: What was the budget altogether on *Haunted Strangler*? You sometimes refer to it as "low-budget" but to me it doesn't look it.

GORDON: Well, it was low-budget by the standards of major Hollywood studio films made in England, like the pictures that Alan Ladd made for [producer] Albert Broccoli. The budget on *Haunted Strangler* I can't really recollect individually, because *Haunted Strangler* and *Fiend Without a Face* were made back to back; in fact, the productions overlapped. They were both made at the same studio, and we only had a production budget for the two films together. Exclusive of the dollar payments to artists who came over like Karloff and Marshall Thompson [star of *Fiend Without a Face*] and their living expenses, the sterling cost of production for the two films was approximately £80,000.

Q: And the cost of making movies must have jumped up when MGM got involved on your second pair, *First Man Into Space* [1959] and *Corridors of Blood*.

GORDON: Yes, *Corridors of Blood* was a much more expensive picture.

Q: Where was *The Haunted Strangler* shot?

GORDON: Not far from London at Walton Studios, which was located at Walton-on-Thames. It was one of the oldest studios in England still to be functioning. Almost all of the *Haunted Strangler* exteriors were shot on the back lot and in the area behind the studio — the prison graveyard scenes, for instance. Walton Studios was originally called Nettlefold Studios, beginning in the days of silent films. Walton Studios was used extensively by independent British production companies that did not want to, or could not *afford* to, go into major studios like Rank or Elstree. Incidentally, that's where *Mother Riley Meets the Vampire* [1952] with Bela Lugosi was shot. [*Editor's note: Gordon extensively discusses his role in the making of* Mother Riley Meets the Vampire *in the book* Science Fiction Confidential *(McFarland, 2002) by Tom Weaver.*]

Q: In *Haunted Strangler*'s pre-credits sequence, when we get too-dark glimpses and from-behind glimpses of Dr. Tenant…that's not Karloff, correct?

GORDON: No, it's not Karloff. That was intentional. I think Karloff would have been too easily recognizable, even from the back. We didn't want the audience to make any connection between the doctor in the pre-credits sequence and Boris Karloff's character James Rankin until it becomes apparent in the story.

Q: Where does a medium-budget movie like yours get such excellent period costumes?

GORDON: There were many companies in England, as there were and still are in Hollywood, that specialized in providing costumes for movies that could not afford to have them designed or made especially for the individual artists. In England, one very well-known one was Bermans. I forget now which one we used for *The Haunted Strangler*.

My brothel's keeper: Cora (Jean Kent), star attraction at that den of iniquity The Judas Hole, shows some leg as Rankin (Karloff) tries to keep his mind on business.

Q: What makeup was involved, and what did Karloff have to do to take on the look of the Strangler?

GORDON: We had a lot of difficulty trying to decide what sort of makeup to use for the Strangler. We didn't want it to be something so outrageous that it would be beyond the realm of possibility; at the same time, we were also limited by the funds we had. And in those days, there weren't all the prosthetic makeup appliances that are available today. One day during pre-production we were having a meeting, either in the offices of Producers Associates, or in Karloff's hotel room, or at Walton Studios. At this meeting, Karloff said that he had a suggestion, and "Would you like to see what I propose?" It's perhaps not a very delicate story to tell, but he took out his false teeth and adopted the facial expressions that you see in *The Haunted Strangler*. He suggested that this would be something that *could* be done, it wouldn't cost anything, he would be able to maintain it throughout the film whenever it was needed, and he was happy to do so. And that's how the "look" of the Haunted Strangler came about.

Q: The Strangler's first action scene might be his best: killing Pearl backstage at The Judas Hole, and then doing a John Wilkes Booth from a box onto the stage.

GORDON: Karloff would have liked to try to do the leap from the box to the stage himself, or at least he *offered* to try and do it; and if it didn't work, he said, then we could employ a stuntman in his place. But I absolutely vetoed that idea. It would have been much too risky to let him do it. If he'd injured himself, it would have ruined the whole production.

Q: What are the ins and outs of getting an older actor into a movie, insurance-wise?

GORDON: Provided that he's in reasonably good health, it's just a question of paying extra insurance. If he has any specific problems that could prove to be a real hazard, then that's another matter. But we had no trouble getting insurance on Karloff; just simply the fact that the premium was somewhat higher because of his age than it would have been otherwise.

Q: In 1957 he did have a few health problems right around the corner. His legs gave him trouble, and also the emphysema.

GORDON: I don't remember any problems with the emphysema at all. The problem he had with his legs and with walking of course dated back to *Bride of Frankenstein* [1935], and it was something that everybody knew about, but it never actually interfered with his work. In fact, it gave him a very distinctive walk which many times in other films he used to great advantage, to create a memorable character.

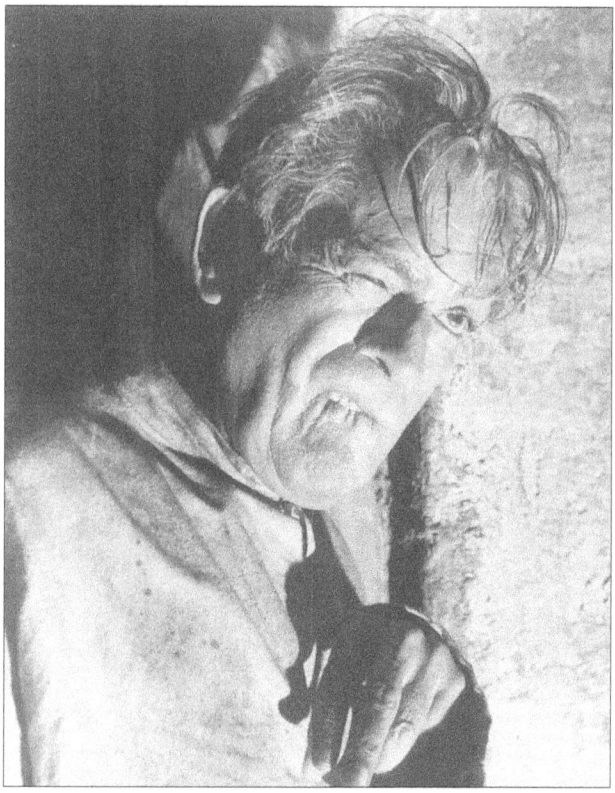

In *Fangoria* magazine, Richard's brother Alex once wrote, "Boris Karloff told me that he preferred to play psychopathic killers without makeup, twisting his face with emphasis on the mouth and teeth to convey their aberration, as in *The Haunted Strangler* and *The Black Room* [1935]."

Q: He was a couple weeks from his 70th birthday in *Haunted Strangler* and yet there was a lot of physical action for him. Okay, it's not him jumping down on the stage, but he runs around a good bit, and in the asylum scene he jumps up and down off a cot and starts a big fire in his cell. Not bad for 70!

GORDON: There were no problems that I recollect. Naturally we made everything as easy as possible for him, but except for one or two things, he did it all, he was a real trouper. Karloff was very enthusiastic about this particular project which he felt would give him a good opportunity to get back to the kind of roles that he was best known for.

Q: This movie — and *Corridors of Blood* — are like an oasis in Karloff's horror career, because he *had* gotten into a rut of small parts in so-so horror pictures and big parts in bad ones. You got the feeling that he knew that *The Haunted Strangler* was a cut above the kind of stuff he was doing lately?

GORDON: Yes, and I think that was why he was so keen on Jan Read's story *Strangle Hold*, because he saw in it the possibility of going back to making a better-class horror picture in which he would be the central character, and which would give him a chance to do some real acting. In his recent horror pictures like *The Strange Door* [1951] and *The Black Castle* [1952], he was just a supporting player and he was obviously being used for his name only. He really had nothing to do in them that was any kind of a challenge, nothing to do that would give him any real satisfaction.

Q: Elizabeth Allan played his wife in *Haunted Strangler*; she had been in a 1932 English version of *The Lodger*, and also MGM's *Mark of the Vampire* [1935].

GORDON: I of course was very thrilled at the prospect of getting Elizabeth Allan because I knew her whole Hollywood history, and particularly her association with Bela Lugosi on *Mark of the Vampire*. But when we met, and I got to know her well enough to speak to her socially and not just about the film we were making, I'm afraid that whenever I started to ask any questions about her career in Hollywood or about the pictures she made there, she absolutely refused to talk about it. She had made it a rule to tell everybody that she was *not* going to talk about her Hollywood career. Otherwise, she was friendly enough, and she got along very well with Karloff. Imagine having co-starred with Lugosi, Atwill and Rathbone in Hollywood's heyday…

The prison governor was played by Leslie Perrins, a popular British stage and screen actor going back to silent and early sound days. He was always a great favorite of mine when I was a kid; whenever Alex and I saw him in a movie, where he almost always played villainous roles, we enjoyed him enormously. So I made a special effort to get him for the role of the prison governor, and it was quite thrilling for me to meet him and to be able to talk to him about "the old times"

and all of that sort of thing. It was his last film, and he died in 1962.

The Scotland Yard superintendent was played by Anthony Dawson. *Haunted Strangler* was the only picture I made with Anthony, but he was a very interesting actor. I met him originally when he was appearing on Broadway in Maurice Evans' production of *Dial M for Murder* [1952-54]; he had an introduction to me from

Movie buff Gordon was keen to hear Elizabeth Allan talk about her earlier screen credits — but the actress, unhappy about her treatment by Hollywood, wouldn't go down Memory Lane.

a mutual friend in England when he came over to do that play. We got to be very good friends, which is the reason that some time later, when I was casting *The Haunted Strangler*, I got in touch with him and offered him the role of the superintendent, which he was quite glad to accept. He had already met Karloff backstage at *Dial M for Murder*.

I think this is quite an interesting story: When *Dial M for Murder* was going to go on tour after its long Broadway run, Maurice Evans was trying to recast the role of the Scotland Yard inspector that had been played on Broadway by John Williams. The suggestion was made that Boris Karloff would be a very good choice to play the role on the tour, and in fact Karloff went to a reading, and it all seemed to go very well. But then Maurice Evans was persuaded that if they went on the road with Karloff advertised as being in the cast, it would spoil the suspense of the play: Everybody coming to the theater would surmise that he was not really a Scotland Yard inspector and take it for granted that he was going to turn out to be the villain, and that would throw the whole thing off balance. So they decided not to go ahead with the idea of casting Karloff. Alan Napier, a great friend of Karloff's, took the role and played it in the *Dial M for Murder* touring company.

But Anthony and Karloff became friends at that time, so Anthony was very happy when we cast him in *The Haunted Strangler* with Karloff. I remained friends with Anthony for a long time after that. He played a supporting role in *Dr. No* [1962], the first of the James Bond films, and while the *Dr. No* company was on location in Jamaica, he and I were corresponding from time to time. I will never forget a letter I received from him one day, complaining that the production of *Dr. No* was in complete disarray; he said that it seemed to him that nobody knew what they were doing; and he predicted that the film would be a total disaster *if* in fact it ever saw the light of day [*laughs*]. I kidded him about that for the rest of his life!

Q: Two other *Haunted Strangler* cast members: Jean Kent and Vera Day as the Judas Hole girls, Cora and Pearl?

GORDON: They were both extremely pleasant to be with. I was particularly thrilled to have Jean Kent, because she was a star in England at the time. She had been in a number of big and important Rank films, she had a starring vehicle called *The Woman in Question* [1950] which was a great success; and I thought it was quite a coup for us to be able to get her to play in *The Haunted Strangler*. She was very charming, very cooperative, and I have only the happiest memories of her.

Gordon gave his good friend Anthony Dawson the substantial role of Scotland Yard Superintendent Burk. In this non-*Strangler* shot, Gordon is seeing Dawson off as the actor prepares to sail from New York to England.

Q: And Vera Day? She was not only in *Haunted Strangler* but also in another picture you had something to do with, *Womaneater* [1958].

GORDON: I've been accused of "having something to do with" the making of *Womaneater* before [*laughs*]; that's because I once acquired its American distribution rights in order to put it on a double-bill with a film I *did* co-produce, *Escapement* [aka *The Electronic Monster*, 1958], for distribution through Columbia Pictures. I didn't come into contact very much with Vera Day during *The Haunted Strangler* because of my working on *Fiend Without a Face*, but as I remember her, she was also very charming, very gracious and very cooperative.

Q: In an interview, Karloff once said that he thought "very, very, very highly" of *Haunted Strangler* director Robert Day. Day got three "very"s!

GORDON: Day was remarkably assured in everything he was doing. He was very low-key, he got along very well with Boris Karloff, he really did his homework, and was prepared every day on the set for whatever was going to be done. There was an immediate rapport between him and Karloff. I think the movie benefited from that. It shows in Karloff's performance, and perhaps it shows in Karloff's willingness to exert himself more physically than he might otherwise have done. We got along very well with Robert Day, and because of that, we put him in again as the director of not only *Corridors of Blood* with Karloff but also *First Man Into Space*.

Q: Did you get to have lunch with Karloff every day on *Haunted Strangler*?

GORDON: No, because on many days he had to rest at lunchtime in order to be able to handle the chores for the whole day. Also, *I* was not there every day during the shooting, because at the same time *Haunted Strangler* was shooting, we were preparing *Fiend Without a Face* and I was very much occupied with that. So I wasn't

Amidst dead man's bones, Rankin (Karloff) finds the surgical scalpel that proves his case — *and* proves his undoing.

always present; in fact, because I had a good knowledge of German, at one point I went to Munich for a couple of weeks in connection with the *Fiend Without a Face* special effects. So during that time, of course, I was away from the Karloff production altogether.

Q: When you *would* go out with Karloff, what was his favorite meal?

GORDON: One of the things Karloff most enjoyed at lunchtime was grilled kidneys, which he used to have for *breakfast* in his younger days. He enjoyed that very much as a luncheon special.

Q: One of the little gripes I have with *Haunted Strangler* is that Karloff's character *was* Dr. Tenant; now he's Rankin but he's interested in Tenant without knowing that he *was* Tenant; and he's going around to all of Tenant's old friends asking them about Tenant. All these people, as he comes through the door, should be saying, "Hey! It's Dr. Tenant! Where've you *been*?" — but not one of them does!

GORDON: That was a popular convention that was used in many horror pictures and in many thrillers. It applies, to some degree, even to *Dr. Jekyll and Mr. Hyde* and other stories of that kind. It's always surprised me that even in some very big movies, when some character disappears and comes back after a long time, looking to the audience pretty much like he did before, nobody in the film takes the slightest notice of it or gives any sign of recognition. *The Count of Monte Cristo* [1934] is a very good example, because there's a man who doesn't even change except that he's a few years older, and quite obviously is the same person. I think that's just one of those "movie conventions" that one has to accept without questioning it too much.

Q: Do you recall that "John C. Cooper," aka John Croydon, wrote a novelization of *The Haunted Strangler*?

Rankin (Karloff) gives the doubting Dr. Johnson (Desmond Roberts) some first-hand proof of his re-emerging Jekyll-and-Hyde tendencies.

GORDON: Yes, it was very common practice in those days, particularly with the horror and exploitation films, to get a paperback house to publish a novelization which would be illustrated on the cover, and sometimes inside the book, with scenes from the film.

Q: In the novelization, the Strangler does a lot of tearing-off of women's clothes; and he also kills a number of prostitutes. A "Jack the Ripper connection" is played up in the blurb on the back cover. I asked Jan Read to sign my copy — several other *Haunted Strangler* veterans had signed it. But he wouldn't!

GORDON: Unfortunately, the demands of the paperback publishers were always that the book had to be much stronger than the film; usually more on (what I would call) the pornographic side. I was never very happy about that, but it *was* a promotional tool that was commonly used by distributors.

Q: Did you have any censor trouble over *Haunted Strangler*? There are several scenes of violence way ahead of their time in 1957 — right to the very end of the movie, with Rankin's blood running down the tombstone!

GORDON: There were some censor problems, both with the British Board of Film Censors and with the MPAA, or the Hays Code as it was known, and we had to tone down one or two scenes. We did some minor trims in the U.K., and some other scenes had minor trims in the United States, but nothing really that seriously affected the picture. But we hadn't had to go through the process of submitting the script in advance to the censors, which the major studios used to do; we were operating as an independent.

Q: Why did the shooting title *Strangle Hold* fall by the wayside?

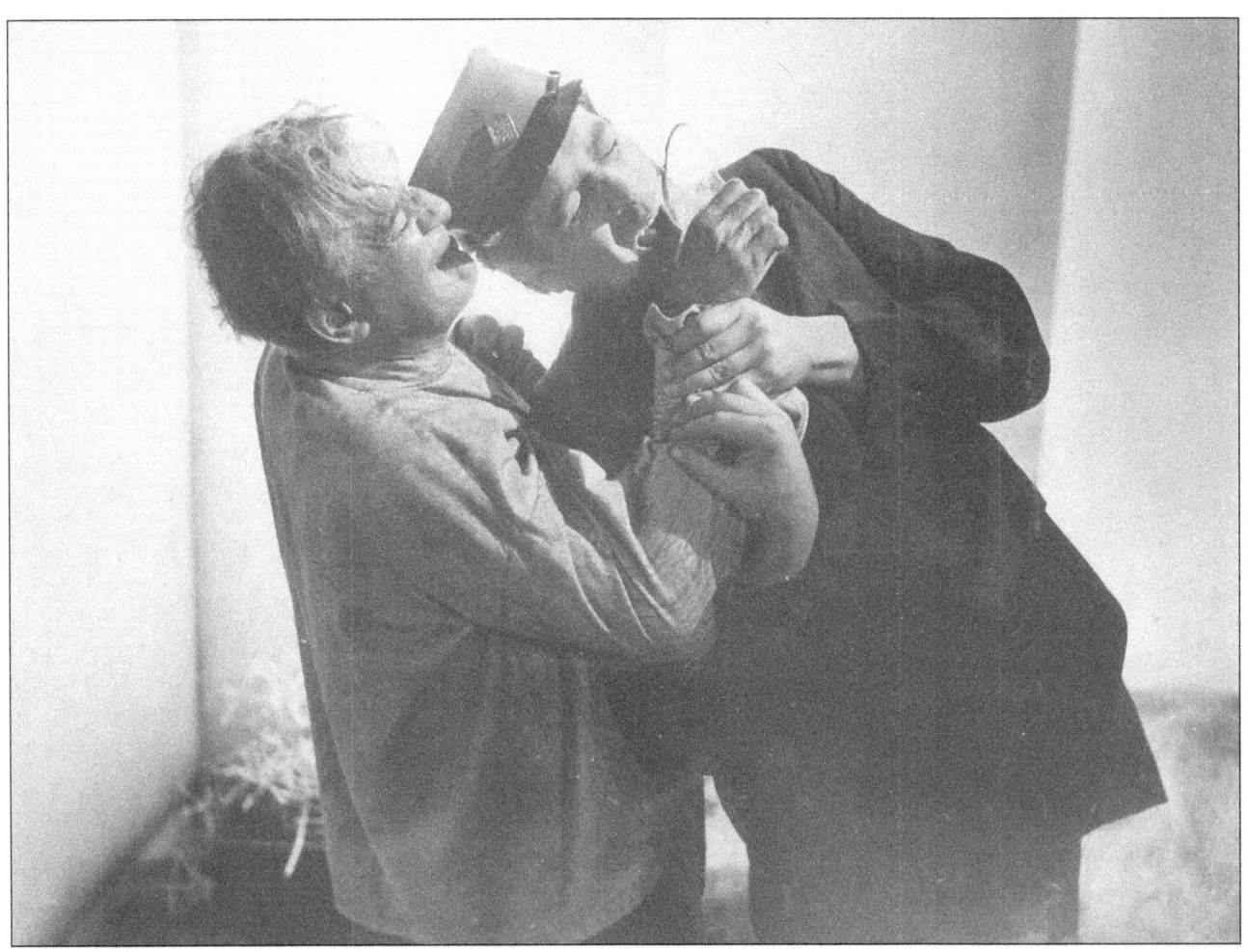

The Strangler (Karloff) escapes his Coldbath Fields padded cell after spoiling the looks of a guard. So that *Haunted Strangler* would not be mistaken for a reissue of a Karloff oldie, publicity materials stressed in bold print that the movie was ALL-NEW.

GORDON: Because we found that everybody's immediate reaction to it was that our movie must be a wrestling movie [*laughs*]! So *that* was no good. John Croydon suggested *The Judas Hole* as a title, because so much of the action takes place in that cabaret. But we didn't like that, it didn't seem suitable, and we discarded that very quickly. Eros Films in England decided to call it *Grip of the Strangler*; but when I made the distribution deal with MGM, Arthur Canton of their New York publicity and advertising department also said that *that* title sounded more like a wrestling film. [*Editor's note: In the 1950s, Ed "Strangler" Lewis, though retired, was still one of pro wrestling's most famous names.*] So Canton came up with the title *The Haunted Strangler*, which suited me very well. Canton, incidentally, was quite a well-known name within the business; he was an independent film distributor early in his career, and then went into publicity. He worked on the marketing campaigns of such films as *On the Waterfront* [1954], *Lawrence of Arabia* [1962] and *The Bridge on the River Kwai* [1957]. He was a nice guy and I knew him for a long time.

Q: Talk about the release of *Haunted Strangler* and *Fiend Without a Face*.

GORDON: As I mentioned earlier, when I set up the production of the two pictures, part of the financing was provided by Eros Films, which in return got the distribution rights for the United Kingdom. When the pictures were completed, I made a deal with MGM for the distribution in the rest of the world for the two films combined; this was the era when the major studios were beginning to acquire and release outside, independently produced pictures. I had some difficulties with MGM on how the publicity, the promotion and the selling of the films should be handled. *Haunted Strangler* and *Fiend Without a Face* opened out of town, not in

New York City's horror salon The Rialto began playing host to Strangler and its co-feature Fiend Without a Face on July 3, 1958. The New York Daily News called Strangler "a picture that measures up with many of [Karloff's] very best," a sentiment also found in other reviews.

New York City, and Arthur Canton asked to go on the road and help to promote them. I said, "Certainly, I'd be delighted to do that." One of the places they sent me was Detroit, where the program was scheduled to open at the Adams Theater, a cinema that played all-MGM product. The Adams was a very high-class theater located in one of the most upscale parts of the city, not in the downtown area where most of the larger movie theaters were located and where horror and exploitation pictures were played. Just a few days before the show was due to open, I went to the Adams to talk to the manager, to discuss exploitation possibilities. I found that he was very unhappy with the idea of playing this double-bill because his theater was the MGM prestige theater in the city and he felt that he was catering to a different type of audience, so he wasn't prepared to be very cooperative. I told him that I thought a very good way of promoting *Haunted Strangler* and *Fiend* would be by putting a coffin in the theater lobby, with a fake body in it, so that audiences going to see the current program would have to step around the coffin in order to gain admittance to the auditorium. I also suggested dressing up the lobby a little bit with creatures of some kind. These were old and corny ideas, but they always worked in the '30s and '40s, and I saw no reason why they shouldn't work in the '50s. However, the manager was absolutely horrified, because the theater was playing *Gigi* [1958] and other such MGM product. He looked at me with great distaste and remonstrated with me: "Surely you don't expect my patrons, who come to see *Gigi*, to step around a coffin?" I realized that I had no argument that would convince him otherwise, so it was a lost cause.

When I came back to New York after having been in Detroit, Baltimore and several other cities, I went in to see the MGM sales manager. I told him the story of my experiences in Detroit and how disappointed I was, and I said that I felt the pictures should have opened at the Broadway Capitol Theater in downtown Detroit, which was making a fortune with the American International double-bills. The program there could have taken in a great deal of money, whereas at the Adams Theater it just barely got by. Well, the MGM sales manager received me with stony silence; and then he looked at me and said, "There's one thing you must remember, Mr. Gordon: *You are now at MGM.*" Well, when he said that, I tucked my tail between my legs and retreated like the villagers who saw the Frankenstein Monster coming down the high street. And I would swear that at that moment, the portrait of Louis B. Mayer that was hanging on the wall over his desk, smiled slightly in derision at the way I behaved [*laughs*].

Q: But in New York they did play at the Rialto Theater in Times Square.

GORDON: Yes, the Rialto, a house that specialized in running horror and exploitation pictures, and *there* I

Part of the Rialto's elaborate front-of-house display. The two films did hold-over business there.

was able to work with the management with somewhat greater success. We decorated the lobby with photographs of Boris Karloff in all his famous roles, from the Frankenstein Monster and Fu Manchu to his latest films; and we also had a Fiend from *Fiend Without a Face* on display in the street, in a glass cage. At the Rialto, the two pictures did much better. From there they went into general distribution and played on the Loews circuit all over the country, and then they were quite successful.

When we finished up making *Haunted Strangler* and *Fiend Without a Face*, I was very proud of having produced a picture with Boris Karloff, and of course *Fiend Without a Face* too. I felt as though I was "on my way," that there were more pictures to come. And of course I had not forgotten that I had an option on Karloff's services for a second picture…[*The Karloff-Gordon saga continues with* Corridors of Blood *on page 80.*]

THE HAUNTED STRANGLER RADIO SPOTS

#1: [*The groaning and wheezing of the Haunted Strangler is heard.*]

ANNOUNCER'S VOICE: Hear that sound? Frightening, isn't it? It's the Haunted Strangler. And here to tell you about him is Boris Karloff.

KARLOFF'S VOICE WITH SLIGHT ECHO EFFECT: Hello. The Haunted Strangler…he goes around at night, and he comes quietly up behind you and then… Well [*fiendish laugh*], you can *imagine* what happens. But why imagine? *See The Haunted Strangler.* And by the way, on the same movie program, there's a second masterpiece of horror, *Fiend Without a Face*. It's about weird little creatures made by atomic energy…loathsome things that kill you by eating your *brains*.

ANNOUNCER'S VOICE: Don't miss Karloff, King of the Monsters, in *The Haunted Strangler*, plus *Fiend Without a Face*. Both terrifying hits from MGM!

…

#2: Hello. This is Boris Karloff. Oh, *don't* go away, because I have a warning for *you*. About the Haunted Strangler. What's that? You're *not* frightened? Oh, but you *will* be when you see my new picture, *The Haunted Strangler*. It's about the monstrous man who couldn't resist his savage impulse to throttle pretty young girls — or anyone *else* who got in his way. A killer, obsessed by strange desires that led him inevitably to madness — and *murder*. It's an experience in suspense, an adventure in horror. *The Haunted Strangler*. [*Fiendish laugh*] It's a *killer*!

ANNOUNCER'S VOICE: Don't miss Karloff, King of the Monsters, in *The Haunted Strangler*, plus *Fiend Without a Face*. Both terrifying hits from MGM!

FUN FACTS

Blooper!: *The Haunted Strangler* is set in 1860 but in Scotland Yard's Lost Property Room is a very old-looking box labeled **Jack the Ripper** — the London serial killer of the late *1880s*.

On the shelf below the **Jack the Ripper** box is one marked **Constance Kent**. That box looks equally old even though teenager Constance's crime (the murder of her three-year-old half-brother Francis) occurred the same year *The Haunted Strangler* was set (1860). In 1945, John Croydon associate-produced the anthology horror film *Dead of Night*; the episode "Christmas Party" features the ghost of little Francis Kent as a character, and Constance is mentioned.

At MGM's request, on April 17, 1958, Gordon's contract with Karloff was modified so that MGM

Photos of Karloff in some of his more memorable movie roles adorn the Rialto's doors. According to a *New York Post* review, "The famed House of Horrors is knee-deep in gore."

had the right to bill the actor simply as KARLOFF in all advertising and publicity. Ultimately, however, the studio never followed through on that idea.

Many of Gordon's movies feature "tribute moments" to the horror classics he grew up with. There's one such moment in *Haunted Strangler* when madhouse inmate Rankin imagines he sees the tall flame in a gas lamp turn into his scalpel; it should make oldies fans recall the climax of *The Old Dark House* and mad Saul's (Brember Wills) discourse about the fact that "flames are really knives."

FIEND WITHOUT A FACE
1958

CREDITS

Executive Producers	*Richard Gordon & Charles Vetter Jr.*
Produced by	*John Croydon*
Directed by	*Arthur Crabtree*
Screenplay	*Herbert J. Leder*

Original Story "The Thought-Monster" by Amelia Reynolds Long
(published in the March 1930 issue of Weird Tales *magazine)*

Lighting Cameraman	*Lionel Banes*
Editor	*R.Q. McNaughton*
Music Composed by	*Buxton Orr*
Music Conductor	*Frederic Lewis*
Set Designer	*John Elphick*
Special Effects	*Ruppel & Nordhoff and Peter Neilson*
Assistant Director	*Douglas Hickox*
Makeup	*Jim Hydes*
Hairdressing	*Barbara Barnard*
Camera Operator	*Leo Rogers*
Dress Supervisor	*Anna Duse*
Sound Recordist	*Peter Davies*
Dubbing Editor	*Terry Poulton*
Continuity	*Hazel Swift*
Second Unit Photography	*Martin Curtis*

74 minutes

CAST

Marshall Thompson	*Major Jeff Cummings*
Kynaston Reeves	*Prof. R.E. Walgate*
Kim Parker	*Barbara Grisselle*
Stanley Maxted	*Col. Butler*
Terence Kilburn	*Capt. Hal Chester*
James Dyrenforth	*Mayor Hawkins*
Robert MacKenzie	*Constable Howard Gibbons*
Peter Madden	*Dr. Bradley*
Gil Winfield	*Dr. Warren*
Michael Balfour	*Sgt. Kasper*
Launce Maraschal	*Deputy Mayor Melville*
R. Meadows White	*Ben Adams*
Kerrigan Prescott	*Atomic Engineer*
Lala Lloyd	*Amelia Adams*
Shane Cordell	*Nurse*

SYNOPSIS OF THE SHORT STORY

"The Thought-Monster" by Amelia Reynolds Long

A farmer lies dead in the woods; on his face is a look of horror "that made the flesh creep on those who found him." This tragedy is followed by the identical deaths of a stranger, two boys, a woman and the town mayor. The townspeople bring in Gibson, a New York detective who theorizes that the deaths were caused by an escaped lunatic so hideous that the sight of him frightens beholders to death. One night, Gibson and a half-dozen townsmen lie in wait in the woods for The Terror; when morning comes, Gibson is missing. "Then, about a week later, he wandered into town — a mouthing, gibbering idiot!"

After more horrific events, psychic investigator Michael Cummings arrives in town offering to try to solve the mystery. He is certain that a supernatural force is at work and yet begins to suspect Walgate, a reclusive scientist who lives in an old rambling place a half-mile outside town. Cummings and local physician Dr. Bradley pay a call on Walgate and discuss the possibility that the killings were done by a psychical force. At Cummings' suggestion, the townspeople put violet-shaded lights (fatal to supernatural things) outside their houses at night.

One day Cummings and Bradley receive a call from Walgate, who asks them to come to his house in a half-hour, walk in and read the manuscript they'll find on a table. Following these instructions, Cummings and Bradley arrive at the house and find the manuscript — actually entries from Walgate's diary, which starts about a year earlier and describes Walgate's interest in the material existence of thought. According to Walgate's entries, he became able to move small objects with the power of thought, and then decided to create a mental being via the concentrated power of pure thought. Walgate had an architect build within his house a room lined with lead (lead would prevent the escape of the thought-monster he planned to create). One day a housekeeper disobeyed orders and left open the lead room door, which allowed the invisible thought-monster to escape; that was the point at which the killings began. Walgate soon realized that the thought-monster shared the house with him, and began to suspect that it was responsible for all the deaths. He confirms his theory by secretly opening the coffin of the mayor and examining his body. ("One glance at his blackening face showed me that he had died an imbecile. My suspicions were right; the thought-monster is a mental vampire, feeding upon the minds of its victims!") At that point, Walgate decided to sacrifice himself in order to destroy the thought-monster: He devised a plan that involved having his lead room fitted with violet lights,

Cover of the March 1930 issue of *Weird Tales* magazine that featured Amelia Reynolds Long's "The Thought-Monster" — and also a poem by H.P. Lovecraft, "The Ancient Track."

luring the thought-monster, sealing the door and turning on the fatal violet lights. This is the point at which Walgate's manuscript ends.

The final four paragraphs of the story:

[Cummings] passed the doctor and led the way down the hall, stopping before the last door. Slowly he turned the knob, and pushed the door open a few inches. A bar of vivid purple light fell across his face.

"Is it all right?" the doctor whispered, close behind him.

"I think so." *Cummings opened the door a bit further. In the room beyond was an atmosphere of snapped tension, of climax that had passed.*

They stepped across the threshold. And then they became aware that the room still held a living occupant. From the far corner, his clothing wrinkled and torn, his hair and trimmed Vandyke beard in disarray, there shambled toward them a helpless, mindless idiot!

SYNOPSIS OF THE FILM

In Winthrop, Manitoba, a remote section of the Canadian backwoods, a USAF base uses atomic power as part of secret experiments to boost the range of their Russia-watching radar equipment. When the body of a local farmer is found in the woods, the simple, superstitious locals — already worried about radioactive fallout — blame the activities at the base. The situation hits critical mass as another farmer, his wife and the mayor join the list of victims, killed by an invisible force attacking the backs of their necks. An autopsy shows that the brain and spinal cord of one victim have been sucked out through two holes in the back of the skull. "It's as if some mental vampire were at work," gasps air base Major Jeff Cummings. Cummings' other pressing problem is the way their radar experiments are hampered by inexplicable drains on their power supply.

Cummings meets (and fancies) Barbara Grisselle, sister of the dead farmer. Barbara works as a secretary for Prof. Walgate, an elderly eccentric recluse who writes books on far-out subjects like the materialization of thought. The major begins to suspect Walgate and eventually pressures him to come clean: According to Walgate, his recent work involved an attempt to detach a thought from his conscious and to give it a separate entity of its own. In flashbacks we see that, via his lab equipment, he diverted a portion of the air base's atomic energy; combining this with the power of his mind, he materialized a being (invisible, like thoughts) which escaped and multiplied.

At the base, the Fiends kill the reactor control room workers and take over, revving up the power to the point that they become visible and we see that they are human brains (with "antenna") that push themselves along with their snake-like spinal cord "tails." Dozens of Fiends lay siege to Walgate's house, where Cummings, Barbara, base security man Capt. Chester and others try to hold them off. When shot, Fiends spurt blood and goo and quickly expire.

Realizing that shutting down the reactors will cause all these "energy vampires" to die, Cummings sets out for the base as Prof. Walgate gives his life to create a diversion. Cummings sets a dynamite charge in the control room, destroying the atomic energy plant. At Walgate's house, one of the Fiends launches itself at Barbara and wraps itself around her neck when the life-giving power ends. Like all the others, it drops in its tracks and dissolves into a puddle of slime.

RICHARD GORDON ON *FIEND WITHOUT A FACE*

Q: Have you found *Fiend Without a Face* to be your most popular picture?

RICHARD GORDON: Yes, I think it *has* become the most popular picture of all those I made over the years, because it's been in continuous distribution. It's forever playing in film festivals and at midnight showings, and on television, and also has been out on VHS, laserdisc and DVD.

Q: What's the secret to its ongoing popularity?

GORDON: Undoubtedly the Fiends themselves, which were considered quite revolutionary in their time, and also went beyond the type of special effects that were commonly used in those days. I think they have stuck in everybody's mind and become the secret to the picture's success; fans are always talking about them. When I go to purely social gatherings and talk about films I made, it's amazing how often somebody will ask, "Did you ever make a picture that I would remember?" and I mention *Fiend Without a Face* and they say, "Oh, yes, that was a picture that frightened me to death when I was a child!" or "It gave me nightmares" and so on. In fact [*laughs*], a few years ago, a Xerox machine repairman came to my office to fix the machine, and as he was leaving, he asked, "What do you guys do here?" I told him that I made movies, including horror movies. Well, he started talking about the ones he loved as a kid, the *Nightmare on Elm Street*s and so on, but then he added that the one that *really* got to him was the one where people were being killed by something invisible, and at the end they turn out to be flying brains. I told him, "Wait a minute," and I went into an adjoining room and came out with one of the brain reproductions. Needless to say, he was very surprised. And as he was leaving, I gave him a *Fiend Without a Face* DVD!

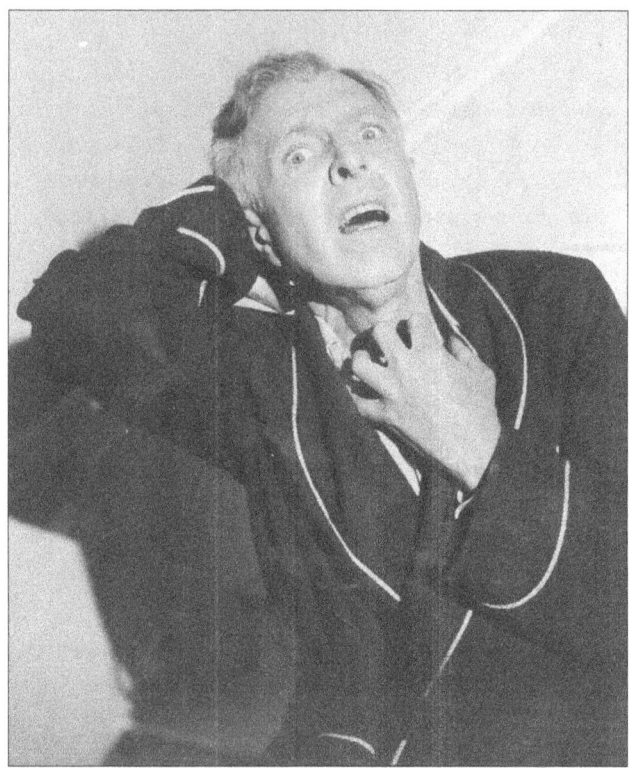

In *Fiend Without a Face*'s early reels, victims succumbed to invisible attackers: a farmer's wife (Lala Lloyd), the town mayor (James Dyrenforth) and an atomic engineer (Kerrigan Prescott).

Q: I notice that the siege at the end of Joe Dante's *Small Soldiers* [1998] was practically a takeoff on *Fiend*, with the Small Soldiers substituted for the Fiends.

GORDON: Yes, there've been a lot of filmmakers, directors especially, who remember the film very affectionately. Some have requested the use of clips from the film for productions of their own, because the Fiends are so instantly recognizable.

Q: How do you feel when a movie like *It Came from Hollywood* [1982], a "celebration" of the *worst* movies ever made, asks for clips from *Fiend Without a Face*?

GORDON: I didn't really mind that, because...first of all, of course, we got well paid for it [*laughs*]. And it wasn't only *Fiend Without a Face*, they also asked for clips from other films I made, like *First Man Into Space* [1959].

Q: And *The War of the Worlds* [1953] and *The Incredible Shrinking Man* [1957] and other very good pictures were also represented in *It Came from Hollywood*, so you were in pretty good company.

GORDON: Yes, I must say that didn't bother me at all.

Q: *Fiend Without a Face* was one of quite a few movies that you made in the 1950s for your own companies.

GORDON: I formed Amalgamated Productions in 1956 when I was 30 years old. I started it in partnership with an American friend of mine, Charles Vetter Jr., whom I had met in connection with my other business of distribution. Chuck had a television studio in New York and was making TV commercials, and wanted to get into feature pictures. We had become associated on an English film that I imported, *The Gelignite Gang* [1956] with Wayne Morris, which I retitled *The Dynamiters*. Chuck wanted to acquire the distribution rights for the United States, and we initially clashed when we met because I had other plans for setting up its release here. But then we formed a friendship and decided to go into partnership together. We started Amalgamated Productions Inc., and in the first year of Amalgamated's existence, we arranged seven films [mostly crime stories] to be co-produced in England with independent producers over there; to star in these films, we brought over American actors such as Zachary Scott, Pat O'Brien, Wayne Morris and Keefe Brasselle. Most of the scripts came either from America or were stories that originated in America, and were then transposed into English settings.

Q: You and Vetter were both New York–based as all this took place.

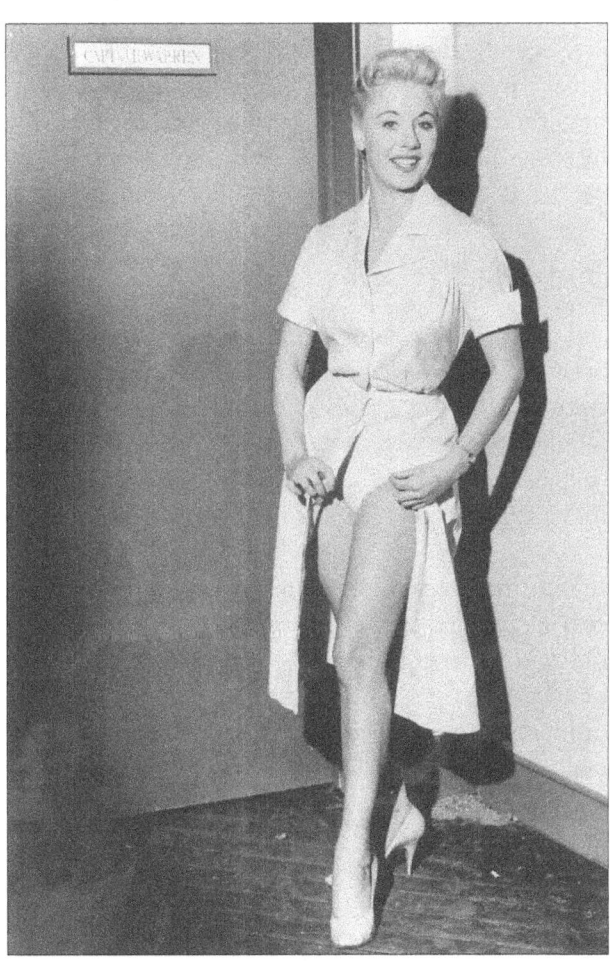

Shane Cordell, who has a one-line bit as a nurse in an office scene, shows a little skin in a marvelously cheesy cheesecake shot.

GORDON: Yes. I was a British subject — in fact, I'm still a British subject *now* — and so we were able to function in England quite easily. When we decided to go into productions of our own and eliminate the co-production partners, we formed Producers Associates Ltd. in England as a British company, and its first two productions were *Fiend Without a Face* and the Boris Karloff picture that was called *Grip of the Strangler* in England, and retitled *The Haunted Strangler* for the American market.

Q: Your brother Alex made a lot of his early movies for AIP in Hollywood. You were never tempted to "go Hollywood"?

GORDON: Never. When Alex and I came to the United States at the end of the 1940s, I settled in New York very quickly and started my professional career distributing pictures from overseas in the United States and representing foreign producers, helping them to set up productions and to get American actors and so on. Alex was more anxious to get into production on his own, and decided that he would have a better chance in Hollywood. So he went out there and eventually he teamed with Jim Nicholson and Sam Arkoff at American International Pictures.

Q: You grew up on horror pictures and have always been a great fan of horror pictures, but it wasn't until Boris Karloff practically *asked* you to make a horror picture, *The Haunted Strangler*, with him in the lead, that you finally got into making horror and sci-fi movies. Why was there an initial delay?

GORDON: Because we were starting out with these co-productions of very low-budget pictures, and it didn't really seem practical to try and make horror or science fiction films on that level. Also, those co-productions were made just before Hammer Films really brought about the renaissance of making horror films in England; the circuits were looking for second features that had more general content. And *that* was the market that, in our initial efforts, we were trying to reach.

Q: *Fiend Without a Face* was based on the story "The Thought-Monster," published in *Weird Tales* magazine, written by a teenager. How did this become your first horror-science fiction movie?

GORDON: While my brother was at American International, a lot of properties were being sent in for consideration. And whenever Jim Nicholson and Sam Arkoff turned down something for whatever reason, and Alex thought it might be suitable for what I was doing in England, he would submit it to me and tell me, "If you can use this, I can get it for you." "The Thought-Monster" was the brainchild — pun intended! — of a young girl called Amelia Reynolds Long, written in 1930, and it was one of the properties submitted to AIP by Forrest Ackerman, who later became well-known for editing *Famous Monsters of Filmland* magazine but who was then acting as an agent for writers from *Weird Tales, Astounding Science Fiction* and all these old pulp magazines. AIP turned it down, but Alex felt that it would be an excellent subject that could be made just as well in England and sent it to me. Chuck and I decided that it *would* be a very good property for us, and so we acquired it through Alex, via Forrest Ackerman. We paid $400 to buy the story outright; and then, to write the screenplay, we hired an American by the name of Herbert Leder, whom Vetter knew through his TV commercials. We paid Leder $2500 to write the screenplay.

Leder was a very nice man who had been quite successful with TV commercials, and was anxious to get into feature films. One of the reasons he was so happy to write the script for *Fiend Without a Face* was that he hoped to direct it. That did not work out, because he was an American and he wasn't acceptable to the British finance and the British distributor, Eros Films, who was involved in the making of the film with us; and also, we would not have been able to get him a labor permit, which was necessary at the time. Later he did go to England and set up two productions of his own, a science fiction-horror film called *The Frozen Dead* [1967] and the other one a horror film called *It!* [1967]. He died in 1983.

Q: Was it Leder who came up with the title *Fiend Without a Face*?

GORDON: No, actually it was my brother, who had a great deal of experience in coming up with titles of this kind at AIP, where they usually came up with a title and sometimes a poster before a film was even written. Alex suggested the title *Fiend Without a Face* — which I very gratefully accepted [*laughs*].

Q: In "The Thought-Monster," you never see the monsters.

GORDON: It's a great short story when you read it, but it really wouldn't have lent itself to making an acceptable film. First of all, it was too old-fashioned, it quite obviously belonged to another era, and we wanted something modern that would also appeal to young people. And obviously the Fiends had to be shown, otherwise it wasn't going to work as a movie. So we decided to just use the basic ideas of the story and really wrote an entirely new script, with a background of atomic radiation and the things that were popular in the 1950s.

Q: "The Red Menace" was worked in.

GORDON: Yes, the Cold War, and the suspicion against foreigners, and all of those elements that were part of filmmaking in the '50s.

Q: Were those all Leder's ideas?

GORDON: Mostly yes. We all worked on it, but he came up with the new storyline.

Q: How long had you been a fan of science fiction?

GORDON: My first exposure to "science fiction," although we did not call it that when I was growing up in England, was reading the works of such noted authors as Sir Arthur Conan Doyle (when he was not writing about Sherlock Holmes), H. Rider Haggard (when he was not being historical), Edgar Rice Burroughs (in between his Tarzan stories) and Jules Verne (who probably started it all). There were movies like Fritz Lang's *Metropolis* [1927] from Germany, and Fox's *Just Imagine* [1930] from Hollywood, but I did not become addicted to it on the screen until I was exposed to the adventures of *Flash Gordon* [1936] and *Buck Rogers* [1939]. Buster Crabbe became my boyhood hero and I began to seek out "the cinema of the fantastic." I even started a Buster Crabbe fan club which I ran for some years until I joined the British Navy in World War II.

Q: Where'd the money to make *Fiend Without a Face* and *Haunted Strangler* come from?

GORDON: In those days, the financing for low-budget films in England was a fairly standard procedure. You got a United Kingdom distributor who undertook to release the films in the U.K. and would guarantee 70 percent of the sterling production cost, which was discountable at a bank. If you had any kind of a track record or were able to satisfy the requirements, the National Film Finance Corporation, which was formed by the British government to encourage film production, would put up another 20 percent. The producer had to be responsible for the rest and any overages, although that in turn was covered by getting a completion guarantee. And the producer was responsible for any American expenses, or any other elements that were not directly connected with the production of the films in England. *Fiend Without a Face* and *The Haunted Strangler* were made back to back and it was intended for them to go out as a double-bill, and they were financed [in this manner described above] through Eros Films Ltd.

Flying brains attack in a climax that ranks with the most startling (and ahead-of-its-time-gory) of the Monster Boom era.

Q: Two young guys — you and Vetter — getting together and making movie after movie for worldwide theatrical release in the 1950s…is this even do-able any more in the 21st century?

GORDON: I don't think it's possible at all today and I don't think it's been possible for some time. One of the reasons I stopped production in the 1980s was because, first of all, production costs skyrocketed; and then a whole new factor became involved, which was marketing costs. In the case of low-budget films, marketing costs very often exceeded the cost of the production of the film itself.

Q: Did you have a hand in casting *Fiend Without a Face*?

GORDON: Yes I did. I cast Marshall Thompson in the leading role, and I was particularly keen on getting a British character actor whose work I knew well, by the name of Kynaston Reeves, to play Prof. Walgate, who turns out to be the man behind the Fiends. And also I approved Kim Parker as the leading lady.

Marshall Thompson was a wonderful guy to work with. I was introduced to him through Alex, because Marshall had been under consideration at AIP for a couple of pictures. When we were casting *Fiend Without a Face* and considering various Hollywood actors, Alex suggested Marshall. I met him in New York and I was immediately struck by his willingness to come to England and work on a low-budget picture under the conditions which we outlined to him. In fact, I signed him to a two-picture deal; that is to say, I signed him to do *Fiend Without a Face* with an option for another film. It worked out so well that not only did we exercise the option and *make* the other film, which became *First Man Into Space*, but I did a *third* picture with him called *The Secret Man* [1958] while he was in England.

Q: He went to University High School in West L.A., where one year behind him was his *Fiend Without a Face* co-star Terence Kilburn. Kilburn tells me they knew each other a little in high school, and he remembers going to see the school's production of *Our Town* starring Thompson.

GORDON: Marshall had a real Hollywood background. He was put under contract by MGM at quite a young age, and began working there in the mid-1940s, but after a few years, roles started to dry up for him there, and he became an independent.

Q: According to his obituary, he studied for the clergy.

GORDON: He was a *very* religious person. He was also a great family man. He was forever excusing himself on the set, calling his wife to make sure that everything was all right at home. He never really, shall we say, "lived it up" while he was in England, although his wife never joined him there.

Q: [*laughs*] The perfect opportunity!

GORDON: Yes indeed! And in order to keep him relaxed, we tried to *give* him the opportunity [*laughs*], but he didn't bite. He was quite happy just to be a homebody. While he was in England doing those pictures for me, he and I stayed simultaneously in apartments at Dolphin Square [an area of London near

Marshall Thompson, a Michigander and a former MGM contract player, starred in three of the five Producers Associates films. Here in an eerie horror movie-like scene in *Fiend* he explores, and becomes trapped, in a subterranean mausoleum.

the Thames]. In 1992, I was quite sorry to hear that he had died at the age of 66. Although we'd had a very good working relationship, by that time I'd lost track of him because not too long after we finished making our films, he went off to Africa and got involved in the *Daktari* television series, and after *Daktari* he was making television series elsewhere, and he just seemed to drop out of the mainstream of feature filmmaking, and I just never had the time to keep up the relationship. But I have very fond memories of him.

Q: His *Fiend* co-star Terence Kilburn was born in London; came to the U.S. as a kid and acted in movies at MGM; and then in 1957 returned to England for the first time as an adult and started directing for the stage, and of course acting in movies and on TV. When I asked him for his impressions of *Fiend*, he told me, "Well, I don't care much for horror movies, so my impressions were not particularly positive!"

GORDON: We tried to avoid using actors who looked down on horror pictures, because I think if the actor isn't "in tune" with the type of picture you're making, it's going to be very difficult for him to give a performance that would be acceptable to us. I was, however, happy to have Terry Kilburn in *Fiend* because of his background playing in films such as *Goodbye, Mr. Chips* [1939] and the American version of *A Christmas Carol* [1938]; I felt he was a recognizable name, which was always something helpful in pictures of this kind, and we really had no other names except Marshall Thompson. Kilburn already knew Marshall and I thought it was a very good idea to cast him, and that he would be very acceptable to American audiences. And since he was English-born, we didn't have the problem of getting a labor permit for him or having to pay him in U.S. dollars and all the things that were involved with American actors.

Q: He told me that he thought nobody'd ever see the quickie movies (like *Fiend*) he made, that they wouldn't even get released in the major cities; "Little did we know that pictures like *Fiend Without a Face* would find immortality on television."

GORDON: *Fiend Without a Face* played all *over*, it had a complete circuit release in England as a double-bill with *Grip of the Strangler*, and under the worldwide distribution of MGM it played in many major cities. There was no evidence of this kind of attitude on Terry Kilburn's part while we were making the film. Probably because he'd been a professional actor since he was a child, he was one of those people who, whatever he thought of the project, once he agreed to do it and signed for it, he treated it with the same respect as he would have any other kind of picture.

Q: How were you able to line up so many American-sounding actors for *Fiend Without a Face* and *First Man Into Space*? Was there an American acting community in England that you drew from?

GORDON: Yes, that was something I started doing right away, when we were making our co-productions. I knew from my experience in distributing British films in the United States, before I got into production myself, that there was always a problem with English accents in these films, particularly the films that were not so-called "art house pictures" but directed at a mainstream audience. American distributors and also critics were complaining about the difficulty of understanding the accents in certain parts of the United States. So right from the beginning, I looked for the American and Canadian actors who were living in England and working in television and film and on the stage and the radio. Because they were living over there, they did not require labor permits, and there was no problem using them in our pictures. We would round up as many of these people as possible, particularly when we were making a film like *Fiend Without a Face* that was supposed to have a North American background. In one or two minor instances, when the accents didn't seem to work, we had to dub them later with other actors. But generally it worked very well. I used the same supporting players in several different films because of their ability to portray Americans.

Q: Do you think *Fiend Without a Face* and *First Man Into Space* "got away" with their American settings?

GORDON: I think in *Fiend Without a Face* we did. Just to cover ourselves a little bit, we set it in Canada, so that explains some of the accents. Also, we felt that it would be more acceptable in the American market if it had a North American setting. When I made *First Man Into Space*, it was a different problem because the whole picture took place in New Mexico, and this was somewhat difficult to fake in England.

Q: Leading lady Kim Parker — what memories?

GORDON: Kim Parker subsequently married an actor by the name of Paul Carpenter, who became quite popular as a star of English B movies. She tended to be somewhat difficult in her conversation. We were shooting *The Haunted Strangler* at the same time as *Fiend Without a Face*, and there were occasions when she and Boris Karloff went together by chauffeured car to the location or studio. One day Boris Karloff took me aside and said that he really didn't mind sharing his car and driver with Kim Parker, and she was a very charming lady, but some of the stories she was telling and some of the language she was using…he really found rather difficult to accept. He asked me to either have a word with her about it, or perhaps I could arrange for somebody *else* to ride to the studio with him. But she was very nice, and very cooperative. The scene in *Fiend Without a Face* where she's taking a shower as Marshall Thompson arrives at her home, and she comes out wrapped in a towel — I must say, I cringe when I see it now. At the time, it was supposed to add a little sex to the picture; and the MGM publicity department seized on it, using an image of her in the towel in the advertising. But when you look at that scene today, it's really quite ridiculous. It's one of those scenes that you realize was obviously put in for a specific purpose —

Q: A purpose which it no longer serves!

GORDON: [*laughs*] Exactly! And it's a scene that actually has nothing to do with the rest of the movie whatsoever.

Q: One thing that's "wrong" with *Fiend* — if I'm allowed to mention things I think might be wrong — is that there's no one to suspect of being behind the Fiends *but* Kynaston Reeves. Would you agree that that's a problem with the picture?

GORDON: It's a problem with the *story*, yes, because there aren't really any other characters that are built up as suspects. That is one of the reasons why I was against having Prof. Walgate played by a recognized villain actor, or an actor of horror pictures; if we *had*, everybody would have known from the first time he came on that he was going to turn out to be the man behind it. We tried to play that down by having an actor like Kynaston Reeves cast against type, and playing it initially as a very sympathetic character that no one in the audience would have any reason to suspect. And hopefully the action was keeping them so engrossed that they didn't realize that there *were* no other suspects [*laughs*], until it was too late!

Pretty Kim Parker gave *Fiend* its requisite dash of sex appeal.

Q: Was he made-up to look older than he really was? He looks like he's at death's door!

GORDON: Well, he's supposed to be playing a man who's had a heart attack and is subject to strokes, and is pretty well at the end of his physical tether. Kynaston Reeves was an actor who'd been around since the early 1930s; one of his first films was a British horror film called *The Lodger* [1932], the story of Jack the Ripper, in which he played a supporting role. He played in a lot of *very* well-known British pictures like *The Prime Minister* [1941], *The Guinea Pig* [1948] and *The Mudlark* [1950], and he also was well-known on the stage. I had seen him some years earlier in a film called *Housemaster* [1938] and I was particularly impressed with his performance; he played the headmaster of a school who was unusually nasty to both his teachers and his pupils. I'd always remembered that performance and I'd always thought it would be nice to have him *in* a movie, if I ever got around to it. He died in 1971.

Q: Some of the other behind-the-scenes *Fiend Without a Face* people, like director Arthur Crabtree and the producer, John Croydon — what can you tell me about them?

GORDON: John Croydon was one of the most experienced production executives in the British film industry. His career went back to the early sound film days. When Chuck Vetter and I formed Producers Associates Ltd. to make these pictures, we felt we needed a British production executive to come on board with us, and we were fortunate to be able to get John Croydon, who agreed to join the company and to supervise the production of our first group of films. I must say it was a very happy experience. I don't think we would have succeeded as well as we did — or as well as I *imagine* that we did [*laughs*] — without his full cooperation.

Q: You were associated with him for quite a long time after that.

The atom-powered predators become visible and besiege our heroes. "[The ending] is pretty strong for even the strongest of stomachs and constitutions," warned the *Motion Picture Exhibitor*. Pictured: Peter Madden and Launce Maraschal.

GORDON: Yes, I was. He was not only a production executive who knew every aspect of the film business, he was also a writer: Under the pseudonym John C. Cooper, he wrote a series of paperback detective novels that was very popular in England, and he also collaborated on the scripts of a few of my films [*The Haunted Strangler*, *First Man Into Space* and 1966's *The Projected Man*]. You'll see his name in the writing credits as John C. Cooper, as distinct from John Croydon as producer of the pictures.

Q: What was the reason for the pseudonyms? He was just *one* of the people who wrote for you under pseudonyms.

GORDON: Well, it wasn't only the people who wrote pictures for *me*; you make it sound as though —

Q: [*laughs*] It was a conspiracy!

GORDON: Yes, a conspiracy that they didn't want to be associated with Richard Gordon [*laughs*]! No, it was commonplace for producers, directors and other people in the industry, when they also engaged in another career such as a writer, to use pseudonyms in order to keep the two things distinct. Also, when the screen credits appear, you do not want to give the audience the impression that a picture was just a one-man job, that one man did everything. This happened not only with John Croydon: Under the name of George Barclay, Ronnie Kinnoch co-wrote the script of my *Devil Doll* [1964]. Chuck Vetter also wrote screenplays and stories under the name of Lance Z. Hargreaves and collaborated on some of the scripts that we did [*The Fighting Wildcats* and *The Crooked Sky*, both 1957, *First Man Into Space* and *Devil Doll*]. And we acquired two properties from Brian Clemens when he was writing under the pseudonym Tony O'Grady, *The Secret Man* and *Curse of the Voodoo* [1965]. So, you see, it was all a very incestuous sort of undertaking!

Q: And *Fiend*'s director, Arthur Crabtree?

GORDON: He was a very experienced director who had started as a cameraman. He directed some very important pictures in England like *Madonna of the Seven Moons* [1945] and *Caravan* [1946], and I had used him as a director on one of the co-productions that we did prior to the making of *Fiend Without a Face*: *West of Suez* was the title of the original script, but I retitled it *The Fighting Wildcats* and we released it through Republic Pictures in the United States. *Fiend Without a Face* was the first horror picture that he made, and as a result of it, he was subsequently able to get the job of directing Herman Cohen's film *Horrors of the Black Museum* [1959].

Crabtree was a nice, cooperative guy. He had a cameraman's eye for direction. He was in his late 50s at the time when we made *Fiend Without a Face*, and the only time he really felt that he wasn't quite on top of things was when it came to the special effects shooting, because he just couldn't visualize how the special effects were to be done and how to shoot them, and he needed some help there. But other than that, he was very good, and he kept the picture on schedule and on budget. He died in 1975.

Q: Amelia Reynolds Long, who wrote the original story for *Weird Tales* — -was she still around in 1957 when you made the picture?

GORDON: Yes. But I never met her, because I was dealing through Alex with Forrest Ackerman, who was representing her.

Q: Did you ever even talk or correspond with her?

GORDON: Well [*laughs*], that's a story in itself. When it came to writing the contract with MGM for the distribution, we supplied MGM with all the underlying documents. Ben Melniker, who became an executive producer on the *Batman* movie series, was at that time the head of MGM's legal department. When he read my agreement with Ackerman, where we bought the picture rights for $400, Melniker asked me to come discuss it with him at MGM's building in Times Square. He couldn't believe that anybody could buy the film rights to a story and only pay $400 for them; he thought there must have been some under-the-table deal or some other arrangement that didn't reflect itself in the documents. I assured him it was so, but with his background at a major studio, he was so suspicious of the whole thing that he insisted on my contacting Amelia Reynolds Long and getting from her a letter confirming that this *was* in fact the deal, that we did in fact have the rights. Ackerman arranged for me to speak with her on the telephone, and found that she was absolutely thrilled at the thought that a picture had been made of her story and was going to be distributed by a company like MGM. She was perfectly willing to give us any kind of letter that we wanted, and I got the necessary document. Later I spoke to her once more, after the film was released and she had seen it, and she said she was delighted with what we had done. Even though it bore not *too* great a resemblance to her original story, she thought it was all very exciting and she was quite happy with it.

Q: Where was *Fiend Without a Face* shot?

GORDON: We shot *Fiend Without a Face* and the Boris Karloff film back to back at a relatively small studio called Walton Studios, which prior to being named Walton was known as Nettlefold Studios. It was one of the oldest independent studios in England, constantly in use by both major companies and independents. The location shooting for *Fiend Without a Face*, the forest scenes, the woods, the town, etc., were all in the immediate vicinity of Walton Studios. There was also an American military base and a British army post where we were allowed to do some shooting.

Q: Your budget and shooting schedule?

GORDON: The budgets were actually combined for the two pictures, because the plan was that *The Haunted Strangler* would be shot first, and as soon as its principal photography was finished, the principal photography of *Fiend Without a Face* would commence. And so there was a combined budget, and the original scheduled production cost for the two films together was approximately $300,000. Which of course sounds ridiculous by today's standards, but was quite a lot of money at that time, and I would say was about on a par with what companies like American International were spending on their pictures in Hollywood.

Q: Oh, I bet most AIP pictures cost a lot less than that. I'm sure there were a lot of *$50,000* AIP movies in there!

GORDON: Yes, I think that is true of the beginning of American International's history. Well, I must admit that Amalgamated Productions, *my* company, when we made the co-productions, we were making the pictures for $50,000 or even less [*laughs*]. It was always the addition of an American actor, which involved not only the actor's salary but his transportation back and forth plus his living expenses while he was active in England, that added to the cost, and naturally made it somewhat higher than it would have been otherwise. And in the case of Boris Karloff, it was a matter of paying a star salary as opposed to paying just an actor's salary.

Q: Was he the highest-paid of all the actors you imported?

GORDON: Yes he was, although Zachary Scott tried to outdo him. But that's another story [see page 68]! *The Haunted Strangler* had a shooting schedule of four weeks for principal photography, and then *Fiend Without a Face* was to follow immediately with three weeks of post-production. Some of the shooting overlapped; *The Haunted Strangler* was still in post-production when *Fiend* started its principal photography. We had a crew which was signed for two pictures, to do them back to back, on the basis of seven weeks of shooting. This was how we kept costs to a reasonable level. We couldn't use the same director for both films because the director of *The Haunted Strangler*, Robert Day, was still involved in post-production while *Fiend Without a Face* was shooting. But a lot of the crew were the same in both pictures.* *Fiend* was supposed to be the second feature in the double-bill, and had a shorter schedule and a lower production cost. As it turned out, the combination went over budget largely because of *Fiend Without a Face* and its special effects, and *Fiend* ended up costing slightly *more* than *The Haunted Strangler*. But that was only because of the complications of the special effects, which were more expensive than we had anticipated and took much longer to do than we had anticipated.

Q: The gory *Fiend* finale was very much ahead of its time. Did you worry about how the English censors, who could be kinda squeamish, would react to it?

GORDON: We knew that we were going to have some censor problems. The situation was that we couldn't afford to shoot extra scenes or shoot scenes twice in order to cover all possible exigencies. And also, in distributing around the world, every country has different ideas about what's acceptable and what isn't and how far you can go with horror. So we shot it the way we thought it would be most acceptable, but we were prepared for the fact that some of the Fiend shots might be reduced in England and/or in the United States; we

---

* Involved on both movies, in addition to producers Gordon, Croydon and Vetter, were lighting cameraman Lionel Banes, camera operator Leo Rogers, set designer John Elphick, assistant director Douglas Hickox, makeup artist Jim Hydes, hairdresser Barbara Barnard, dress supervisor Anna Duse, continuity girl Hazel Swift, dubbing editor Terry Poulton, composer Buxton Orr and conductor Frederic Lewis.

didn't think that would present a problem because once you saw the Fiends and once they went into action, there was plenty there. The elimination of a few shots here and there wouldn't make that much difference. Now, shooting the picture in black-and-white was quite a different thing than if it had had to be shot in color. I have no doubt that, if we'd shot it in color, we would have had to play down the effects considerably, otherwise it would have been too gory. As it was, it got an X Certificate in England.

What I *wasn't* prepared for was that, when the film was released in England and it opened by itself at the Ritz Theatre in Leicester Square, the newspapers would be so offended by what they considered the excessive gruesomeness of the picture, that they made a major issue of it in the reviews, and it got to the point where somebody brought up in Parliament the fact that the British Board of Film Censors did not seem to be fulfilling its obligations in preventing the showing of a film like *Fiend Without a Face*, which was a "disgrace" to the British film industry, and obviously was influenced by the kind of pictures that were being made in America — pictures which they didn't think should be shown in England either.

Q: When newspapers are saying that your movies are too revolting to be called entertainment, and when somebody in Parliament says it's a crime that your movie got released, what goes through a producer's mind?

GORDON: What went through *my* mind was that I could never have afforded to buy that publicity, if it hadn't come my way free, and that it was the best possible thing that could happen to the picture. Which perhaps is a cynical attitude, but we were in the business to make a box office success and to make money and to be asked to make additional films, and this seemed to be playing right into our hands, as it were. In those days, none of the censors, not even the Catholic Legion of Decency, realized that the more they complained, the more people would want to see the pictures. The "forbidden fruit" [syndrome].

Q: Was it cut in England?

GORDON: It wasn't cut much. The scenes of the Fiends being shot and disintegrating were shortened; that was really *all*, because the scenes when the Fiends are invisible and are doing their killings are not excessively gory. In the United States, where it was distributed by MGM, of course the picture had to be submitted to the Motion Picture Association for approval, to get a Code seal. They also shortened some of these scenes. There were *some* countries, fortunately not any of the major territories, where the picture was banned altogether, simply on the basis that it was too grisly to be shown.

A Fiend catches up with its creator at a recent Monster Bash convention. PHOTO COURTESY GORDON REID.

Q: *Variety* wrote that *Fiend* "oozes and gurgles with Grand Guignol blood and crunching bones, easily one of the goriest horror pictures in the current cycle." And according to *Motion Picture Daily*: "This entry in the science fiction, horror division, sweepstakes is well and logically constructed, capably acted and directed with an eye toward building suspense." But I've seen more reviews that were in line with *Harrison's Reports*: "During the final fifteen minutes, [the picture] is just plain revolting, to an extent that even those with strong stomachs may not be able to take it.… What gives one a feeling of revulsion is the fact that, as the 'brains' are shot down by the different principals, they fall lifelessly to the ground and ooze slime. All this is depicted so vividly that it makes the viewer sick to his stomach.

Because of its excessive gore, the picture is too unpalatable to be classified as entertainment."

GORDON: At the time, I thought these reviews could only help us. They certainly weren't going to stop MGM from distributing the picture. And the publicizing of such elements has always been a draw to the public, rather than preventing them from coming to see the film.

Q: Some of these reviews were written not for the public but for exhibitors.

GORDON: Exhibitors were not concerned at all.

Q: The Fiend sound effects — the heartbeat sound and the slurping and the noise like something being dragged...just terrific!

GORDON: I think they worked very well, and when I see the film today I think they *still* work well. I used some similar sound effects for the Silicates in *Island of Terror* [1966]. It's the first part of *Fiend Without a Face* that, I think, dates it, because it's rather slow-moving, it takes a long time to get into the story, and that's not the way pictures are made today. Today the theory is that if you don't have a lot of things happening right at the beginning of the picture, you're going to lose your audience. So I think the first part of *Fiend* is somewhat dated in its pace, but hopefully holds the interest still.

Q: Why do brains have heartbeats in your movie?

GORDON: To make them more frightening. And also, because while they're invisible, you need *something* to convince the people that there is a force at work. You'll notice that once we get into the Fiends materializing and interacting with the human beings,

Among the many vintage movie monsters making cameos in Looney Tunes: Back in Action (2003) were the Metaluna Mutant, Robot Monster, Triffids and — here seen battling star Brendan Fraser — a Fiend (created by the Hollywood special effects studio KNB EFX).

the heartbeats are practically eliminated. The brains were all manufactured in Munich, which is where the special effects were created. There was a German team of special effects men who called themselves Ruppel & Nordhoff, who had done some work in England, principally for the Rank Organisation. They specialized in combining live-action with rear-projection, and also traveling mattes which were used in a lot of the Rank war films — shooting airplane sequences and battles in the sky with models. John Croydon had met these people during his work at the Rank Organisation and introduced them to me, and they immediately reacted very favorably to the project of *Fiend Without a Face* and came up with some suggestions. We made a deal with them and they created the special effects in their Munich studios where I spent a great deal of time while principal photography under John Croydon's supervision was going on in England. Towards the end of the shooting, some of the effects shooting was moved to Walton Studios. When the Fiends become visible and interact with human beings — *that* had to be done in England, because we couldn't recreate the sets in their special effects studio in Munich. Also it would have meant taking all the actors in that final scene to Munich, which wouldn't be practical. It was easier to bring Ruppel & Nordhoff and their special effects to England. The two gentlemen arrived with trunks full of Fiends of all different sizes [*laughs*], which they'd brought with them to be used for that final sequence.

Q: Was Nordhoff really a baron, as he liked to call himself?

GORDON: Nordhoff called himself Baron von Nordhoff and claimed he was an Austrian. I never checked into it because — well, because it didn't make any difference to me [*laughs*]. But thinking back on Josef von Sternberg, who was not really named von Sternberg, and Erich von Stroheim, who was not really named von Stroheim, I believe it's very likely that Nordhoff was not von Nordhoff. He was a very theatrical character, very eccentric, and if that's what he wanted to call himself, we didn't care. Ruppel was a much quieter and more reserved person.

Q: John Croydon, writing in *Fangoria*, said of Nordhoff: "Flo is a strange, likable man. A little crazy, as his features and behavior suggest, with a penchant for eating vases of tulips when in his cups."

GORDON: I never saw him eating tulips, I have to admit. I did see him, once or twice, in his cups, but perhaps it was when tulips were out of season [*laughs*]. So I can't bear witness to that!

Q: Croydon also wrote in *Fango*, "Many grotesques have flown from [Nordhoff's] pen and brush — a little Dali-esque, a little Picasso-esque, always fascinating. A mind easily adapted to the creation and birth of a Fiend."

GORDON: That is absolutely correct, and that of course is what sold us on employing Ruppel & Nordhoff to do the special effects. One day early on, John Croydon and I were having lunch with them at Walton Studios, discussing the project — this was before we had made a commitment. John was describing the story of *Fiend*, and all the time he was talking, Nordhoff was sitting there doodling away on little pieces of paper. We thought he was just being slightly distracted and not paying too much attention, but at the end of John's recounting of the story, Nordhoff suddenly turned over these pieces of paper and asked us to look at them. As he was listening to the story, he had been creating the Fiends in his mind and then putting them down on paper, and they were very much like the Fiends as they appear in the final picture! That of course was the clincher, and we immediately signed them. So Nordhoff came up with the "look" of the Fiends, which was then inserted into the script.

Q: Spinal-cord tail and all?

GORDON: Yes. I have to give Nordhoff credit for *all* of those things. The description of the Fiends in the original screenplay was left very loose because, until we had signed a special effects expert and worked with him, we didn't really know ourselves what they were going to look like in the finished picture. And of course in the original story "The Thought-Monster" the Fiends are never visible so they're never described, and there was nothing to go on.

The Ruppel & Nordhoff studio in Munich was relatively small and in the basement of a building in which one of them lived, I forget now which one. The Fiends were animated by the stop-motion process, which was used in *King Kong* [1933] as a technique. If it was good enough for *King Kong*, it was good enough for *Fiend Without a Face* [*laughs*]! Doing the work were Ruppel and Nordhoff, and one assistant. The shots that didn't involve the interaction of humans or show too much of the location or set where they were taking place, were photographed there in Munich. We would look at rushes every day and make sure they were all right, because it was done on a trial-and-error basis. If something didn't look right, it had to be re-done.

Q: When the Fiends are killed, they make quite a mess.

GORDON: A combination of stage blood and raspberry jam was used to represent the blood coming out of them when they were shot. Later in the scene, each "dead" Fiend was replaced with a gooey mess which was supposed to be their total disintegration. Then, for the shots where you see the gooey mess gradually dry up and then disappear altogether, we simply used a hairdryer to clear up the mess. Again, it was done with stop-motion photography.

Q: What were some of the publicity ploys MGM used in the U.S. during *Fiend*'s theatrical run?

GORDON: After *The Haunted Strangler* and *Fiend Without a Face* were completed, I made a worldwide distribution deal with MGM — "worldwide" excluding only the U.K., where Eros Films released them. Next I was put together with MGM's publicity department to work out the ad campaign. I had certain problems with MGM. I mean, it was a great coup for Chuck Vetter and me that the first two films we ourselves actually produced were picked up by MGM for worldwide distribution. MGM had not up to that time been in the habit of distributing independent pictures, certainly not low-budget independent pictures, but the management that was there at the time, which had fairly recently been installed, decided that they needed that kind of programming in order to keep up with the developments in the business, and so they were very happy to get the films.

Q: The "problems with MGM" you mention included people like the Detroit theater manager who didn't like having to play your pictures and wouldn't ballyhoo them [see page 39 for the full anecdote].

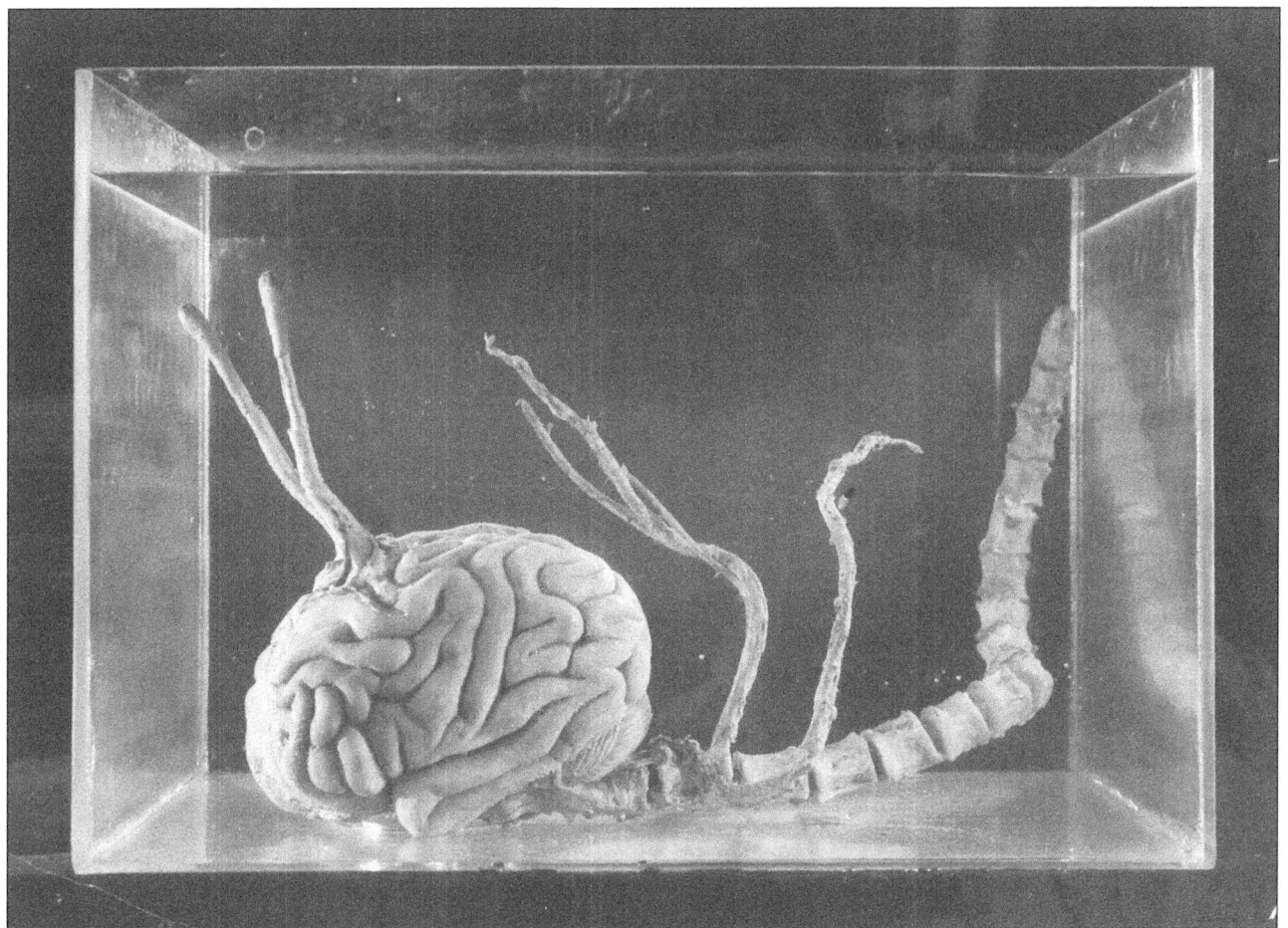

A close-up look at a Fiend, encased in glass for its in-person debut at Manhattan's Grand Guignol, the Rialto Theater.

A Fiend "takes Manhattan" as throngs of curiosity-seekers gawk at the display outside the Rialto.

GORDON: That's correct. However, when it came to the New York opening, we were able to arrange for the double-bill to open [on July 3, 1958] at the Rialto Theater, which was then known as the House of Horror in New York because all the horror and exploitation and science fiction pictures used to play there. We built a very elaborate theater front based on Karloff and the Fiends, and we got hold of one of the full-scale models of a Fiend —

Q: An actual, used-in-the-movie Fiend?

GORDON: Yes. We put it in a glass case in the street outside the theater. Every few minutes, the Fiend would move its motor-activated tail as a tape played the sounds that the Fiends make in the movie. Well, this attracted a tremendous amount of attention in Times Square, and there were crowds gathered around the Fiend display at all times — so much so that after two days, the police made us take away the display because they said we were disrupting the traffic and flow of Times Square pedestrians, and this couldn't be allowed. The theater had no lobby that was suitable for this kind of thing, so that was the end of that. But the program did very well there; *wherever* it played in suitable locations, it did very good business. Overall it obviously did very well for MGM because they then joined with Producers Associates in the financing and production of our next two pictures: my second Boris Karloff film *Corridors of Blood* [made in 1958, released in 1962] and my second Marshall Thompson film *First Man Into Space*.

Q: Is it true that there's a print of *Fiend Without a Face* in the Museum of Modern Art's permanent collection?

GORDON: Yes, absolutely. In fact, the Museum of Modern Art requested prints of the four films we did with MGM, as representative of independent production distributed by what was then Hollywood's leading studio.

Q: Over the years you've occasionally talked of remaking *Fiend*.

GORDON: I've always had the desire to remake *Fiend* in color and on a bigger budget. The difficulty is to come up with a script that is feasible in today's climate. You can't just remake the old picture scene by scene in color and on a bigger scale; I think it's been proven with several recent pictures that tried to go that route (like the 1998 *Psycho*) that it just doesn't work. We've made attempts with several different writers and we haven't come up with anything that's really satisfactory. If you move too far away from the original story, then all you're doing is using the title and making a brand new picture, which is only going to alienate people who have fond remembrance of the original film. And if you

The 1999 Manchester Festival of Fantastic Films was the scene of another Gordon-Fiend reunion.

stick too close to the original film, then you're going to have something that's outdated and isn't going to work. Something else that worries me is the fact that, with special effects being the way they are today, we would have to go so far overboard in presenting the gruesome aspect of it that it wouldn't be fun any longer.

Fiend Without a Face has acquired quite a reputation over the years and it's become a cult movie. I've been lucky enough to be invited to a number of festivals devoted to horror and science fiction films in recent years, to introduce the film and to speak about it, and it always get a very warm and friendly reception.

Q: You were presented with a newly made Fiend at a recent Manchester [England] Festival of Fantastic Films.

GORDON: Yes, in 1999 they surprised me by marking the 50th anniversary of Gordon Films Inc., and part of the celebration was a gigantic 50th anniversary cake that they rolled out, with a full-sized rubber reproduction of a Fiend on the top. I was left speechless, which (as you can tell from listening to me today) is something that doesn't usually happen [*laughs*]! But I was so unprepared for it that I really didn't know what to say. It was a wonderful moment and a very nice tribute to the picture.

FIRST MAN INTO SPACE
1959

CREDITS

Executive Producer...*Richard Gordon*
Produced by..*John Croydon & Charles Vetter Jr.*
Directed by...*Robert Day*
Screenplay..........*John C. Cooper [John Croydon] & Lance Z. Hargreaves [Charles Vetter Jr.]*
Original Story..*Wyott Ordung*
Photography...*Geoffrey Faithfull*
Editor...*Peter Mayhew*
Production Manager...*George Mills*
Electronic Effects..*Sound Drama*
Music Composed & Conducted by..*Buxton Orr*
Sound Editor...*Peter Musgrave*
Sound Recording...*Terence Cotter*
First Assistant Director..*Stanley Goulder*
Camera Operator..*Frank Drake*
Continuity..*Kay Rawlings*
Location Manager..*John George*
Wardrobe...*Charles Guerin*
Hair Stylist...*Eileen Warwick*
Miss Landi's Dresses Supervised by Anna Selby-Walker

Uncredited

Special Effects..*K.L. Ruppel*
Rocket Model Maker..*Peter Bestehorn*
Second Unit Footage.................*Alex Gordon, John Carpenter, and possibly Ed Wood*
Production Secretary..*Margery Warnes*
Second Assistant Director...*Claude Watson*
Focus..*Les Paul*
Clapper/Loader...*Peter MacDonald*
Sound Maintenance..*Brian Hunter*
Boom Operator..*Claude Hitchcock*
Art Director..*Denys Pavitt*
Buyer..*John Bigg*
Construction Manager...*Peter McGoldrick*
Assistant Editor..*George Saxby*
Still Cameraman..*Norman Hargood*
Production Accountant..*Arthur Tarry*
Makeup..*Michael Morris*
Chief Electrician..*Tom Chapman*
Assistant Electrician...*Tom Cookson*
Chief Props..*S.A. Davis*
Props...*W.R. Hill & C.W. Burgess*
Grip..*W.R. Venn*
Stagehand..*J. Lithgow*
Carpenters..*Harry Arbour, G.J. Moody & Jim O'Neill*
Painters..*P.W. Vaughan & W. Hawkes*
Rigger..*L. de Rose*
Publicity..*Philip Ridgeway Associates Ltd.*

77 minutes

CAST

Marshall Thompson	Comdr. Charles Ernest "Chuck" Prescott
Marla Landi	Tia Francesca
Bill Edwards	Lt. Dan Milton Prescott
Robert Ayres	Capt. Ben Richards
Bill Nagy	Police Chief Wilson
Carl Jaffe	Dr. Paul von Essen
Roger Delgado	Ramon Guerrera — Mexican Consul
John McLaren	Harold Atkins — State Department Official
Spencer Teakle, Chuck Keyser, John Fabian	Ratings Control Room
Richard Shaw	Witney
William R. Nick	Clancy
Helen Forrest	Secretary
Rowland Brand	Truck Driver
Barry Shawzin	Mexican Farmer
Mark Sheldon	Doctor
Michael Bell	State Trooper
Sheree Winton	Nurse
Franklyn Fox	Chief Petty Officer
Laurence Taylor	Shore Patrolman)

Uncredited

Bonar Colleano	Voice of Lt. Dan Milton Prescott)

SYNOPSIS

Lt. Dan Prescott, test pilot of the Navy's newest rocket, the *Y-12*, takes off from the U.S. Naval Air Development Center in Alvega, New Mexico. Once underway, daredevil Dan decides to set a new altitude record and, despite radioed instructions to turn back from his brother Comdr. Chuck Prescott, he soars ever farther into space. No sooner does the *Y-12* return to Earth via parachute than Dan goes AWOL, leaving the landing site for a tryst at the apartment of his Italian girlfriend Tia.

Despite his unpredictability, Dan is next assigned to pilot the *Y-13* — and again his craving to be a record-breaking hotshot clouds his judgment. Disobeying Chuck's orders, he flies beyond the planned altitude and even fires his emergency booster rocket in order to become the first man to reach outer space. In space, however, the *Y-13* flies into a cloud of meteorite dust and Dan is forced to press his ejector button. Back at the base, all must assume that he has lost his life. Chuck tries to comfort Tia, who is on the staff of Dr. von Essen of the Aviation Medical Dept. at the University of Albuquerque.

When the *Y-13* nose section lands near a local farm, Chuck rushes to the scene to examine it. Metallurgic tests show that the craft is now encrusted with meteorite dust. Soon a monster is killing cattle for their blood, and even slays a New Mexico State Hospital nurse during a blood bank break-in. Finding shiny specks of meteorite dust in the wounds of both the animal and human victims, Chuck realizes that his brother Dan is the monster.

His body and brain starved of blood because of exposure to cosmic rays, Dan is hideously encased in a coating of bulletproof meteorite dust. In search of Dr. von Essen, he bursts into the Aviation Medical Dept. building, gasping as he struggles to breathe in Earth's atmosphere. Heard over the public address system, von Essen's calming voice directs the hulking monster through the darkened hallways to the high-altitude chamber, in which he is sealed so that he can breathe more easily. Chuck also enters the chamber even though he cannot live long in its now-rarefied atmosphere. Again able to breathe properly, think and speak, Dan submits to metabolism and blood pressure tests as he relates the details of his harrowing experience in space. "I'm sorry things had to happen this way," he gasps out to Tia, "but, you see, I — I just *had* to be the first man into space!" Dan drops dead to the floor and Chuck weakly staggers from the chamber.

RICHARD GORDON ON *FIRST MAN INTO SPACE*

RICHARD GORDON: We first signed Marshall Thompson to appear in *Fiend Without a Face* [1958], and he was so helpful and cooperative and such a nice guy that when it came to planning *First Man Into Space*, I decided to use him again. But there was going to be a considerable interval between the making of the two pictures, during which he was going to go back to Hollywood as he really didn't want to hang about London with nothing to do. I thought if we could come up with a screenplay that would appeal to him, that we could shoot quickly and easily *between* these two pictures, we would have an extra film with him. I found a screenplay called *The Secret Man*, written by one "Tony O'Grady," which actually was a pseudonym for Brian Clemens, who later became famous for writing many of the *Avengers* television scripts. We made that movie [in November 1957] while *Fiend Without a Face* was still being edited, and *First Man Into Space* was in preparation.

Q: All of your early pictures had American stars, and your brother Alex was the one who hooked you up with a number of them. Was it he who introduced you to Marshall Thompson?

GORDON: Yes, Alex, who was working at American International in Hollywood at the time, was dealing with a lot of actors like Marshall Thompson, John Agar, Richard Denning and others who were appearing in his pictures. As I was planning my films, I used to consult with him on who was available and get his take on what his experience in working with these people was. He highly recommended Marshall to me, so that was how we came about casting him in *Fiend Without a Face*.

At a reception for the Producers Associates movie *The Secret Man*, guests included actors John Loder and Marshall Thompson, unidentified woman, writer-producer-director Ronald Kinnoch and executive producers Gordon and Charles Vetter Jr.

Q: Funnily enough, Thompson ended up being in three of your pictures and *none* of Alex's!

GORDON: That's correct, but they had many discussions about doing movies together, which for one reason or another didn't materialize.

Q: Did you pay him a little more each time he starred in a picture for you, as you did with Boris Karloff?

GORDON: No, Marshall's salary for *First Man Into Space* was the same as for *Fiend Without a Face*. Actually, the first time that happened with me was with Zachary Scott who, I want to say right up front, was very nice. But I made a picture with him called *The Counterfeit Plan* [1957] which went over so well in the United States and England that we decided to do a second picture with him, *Man in the Shadow* aka *Violent Stranger* [1957]. The only *slight* run-in I had with Zachary was that, when it came to the second picture, he demanded a higher salary than for the first one. I had paid him $25,000 to make *The Counterfeit Plan*, and when I asked him to come back to England and do another picture, his agent said that he wanted $27,500. These figures today seem ridiculously low, but at the time they were normal figures for that kind of low-budget picture. After some argument I gave in and we agreed to $27,500. When Zachary came back to London to do the second picture, I sat down with him and one of the questions I asked him was, "Zach, why did you give me such a hard time by asking for an extra $2500? It doesn't mean that much to you but it meant a great deal to *us*. You enjoyed coming to England for *The Counterfeit Plan* and I know you *wanted* to do another film so, really, why did you insist on that?" And he said, "I'll tell you something that may be very helpful to you in your career in the future: Never work for the same guy twice for the same salary!" [*Laughs*]

Q: Who came up with the idea for *First Man Into Space*?

GORDON: It originated as a screenplay called *Satellite of Blood* that had been written on speculation by a writer in Hollywood, Wyott Ordung, whom again Alex knew. Ordung was among those writers who were doing pictures for people like Roger Corman and Herman Cohen and so on. Alex sent me the screenplay, because it was something that AIP decided not to do, and I liked it very much. We decided to use it as the basis for a film about space travel, because at that particular time, the late 1950s, space travel was very hot in the news. There was a lot of talk going on about it, there was a lot of real-life activity connected with it, and we thought it would be a very timely subject for a movie.

Q: How "into" the space race were *you* at the time? Were you watching the liftoffs on TV and so on?

Marshall Thompson never gets as much as a foot off the ground in *First Man* but that's all right; he'd just gone to Mars and back in *It! The Terror from Beyond Space*, shot about a month prior.

GORDON: I was watching it, but it wasn't something that I was so terribly interested in that I was absolutely *wedded* to it.

Q: Taking advantage of real-life headlines — that's something that exploitation moviemakers historically *do*, yes?

GORDON: We were *always* looking for real-life situations that could be exploited dramatically in movies, while they were still a hot topic.

Q: Once you had Ordung's script in hand, what was the next step?

GORDON: To do a rewrite of the script, so that it would fit within our budget requirements, or I should say our budget limitations [*laughs*], and also taking into account the fact that were making the film in England although the story was of course set in America. There was a considerable amount of work to be done on the screenplay before it was ready to be filmed.

Q: Interviewed in *Fangoria,* Ordung said that, of all his films, *First Man Into Space* was his favorite.

GORDON: That was actually quite flattering, because the finished picture was quite a distance removed from his original.

Q: How involved was MGM in the making of the picture?

GORDON: I had previously done a deal with MGM for *The Haunted Strangler* [1958] and *Fiend Without a Face*, which I produced independently but then licensed to MGM for world distribution. They were very pleased with those films, so they asked us what else we were going to do, and I mentioned this project among others. They said that, subject to their approval of the final script and the budget and all the usual things that major studios demand, they would be willing to finance this picture in exchange for having the world distribution rights. MGM had no direct involvement in the shooting of *First Man Into Space* apart from the use of their studio for some of the interiors, and they did not in any way interfere with the making of the film as long as it did not exceed the agreed budget since they were financing the picture 100 percent. By their "Hollywood studio standards," it was a very small investment.

Q: There being a blood-drinking monster in your movie, wouldn't Ordung's title *Satellite of Blood* have been more descriptive and exploitable?

GORDON: We didn't want to sell it as a horror picture, because the whole idea was to cash in on the interest in space travel. *Satellite of Blood* would have sounded

Canadian actor Bill Edwards enjoys a cigar as he prepares to soar into the wild blue soundstage.

like a picture possibly about vampires from outer space, that kind of thing, and we wanted to tie this picture in with the subject that was very much in the headlines of newspapers around the world at the time. We thought *First Man Into Space* would be a much more appropriate title.

Q: With the space program going great guns, did you worry that maybe there *would* be a first man in space before your picture got out?

GORDON: A real-life first man in space might have *increased* our picture's box office potential. But we were fairly confident that we were ahead of the game, so to speak, and that we would have the picture out before a man actually successfully went up into outer space.

Q: Was there as much of an emphasis on space travel as on the monster in Ordung's script?

GORDON: I don't remember how much "space travel" was described in any detail in Ordung's original screenplay, but Chuck Vetter was very knowledgeable on the subject and undertook to do whatever rewrites were required. Chuck was an American who had been quite successful in the production of commercials for television in the United States. When we met and we found that we hit it off quite well together, we decided to go into this whole scheme as partners, so that we would be able to go straight from one picture to another and divide the duties between us, rather than either competing with one another or working solo and therefore never being able to start a second picture until everything to do with the first picture was completed.

Q: *First Man Into Space* director Robert Day told me he hated the monster. He said he put forward the idea that the pilot should come back from space with an aberrated brain, not as a monster.

GORDON: I was not, at the time, worried about Robert Day's opinions of the "monster" aspect of the script. It was what I, and also Chuck Vetter, wanted, and what MGM accepted, and we felt it was a good, topical, "Hammer kind of movie" that satisfied us entirely.

Q: Why don't you get on-screen credit on your early pictures?

GORDON: *My* aim in forming Amalgamated Productions and, later, Producers Associates was to create a company that would have some identification, and would turn out pictures the way Jim Nicholson and Sam Arkoff were making pictures at American International. In order to attract producers like John Croydon to come in with us, I preferred to have *them* get the credit. I felt that I was acting as executive producer, which in those days you generally didn't put on the screen. I was promoting the company rather than the individual. Also, in those days it wasn't the normal practice that every picture had multiple producers and various executive producers and five *other* producers who really had nothing to do with the making of the picture. I was fortunate to have John acting as line producer on the first few pictures, he was entitled to the credit, and I didn't want to take anything away from him. It didn't seem to me to be so important for me to see *my* name up on the screen, which wouldn't mean anything to anybody else anyway. I was very fortunate to establish a good relationship and friendship with John, and to have him come on board to take charge of the actual production on a day-to-day basis.

Q: Where was *First Man* shot?

GORDON: There was no "one place" where the whole production was put together. It was shot on different locations in and around London and in the countryside. Most of it was shot in a mansion near Hampstead Heath, which is an area similar to New York's Central Park. Some of the exteriors, like the scene where the police car is chasing the monster's car, were shot on Hampstead Heath itself. And then finishing touches were done at the MGM Studios. Of course there was a certain amount of stock footage that we obtained from the United States. Also, my brother Alex shot some footage for me to use as establishing shots. That was done in California and the footage was cut into the picture.

Q: For movies like *Fiend Without a Face* and *First Man Into Space* you had to round up a lot of cars with steering wheels on the left, American-style.

GORDON: Just as there was in England a pool of supporting actors who were able to "speak American," there were also a number of companies that specialized in servicing film production needs, and could supply American cars with steering wheels on the left side, and whatever else was needed in the way of American hardware, to add to the believability of English films that were purported to take place in an American setting.

Q: Your *First Man* special effects were done in Munich.

GORDON: K.L. Ruppel, who had been our special effects man on *Fiend Without a Face* and was responsible for shooting the Fiend footage, had a Munich studio where he did a lot of effects work. We used his services to design and photograph the *First Man Into Space* rocket models and other such footage that needed to be inserted into the picture. I thought they did a very good job on it, considering our budget limitations, and also the short space of time during which the picture had to be made.

Q: *First Man Into Space* is similar plot-wise to Hammer's *The Quatermass Xperiment* [aka *The Creeping Unknown*, 1955]. Do you happen to know if anyone involved in the writing of *First Man* may have taken a few tips from *Quatermass*?

GORDON: I think inevitably that happened. Not in the case of Wyott Ordung when he wrote *Satellite of Blood*; but when his screenplay was rewritten by us in England, where *Quatermass Xperiment* had been a great success already, certainly the writers who worked on it (and Chuck Vetter was one of them) would have been influenced by that, and probably tried to emulate it a little bit.

Q: When we see the monster, how much of the time is it Bill Edwards in the monster suit?

GORDON: Most of the time it was Edwards, but there were occasions when he had to wear the suit for a very long period of time, and it became too much for him because of the difficulty of breathing and the heat inside the clothing. He would beg off, and we would have a stuntman standing by to take over. But

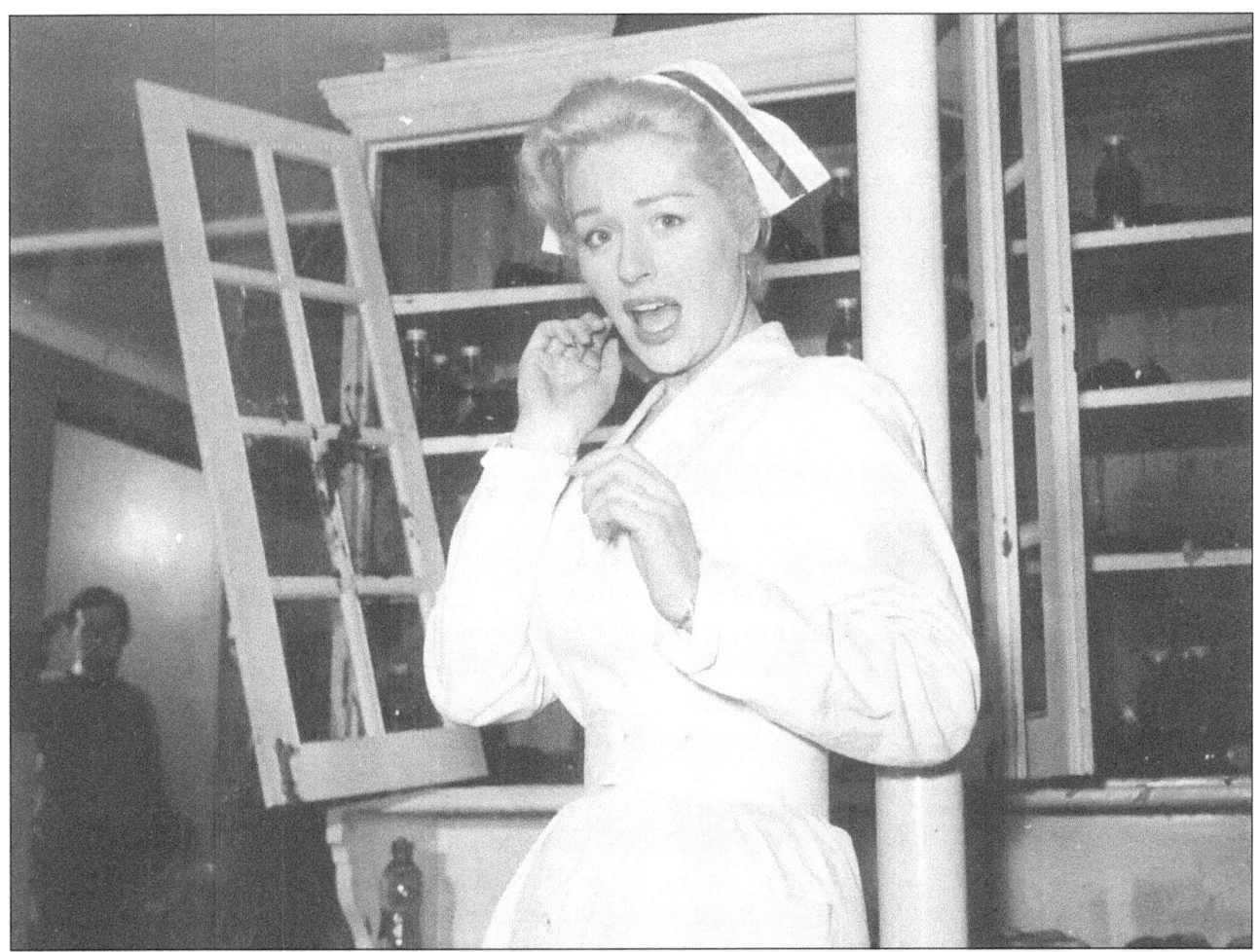

Glamour girl Sheree Winton as the blood bank nurse who becomes the monster's first victim.

Bill did as much of it as he possibly could, and I was very grateful to him for that.

Q: To me, it sounds like Edwards' lines have been dubbed-over throughout the entire movie. Was it his performance, or could he not maintain the American accent, or...what *was* the problem?

GORDON: At this late date, I can't recall the reason we had to replace all his dialogue. I *can* tell you that the dubbing was done by an American who was living in England and had become quite a successful actor, by the name of Bonar Colleano. He was a member of the well-known circus and vaudeville family, and had appeared on the London stage in *A Streetcar Named Desire* with Vivien Leigh, *A Bell for Adano* and *Will Success Spoil Rock Hunter?*

Q: Even when *First Man Into Space* was brand-new in 1959, audiences were hearing the voice of a dead man when the monster spoke: Colleano died in a car crash in August 1958.

GORDON: He was a very nice guy and very helpful. In fact, I had mentally made a note that in some future picture I would like to use him, because I thought he would also appeal to American audiences. But unfortunately, of course, it never happened.

Q: *First Man Into Space* has a good Buxton Orr music score.

GORDON: We employed Buxton Orr for the Boris Karloff picture *The Haunted Strangler*, which I think was the first of the movies I was involved in that actually had an original score specially written for it. Buxton was a serious composer and also a conductor of classical music who had done a few films, but was not one of those composers who had done it so many times that all you got was a variation on something he'd done before, for another movie. John Croydon made the contact with Buxton and we made a deal with him to do the music for both *The Haunted Strangler* and *Fiend Without a Face* because those two movies were shot back to back anyway, and employed a lot of the same talent behind the cameras. It worked out quite well, we were very pleased with his scores, especially for *The Haunted Strangler*, and so when it came to doing *First Man Into Space*, we asked him if he would be willing to come back and do another picture. He was quite pleased to do it, especially when he heard that it was going to be distributed by MGM worldwide as he felt that that might be a good career move for him.

He was very cooperative, but he was very much of a loner. He kept to himself, didn't socialize with anybody. He was very serious about the work he was doing, and he didn't really encourage us or anybody connected

In the role of Dan's girlfriend, international model turned actress Marla Landi added a touch of exotica. She's now Lady Dashwood, widow of Sir Francis Dashwood — a descendant of the English rake who founded the infamous Hellfire Club!

with the production to become too familiar with him. We paid him £500 to do both the composing of the score and also to conduct it when it was recorded. The deals were usually that the composer received a relatively small amount of money but in return for that, he retained all of the ancillary rights such as recordings, performance rights and any other sources of income that could be derived from the music other than the actual playing of the music on the soundtrack of the film. In other words, *we* had no rights to put it out on records or anything like that.

Q: The leading lady Marla Landi — how did you find her?

GORDON: Marla Landi, who was born and raised in Turin, Italy, was a top model whose picture had been seen in fashion magazines throughout the world. She was now trying to make a career as an actress in England; a number of French, Italian and German

First Man's "first lady" Marla Landi and the boss (Gordon).

actresses were then working in England, trying to establish themselves in the British film industry, because in their own countries the industries were lagging very far behind. Marla was brought to my attention by Jimmy Carreras, the head of Hammer Films, with whom I was on very friendly terms. He had used her or was planning to use her in a couple of pictures, including the Peter Cushing *The Hound of the Baskervilles* [1959]. So Marla and I met and, as I didn't want a typical English actress for the film which had an American setting, I thought it would be very suitable to have somebody like Marla Landi play the role. I liked her chemistry with Marshall Thompson in the romantic scenes, and with Bill Edwards in the earlier part of the picture.

Q: As director, you brought back Robert Day from *Haunted Strangler*.

GORDON: When we were preparing *The Haunted Strangler*, Day had just directed Launder and Gilliat's film *The Green Man* [1956], a comedy-thriller with Alastair Sim which became a sleeper and had considerable success in England. Day got very good notices for it, and was anxious to continue with his directing career. (Prior to that, he had worked as a cameraman for some years.) We made a deal with him to direct *The Haunted Strangler* and it worked out very successfully, so we asked him to join us again when it came to doing *First Man Into Space* and *Corridors of Blood*, especially because he got on very well with Boris Karloff during *Strangler*.

Q: Geoffrey Faithfull, your cameraman on *First Man* and a couple of your other pictures — he goes back to the days of the dinosaurs!

GORDON: Yes, he had a wonderful career as a cameraman over there in England, dating back to silent pictures. He also was the cameraman on the picture I did with Pat O'Brien, *Kill Me Tomorrow* [1957], and on *The Secret Man*, so I knew him and he seemed a very logical person for us to hire. He was very good at shooting low-budget movies quickly and economically, but giving them a look that made them appear far more expensive than they actually were.

Q: A couple of the reviews *First Man* got in 1959 complained about the long build-up to the monster scenes — we don't see him 'til the movie's more than half-over. Is that a fair criticism?

GORDON: I didn't feel that it was, because we thought that the build-up to the mission of *being* the first man into space would be of great interest to audiences, and that they would be interested in the scientific jargon and all of those things. I didn't feel that it took too long to get to the monster, no.

Q: The *First Man Into Space* press materials are full of funny suggestions for theater owners — a lot of publicity stunts and contests and so on, all tied to the movie. I was born in 1958, I missed out on *all* this stuff. Everything about moviegoing seems like it was more fun back then.

GORDON: It was a *lot* of fun back then. And it was customary for *all* pictures, not only horror and science fiction pictures and not only lower-budget movies, but *all* pictures to come out with campaigns of the type you're talking about, that were available to individual theater owners to promote the pictures. That side of the business has disappeared completely. Once it did, the only way a picture was promoted was over television and with a few interviews, and everything else had to take care of itself. I think that helped to make the moviegoing experience a lot less interesting than it was in those days.

Q: Straying from the subject of *First Man Into Space* for just a few moments…can you talk about your moviegoing days as a kid in England?

GORDON: When my brother Alex and I were growing up in London in the 1930s, moviegoing was divided between three kinds of cinemas. There were the glamorous palaces where the biggest and best pictures had exclusive first runs; the neighborhood circuits with their weekly double feature programs; and what we called the flea pits — small, independent halls that ran whatever product they could get, usually changing their programs three times a week. There were also the Saturday morning matinees for children that usually showed a B Western or action picture accompanied by a serial and a variety of shorts. Alex and I were avid readers of weekly fan magazines like *Picturegoer* and *Film Weekly*, and others directed particularly at children, such as *Boys' Cinema* and *Film Fun*. Fan clubs would advertise in those magazines and we joined many of them, which led to our starting our own fan club to honor cowboy idol Gene Autry and other Western stars of the period.

My earliest recollection of being taken to a cinema is of a jungle documentary called *Simba* [1928] at the end of the 1920s. Not long after, I clearly remember seeing a large-scale Western with Richard Dix called *Redskin* [1929]. In the mid-1930s, I was taken to see my first quasi-horror film, Fritz Lang's *The Testament of Dr. Mabuse* [1933]; being a foreign-language film with English subtitles that was deemed an art house picture, it escaped the British Censor's "For Adults Only" rating accorded to most horror films. I think it's the only horror film that ever actually gave me nightmares. I was not allowed to see the original *Frankenstein* and *Dracula* [both 1931] or even *King Kong* [1933], until many years later when they were reissued. I bluffed my way into *Son of Frankenstein* [1939] by showing an identity card, on which I had altered my birth date, to the box office cashier. Some horror films, like Tod Browning's *Freaks* [1932] and the Charles Laughton starrer *Island of Lost Souls* [1933], were at that time banned from English cinemas altogether and did not get a showing until some 30 or more years later.

Many incidents from those days are still clearly

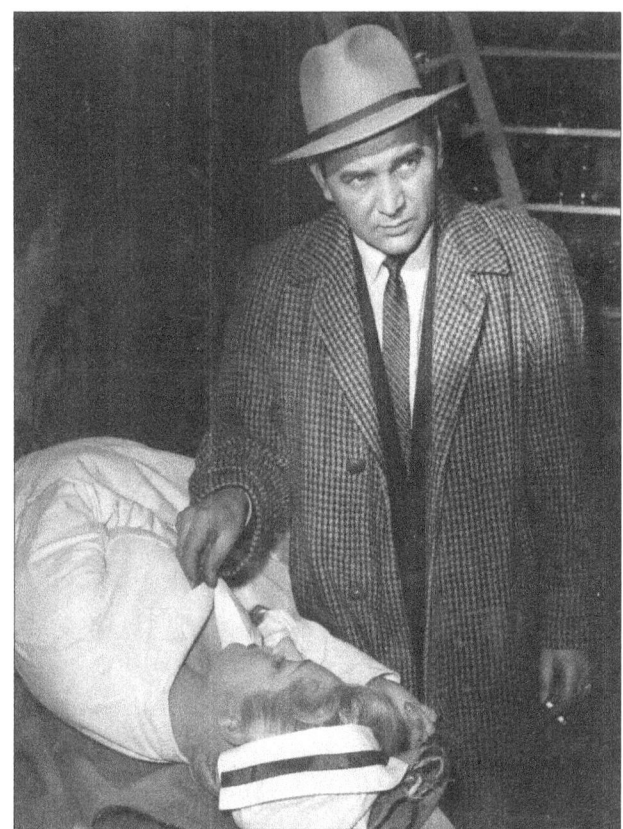

The *First Man* scene in the wrecked hospital room must be the bloodiest in any vintage horror film (covering the floor and dripping off shelves, walls and cabinets). In this family-friendly publicity photo, however, the police chief (Bill Nagy) isn't in danger of finding even a drop on the slashed-to-death nurse (Winton).

etched in my mind. When cinemas enjoyed full houses, they were allowed to sell "standing room only" tickets, and I remember seeing a double-bill of *Frankenstein Meets the Wolf Man* [1943] and another Universal horror film while standing at the back of the stalls for the entire program. During a run of one of the *Flash Gordon* serials, which we attended weekly, the cinema was struck by a bomb shortly after running the next-to-last chapter. It took me a year to catch up with the final episode at another location.

Gone with the Wind [1939] came to London and opened in a legitimate theater as a roadshow presentation with advanced-ticket prices for two performances daily. It was then moved to MGM's flagship cinema, the Empire in Leicester Square, and eventually moved again to their second first-run house, a much smaller venue called the Ritz, also in Leicester Square, where it ran for more than a year. Because of British Quota regulations, the cinema also had to show a British film, so MGM put in *Busman's Honeymoon* [1940] with Robert Montgomery, screened only after *Gone with the Wind*'s second daily performance; few people stayed on to watch it. On the night that Alex and I were there, we were the only remaining patrons. The manager tried to persuade us to accept free tickets to a future show in return for leaving so he could close the doors early. We refused and they had to run *Busman's Honeymoon* just for the two of us.

Reissues of famous films always remained a big attraction. A special event was a late 1930s revival by Paramount of the Rudolph Valentino silent classic *The Sheik* [1921] with a full symphony orchestra in the theater pit to provide musical accompaniment. The co-feature was also a reissue, *The Love Parade* [1929] with Maurice Chevalier and Jeanette MacDonald. To Alex and me, as children, the reissues were of course also always new. When something was shown that we particularly liked, such as Frank Capra's *It Happened One Night* [1934] at the Rialto in Coventry Street, we went two days running.

For many important first-run presentations, especially spectacles like Cecil B. DeMille's films and such pictures as *The Lives of a Bengal Lancer* [1935], the theaters would enact short prologues on the stage before the start of the film. Other examples of showmanship included nurses in the theater and ambulances waiting

In real life, the headline-making "first man into space" was Soviet cosmonaut Yuri Gagarin, soaring to fame in April 1961. According to his book *Road to Outer Space*, as he re-entered the atmosphere, his rocket was in the center of — no, not a meteorite dust cloud, but "a whirl of flames." Fortunately the rocket jockey did not return as a monster, as Dan Prescott (pictured) did.

in the street outside to promote a new horror film, or live dance acts in the foyer when there was a big new musical. It was an era of movie magic that left indelible impressions on all of us who were fortunate enough to participate. And it was a lot more glamorous than sitting in front of a television screen with a bottle of beer.

Q: When you mention B-pictures and serials, I assume your parents didn't always attend with you.

GORDON: Alex and my cinema-going was divided between the films our parents wanted to see, and to which they took us every weekend, and the flea pits where Alex and I went on our own. Alex and I also tried to go to various Saturday matinee children's programming which usually consisted of a Western, a chapter of a serial and some assorted shorts. When World War II started and London was constantly on the alert for the German enemy planes, Alex and I were more restricted from going out alone, particularly in the evenings. All cinemas were equipped with the sirens that notified audiences of the alerts and then the "all-clear" warnings. Alex soon was drafted into the Army but I had a few years still to go before I was old enough. I was particularly interested for a while in serials and wanted to see the 15 episodes of *The Amazing Exploits of the Clutching Hand* [1936] with Jack Mulhall, which was produced by Louis Weiss and released in England by New Realm Pictures. The only cinema I could find that was running the serial weekly was in London's Chinatown, known as Limehouse, where it was part of the program on several days every week. I was strictly forbidden to go out alone after school at night not only because of the threat of the air raids but also because Limehouse was considered too dangerous for a young boy to visit it alone. I suppose now that it was the equivalent of New York's Hell's Kitchen. Nevertheless, I made it through all 15 episodes after school hours and by pretending that the school was requiring me to be present at various classes in the late afternoons or early evenings.

Test pilot Dan goes up into space full of The Right Stuff and comes back covered in The Wrong Stuff (meteorite dust), to this hapless cop's dismay.

Q: Getting *back* to *First Man Into Space*: It was originally intended to go out on a double-bill with *Corridors of Blood*.

GORDON: When we made *The Haunted Strangler* and *Fiend Without a Face* and MGM took the pictures for distribution, and we were then planning *First Man Into Space* and MGM offered to finance the picture against

Capt. Richards (Robert Ayres) avoids a swipe by the *First Man Into Space*.

the world distribution rights, naturally they wanted a second picture to be part of the package, because in those days, practically all theatrical exhibition was still done via double-feature programs. So, yes, the idea was that *First Man Into Space* and *Corridors of Blood* would go out together, as a follow-up to *Haunted Strangler-Fiend Without a Face*. It was logical thinking: We would have a Karloff picture that was a horror picture and a Marshall Thompson picture that was science fiction, programmed together; it had worked the first time, and everybody thought it would be a good idea to try and make it work again.

But what actually *happened* was that *First Man Into Space* was shot ahead of *Corridors of Blood* and finished long before *Corridors of Blood* really got underway. MGM saw the finished film and, with everything that was going on in the newspapers every day about space travel and the anticipation of someone really going into outer space, they came back to us and said, "Why don't we release this film as a solo picture immediately, and take advantage of all this publicity? Later on, when *Corridors of Blood* is done, we'll find another picture to play with it." Chuck and I decided to go along with that.

Q: *First Man Into Space* had its premiere in Albuquerque, New Mexico, with ads proclaiming "Filmed in Albuquerque."

Within two days after Russia's October 1957 launch of Sputnik 1, *43* films on satellites and spaceships were announced. *The Flame Barrier* (1958) with Arthur Franz was the first to go into production but *First Man* may have been second. Unfortunately, foot-dragging MGM didn't have it in theaters until 1959!

GORDON: Well [*laughs*], let me tell you the story behind *that*! We set the story of *First Man Into Space* in New Mexico because that was where a lot of the experimental work was being done with space travel, and we wanted an American setting. My brother Alex shot some exterior footage in California for us; we also got some stock footage; and I think we came up with a very satisfactory resemblance to New Mexico in the film. *However*, when the picture was turned over to the MGM publicity department for distribution, someone had the bright idea that since the film took place in Albuquerque and presumably was shot there (they never asked me about it), it would be a terrific stunt to have the world premiere *in* the city where the picture was filmed. So they planned this whole, very elaborate [March 4, 1959] premiere in Albuquerque and arranged with Marshall Thompson to be there in person to promote the picture. And, as you will see in the advertising at the time, they had catch lines like "SEE THE FIRST MAN ROAR INTO OUTER SPACE FROM ALBUQUERQUE"; "SEE! Scenes of Alameda… The University… Sandia Base… New Mexico State Police in Action!" and so on. Of course the people who saw the picture at its world premiere were very quick to see that it wasn't genuinely filmed in Albuquerque, and we got a lot of laughs where it wasn't intended. But it did not spoil the success of the film.

Q: So *First Man* was a success, yes?

GORDON: We were lucky that we came along at the right time with the right picture, and so we had a very good success with it. This doesn't always happen. I don't regret anything to do with the making of the film, or any of its inaccuracies, like what might happen to a man as a result of space travel. I think it was just a very entertaining picture, and I'm quite satisfied with it.

Q: And, just to finish up on Marshall Thompson, did *The Secret Man* ever get much of a release?

GORDON: Overseas, yes. It was never released theatrically in the United States, although it did have a few television showings. Then in 2009, at Cinefest [a yearly convention for old-movie fans in Liverpool, New York], they showed my 16mm print of *The Secret Man* and I introduced it, pointing out that "theatrically," this was the first time it had been legally shown in this country. My greatest fear was that at the end of the screening,

This shot from executive producer Alex Gordon's *The Lawless Rider* (1954) provides a look at actor-stuntman-writer-producer John Carpenter, head of *First Man Into Space*'s California second unit. Also pictured is Alex himself, appearing on camera for the only time in a movie.

some people might say that it would have been better to let it stay buried [*laughs*]! In my intro, I declared that I would stay seated throughout the movie, because if I walked out, it might *start* something! I'm happy to report, however, that it was a packed house and most of the people stayed in their chairs, right to the end.

GUEST INTERVIEW: ALEX GORDON ON THE *FIRST MAN* SECOND UNIT

When Richard was in England putting into production his picture *First Man Into Space*, he had a problem: He needed some car drive-throughs and run-bys on roads that looked like they could be in New Mexico. He asked me if I could possibly get those shot for him over here and send the footage over so they incorporate it into the picture. I said, "Sure!"…but I didn't quite know how I was going to do this because I was not at a studio, so I couldn't use a studio crew; I'd have to hire the people. And of course we didn't have really any money to spend on this, we had to "steal" it.

Suddenly I got a brilliant idea: Johnny Carpenter, the actor with whom I was involved in my very first film *The Lawless Rider* [1954], was working mostly non-union, and he knew all these other people that he could pay off with…oh, I don't know, a pizza lunch [*laughs*]. I asked Johnny, "Do you think you could round up a crew and could we go out maybe on a Saturday, maybe around Iverson's Ranch? We just need to shoot some run-bys with cars." So Carpenter and some of his cronies, and it could even be that Eddie Wood was amongst them, went out to Iverson's Ranch with me and we shot these run-bys. It cost very little money, I think the total was about $500, and we were able to provide that footage to Dick.

FUN FACTS

While perhaps only New Mexicans could know for sure that *First Man Into Space* wasn't actually shot in their state, even non-residents might sense something amiss if they noticed in the movie not one but *two* signs which spell "authorized" the English way: authorised. Chief Wilson of the State Police (played by Bill Nagy) pronounces Alvarado Al-va-*ray*-do. The front page of the *Santa Fe Daily News*, seen in an insert shot, includes the *very* English-sounding story headline CLIPPIE NANCY MAY BE "SENT TO COVENTRY."

In the first shot of the Dirk Bogarde-Olivia de Havilland drama *Libel* (1959), as the camera pans around Piccadilly Circus, plainly visible is the London Pavilion marquee advertising its current attractions *First Man Into Space* and *High School Confidential!* (1958).

From the files of "You're safer flying (even in space!) than driving": In 1958, Bonar Colleano (who provided the voice of Dan as man *and* monster) died while en route home from a Liverpool theater when his car smashed through a fence. Fifteen years later, Roger Delgado (who had a comic relief role in *First Man* as a Mexican consul) died in central Turkey where he was making a movie for French TV; his chauffeur-driven car overturned at a sharp corner, also killing another passenger.

CORRIDORS OF BLOOD
PRODUCED IN 1958
RELEASED IN 1962

CREDITS

Executive Producer	*Richard Gordon*
Produced by	*John Croydon & Charles Vetter Jr.*
Associate Producer	*Peter Mayhew*
Directed by	*Robert Day*
Screenplay	*Jean Scott Rogers*
Photography	*Geoffrey Faithfull*
Music Composed & Conducted by	*Buxton Orr*
Art Director	*Anthony Masters*
Editor	*Peter Mayhew*
Production Manager	*George Mills*
Assistant Director	*Peter Bolton*
Camera Operator	*Frank Drake*
Sound Recordists	*Cyril Swern & Maurice Askew*
Dubbing Editor	*Peter Musgrave*
Continuity	*Susan Dyson*
Makeup	*Walter Schneidermann*
Hairdresser	*Eileen Warwick*
Dress Designer	*Emma Selby-Walker*
Wardrobe Mistress	*Doris Turner*

86 minutes

CAST

Boris Karloff	*Dr. Thomas Bolton*
Betta St. John	*Susan*
Christopher Lee	*Resurrection Joe*
Finlay Currie	*Superintendent Charles Matheson*
Adrienne Corri	*Rachel*
Francis De Wolff	*Black Ben*
Francis Matthews	*Dr. Jonathan Bolton*
Frank Pettingell	*Dr. Blount*
Basil Dignam	*Chairman*
Marian Spencer	*Mrs. Matheson*
Carl Bernard	*Ned, the Crow*
John Gabriel	*Baker — Dispenser*
Nigel Green	*Insp. Donovan*
Yvonne Warren [Romain]	*Rosa*
Howard Lang	*Chief Inspector*
Julian D'Albie	*Bald Man*
Roddy Hughes	*Man with Watch*
Robert Raglan	*Wilkes*
Charles Lloyd Pack	*Mr. Hardcastle*
Anthea Holloway	*Addie's Mother*
Bernard Archard	*First Dresser*
Frank Sieman	*Evans — Night Porter*
Charmian Eyre	*Ellen*

Uncredited

Gilda Emmanuelli	Addie
Peter Perkins	Sailor
Ivor Collins	Peter – Coachman
Brian Wilde	Blount's Assistant
Robert Brian	Tapster
Stan Simmons	Stoker
Fred O'Malley	Cook
Ken Buckle	Butcher
Stratford Johns	Workman
Skip Martin	Midget

Footage Deleted

Josephine Bailey	Child

SYNOPSIS

In 1840 London, before the discovery of anesthesia, surgical operations are scenes of horror, with hospital physicians cutting and sawing away at fully conscious patients. Dr. Thomas Bolton is determined to discover a means to perform painless surgery, but his colleague Dr. Blount scoffs, "You can't have operations without screams. Pain and the knife are inseparable." One day while caring for charity patients in Seven Dials, a notorious slum, Bolton is summoned to attend a sick man at the nearby tavern-lodging house of the roguish Black Ben. Bolton arrives to find the man dead, and signs a death certificate. He has no idea that he has been duped: Black Ben, his wife Rachel and their crony Resurrection Joe commit murder in order to sell fresh bodies to Blount, who teaches an anatomy class.

In his home laboratory, Bolton works to develop a gas that will render surgical patients unconscious; he inhales the gas and makes a notebook record of every experiment. Late one night, as a result of the inhalations, he bursts into uncontrollable laughter and wrecks his lab. As the gas effects wear off, his niece Susan points out that he has gashed his hand. Knowing that he felt no pain, Bolton realizes that he has succeeded. A demonstration at the hospital is arranged: With the eyes of dozens of medical men and students upon him, Bolton cuts into an abscess on an anesthetized man's arm. But the man revives too early, sees that the operation is in progress and lets out a scream. When onlookers laugh, the enraged patient runs riot. Bolton slinks away to a chorus of laughter and boos.

In his chemical experiments, Bolton now begins using opium; one night, in a gas-induced daze, he goes to Black Ben's, where a pickpocket takes his notebook. Now addicted to his inhalations, but no longer able to access the hospital dispensary, Bolton agrees to sign phony death certificates for Black Ben in exchange for the chemicals he needs. Under cover of darkness Bolton and Resurrection Joe break into the hospital dispensary; Joe kills a night porter who catches them in the act. Bolton's Jekyll-Hyde existence takes a toll on his mind and body; he horribly bungles a surgical operation on a little girl, and his son Jonathan must take over. The hospital suspends Bolton.

Hiding from the law, Bolton works in a new lab in an upstairs room at Black Ben's until Ben and Joe decide he's outlived his usefulness; Joe goes in for the kill. At that moment, police raiders burst into the tavern below, creating pandemonium. Joe stabs Bolton, who retaliates by flinging vitriol in his face; Black Ben attempts a rooftop escape and plunges to his doom. Susan and Jonathan hurry to the bedside of the dying man, who gives the notebook to Jonathan and begs him to carry on the work and prove that pain and the knife *can* be separated.

In the final scene, hospital operating room onlookers watch in awe as Jonathan performs surgery on a fully anesthetized patient. Nearby is a display case containing Bolton's notebook, glass retort and inhalator, and a nameplate that reads, "**IN MEMORY OF THOMAS BOLTON — 1778-1841.**"

RICHARD GORDON ON *CORRIDORS OF BLOOD*

RICHARD GORDON: In 1956 I had started to make pictures in England by setting up co-productions with independent British companies and furnishing

American actors and other facilities to produce the pictures. I did seven pictures that way, with actors like Zachary Scott, Pat O'Brien, Wayne Morris and Richard Denning. After a while, I felt I was ready to move on and start producing my own pictures, and so in partnership with a young American, Chuck Vetter, we started a production company in England called Producers Associates Ltd., with its American counterpart called Amalgamated Productions. *The Haunted Strangler* with Boris Karloff was the first film we made ourselves.

Q: Followed by *Fiend Without a Face*, a science fiction picture with Marshall Thompson.

GORDON: We made *The Haunted Strangler* and *Fiend Without a Face* back to back, to be put out as a double-bill, because everything in those days was double-feature programming. Then we followed that with two other pictures which were also originally intended to go out as a double-bill, *First Man Into Space* and *Corridors of Blood*. But for reasons that we can go into later, they ended up being distributed individually.

Q: You've told me that you had a clause in your first Karloff contract concerning a possible second picture.

GORDON: When I made the *Haunted Strangler* contract with MCA [Karloff's agents], it included an option to make a second picture within a specified period of time, and subject to our finding a script that Boris would approve. That is how we were able to do *Corridors of Blood*.

Q: But before you settled on *Corridors*, you had a couple different ideas as to what the second picture would be. The first thing you came up with was *Dracula's Revenge* with Karloff as Dracula.

GORDON: MGM suggested that, if we were going to make another picture with Karloff, we should do a CinemaScope color version of *Dracula*. But there was something that everybody overlooked, including MGM who had come up with the *Dracula* idea: When we went into the question of copyright, it turned out that we weren't free to make such a picture. Both the novel *Dracula* and the character were still owned by

 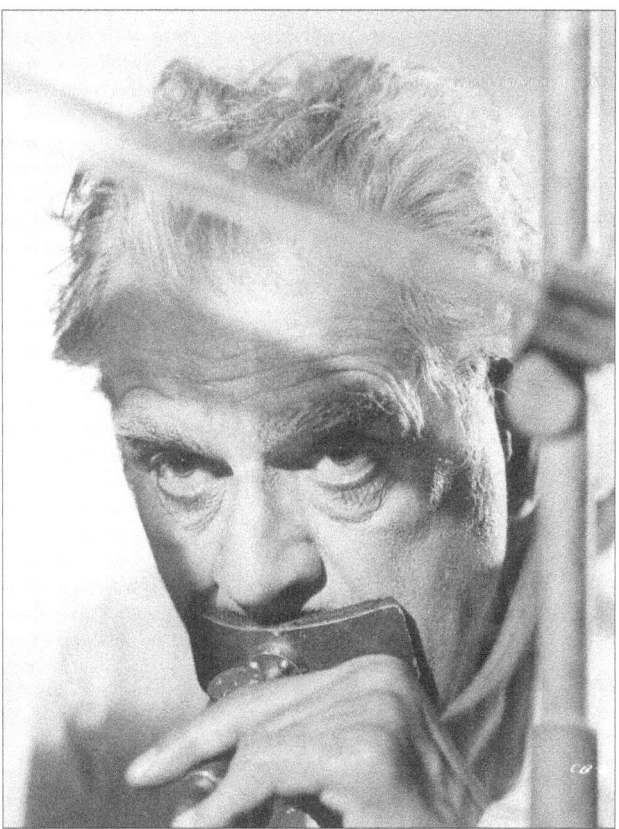

In *The Man With Nine Lives* (1940), a physician says of the miraculous "frozen therapy" work pioneered by Dr. Kravall (Karloff on left), "There's been nothing like this since the discovery of anesthesia." Eighteen years later, in *Corridors of Blood*, Karloff (right) would pioneer *that*, too!

Universal. In fact, it was very shortly thereafter that Universal partnered with Hammer to make the Christopher Lee *Dracula* [aka *Horror of Dracula*, 1958].

Q: What was Karloff's reaction to your idea that he play Dracula?

GORDON: His reaction was that if we would try to present the story more or less as it was in the Bram Stoker novel, rather than simply remake the famous version with Bela Lugosi, that it would be a very interesting project that he would be happy to participate in. But it didn't work out.

We then began looking around for other subjects, because by that point I had exercised the option on Karloff's services, and there was a limited period of time in which I had to make a picture before he had to get back to the United States to fulfill other commitments. We had an idea to take a story of Edgar Allan Poe's, "The Facts in the Case of M. Valdemar," and prepare a script that would be suitable; but there were too many problems in trying to get it done, and so we abandoned that. At that moment, [producer] John Croydon introduced us to a young English writer whom he knew, Jean Scott Rogers. Jean was preparing a screenplay based upon the factual history of the discovery of anesthesia, set in the days when surgeons were still looking for ways to make operations more safe and less painful. She was still working on the script at the time, and hadn't yet reached the point where she was sending it out for people to read. She had some very good ideas, and we eventually made a deal with her.

Q: And I'm sure that once she knew she was writing it for Karloff, that it became somewhat more "horrific" than if she'd been writing it for a star *not* associated with horror pictures.

GORDON: That's right. Karloff liked the script immediately. He felt that the historical background and the seriousness of the subject would be a welcome change from making "just another horror picture."

Q: Seeing *Corridors of Blood* many times while growing up, I "took the movie at its word" and assumed that the real-life inventor of anesthesia was English. But the rest of the picture, where he becomes an addict and a Jekyll-and-Hyde character...I figured *that* was all made-up. Now I come to find out that the one thing I "bought" — that the inventor was English — is *wrong*: The first painless operation was performed by an American near a slave plantation in Georgia. And the part that I thought was made-up is *true*: One of the early developers of anesthesia *did* become a chloroform addict and did lead a horrific Jekyll-and-Hyde life! In the movie there are several re-enactments of experiments and demonstrations that actually happened.

'Twould appear that *Corridors* scripter Jean Scott Rogers based Karloff's character on New England dentist and anesthesia pioneer Horace Wells (1815-48). After many setbacks, he became a down-and-out chloroform addict who went to jail for throwing acid at prostitutes!

GORDON: Jean Scott Rogers has to get the credit for that, because all those elements were in her screenplay from the time when we first read it. I never knew the real-life background of the history of anesthesia until then. Quite clearly Jean did her research.

Q: Did you need to submit the script to Hollywood's Breen Office, since it was going to be an MGM release?

GORDON: Fortunately we didn't, because it *wasn't* considered an MGM picture: It was from the beginning an independent picture that would eventually be distributed by MGM. Since there was no obligation on our part to submit it to the censors, we decided it would be best *not* to do so. We didn't want to start running into any difficulties that would cause delays in the start of shooting.

Q: Did you have to fly Karloff over from America for *Corridors*?

GORDON: No, at that point Karloff was in England, setting up a home where he intended to live from that period on.

Q: MGM released *Haunted Strangler* and *Fiend* but had nothing to do with the physical production of those movies. How involved were they on *Corridors* and *First Man Into Space*?

GORDON: What happened was that MGM was very pleased with the way *Haunted Strangler* and *Fiend Without a Face* looked, and with the budgets that enabled us to make those pictures; and so they proposed that they would be willing to finance our next program. They didn't in any way interfere with the making of *First Man Into Space*. But they did insist that *Corridors of Blood*, because of the nature of the subject and its backgrounds, should be made at the MGM Studios in Boreham Wood, and not at an independent studio.

Q: *Haunted*, *Fiend* and *First Man* were all shot at independent studios, yes?

GORDON: That's correct. We certainly could never have afforded to build sets of the kind seen in *Corridors of Blood* at an independent studio, if we were making the picture on our own.

Q: When *Corridors of Blood* began shooting on May 12, 1958, *Doctor from Seven Dials* was the shooting title.

GORDON: Yes, the script was called *Doctor from Seven Dials*. Seven Dials was a slum area in London where, in the 1840s, the sort of happenings portrayed in this film [the scenes at Black Ben's] could very easily have taken place. However, we felt that the title *Doctor from Seven Dials* would not mean anything to international audiences; moreover, it didn't in any way suggest a horror film or the kind of picture we were making. So various other titles were under consideration, and eventually we came up with *Corridors of Blood*. I can't honestly remember right now who suggested it. But that was the title under which we contracted with MGM.

Q: Jan Read, screenwriter of *Haunted Strangler*, told me that he was approached about writing *Corridors*. He also said that he felt the title was a takeoff on a hospital picture he had written, *White Corridors* [1951].

When Boris Karloff played a father, he almost invariably had a daughter; *Corridors* was one of the rare movies when he had a *son* (played by Francis Matthews). Can you name another?

GORDON: *White Corridors* was produced by John Croydon, which is where John originally met Jan Read; *White Corridors* was considered quite a classic British film in its day. But as to Jan's claim, no, it couldn't have happened that way; over the years, Jan must have become confused. Jan couldn't have been approached about writing the *Corridors of Blood* screenplay because the script was in the process of being written, by Jean Scott Rogers, at the time when it came to our attention. It *is* possible that someone at some point might have asked Jan if he would like to review the screenplay and make suggestions for modifications or offer ideas to add to it. But I have no recollection of that.

Q: John Croydon wrote in *Fangoria* that working as a tea boy on the set of *The Ghoul* [1933] was the first time he met Karloff. Was Croydon a fan of Karloff and/or horror movies?

GORDON: Even though he associate-produced the classic anthology horror film *Dead of Night* [1945], John was not particularly a fan of horror movies. But he did have very pleasant memories of having met Karloff on *The Ghoul*. By the time we were making these pictures, *The Ghoul* was considered a lost movie in England; there seemed to be no material in existence on the film whatsoever. Neither my brother Alex nor I had ever seen it, and as always in such cases, we were most anxious to try and *find* a way of seeing it, if ever a print surfaced. At one point, I approached the Rank Organisation and indicated that I would like to buy from them the remake rights of *The Ghoul*. I had in mind, of course, that it could be another vehicle for Boris Karloff, but I approached them as much in the hope of their finding a print and screening it for Alex and me as for any other reason! However, they said they couldn't find any material, and that there was no way of making a deal with us. Another company subsequently secured the rights to *The Ghoul*, going back to the original novel by English writer Frank King rather than worrying about the Karloff film, and they made a comic version which was quite awful [*What a Carve Up!*, aka *No Place Like Homicide!*, 1961].

Q: Playing a supporting part as a tavern girl in *Corridors* is Yvonne Romain, who later starred in your *Devil Doll* [1964].

GORDON: It was very pleasant working with her. She was very cooperative, and it was a very good experience. In fact, *almost* without exception, everyone in the cast of *Corridors of Blood* was extremely cooperative, and it was a very happy set from that standpoint.

Q: "Almost without exception."

GORDON: Yes, we'll get to that! Francis Matthews [playing Karloff's surgeon-son] was recommended by Jimmy Carreras, the head of Hammer Films, because Matthews was doing some work for Hammer as well. I followed up on that suggestion. Jimmy Carreras was always very helpful to me. Whenever he could give me any advice or suggest anything that he thought would be useful for me, he did so without thinking in terms of the fact that I might eventually become a competitor of his in the making of horror pictures in England.

Q: You were in the process of making four in a row and yet there he was helping you every time you turned around — that *was* nice of him!

An increased budget enabled Gordon to enlist the services of high-class actors (including Finlay Currie, pictured) in supporting roles.

GORDON: In those days, people tended to act that way. Today it seems to be it's just the opposite, that whenever anybody meets somebody new who is a potential competitor, they want to cut his throat rather than to give him any assistance [*laughs*]!

Q: Receiving special "And" billing in *Corridors of Blood* is Christopher Lee, in the first of his two movies with Karloff.

GORDON: When we were casting *Corridors of Blood*, I was invited by Jimmy Carreras to a screening of *The Curse of Frankenstein* [1957] at Hammer. Carreras pointed out to me the characterization of Christopher Lee as the Creature and he said that, since I was about to make a picture with Boris Karloff, he thought it would be a very good idea if I tried to engage Lee to play in the film. Carreras was quite sure that Lee would soon come into much greater prominence, and that it would be to my advantage eventually to have a film that co-starred Boris Karloff and Christopher Lee. I thought that was a very good idea and I arranged to meet with Lee at the production offices at Producers

Frank Pettingell as Dr. Blount, the arrogant naysayer with the refrain "Pain and the knife are inseparable." Hard as it may be to believe, in olden days there actually *were* physicians opposed to painless surgery.

Associates. That meeting resulted in my signing him to play the part of Resurrection Joe. In the original script, Resurrection Joe was a very minor character, and we had to rewrite and expand it in order to make it suitable for Lee and to justify the co-star billing. I found Lee somewhat pompous in his approach to the whole situation, and it wasn't the happiest of experiences. But he gave an excellent performance in the picture, and of course he *did* come into greater prominence and that's added to the residual value of the picture.

Q: In later years he was a neighbor of Karloff's in London, and claimed to be a great friend of his. Did you observe how they got along during the shooting?

GORDON: They seemed to get along perfectly well, but during our initial interview he did make the remark that he felt that people talking about the Frankenstein Monster in future years would be more likely to be referring to his performance in *The Curse of Frankenstein* than to Boris Karloff's creation of the character in the original *Frankenstein* [1931]. I thought this was hardly a pleasant approach to the subject of co-starring with Karloff in *Corridors of Blood*, but I didn't say anything about it. And I'm quite sure he never made any such remark to Karloff in person.

Q: Finlay Currie, who played the superintendent of the hospital in *Corridors*, was one of several excellent character actors you hired.

GORDON: The deal with MGM had its advantages and its great *dis*advantages — and we'll talk about the *dis*advantages in a minute [*laughs*]! But one of the advantages was that we had a budget and a studio where we could afford to employ a number of English character actors of a caliber that, under other circumstances, we might not have been able to engage. For instance, Finlay Currie, whom everybody will remember from his role as the convict in David Lean's *Great Expectations* [1946], but who was also a major star in British films for many, many years. Then we also had Frank Pettingell [as the sardonic Dr. Blount], a wonderful actor of both stage and screen in England. And there were several others, like Basil Dignam [as the hospital chairman], who were all top-flight British personalities that we were able to engage. Dignam was later the star of my *Naked Evil* [1966].

Nigel Green [as a Scotland Yard inspector] was an up-and-coming actor in England at the time. John Croydon suggested we cast him rather against type as the inspector, and it turned out to be an excellent idea. I think, in the few scenes that he has, he gives a very convincing performance. But unfortunately, his career didn't go very far, and he died at an early age.

Q: Whenever a movie starts out with Karloff as a nice-guy scientist trying to do something for the good of humanity, you just know it's all going to go to Hell in a handbasket and he's doomed. He made *so* many of those!

GORDON: That *was* the way he was cast in pictures much of the time. In fact, I suppose in a way it even applies to the characterization of the Frankenstein

Monster, which is what made it such a moving performance; you felt more sorry for him than terrified by him. That was a great difference between Boris Karloff and Bela Lugosi. In many of Karloff's films, although he played the villain, there was always some element that made you either feel sorry for him or at least understand what caused the villainy. Whereas with Bela Lugosi, when *he* played the villain, which he did in most of his pictures, he played it with such relish that it was almost as though he wanted the audience to hate him from beginning to end!

Q: *The Black Cat* [1934] being a major exception.

GORDON: Exactly, and it worked extremely well in that particular instance. That's why *The Black Cat* is one of my favorite pictures; I thought the juxtaposition of roles [Boris as an all-out villain, Bela as a sympathetic character] was such an interesting idea. It was an instance of Karloff playing a sinister and fanatic villain in such a manner that you could in no way whatsoever feel sorry for him.

Q: How much did you pay Karloff on *Corridors of Blood*?

GORDON: The deal with Karloff for *Haunted Strangler* was $27,500, and that was for a minimum guaranteed period of four weeks. At that time it was common, when you had an option on an actor's services for another picture, that the fee would be somewhat higher if the option was exercised, and in this instance we paid Karloff $37,000 when he agreed to do *Corridors of Blood*. It was, of course, also for a longer shooting schedule than *Haunted Strangler*.

Q: You told me that, on the *Haunted Strangler* set, Karloff would rest up at lunchtimes, so you couldn't socialize with him then.

GORDON: At the MGM Studios they had of course a fairly elaborate restaurant that was available to everybody who was shooting at the studio, but we didn't really have any lunches together. Karloff *was* very much under a strain, because of the physical activity involved with the film, and he tended to want to be by himself when he wasn't in front of the camera; not to socialize. The atmosphere was not as relaxed as it was during the shooting of *The Haunted Strangler*.

Q: So you did most of your socializing with him in New York.

GORDON: I visited him a number of times in New York, where he had an apartment at the Dakota, the building where *Rosemary's Baby* [1968] was shot —

Q: And where John Lennon was also shot!

GORDON: I not only visited Karloff at the Dakota but also Zachary Scott, with whom I made two pictures as co-productions before I started making my own films; he lived there with his actress-wife Ruth Ford. So I knew the Dakota quite well. Fortunately I never tried to visit John Lennon there [*laughs*].

Q: Karloff was always such a gentleman in his interviews. Did he let his hair down and let you know which past pictures of his he did and didn't care for?

GORDON: He did talk about some of his other pictures, particularly if he was asked about them, and naturally always expressed his gratitude to Universal for the making of *Frankenstein*, which was the beginning of his starring career. He quite clearly didn't like pictures of the caliber and type of *Voodoo Island* [1957] and *Frankenstein 1970* [1958], because he felt that these were pictures which had no artistic merit whatsoever. But he didn't denigrate the producers for *making* them or anything like that. If one asked him about a picture like *The Mask of Fu Manchu* [1932], he simply started laughing, because he thought the whole thing was a total disaster. His clearest memory of the making of *Fu Manchu* was of the scenes in which he had to play with a giant snake wrapped around him. He said that, in the heat of the arc lamps, the snake gave off such a stench that it was hard for him to concentrate on what he was doing.

Q: Starting in the '50s, Karloff expressed in interviews his disappointment with the rising levels of gruesomeness in horror movies. I bet he wasn't overjoyed with the new "sexual frankness" either.

GORDON: Off-screen he was, needless to say, exactly the opposite from his villainous roles: He was a highly educated, intellectual Englishman. As for his attitude toward the sexual frankness, I can recall that on one occasion when we were talking about the theater and current plays, he said that *Blue Denim* [1958], a then-current hit about a pregnant teenage girl [Carol Lynley], was *not* the kind of thing that ought to be playing on Broadway, because of its theme. And, yes, when horror films started to turn ultra-violent, he turned against them completely, and felt that it was a betrayal of the whole idea of making horror films. He thought that they were disgusting, and possibly something that he no longer wanted to be associated with. Well, some years later, after Karloff's passing, *I* began to get to that point as well. Horror films became *so* explicit. My own film *Inseminoid* [1981] already had more gore than I was comfortable with. Needing to make movies with that amount of gore, to satisfy the demands of the marketplace…it just wasn't fun any more.

Q: In your presence, did Karloff ever put down Bela Lugosi and/or did Lugosi ever put down Karloff?

GORDON: Karloff never "put down" Lugosi. Boris Karloff felt *sorry* for Bela Lugosi and did often refer to him as "poor Bela" — but not in a sarcastic or derogatory sense. He simply felt that Bela had been his own worst enemy in choosing the type of roles that he did, and in making no effort to lose his extremely heavy foreign accent, which at that time in Hollywood immediately relegated him to playing only villainous roles. So Karloff thought it was a shame that Bela did not have a better Hollywood career, considering the fact that in Hungary, as a younger man, Bela had been a star of plays by Shakespeare and others, he played Romeo and Hamlet, and he was far from being what he later came to be considered, a melodramatic horror actor.

Bela Lugosi was a little more outspoken in his criticism of Karloff. Certainly not in the way Martin Landau [playing Lugosi] acted and spoke in the film

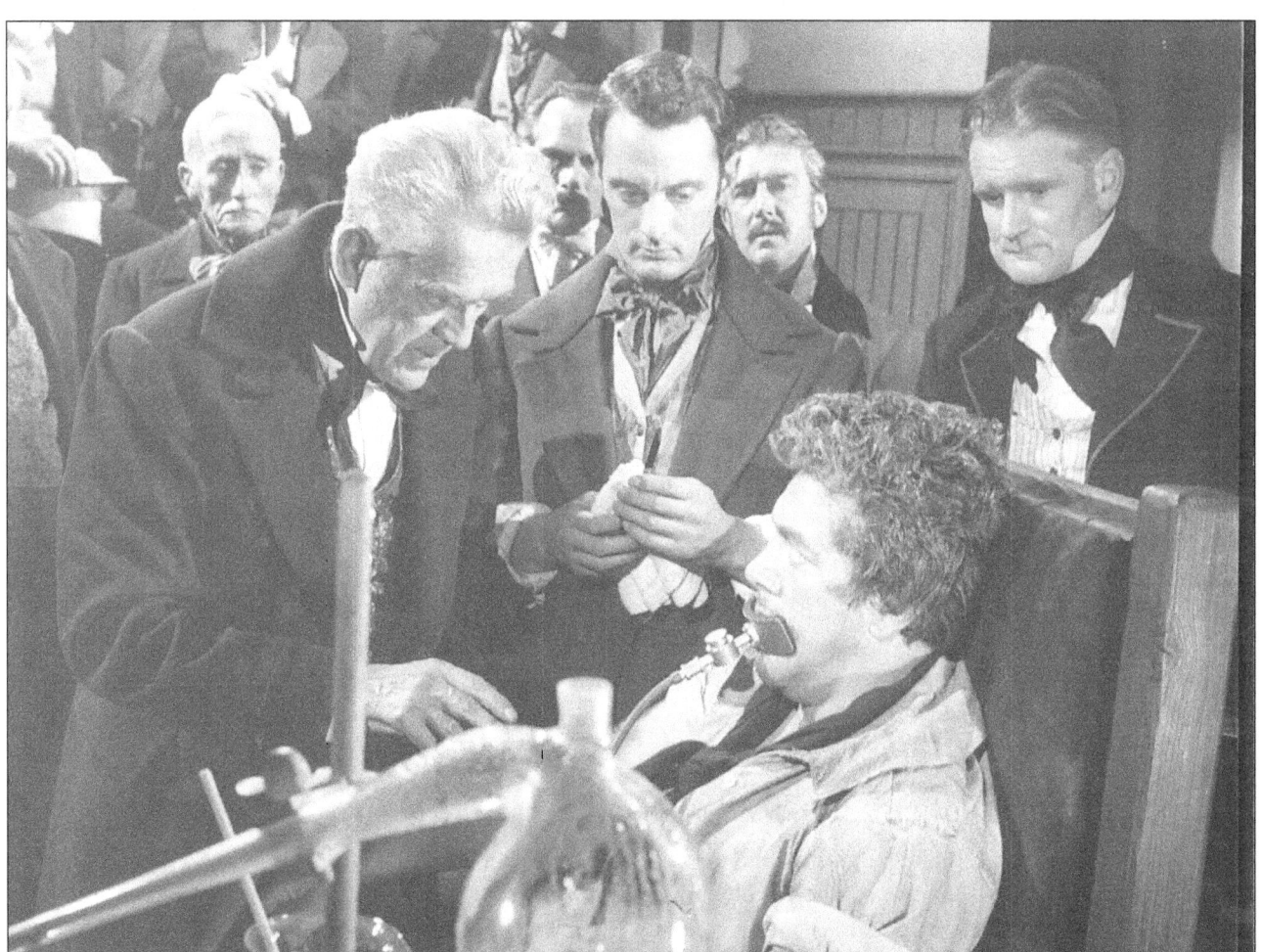

Father-and-son Boltons (Karloff and Matthews) prepare to anesthetize a patient, a demonstration that will turn out disastrously. The scene was no doubt based on an exhibition of the effects of nitrous oxide that took place in Hartford, Connecticut, in 1844, with identically riotous results; the administrator that evening was Gardner Colton (rhymes with Bolton). That fiasco was also recreated on screen in writer-director Preston Sturges' *The Great Moment* (1944).

Ed Wood [1994], using language that Bela would never have used at any time in his life; but Lugosi obviously was envious of Karloff's success. By the time I met Lugosi and worked with him, he had convinced himself that in his own way he was partially responsible for Karloff's success because he, Lugosi, had turned down the role of the Frankenstein Monster when it was offered to him at Universal, and it was as a result of that that director James Whale gave the part to Karloff, and Karloff became an international star.

Q: Can I get you to re-tell your famous story about the autographed Karloff photo in your office?

GORDON: Yes, I used to have autographed photos of all the people with whom I was associated hanging in my office. And I discovered early on that when Bela came to my office and saw his picture hanging next to Boris Karloff's, that he got very upset about the idea [*laughs*]! So after that, whenever there was an appointment for Bela to come up to my office, I would take down the picture of Karloff and substitute somebody else — and then hang it up again after Lugosi left!

Q: Mrs. Karloff — was she on the sets of *Haunted Strangler* and *Corridors* much?

GORDON: On the days when Karloff was working, Evie was there almost all the time. She was extremely protective of him, very concerned about looking after him: to make sure that he was comfortable, to be there if any problems arose, and so on. But in a *nice* way, not in any way to interfere with what was going on, or to complain to me or to John Croydon or to make suggestions that would make it uncomfortable for us. She just wanted to be sure that Boris was fully protected, that he was given the consideration to which he was entitled, and that everybody was behaving towards him the way she thought they should. And so I was very glad about her presence, because I felt it was a steadying influence on everybody. Naturally there *are* tensions when you are producing a picture under the limitations and difficulties that we had here, so I think it also *helped* Boris: He did not resent her presence, he did not feel that she was trying to in any way interfere with him or dominate him. I think he appreciated very much that she wanted to look after him, and he never had any arguments or dispute with her about that. I found her to be a very, very nice lady, and I remained in touch with her for a number of years after Boris died, and I was very sorry when eventually I heard that she had also passed away.

Q: Speaking of "tensions": John Croydon in *Fangoria* wrote about an incident on *Corridors* where director Robert Day tried to embarrass him and Croydon turned the tables and embarrassed *Day*; and he wrote about butting heads with Karloff now and then. He didn't make *Corridors* sound like a particularly fun set!

GORDON: There was a lot of tension on the set at times, and there have been a lot of different interpretations as to where those tensions came from. I must admit that, although John Croydon was a wonderful person and I was very happy to be working with him, I think that he was really responsible for some of the things that happened on the set. Robert Day was a superb director, he knew exactly what he wanted to do and in a very quiet, understated manner he usually achieved it. He got along very well with Boris Karloff, there was an immediate rapport between them. I think that Croydon ended up being somewhat jealous of their friendship, because he felt that he [Croydon] was being pushed aside. Also, he didn't always approve of the decisions that Robert Day was making — which he shouldn't have voiced, because once you're in production on a picture with a director of that caliber, you let him get on with it, and only start to interfere if things go wrong. So there *was* tension, Croydon tried to create problems which should never have existed, and Karloff and Robert Day together sort of sided against him. But it in no way interfered with the completion of the picture or in any way increased its budget or caused delays or anything like that. It was just a clash of personalities.

Q: Croydon also wrote that, subsequent to the making of these two pictures, he had many pleasant get-togethers with the Karloffs, so I assume everything was patched up.

GORDON: Well, that shows you the inconsistency of his attitude: Originally he was delighted to be working with Karloff [on *The Haunted Strangler* and *Corridors of Blood*] because it reminded him of the days when he was a tea boy on the set of *The Ghoul*. Then came this friction at the MGM Studios which caused a rift between them. Then, and I don't doubt it if that's what Croydon wrote in his *Fangoria* article, they became friends again; and perhaps they did have a happy relationship together, I don't really know about that.

Q: Did Croydon and Karloff stay on speaking terms throughout the making of *Corridors*, or were they ducking each other by the end?

GORDON: They were not ducking each other, but there *was* a moment when Croydon refused to address Karloff directly and would turn to me or to Chuck Vetter to say, "Would you please tell Mr. Karloff [this or that]," which was an indication of his stubbornness.

Q: With Karloff within earshot, or Karloff half a stage away?

GORDON: No, it was within earshot, Karloff was well aware of the situation. But Karloff was not the kind of person to either take advantage of it, or to take offense at the risk of causing delays or hurting the picture. So he overlooked it.

Q: Robert Day did a good job on *Haunted Strangler* and *Corridors*; they stand out in the last 20, 25 years of Karloff's career as practically his *only* good horror movies. Were you enough of a Karloff fan that, throughout the '60s, as his movies got worse and worse, that you'd go see each new one?

GORDON: I always went to see Karloff's movies. I was a fan of his from Day One. And I agree with what you say, Robert Day *was* an ideal director for these pictures. We were very fortunate in that respect. And I think Karloff was aware of the fact that, when he agreed to make these two pictures in England, this might be his last chance to make pictures of a quality that he considered worthwhile. That's why he put so much effort and so much enthusiasm into them. In fact, at the risk of physically making himself too tired or perhaps debilitating his health, he rallied and, I think, gave two wonderful performances in these films.

Q: Would you like to talk now about the *dis*advantages of the MGM deal?

GORDON: Yes, I'd like to very much, and I'd like to set the record straight, because there have been so many different stories about why the distribution of *Corridors of Blood* was delayed for such a long time. The arrangement with MGM was that they had financed *First Man Into Space* and they were going to finance also *Corridors of Blood*, provided that the film was made at their studio, which automatically meant that it would have a considerably higher budget than otherwise. In fact, the budget was close to £90,000, not including Karloff's salary and American expenses, and that was almost more than the budget of *Haunted Strangler* and *Fiend Without a Face* combined.

We started the picture at MGM, and MGM was putting up the money as it went along. As was fairly common among production deals at that time, there had been an agreement with MGM about how this was all going to take place, but a formal contract had not yet been signed when we actually began shooting. Several weeks after we started *Corridors of Blood*, there was a complete change of management at the MGM company in the United States; new people came in and took over, and one of their first decisions was that they no longer wanted to release the kind of pictures that the previous management had been acquiring from outside producers. *Corridors of Blood* was one of the pictures that they felt they no longer wanted to release. So right in the middle of production, MGM notified us that they wanted to pull out of the production-distribution agreement.

I consulted my lawyer in New York about my position. He was Irwin Margulies, whose firm Margulies & Heit was a leading adviser to independent producers, including Sam Spiegel and Samuel Bronston. Margulies advised me against starting legal proceedings which could only result in a shutdown of the production that would have been disastrous for me. The whole project would have collapsed because of time restrictions. He therefore negotiated an agreement with MGM whereby they let me finish the film with an understanding that their investment in it would be repaid from distribution proceeds. With Irwin's help, I raised the necessary financing to finish production and complete delivery to MGM.

Q: Did you make Karloff aware of what was going on?

GORDON: Yes, Karloff was aware of it, because, while working out all of these difficulties, Amalgamated Productions fell behind in paying him his salary which was spread over the period of shooting in England. He truly came "to save my life" by agreeing to defer the moneys owing to him until I had time to sort out my problems. We had an understanding that the film would not be released before he was paid. It was another reason why I loved him dearly and I never forgot his gesture.

Q: So Karloff knew about MGM stepping out — but did the crew and the rest of the cast know, or did you keep this under your hat?

GORDON: We tried *not* to make it known to everybody else. If they knew, the morale would have dropped.

Q: Their feeling might have been "Here we are making a movie that may not even get released."

GORDON: Yes. Or "Here we are making a movie and we may not even get paid next week!" We had to avoid *that* kind of thing.

Q: Naturally you had to continue *at* MGM, you couldn't pull out of there in the middle of shooting.

GORDON: That's correct. MGM did agree that, provided we came up with the remaining financing on our own, they would leave us alone with regard to the money they had already put up, until the picture went into release, and then we would then have to repay them from the receipts. I was in no position to say no. After *Corridors* was completed, it remained MGM's property while we were trying to find a solution to the problem.

MGM decided that they would release *First Man Into Space* by itself [in 1959] because of the current interest in space travel, and after that, *Corridors of Blood* stayed on the shelf for a considerable period of time. Margulies had earlier been my adviser in the sale of *The Counterfeit Plan* [1957] to Warner Brothers and he arranged for them to look at *Corridors of Blood* with the possibility that Warners would take over the distribution outside the U.K. But once Warners screened it, they made an offer only to purchase it *outright*, at a price that would not have been sufficient for us to reimburse MGM for their outlay, let alone the additional money that we spent completing the film. "Outright" is the key word; an outright sale would have cut off

Karloff gets impassioned opposite his on-screen son (Matthews) in *Corridors*. According to Gordon, Karloff liked this medical thriller's script immediately because he felt that the serious subject and historical background would be a change from making "just another horror picture."

any chance of us getting further income, and we would have been left in the hole, with no place to go to recover the rest of the expense.

Then, some time later, there was another upheaval in the MGM hierarchy in the United States. Someone else was put in charge of distribution, and a decision was made to set up a separate unit, rather like the "Classics" units that the major studios have in place now; but it was not for the distribution of *classic* films but rather for the distribution of those films which had ended up on the shelf at MGM, films which the previous management didn't want to release. A former exhibitor named Fred Schwartz was in charge of the operation. Finally, *Corridors of Blood* was going to be released; but because double-bills were the norm in those days, the question then became, what to release *with* it? *I* didn't have another picture; and after my experience with MGM, I wasn't about to *make* them one [*laughs*]. So Fred Schwartz acquired the Italian film *Lycanthropus* [1961], retitled it *Werewolf in a Girls' Dormitory*, and double-billed it with *Corridors of Blood* as a horror program of the type with which American International Pictures and other such companies were having so much success. I thought it was a pretty awful idea, because I saw *Werewolf in a Girls' Dormitory* and I felt that this was not a picture that could be suitably paired with *Corridors of Blood*, which was much more seriously intentioned. But I could not object to it. I was just concerned about getting *Corridors of Blood* out into distribution, I didn't want it to remain on the shelf any longer.

This separate unit of MGM's, which went under the name of Altura Pictures, went ahead and released the double-bill. I must say that, if the distribution had been by somebody like American International, they probably would have made a much greater success of it than MGM, who were really rather ashamed of the whole thing, and trying to sweep it under the carpet. But that was why *Corridors of Blood* was not released for such a long time.

Q: It must have been *such* a relief, having *Corridors of Blood* in theaters and putting that whole thing behind you.

GORDON: Absolutely. We had paid the rest of *Corridors'* production costs by getting a bank loan, and we were paying interest on the money. It was a Catch-22 situation where MGM wouldn't let us release the movie until they were paid back, but the only way to pay them back was to release the movie.

Q: What a lousy thing for a giant company to do to a couple young independent producers.

GORDON: It was. It was the worst experience I ever had, *any*where in my career.

Q: You have a story about screening *Corridors of Blood* for Mr. and Mrs. Karloff.

GORDON: One of the early rough cut screenings was set up at the MGM Studios, and Karloff was still in England because there was always the possibility that there might have to be some retakes or some additional voice dubbing. So of course Boris was there and so was Evie. We were watching the film and as it came towards the end and the scene where Dr. Bolton [Karloff's character] dies, I looked over at Evie to see how she was reacting, and she was sitting there *crying*. Which I thought was rather touching.

Karloff liked *Corridors of Blood* very much. Well, let me put it this way: He liked *making Corridors of Blood*, and I think perhaps he favored it over *Haunted Strangler* because of the circumstances of working at the MGM Studios, and because of the bigger budget. Also, I think the seriousness of the historical story made it a more interesting picture for him.

Q: When MGM released *Corridors of Blood* and *Werewolf in a Girls' Dormitory*, they were advertised as "Nervo-Rama Shockers."

GORDON: I think "Nervo-Rama" was intended to suggest that the two pictures would put your nerves on edge. As far as I'm concerned, I think MGM had a *nerve* in putting those two pictures together [*laughs*]! *Werewolf in a Girls' Dormitory* might have been all right on its own, but it was so inferior to *Corridors of Blood* that it upset the balance of the double-bill.

Q: In connection with these two movies, in Manhattan on April 15, 1963, exhibitors were invited to a luncheon at the Chateau Henri IV Restaurant. They were taken by horse-drawn hearse from MGM's Times Square headquarters to the restaurant and chose from a menu that included Zombie Zoup, Hungarian Ghoulash, Braised Brains, Soft-Boiled Eggtoplasm, etc. The pressbook is full of pictures of the event. Can I find you in any of them?

GORDON: No, you can't. Not because I was boycotting, but because I wasn't in New York at the time, I was in England preparing to make *Devil Doll*. But you can see from the photos that MGM actually built its campaign for the distribution of the program mostly around *Werewolf in a Girls' Dormitory* rather than around *Corridors of Blood*. And of course it was MGM who had the idea of having a song composed, "The Ghoul in School," and adding it to the soundtrack of *Werewolf in a Girls' Dormitory*. It certainly wasn't on the soundtrack of the original film; *Werewolf in a Girls' Dormitory* was an Italian film that was dubbed into English!

Q: And now that *Corridors* was in distribution, you finally started seeing some money — I hope!

GORDON: When *Corridors* was eventually released by MGM, all revenues accruing to me were used, in the first place, to reimburse MGM's investment, and secondly to repay the outside financing that Irwin Margulies had helped to arrange for the completion of the film. By the time this was all paid off, the picture had already been licensed by MGM to television and eventually the remaining income was paid to Amalgamated.

Q: Why doesn't MGM still control it today?

GORDON: In those days, the situation was very different from what it is today when the major studios acquire a picture that was independently produced. You have to remember that in the late 1950s, even television was only considered a very secondary source of income for films that were being released theatrically. There was no such thing as home video and all the other ancillary rights that are considered important today, and the attitude of most major studios, when they acquired a picture, was that the film would be good for five or ten years, but after that, it would really

Within two months of the U.S. release of the *Corridors-Werewolf in a Girls' Dormitory* twin bill, *Variety* was reporting that MGM "had a decided hit on its hands."

have no further value, and they had no interest in keeping it in their library. So I was able to negotiate a deal with MGM whereby all the pictures which I did which they distributed [*The Haunted Strangler, Fiend Without a Face, First Man Into Space* and *Corridors of Blood*] were licensed to them for only 12 years, and at the expiration of that period, all rights reverted to me, all materials were returned to me, and I remained the copyright owner of these films, which has stood me in very good stead, and which is the reason I'm still able to distribute the pictures today.

Q: These are not the *only* pictures of yours where you've retained the rights.

GORDON: Because I made most of my pictures independently and then licensed them for distribution after they were completed, I was able to make the deals on that basis. The exception was when I did *Island of Terror* and *The Projected Man* [both 1966] as a double-bill and Universal came along and purchased the American distribution rights; there was no way that they would give me the kind of deal I was looking for, unless they were given outright ownership of the rights for perpetuity. But even in *that* instance, they only acquired the Western Hemisphere rights, and I retained the Eastern Hemisphere distribution rights, which I exploited.

Q: You mentioning the Peter Cushing movie *Island of Terror* makes me want to ask: Everybody talks about what a saint Karloff was, everybody talks about what a saint Cushing was. Who was the bigger saint?

GORDON: They were very similar, and I would say perhaps with credit to the length of his career that one would have to regard Boris Karloff as the bigger saint. But you know that while people talk about what a saint Boris Karloff was and what a saint Peter Cushing was, I don't think that anybody has ever made the comment that Christopher Lee was a saint!

Q: [*laughs*] Christopher Lee is now [2003] in the middle of kicking up a fuss about being cut out of the third *Lord of the Rings* movie, lashing out at his director, *not* going to the premiere…I guess leopards never *do* change their spots, do they?

GORDON: In my experience, no, they don't.

Q: *Corridors* not only has the backdrop of true-life medical history but also Karloff as a character who is reminiscent of his old Columbia "Mad Doctors" and becomes a Jekyll-and-Hyde type; plus there are the Burke and Hare counterparts who make me think of Karloff's *The Body Snatcher* [1945]. While I used to prefer *Haunted Strangler*, lately I lean toward *Corridors*.

GORDON: I have very mixed feelings about *Corridors of Blood*. At the end of the day, I would say that I prefer *The Haunted Strangler*. Although it was more a sort of traditional Gothic horror story than *Corridors of Blood*, *Haunted Strangler* set out to *be* what it eventually *became*. The film came off exactly the way we had planned it, it conformed in all respects to the way we envisaged the project. Also, I think it gave Karloff a wonderful role. *Corridors of Blood*, partly because it was put together in a great hurry as we were under pressure of time, doesn't do a good job of mixing the historical background and the horror elements. It never clearly made up its mind whether it was a picture dealing seriously with the history of research into anesthetics for surgery, or a straight horror picture. I always had the feeling that the Boris Karloff fans who like to see him in horror films wouldn't appreciate the enormous amount of screen time devoted to the historical background, while people who might otherwise be interested in a picture *with* such a historical background would be put off by the title and by the fact that Boris Karloff was in it. So I felt it didn't really work as well as *Haunted Strangler* worked.

Q: When I asked your brother Alex which of the two *he* preferred, he said *Haunted Strangler*, his main reason being that, between the surgeries and all the other gory things that go on in *Corridors*, he just didn't like to watch it. I didn't know that Alex, a producer of horror movies himself, was so squeamish!

GORDON: Well, you see, even us producers of horror movies can always be full of surprises [*laughs*]!

DEVIL DOLL
1964

CREDITS

Executive Producers... *Richard Gordon* & *Kenneth Rive*
Produced & Directed by .... *Lindsay Shonteff*
Screenplay .... *George Barclay [Ronald Kinnoch]* & *Lance Z. Hargreaves [Charles Vetter Jr.]*
Original Story "The Devil Doll" by *Frederick E. Smith*
(published in London Mystery Magazine *#23)*

Photography ....*Gerald Gibbs*
Art Director... *Stan Shields*
Editor ....*Ernest Bullingham*
Production Manager..*Fred Slark*
Camera Operator..*Brian Elvin*
Continuity .... *Barbara Thomas*
Assistant Director ....*Ernie Lewis*
Sound Recorder .... *Derek McColm*
Makeup..*Jack Craig*
Hair Stylist ....*Ann Fordyce*
Wardrobe.. *Mary Gibson*

81 minutes

CAST

Bryant Haliday... *The Great Vorelli*
William Sylvester .... *Mark English*
Yvonne Romain... *Marianne Horn*
Sandra Dorne ....*Magda Cardenas*
Nora Nicholson... *Aunt Eva*
Alan Gifford... *Bob Garrett*
Karel Stepanek ....*Dr. J.C. Heller*
Francis De Wolff.. *Dr. Keisling*

Uncredited
Sadie Corre .... *Hugo the Dummy*
Philip Ray... *Uncle Walter*
Pamela Law..*Garrett's Girl Friend*
Heidi Erich .... *Grace*
Anthony Baird.. *Soldier*
Trixie Dallas ....*Miss Penton*
Margaret Durnell... *The Countess*
Ray Landor.. *Twist Dancer*
Ella Tracey .... *Louisa*
Guy Deghy ....*Hans*
David Charlesworth...*Hugo Novik*
Lorenza Coalville... *Mercedes*
Jackie Ramsden ....*The Nurse)*

SYNOPSIS OF THE SHORT STORY

"The Devil Doll" by Frederick E. Smith

Filling 12 pages in *London Mystery Magazine* #23, the story (told in the first person by a man named Blake) opens with Blake and his wealthy blonde fiancée Marilyn discussing the career of Vorelli, a stage ventriloquist. Vorelli used to have a hypnotist act with a partner named Gardeni, who died on stage during a performance. Rumor has it that since Gardeni died while under Vorelli's hypnotic influence, Vorelli *still* holds his soul captive inside Hugo, the dummy he uses in his *new* act. A devotee of the occult, Marilyn asks Blake to invite Vorelli to perform at her house at her upcoming birthday party.

Blake catches Vorelli's act and is amazed by the finale in which Hugo walks to the front of the stage and, "swaying like a drunken dwarf," thanks the audience. The onlookers are unnaturally quiet except for one woman whimpering in fear. Blake goes backstage and extends the party invitation to Vorelli, who accepts. From an alcove behind a curtain come strange noises and moans and a voice wailing, "Help me, whoever you are. Get me out…Free me, for the love of heaven…" Vorelli pulls the curtains to reveal Hugo in a small cage with a padlocked door.

At the birthday party at Marilyn's father's large manor house in Sussex, Vorelli performs his act. A woman faints and falls to the floor, distracting Vorelli; at that point, Hugo takes a knife off a table and briefly menaces Vorelli with it. Marilyn later tells Blake that if Hugo were to catch Vorelli sleeping, Hugo might be able to get his revenge.

Blake thinks there's a gramophone record and a motor inside Hugo and, planning to prove it, he asks Marilyn to get overnight-guest Vorelli drunk. She does; after Vorelli goes to bed, Blake and Marilyn quietly enter his bedroom. Unlocking the cage, they examine Hugo and see that it *is* a dummy. Vorelli starts to wake up, prompting Blake and Marilyn to leave in a hurry. Later, in bed, Blake realizes that he forgot to padlock the cage door.

A sudden rush of cold sweat soaked my pyjamas…. Slipping on my dressing-gown, I crept down the corridor and into his room. The curtains were drawn back and a single shaft of moonlight was now striking the floor in front of the window. Vorelli appeared to be as I had left him; I could see his dark shape on the bed. Carefully I tiptoed round the foot of the bed to where the cage was standing.

The cage was right in the shaft of moonlight. I drew nearer, then suddenly froze in horror. The barred door hung open and the dummy was gone. For a full half-minute I could not move a muscle. Then, with cringing back, I turned slowly to the bed. I saw now that a smaller shape was lying on the bed beside Vorelli.

Cover of the January 1955 magazine in which Frederick E. Smith's short story "The Devil Doll" was published.

As Blake watches from the shadows, Vorelli awakens, snatches up Hugo and holds it at arm's length, his face twisted with hate and triumph, and then puts the dummy back in its cage.

Several days later, Blake stops in at the theater to see Vorelli; as he enters the dressing room, Hugo reaches through the bars of its cage and begs to be let out, continuing: "The other night…after you left open the cage…he escaped. And I was drunk…helpless. so he robbed me…took my place. Don't you understand? I am Vorelli…" Into the room walks Vorelli-with-the-soul-of-Hugo, who confirms what the dummy said. When Blake steps forward with clenched fists, Vorelli explains, "It would not help him. If you destroyed the dummy, I could easily make another for him. And you will get no help from outside because no one will believe you. No, there is nothing you can do, Mr. Blake. Good night."

I have never told any of this to Marilyn. I dare not. That's why she has so often asked me why I can't bear to watch a child playing with a doll. Because I can't! It turns my stomach over…

SYNOPSIS OF THE FILM

Mark English, an American working as a London newspaperman, is assigned to write a story on the Great Vorelli, a hypnotist-ventriloquist playing to sell-out theater audiences. He attends a performance with his fiancée Marianne, a wealthy society beauty, and for the purposes of his story gets her to respond to Vorelli's call for an audience volunteer. Once under Vorelli's hypnotic control, the shy Marianne wildly dances the twist. Vorelli then brings out his wooden dummy Hugo, whose unexpected talents include walking unaided to the footlights. As master and dummy talk, their sarcastic, mutually antagonistic repartee fills the air with tension. In his dressing room, Vorelli keeps Hugo in a steel cage covered with a cloth.

Marianne's Aunt Eva is about to host her annual charity ball in their palatial home; at Mark's request, Marianne visits Vorelli in his theater dressing room and asks him to come and perform. Aware that Marianne is one of the richest women in England, he accepts. At the ball, there is again a macabre quality to the intense exchanges between Vorelli and Hugo; at one point, the dummy threatens its master with a knife. Mark sneaks into Vorelli's guest bedroom and examines Hugo, satisfying himself that it *is* a wooden puppet. Later that night, there's some partner-swapping: The Svengali-like Vorelli mentally summons Marianne to his room; as he is undressing her, Mark also has a visitor in *his* guest bedroom: Hugo, who wakes him by entreating, "Find me in Berlin…1948…"

The plot thickens when Vorelli decides that his blonde stage assistant Magda needs to be replaced with a newer model; he gives Hugo a knife with which it kills Magda while Vorelli is elsewhere for future alibi purposes. Meanwhile, Marianne, who is in Vorelli's power, slips into a delirious semi-coma.

In Berlin, Mark meets Mercedes, a former member of Vorelli's act; she reveals that, in the late 1940s, she and her young partner Hugo Novik were under Vorelli's sinister spell until the night when Novik was killed with a dagger in an on-stage "accident." It is now apparent to Mark that Vorelli, a fanatic on the subject of the mysteries of the east, has imprisoned the soul of the murdered Novik in the dummy Hugo.

Vorelli has the same sort of fate in mind for Marianne, whom he plans to wed and kill for her money,

Gordon returned to filmmaking after a five-year hiatus with this moody chiller.

putting *her* soul into a female devil doll. But his concentration on dominating the mind of Marianne weakens his control over Hugo, who attacks Vorelli in the theater dressing room. By the time Mark arrives on the scene, the battle is over and the tables have been turned: Vorelli is speaking in the placid voice of the congenial Hugo Novik — and the dummy is back in its cage, begging Mark for help *in the voice of Vorelli.*

CURSE OF THE VOODOO
1965

CREDITS

Executive Producers	**Richard Gordon & Kenneth Rive**
Directed by	Lindsay Shonteff
Screenplay	Tony O'Grady [Brian Clemens]
Additional Scenes & Dialogue	Leigh Vance
Photography	Gerald Gibbs
Editor	Barrie Vince
Music Composed & Conducted by	Brian Fahey
Art Director	Tony Inglis
Assistant Director	Bill Snaith
Sound Recorder	Jock May
Makeup	Gerry Fletcher
In Charge of Production	Fred Slark
Camera Operator	Brian Elvin
Casting Director	Ronnie Curtis
Wardrobe	Mary Gibson

83 minutes

CAST

Bryant Haliday	Mike Stacey
Dennis Price	Major Lomas
Lisa Daniely	Janet Stacey
Mary Kerridge	Janet's Mother
Ronald Leigh Hunt	Doctor
Jean Lodge	Betty Lomas
Dennis Alaba Peters	Saidi
Danny Daniels	Simbaza
Tony Thawnton	Radlett
Michael Nightingale	Second Hunter
John Witty	Police Inspector
Andy Myers	Tommy Stacey
Louis Mahoney	African Expert
Jimmy Felgate	Barman
Nigel Feyisetan	Simbaza in London
Beryl Cunningham	Night Club Dancer
Bobby Breen Quintet	Night Club Band
Valli Newby	Girl in Bar

SYNOPSIS

During an African hunting expedition led by heavy-drinking big game hunter Mike Stacey and his friend Major Lomas, an inexperienced hunter takes a shot at a lion but only wounds it. Stacey knows he must finish off the beast and, accompanied by his native gunbearer Saidi, follows it into Simbaza territory, where primitive natives worship lions and practice black magic. The lion attacks and claws Stacey's arm, but he kills it. That night as Stacey, Lomas and others relax in their camp, Simbaza tribesmen appear, and one throws a spear into the ground at Stacey's feet. For killing the lion, Stacey is now marked for death. The next day, Saidi slips into a trance and tries to knife Stacey, but Lomas intercedes. Saidi flees.

In Johannesburg, neglectful husband Stacey learns that his wife Janet has left him, returning to her family home in England with their young son. Stacey goes after them, arriving at Janet's mother's house and asking Janet to meet him at the bar in his hotel that night to discuss a reconciliation. When she stands him up, Stacey gets drunk, meets a beautiful woman, goes to her flat with her and immediately passes out. In his feverish sleep he has a vision of Saidi as a prisoner of Simbaza tribesmen. Walking through a park after leaving the flat, he hears a lion growling; he later sees a Simbaza native dressed in suit and tie, and is chased through a misty park by two spear-carrying warriors. Are these experiences real, or is the infection of Stacey's arm wound making him delirious?

Janet consults an expert on Africa who tells her that Simbaza black magic enables them to hound and haunt an enemy, gradually destroying his mind and body; the only way to save oneself is to seek out and slay the Simbaza who placed the curse. She relays this to Stacey who, despite his weakened condition, decides to do just that. Returning to Africa, Stacey finds the Simbaza camp, saves Saidi and then sets out after the Simbaza who cursed him. When Stacey runs out of rifle bullets, he races back to his Jeep and

Bwana Bryant Haliday and his safari boys trek across the expanses of Darkest Regent's Park — a location so *un*-equatorial, in some shots you see the actors' breath!

speeds after the fleeing Simbaza, ultimately running him over and killing him. The curse of the voodoo has been broken.

RICHARD GORDON ON *DEVIL DOLL* AND *CURSE OF THE VOODOO*

Q: *Devil Doll* was your first movie in five years, after the *Corridors of Blood* mess in 1958. Your longest stretch between movies.

RICHARD GORDON: When I had the *Corridors of Blood* problems with MGM — and they were substantial problems that involved substantial moneys — I was very discouraged, and I wasn't really in the mood to put all my enthusiasm and all my energy into another film right away. And after all, I did have my distribution business Gordon Films Inc. to continue, and that was very active in the 1960s. So it wasn't until a few years later, after I'd properly done everything that had to be done with MGM and I got my feet back on the ground, that I felt it was time to go back to the original plan and start a new British production company and start producing pictures again.

Q: In the '50s you made seven crime pictures lickety-split, and then four horror and sci-fi movies *almost* as rapidly. I assume that if MGM hadn't thrown that monkey wrench into your producing career, you'd have made a lot more movies in the five years between *Corridors* and *Devil Doll*. A *lot* more movies.

GORDON: Yes, absolutely. But I ran into all that MGM trouble, and then that resulted in troubles with my partner Chuck Vetter. Chuck wasn't happy with the way things were going. I should also mention that Irwin Margulies, my attorney at the time, did not get along with Chuck, and vice versa. Also, I think Chuck felt that I was taking all the credit for some things, and that he should have had equal credit, and been given a little more leeway in things that **he** wanted to do. So he decided to step out of Producers Associates. He sold me his interest and went his own way. He then made two pictures for MGM, **The Green Helmet** [1961] and **Battle Beneath the Earth** [1967], and what happened to him after that, I really don't know.

Q: Your "comeback" movie, *Devil Doll* — how did it come about?

GORDON: John Croydon first brought the story "The Devil Doll" to my attention in 1958. It had been written by a man named Frederick E. Smith for publication in *London Mystery Magazine*, an English pulp. Probably Croydon was attracted to it because of its similarity to the famous ventriloquist sequence in the anthology horror film *Dead of Night* [1945], of which he was one of the producers. I liked the story very much, as I'd always been interested in movies with a background of ventriloquism, hypnotism and the like, and I thought that it could be transformed into a very interesting screenplay. So we acquired the rights.

Q: Did you meet Smith at the time?

GORDON: No, it was all done through literary agents. After the rights were acquired, a screenplay was written by Ronald Kinnoch, the production manager on several of my earlier films. Kinnoch was going to direct the film if we got it set up, but then we had those MGM-*Corridors of Blood* problems [that derailed Producers Associates]. John Croydon went on to do something else, and Kinnoch stepped out.

Q: In *Devil Doll*'s on-screen credits, the script is credited to George Barclay and Lance Z. Hargreaves.

GORDON: George Barclay was Kinnoch's *nom de plume*. And then Chuck Vetter, who was also a writer under the name of Lance Z. Hargreaves, had done a final screenplay based on Kinnoch's screenplay, and that's the screenplay we eventually shot.

Q: So by the time you made the movie, in 1963, Croydon, Kinnoch — and of course Vetter — were no longer involved.

GORDON: That is correct. At that point, as sole owner of Producers Associates, I inherited several stories and scripts that had been written for the company, including all *Devil Doll* material.

Q: *Devil Doll* was the first time you used Gordon Films Inc. as one of the production companies.

GORDON: Yes, Gordon Films took over the project, and then entered into a production agreement with a London company called Galaworldfilm that belonged to Kenneth Rive. Ken was a very successful businessman, a distributor of foreign-language and art house movies in England. He had also built up a chain of specialized theaters. In the early 1960s he got into production, because there seemed to be a great demand for British-made independent films in England. He formed a subsidiary company called Galaworldfilm Productions —

Q: Sidney Furie worked for them.

GORDON: Sidney Furie was a *partner*. When I met Ken, he and Sidney had already made two films, one called *During One Night* [1960], the other called *The Boys* [1962], which was a courtroom melodrama with Robert Morley and Richard Todd. Both of them had been directed by Sidney and they had been quite successful. Incidentally, Sidney had also made two horror films in England, *The Snake Woman* and *Doctor Blood's Coffin* [both 1961]. Ken Rive took a great interest in *Devil Doll* and suggested that we do it together, and said that he would bring Sidney in as the director.

Q: *Devil Doll* was always intended to be low-budget, correct?

GORDON: Yes, and Sidney was quite happy to do it that way. But, again, there were certain delays before we could get started, and meanwhile Sidney got an offer to do a big film with Cliff Richard. So he suggested that he would bring in a protégé of his, Lindsay Shonteff. Shonteff would become the director of *Devil Doll* but Sidney would keep an eye on things behind the scenes and supervise the direction of the picture as much as he could, without putting his name on it.

Q: What kind of guy was Shonteff?

GORDON: Like Sidney, he was Canadian. He was extremely cooperative and very pleasant. Naturally he was somewhat nervous; to the best of my knowledge, *Devil Doll* was the first film actually directed by Shonteff. He was very young; in fact, if I may say so, we were *all* young at the time [*laughs*]! But with Sidney's benevolent help and great cooperation from Ken Rive, it all worked very well; in fact, to the extent that we subsequently made another picture with Lindsay Shonteff, *Curse of the Voodoo* — or *The Curse of Simba*, as it was originally called.

Q: Who cast *Devil Doll*?

GORDON: Ken Rive and I more or less cast it together, with one of the small casting agencies to help us negotiate the deals. It was always intended that Bryant Haliday would play the leading role as the Great Vorelli. During pre-production when we were thinking about an actor to play the role of Mark the newspaperman, Kieron Moore's name came up, perhaps because he had been in Sidney's film *Doctor Blood's Coffin*, but Ken told us we could not afford him. We eventually engaged William Sylvester, an actor who had appeared on the stage and made many films in England. I sold a number of them through Gordon Films Inc. to American distributors and television. I suppose he's best-known for starring in *Gorgo* [1961] and for his supporting role in Stanley Kubrick's *2001: A Space Odyssey* [1968].

Q: Some prints of *Devil Doll* have Haliday top-billed and others have Sylvester leading off.

GORDON: Ken felt that it should have William Sylvester on top in England, because Sylvester was better-known. But in the rest of the world, and especially in America, we featured Bryant Haliday as the star. Yvonne Romain was an actress I had already met and knew because she had a supporting role in *Corridors of Blood*, where she was still known as Yvonne Warren. Francis De Wolff and Karel Stepanek were actors that Ken and I selected together from a large pool of very good stage and screen actors who were available to do this kind of work, and happy to do it, and who could be relied on to give very good performances with a minimum amount of problems.

Q: Haliday — like William Sylvester — was an American. He was also a friend of yours from long before the days of starring in your movies.

GORDON: Bryant was a very extraordinary talent who I think would have become a major international star of stage and screen if he hadn't preferred to go his own way. He was born in 1928 in New York City and in his childhood he studied at a Benedictine monastery to become a priest.

Q: In an interview, he claimed that it wasn't until he got out of the monastery and went to Harvard that he saw a movie for the first time, or heard music other than Gregorian chants. Was he exaggerating, or do you think that *was* the childhood he had?

GORDON: I think that's probably true. He was a fascinating character. During his years of study for the priesthood, he won prizes in theology, and went on to teach Latin and Greek. Then he suddenly abandoned that life to study international law at Harvard University.

He became restless again, and at the age of 21 he decided on a career in the theater. He was one of the founders of the Brattle Theatre company at Cambridge,

Bryant Haliday brought intensity to his performance as the sardonic Vorelli — but, when the cameras stopped rolling, could "turn it off at the drop of a hat," says Gordon.

Massachusetts, and he performed in something like 50 productions, from Shakespeare to Shaw; he recorded classical plays; and he founded the Cambridge Drama Festival. Then he and one of his Harvard classmates, Cy Harvey, founded Janus Films, which became the first American distributor of classic foreign movies, including the works of Ingmar Bergman, Fellini, Antonioni and the like. The Brattle Theatre became an art house cinema, and they also operated a cinema in New York City called the 55th Street Playhouse. I met Bryant and Cy Harvey for the first time while I was negotiating with Janus to distribute some of the films that Gordon Films Inc. imported from overseas. Janus also had an affiliation with Ken Rive's Gala Films, and so it was known to Ken as well as to me.

Bryant was very restless, and not content with remaining a business executive. He actually wanted to return to acting, and so he did it by appearing in several French films. We used to meet every year at the Cannes Film Festival and I saw two of his films which were screened there in the market section. They were quite rough thrillers, and I was impressed with his performances as villainous characters. In one of them, *Règlements de comptes* [1963], he played a murderer being chased all over Paris by Daniel Gélin, who was a French star. In the other, *Jusqu'à plus soif* [1962], he was the leader of a band of alcohol smugglers. When I told Bryant of my plans for *Devil Doll*, he expressed great interest as he wanted to switch to English-language films. Ken and I agreed that he would make an excellent Vorelli, and he joined the project.

Q: Did he grow that satanic-looking mustache and beard for *Devil Doll* or were they provided by the makeup department?

GORDON: It's makeup. In the flashback sequences, he appears without a beard. And normally he did not have a beard or mustache.

Q: In an interview, Lindsay Shonteff said Haliday had money in *Devil Doll*.

GORDON: When he agreed to join in the project, he contributed some of the financing for the picture, which was otherwise being financed privately by Ken Rive and myself. He also worked for a minimum salary in order to retain a profit participation in the picture. For many years I used to account to him for his share of the profits from worldwide distribution, and continued to do so to his son after Bryant died.

Speaking of Lindsay Shonteff, I would like to make it clear that Lindsay did, in the end, direct the picture himself even though Sidney Furie was behind the scenes. I don't want it to sound as though Sidney directed the whole film and Lindsay was nothing more than an assistant director. The success of the film on the screen should be largely credited to Lindsay's efforts.

Q: A lot of *Devil Doll* was shot on practical locations.

GORDON: In the opening scene, when you see Vorelli in the car, the car is traveling around Piccadilly Circus, and then it's heading down Park Lane for Hyde Park Corner, and continues up Park Lane to Marble Arch. While it's traveling up Park Lane, if you look very carefully in the background, you can see the Dorchester Hotel and the Grosvenor Hotel.

The theater in which we shot a number of scenes was a famous variety hall known as the Metropolitan Edgware Road, located in a busy thoroughfare in central London not too far from Hampstead where I grew up. At that time [April 1963], it had just been closed down and was about to be demolished. We were able to arrange with the owners to go into this theater and shoot most of our theater scenes and some other sequences there, before the demolition began. And of course they didn't care what we did in there, or even if we knocked down a wall here or there, because it was all going to come down anyway. That was a great luxury and it gave us a lot of extra production value that we probably couldn't have afforded on our budget otherwise.

Incidentally, I knew the theater quite well because it was very popular. During the years of the Second World War, when it was functioning as a variety hall, it was a regular stop for many variety [vaudeville] performers whom I saw at the time, and one of its biggest attractions was an annual visit by the actor Tod Slaughter, doing a series of Victorian melodramas and horror stories for which he was very famous. He was best known for doing *Sweeney Todd, the Demon Barber of Fleet Street*, which was always part of his repertoire and which he also filmed in 1936. I saw him do that at the Metropolitan Edgeware Road, and also plays called *The Murder in the Red Barn*, *The Chinese Bungalow* and *Bluebeard*.

This was at the time when there were German air raids almost nightly, and by law the air raid sirens sounded in the theater when there was an alert so that anybody who wanted to go to a shelter could do so. The all-clear siren also sounded in the theater when an air raid was over. One time when I was there and I was watching Tod Slaughter in *Bluebeard*, the air raid was on. Towards the end of the play, he tried to escape from the police and he ran up the center aisle of the

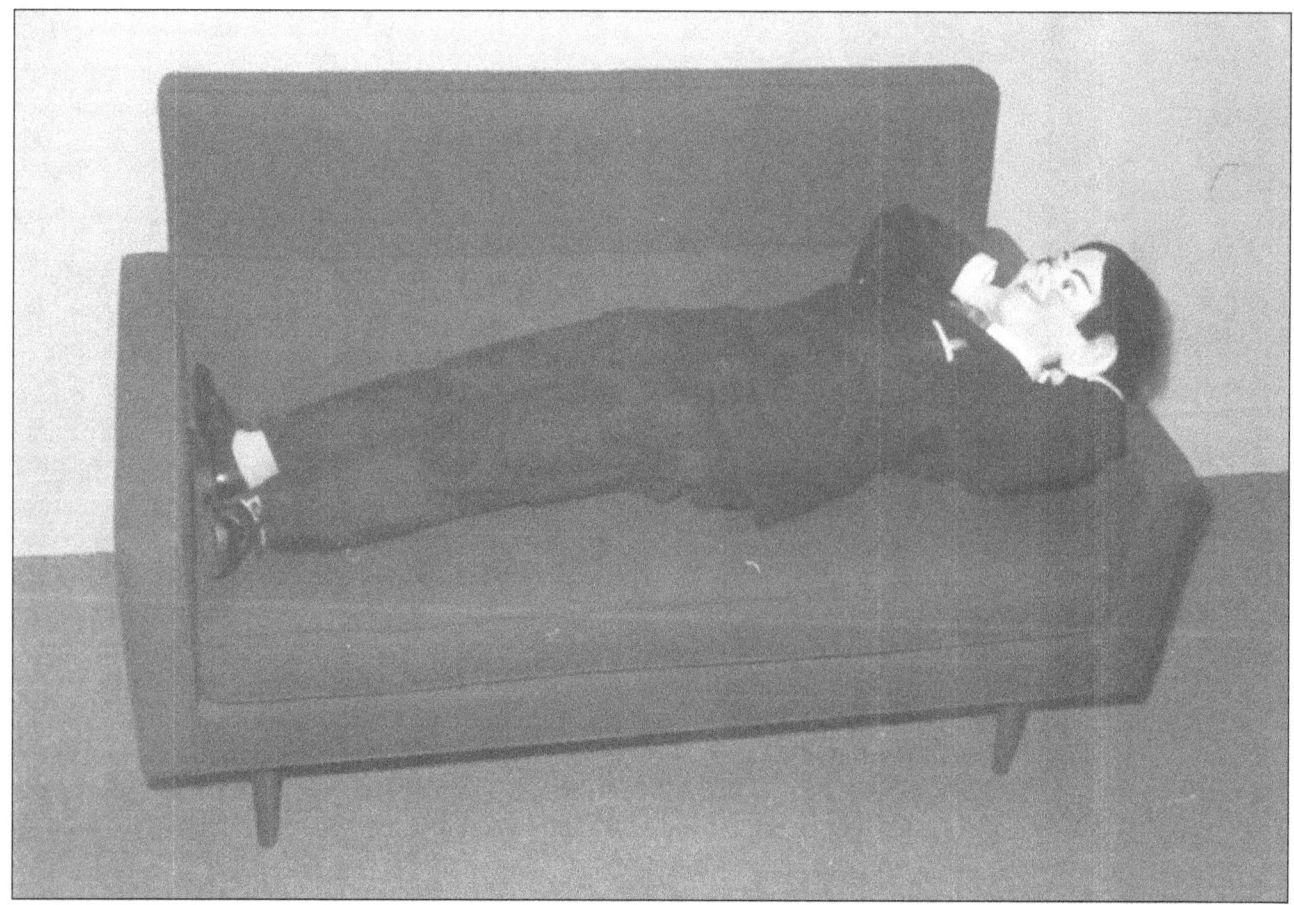

4'1" Sadie Corre relaxes inside her Hugo costume in this gag shot. A veteran dancer and comic performer, Corre (1918-2009) appeared in a number of additional movies, including *The Rocky Horror Picture Show* (1975) and *Return of the Jedi* (1983).

theater, and just as he was about to get to the exit, he was "shot" by a policeman from the stage. I was sitting in the back, and as he was coming up alongside me, the shot rang out — and at that particular moment, the all-clear siren went. And Tod, who was ever the great showman, clutched his breast, collapsed on the floor as he should have done, and said in a very loud voice, "They *got* me — and just as the all-clear came!" The audience loved Tod Slaughter and cheered him loudly. It is one of my great regrets that I never was able to meet him off-stage, even when I saw him some time later in the Grand Guignol melodramas in which he co-starred with Ellen Pollock. John Croydon at one time wanted to sign him up for a serious supporting role in a film called *Champagne Charlie* [1944] but the Ealing Studios, for which John was producing the film, could not get insurance on Slaughter because of his drinking, and it never came to pass.

The dressing rooms seen in *Devil Doll* were the dressing rooms at the Metropolitan Edgeware Road. We furnished them according to our requirements. They were big enough to get cast and crew in; and if one of them *wasn't* big enough, we simply knocked down a wall. Marianne's home in the movie was a country house, at least as far as the exteriors were concerned. I don't recollect which country house it was, because we [low-budget moviemakers] used country houses in England all the time, since it was a much less expensive way of doing it than going into a studio. I have in my mind a jumble of country houses that I used in films, going from my Boris Karloff pictures forward to *The Cat and the Canary* [1978], but unfortunately I can't remember which particular one was used for *Devil Doll*. We also shot *some* of the interiors there, but there was strict control over what you could do if you went into such houses to shoot. In the first place, you had to have extensive insurance coverage to protect the owners of the houses from incurring any losses by what you were doing. Many times we could only use the exterior of a house, and the interior had to be built in a studio.

Q: What was your budget on *Devil Doll*?

GORDON: The sterling cost was £20,000, and then there was an additional dollar cost, estimated at $20,000, which covered Bryant Haliday's salary, my own salary and expenses, our flights back and forth to England, insurance, etc. I don't remember now what the rate of exchange was at the time between the pound and the dollar, but I would say that the final cost of the picture in dollars probably was around 60 to 75 thousand dollars.

Q: Less than your Karloff movies, and even your Marshall Thompson movies.

GORDON: Yes, considerably less. But that was partly due to the fact that the principal persons involved were partners in the film and therefore did not take their full salaries up front. Also, because it was privately financed between Ken Rive, Bryant and myself, we did not have to spend extra money on completion guarantees, overhead, bank interest and such factors which otherwise are normally factored into a budget. The shooting schedule was four weeks, tailored to Bryant's requirements so that he only had to work for two weeks, and we did not have to keep him in London for the full period of time. We shot it partly at a small studio that was very popular with producers of low-budget films, Merton Park Studios in Merton Park, a suburb of London, and very easily accessible for everybody connected with the production. It had existed since the 1930s. The newspaper office seen in *Devil Doll* was a set at Merton Park Studios, as you might guess by the fact that it was so small. It was a very nice studio. We used it again when Bryant and I later did *The Projected Man* [1966], and then some years later I shot the bulk of my film *Horror Hospital* [1973] there.

Q: Did you submit the *Devil Doll* script in advance to the British Board of Film Censors?

GORDON: We didn't do it with *Devil Doll* because we didn't feel that we were going to run into any problems. We did plan to shoot certain scenes that we knew the censor would not approve, but those scenes were designed strictly for use in other countries where the censorship regulations were quite different from what they were in England.

Q: At this point, the mid-60s, what were the folks at the British Board of Film Censors like to deal with?

GORDON: They were very reasonable people, particularly with independent production, because they felt, being under government supervision, that it was part of their duty to encourage production in England, and they would always try to be as helpful as they could. Sometimes — not in the case of *Devil Doll*, but on some other films I took a leaf out of Hammer's notebook and we shot certain scenes rather more explicitly than we intended, in order to give the British Board of Film Censors the opportunity to make some cuts without ruining the picture, and still give us what we wanted to put on the screen in the first place.

Q: That must have come in handy on later pictures like *Tower of Evil* [1972] and —

GORDON: Yes, it was very much true of *Tower of Evil* and *Inseminoid* [1981].

Q: As time went on, the gore quotient in your movies went up, in keeping with modern trends — and also the sexiness. You started with the Judas Hole girls in *Haunted Strangler* and Kim Parker in the towel in *Fiend Without a Face*, and now with *Devil Doll* you're at the point where there's some female nudity. How did you feel about having to "up the ante" sex- and violence-wise in your pictures through the years?

GORDON: In the early days I thought it was fun because it wasn't *so* explicit, and it seemed to me perfectly logical to do it. Although for instance, in the case of the can-can sequence in *The Haunted Strangler*, we had great problems because unless we dressed the girls in a certain way, the performance of the can-can would not have been permitted on the screen [*laughs*], and that was sort of ridiculous. Later on, we had to go further into blood and violence *and* sex because of the requirements of the marketplace, and because Hammer was forever pushing the envelope and becoming more and more explicit with their movies with which we obviously had to compete. I found it became less attractive to do so. And in *Inseminoid*, I really would have preferred to make the movie with *much* less of the explicit gore and sex. But it was dictated by the marketplace. If we were going to compete and get the play dates that we wanted and be able to exhibit the picture in territories around the world, that's what they wanted and we had to comply.

Q: In *Devil Doll*, one flash of partial nudity is provided by Sandra Dorne, who plays Vorelli's assistant.

GORDON: Sandra Dorne had also been in a lot of British B movies. She was a sort of "Diana Dors type," and also reminiscent of Vera Day who was in *The Haunted Strangler*. She was quite used to this sort of thing and it didn't give her any problems. We shot three sequences for *Devil Doll* that were never used in England or the United States: One was an additional theater scene where the Great Vorelli hypnotizes an audience member [Trixie Dallas] into doing a strip tease act. The second was the scene where Sandra Dorne is sleeping in the dressing room and there was a longer exposure of her breast than we see in

Haliday minus the (fake) beard and mustache in one of *Devil Doll*'s flashback sequences.

the domestic prints. The third was an alternate version of the scene set in the American reporter's Alan Gifford German hotel room; in that version, his girlfriend Pamela Law comes out of the bathroom bare-breasted.

Q: There's a topless shot of Law in the *Devil Doll* pressbook.

GORDON: There were two pressbooks, one for use with the overseas version and the other for use with the domestic version. It was never intended to show those three sequences in England or America; in fact, I think those sequences detract from the suspense and intentions of the film. They were there for overseas distributors, particularly in the continent of Europe and in the Far East, to include in the film if they wanted them.

Q: In one *Devil Doll* scene, Vorelli lures Marianne into a guest room and starts to undress her. That scene went no further in any version?

GORDON: No. And also the scene where William Sylvester and Yvonne Romain are driving at night and pull over and start making love in the car; that never

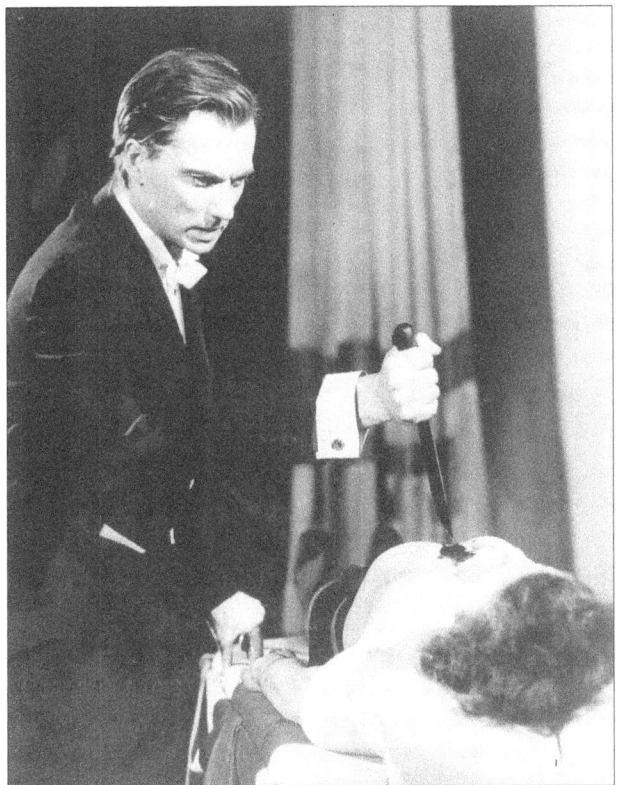

Oops! A gory on-stage…"accident"…makes Vorelli (Haliday), a possessor of mystic powers, the master of Hugo Novik's (David Charlesworth) soul.

went beyond what you now see on the screen. By the way, that Rolls Royce actually belonged to Kenneth Rive. If you watch the end of that scene carefully, you can see the initials KR [on the license plate **KR 38**] on the front of the car.

Q: Can you talk a little about each of the people in the cast?

GORDON: Unlike some actors, like for instance Bela Lugosi who once when he got into the mood for a scene in a picture would try to remain in that mood for the entire time and just retire quietly to his dressing room in between scenes, Bryant Haliday was the kind of actor who could turn it on and turn it off at the drop of a hat.

As intense as he was during the shooting of the scenes featuring him as the Great Vorelli, whenever a scene was over, he would just drop that attitude completely, and the next moment he'd be having fun with people on the set and playing around with the dummy and so forth. I really thought he was ideal casting for the role of Vorelli. With the way that *Devil Doll* was exhibited in the United States where it had a substantial success, Bryant became a recognizable name for fans of horror and science fiction pictures, so it was perfectly logical to use him again in *Curse of the Voodoo* and also, eventually, to have him starring in *The Projected Man*.

William Sylvester was very cooperative and had had so much experience in playing in every type of British picture that it was easy for him to do this role, particularly since he was cast as an American and didn't have to affect any kind of accent. We had no problems with him. In fact, I must say that on this film, we had no problems with *any*body in the cast. Francis De Wolff was wonderful to work with, a complete and absolute pro. The sort of person who knew exactly what he had to do and what he wanted to do when he appeared on the set, and went through it in the most professional way. He was also in *Corridors of Blood*.

Q: Karel Stepanek's character Dr. Heller reminded me of Dr. Van Straaten [Frederick Valk] in *Dead of Night* — a psychiatrist who has a rational explanation for everything, no matter how far-out things get.
GORDON: Karel Stepanek was a typical Continental actor with a very varied background in the theater and screen. Like Francis De Wolff, he arrived fully equipped to do what he had to do, he did it with a minimum of fuss or bother, and that was *it*.

Q: Who played Hugo the dummy?

GORDON: Hugo was actually played by a girl, Sadie Corre, who was brought to our attention by one of the casting people that we had collaborating with us on the picture. She was a midget with a background of working in the circus and in vaudeville. She is inside the costume of the dummy during the scenes where the dummy has to walk and perform other physical functions.

Q: So there were two dummies.

GORDON: There was the dummy that *was* a dummy, which is carried around by Bryant Haliday and which you see propped up in the cage and so on, and then there was a dummy which was actually hollow inside, and that became Sadie Corre's costume when the dummy had to move around.

Q: I once read an anecdote about a prop man walking over to pick up what he thought was the dummy, and it suddenly screamed and lunged at him. Sadie Corre apparently had a sense of humor!

GORDON: I wasn't there at that particular moment, but I remember hearing about the incident with the prop man. Yes, she did have a great sense of humor, and she and Bryant got very friendly. Bryant had somewhat of an impish sense of humor as well, so they used to enjoy playing these tricks on people who were not expecting it.

Q: One early draft of the *Devil Doll* script was set in Vienna. Was there a thought of shooting in Vienna?

GORDON: Only if a German company had volunteered to finance it.

Q: That same draft had an action-full finale with Hugo up in the catwalks of a theater, trying to kill Vorelli by dropping sandbags on him!

GORDON: I thought it was a very contrived ending that didn't fit the context of the picture at all. In fact, I think it *negated* everything that went before, it negated the buildup of suspense and terror and also a feeling of *doom*, so to speak. That ending would have spoiled the whole picture, and we rejected it out of hand. The irony of the ending of the short story, and of my movie, is what makes the ending so interesting: The soul of Hugo is now in Vorelli, and the soul of Vorelli is now in the dummy, and the act is probably going to continue *but with the tables turned*. People coming out of a theater always remember the ending more strongly than anything else about a movie, and I thought the ending would become a great talking point.

Q: There's no composer listed in the on-screen credits.

GORDON: As with so many low-budget British movies, the music was actually what we called library music — that is to say, existing music tracks that were licensed from a music library. There was no individual composer, although some of these tracks were originally composed by people like Malcolm Lockyer and other fairly well-known composers in England. But it was not a specially composed track for the film.

Q: The music that goes along with the Hugo scenes is very much like the ghost music in *The Haunting* [1963], and really enhances those scenes.

GORDON: These libraries in England had a tremendous range of music available, particularly for horror and science fiction films — sinister and *misterioso* motifs. It was always possible to find what you needed.

Q: You mentioned being a fan of movies involving ventriloquism and hypnotism. What were some of the earlier ones that stand out in your mind?

GORDON: I think the first time that ventriloquism was used in a major movie was in a silent film made by the great Lon Chaney in 1925, called *The Unholy Three*, in which he played a circus ventriloquist-criminal by the name of Prof. Echo. Chaney remade it as a sound film in 1930; in fact, it was the only sound film he *ever* made, and he died shortly thereafter. The gimmick was certainly much more effective in a sound film, where they could include scenes in which he throws his voice — scenes which, in the silent version, wouldn't have worked.

Then there was *The Great Gabbo* [1929], an Erich von Stroheim film I saw when I was quite small. Von Stroheim played a character very much like Vorelli in our movie, who comes to believe that he has transferred his soul into the body of his dummy Otto, and the dummy eventually takes control of him. In a British B movie from 1943, *The Dummy Talks* with Jack Warner, a midget poses as a dummy to unmask the killer of a blackmailing ventriloquist; and then of course in 1945 ventriloquism was featured in the anthology *Dead of Night*, in which Michael Redgrave played the ventriloquist who is driven to insanity and murder. That episode was directed by Cavalcanti, a famous Brazilian film director who had made a great career for himself in England doing documentaries and very realistic films, and John Croydon was one of the producers. I have no doubt that Frederick Smith, the author of our short story "The Devil Doll," was influenced by *Dead of Night* because in his story he called the dummy Hugo, the same name that was used for the dummy in *Dead of Night*. And then of course ventriloquism was also used for comic effect in movies with Edgar Bergen and Charlie McCarthy and so on.

Q: Several of the *Devil Doll* reviewers compared it to *Dead of Night*, and a few of them compared it disparagingly, as if you had taken the story. But it's completely

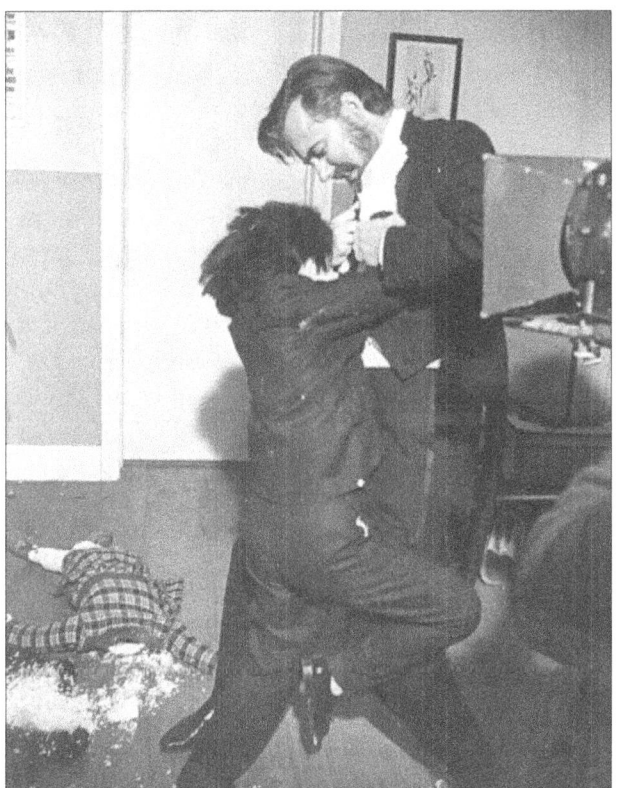

Vorelli (Haliday) and Hugo (Corre) battle it out in *Devil Doll*'s macabre finale.

different: In *Dead of Night*, it's the dummy who gives the orders and the ventriloquist who's the completely submissive one, the opposite of your picture.

GORDON: I don't think that we appropriated anything from *Dead of Night* that we shouldn't have. We retained the name of Hugo for the dummy because Frederick Smith had used that in his published short story. Incidentally, the published short story was called "The Devil Doll," and I decided immediately that we needed to change the title because there was an MGM picture called *The Devil-Doll* [1936] with Lionel Barrymore; it actually had nothing to do with ventriloquism but nevertheless it was still being shown and would appear on television and so on. We didn't want anyone to confuse our picture with that, so we made our title *Devil Doll*.

One of the interesting things about *Devil Doll* is that it's the first time that hypnotism and ventriloquism were brought together and incorporated into one film. Hypnotism in the movies goes back to the days of *The Cabinet of Dr. Caligari* [1919]; and in 1926, Boris Karloff played a Caligari-like hypnotist in a picture called *The Bells*, in which he uses hypnosis to unmask Lionel Barrymore as a murderer. And Barrymore himself used hypnotism to solve the killings in *Mark of the Vampire* [1935]. But I don't think it had ever been used in conjunction with ventriloquism before.

Q: Your movie follows the original short story for a while; goes off on its own into *Svengali* territory; and then returns to the short story for its finale.

GORDON: Yes, I think the *Svengali*-type scenes are inevitable with any film that features a sinister hypnotist, because *Svengali* inspired so many of the stories of hypnotism that were done later.

Q: What can you tell me about the distribution of *Devil Doll*?

GORDON: The production was set up with the intention that Gala Film Distributors would release it in the United Kingdom. It went out in England on a full circuit release on a double-bill with a Paramount picture called *Sylvia* [1965] with Carroll Baker. In America I decided to see where I could get the best distribution arrangements. I screened it for several major companies, but inevitably, even if they liked it and even if they wanted to make a deal, it would have meant giving up all control over the distribution of the picture and more or less losing my rights, except for the percentage of the profits that I might have retained. I decided that I would be better off distributing it independently, and retaining control. Incidentally, there was one very funny incident when I screened it for a top distribution executive of one of the Hollywood major companies. At the end, he turned to me and he said, "Just as a matter of interest, what did it cost you to make the picture?" On the spur of the moment, because I wasn't prepared for such a question —

Q: Before you get to the punchline, remind me what the picture *did* cost to make.

GORDON: The *real* budget was $75,000 or less. But on the spur of the moment, I said, "Well, actually the picture cost $200,000 to produce." He looked at me very admiringly and he said, "Well, you sure got a lot of production value on the screen for that amount of money!"

I was very friendly at the time with a distributor by the name of Joe Solomon. He was based in Philadelphia and distributed independent films, some of which he had acquired from Gordon Films Inc.; one was a film that I imported and we released as *Playgirls and the Vampire*, which became a great success in drive-in theaters and hard tops in 1963. When I screened *Devil Doll* for Joe, he was very keen on it, and we decided to go into a distribution deal together. Joe was *so* keen on *Devil Doll*, and wanted to mount such an extensive publicity campaign, that he took in a Pittsburgh exhibitor as a partner and formed a company called Associated Film Distributors to release it. They put the film out with over 200 prints, which in those days was considered quite a big release, and played it in drive-ins and hard tops with tremendous publicity campaigns, and it was a very big success. We even brought over the stuffed dummy Hugo to make "personal appearances" in theaters where the film was playing. Eventually Joe "inherited" it, and it later got lost.

Joe and I remained friends for years after *Devil Doll*. He later moved to Hollywood and started a new company called Fanfare Films, which continued in distribution, and then he also went into production. As a matter of fact, the first film he produced was a low-budget exploitation picture called *The Black Klansman* [1966], directed by Ted Mikels; I helped to finance it along with a Canadian distributor, Jerry Solway of Astral Films, who had distributed *Devil Doll* in Canada. *The Black Klansman* was not a financial success and so when Joe decided to make another picture, I declined to participate. The second film turned out to be *Hell's Angels on Wheels* [1967] with Jack Nicholson.

Q: Which was a hit, yes.

GORDON: Yes yes yes, very much of a terrific success at the box office, not only because of Jack Nicholson but because of the Hell's Angels. I tell that story only to prove that we all make mistakes [*laughs*]!

Joe Solomon was one of the top showmen in the country at the time. He went on to make a number of successful films; he's probably best remembered now for *Evel Knievel* [1972] with George Hamilton, Sue Lyon and Rod Cameron. After Joe had a very successful career for a while, he retired and went back to live in Philadelphia. He passed away several years ago.

Q: What was *Devil Doll*'s co-feature in the U.S.?

GORDON: In the U.S., it was not distributed with any particular co-feature, because it was sold as a single top-billed picture, and exhibitors were free to play whatever film they wanted to, in support of it. It was always sold on percentage and as the feature attraction.

Q: In some theaters it was on a double-bill with a French picture called *My Baby Is Black!* I hope other theaters paired it with something more appropriate.

GORDON: Sometimes yes, sometimes no [*laughs*]! It was generally played with another exploitation picture. But it didn't really matter because, by distributing *Devil Doll* independently, we could insure that *Devil Doll* always played top-of-the-bill and on percentage, and the other film was usually a second feature for a flat film rental. The picture did so well in the United States and Canada that Sam Arkoff and Jim Nicholson of American International Pictures came to me and solicited me for a deal to distribute the film in Latin America. They had a very successful release of it in the South America countries. Incidentally, in 2002 when I was a guest at the Manchester [England] Festival of Fantastic Films, Frederick E. Smith was also invited and I met him in person for the first time. *Devil Doll* was shown and he and I did a Q&A session together, which was one of the festival's highlights. He said he was *delighted* with the changes we made in the story and with the finished film.

Q: More than one reviewer mentioned the excessive use of big closeups in *Devil Doll* and they deduced that it had been made with TV showings in mind. Any comment on that?

GORDON: In making *any* low-budget movie, one tended to use closeups more frequently and more prominently than otherwise, because it helped to reduce production costs; you didn't have to light and dress up a whole set in order to shoot a scene. There was no intention of making *Devil Doll* or any of my other films with any particular appeal for television.

In the 1970s, I thought it was time to consider a remake of *Devil Doll* on a bigger scale. Ken Rive was quite willing to go along with that, and we had a new screenplay written by a man called Sture Rydman, whom I had met when he wrote and directed two half-hour horror films, *The Man and the Snake* [1972]

Top: Gordon and Haliday at a *Devil Doll* press conference. Bottom: Gala Film Distributors' *Devil Doll* booth at that year's Cannes Film Festival.

and *The Return* [1973], which were based on stories by Ambrose Bierce; Gordon Films Inc. distributed them in the United States. However, Ken and I were not satisfied with the result, and a year later we made an agreement with Stanley Price to write an entirely new screenplay suggested by *Devil Doll*, but with a totally different storyline.

Q: Stanley Price, one of the writers of *Arabesque* [1966].

GORDON: Yes, and also *Gold* [1974] and *Shout at the Devil* [1976], two major films that were shot in South Africa. He had a number of other very interesting screen credits, and he came up with a story that I liked *very* much, and we tentatively called it *Dummy*.

Unfortunately, at that particular moment, William Goldman published his novel *Magic*, which was about a ventriloquist and his dummy, and [producer] Joe Levine acquired the film rights. They expected *Magic* to become a major international success, and so for the time being, no one else wanted to know about a less costly film that was more or less based on the same subject. In fact, Joe Levine at one time showed some interest in possibly optioning our *Dummy* screenplay, but I think it was just as a means of keeping it *off* the screen as he thought we might try to compete with *Magic*. When *Magic* came out, despite Anthony Hopkins and Ann-Margret and handsome production values, it was a total flop. And the result of *that* was that interest in any kind of a picture about a ventriloquist and his dummy evaporated completely for the time being. I still have the screenplay and perhaps one of these days we will be able to get it on the screen. I think it has very interesting possibilities and I've never lost interest in it.

Q: You made your second film with Bryant Haliday, *Curse of the Voodoo*, very soon after *Devil Doll*.

GORDON: When *Devil Doll* turned out so well, Ken Rive suggested that we should go ahead, as soon as

In the 1970s, at Gordon's behest, a couple of screenwriters took stabs at penning another ventriloquist-themed thriller for him, but as of today, Hugo (Corre) is still the only living dummy on his fright film-ography.

we could, and make another picture together; and we agreed that it should be a follow-up vehicle for Bryant Haliday. Among the many scripts on hand was one called *The Lion Man* by Brian Clemens, who had written it under the pseudonym Tony O'Grady. I think it had come to me from one of the agencies…or perhaps it had come to Ken, and *he* gave it to me. Either way, both Ken and I thought that it would be a very suitable subject as a follow-up to *Devil Doll*, and that it could be made using a certain amount of African stock footage and suitable locations in and around London, like for example Regent's Park near the London Zoo. Once again, Lindsay Shonteff directed.

Q: You've mentioned in past interviews that the weather just wouldn't cooperate during production.

GORDON: Unfortunately, it was very cold and there was lots of rain in London. And since we were shooting exteriors which were supposed to be Africa, this was a *big* problem! In fact, if you watch carefully, you can see that it actually *is* raining in the scene where the African natives are chasing Bryant Haliday through the park, and progressively he's getting more and more drenched! The weather really botched things up, and sort of depressed everybody. There's nothing worse when you're shooting a film than suddenly finding yourself in a situation where you have to stand around doing nothing. Somehow we managed it, but the picture did go somewhat over budget [budgeted at £35,000, it jumped to 50,000], and it didn't really turn out the way we'd hoped that it would.

Q: Bryant Haliday is a blond in two of your movies and dark-haired in the other two. What was he in real life?

GORDON: Dark-haired. Probably it was his own idea to "go blond" in *Curse of the Voodoo* and *Projected Man*, but I don't really recollect.

Q: Was he a horror movie buff?

Gunbearer Saidi (Dennis Alaba Peters), captured by Simbaza tribesmen, gets the point that he shouldn't have strayed into their territory.

GORDON: He was a *great* horror buff, and it was his ambition — which unfortunately he never realized — to star in a remake of the classic Hollywood horror picture *The Most Dangerous Game* [1932]. He wanted to play the role that was taken in the original movie by Leslie Banks, and I think he was ideally suited for it. I did in fact try to acquire the remake rights to *The Most Dangerous Game*, but they were in such a legal tangle that it was impossible to clear them, and so that project never came to fruition. He also very much wanted to play the title role in a remake of *Svengali* but I had no way at that time to set up such a spectacular production. However, after *Devil Doll* and *Curse of the Voodoo*, I did make two more films with Bryant, *The Projected Man* and *Tower of Evil*.

Q: Was *Curse of the Voodoo* your first time working with Dennis Price?

GORDON: Yes, and then the second time would have been *Tower of Evil* and the third and last time *Horror Hospital*. He was introduced to me by Kenneth Rive, who knew him from some other project, with the idea that Ken would be able to get him to appear in *Curse of the Voodoo*. I thought this was a terrific idea and, when we met, Dennis and I immediately took a liking to one another. Of course I knew all about his career from *Kind Hearts and Coronets* [1949] onwards. He was delightful to work with…so long as you could keep him sober. We found, particularly on *Horror Hospital*, that you really had to work with him in the morning, because he'd [start in on the drinking] by lunch time, and then it'd be useless to try to do anything with him in the afternoon. But he was a nice guy and very appreciative to get the work.

When the film was finished, the British distribution automatically was with Gala Films, Ken Rive's company. When I got the film to the United States, Joe Solomon wasn't particularly interested in taking it on. I can't recall the details now; I suppose I screened it for the usual list of potential distributors, and Allied

In London, Haliday's holiday turns out horribly when he's stalked by the tribesmen who marked him for death. Or is it all in his head?

Artists would have been one. They picked it up for distribution, to double-bill it with *Frankenstein Meets the Spacemonster* [1965]. I'm afraid I also don't recollect why the title was changed to *Curse of the Voodoo*.

Q: Did you see or hear from Shonteff much after he made those two movies for you?

GORDON: He started an independent production company of his own and produced and directed a considerable number of exploitation pictures in the U.K. and elsewhere in Europe. I remained in contact with him over the years, and I ran into him once in a while at film festivals and film markets overseas. Lindsay and I always remained on good terms but never actually did business together again after *Curse of the Voodoo*. He died in 2006.

As for Sidney Furie, while *Devil Doll* was in post-production, he accepted an offer from Universal to go to Hollywood and direct, as his first American film, *The Appaloosa* [1966], a Technicolor-Techniscope Western starring Marlon Brando. In the years since, Sidney has made a number of pictures in North America.

And after Ken Rive and I made *Devil Doll* and *Curse of the Voodoo*, we sort of each went our own way. Ken was very much involved also in distribution and production of films on the Continent of Europe, and I was anxious to continue with making the kind of films of which I had made a specialty. So we didn't continue to work together although we still remained friends and remained in contact. He died in 2002.

Q: You also stayed in touch, needless to say, with Bryant Haliday, even following his move to France.

GORDON: Yes, after he developed a lot of health problems, he decided to live in France. He spoke French as well as he spoke English; in fact, he'd dubbed his own voice in French for the French versions of *Devil Doll* and *Tower of Evil*. So for a while he worked in

Curse of the Voodoo veterans cavort: right to left, Dennis Price, Gordon, Lisa Daniely, director Lindsay Shonteff and executive producer Kenneth Rive. Rive (1918-2002) went from working as a child actor in German and British silents to importing the best of world cinema to Britain as a distributor-exhibitor.

France, doing dubbing, recordings and theater projects, but eventually he had to stop. He died in Paris in 1996 from the aftereffects of a stroke. At the time of his death, he had been married for some years to an English woman and they had one son, Mark. It was a tragic end for what had started out to be a very promising career as an actor. I visited Mark in Paris after Bryant's death and he took me to the very famous Le Père Lachaise Cemetery, near the Pigalle district of Paris, where his father and many other show business celebrities are buried.

I have a particular soft spot for *Devil Doll* because of Bryant Haliday; he and I were such close friends and we had such a happy working relationship. I think *Devil Doll* is one of my better pictures in terms of the way the screenplay was transferred to the screen and the fidelity of the final version of the picture *to* the screenplay and to the concept. I have very good memories of it.

GUEST INTERVIEW: FREDERICK E. SMITH ON *DEVIL DOLL*

Frederick E. Smith, author of the short story which provided the basis for *Devil Doll*, is an award-winning English novelist who believes that new experiences, new faces and extensive travel are vital to him in his writing career.

After serving in England's Royal Air Force during World War II, Smith and his wife relocated to South Africa, where he worked at a variety of jobs. It was then that his lifelong desire to write became irresistible, and for four years he dedicated five evenings a week to learning the craft. His earliest stories, including "The Devil Doll," were horror tales for the English-based publication *London Mystery Magazine*.

FREDERICK E. SMITH: The idea for "The Devil Doll" grew from my seeing a ventriloquist on the stage in my home town Hull in Yorkshire, England, when I was a child. Perhaps it was also influenced by the two years I spent in India during World War II when, in unusual circumstances, I met an Indian yogi who took me under his wing and helped to cure me of a serious illness I had contracted out there. I met my yogi near the town of Quetta, which was then in British India but now is in Pakistan. It is situated less than 20 miles from Afghanistan, which is so much in the news these days. [This interview took place days after 9/11.] Oddly enough, he did talk about soul transference although, being a very young man in those days, I did not take too much notice of this aspect of his conversation at that time. I feel it almost certain those were the influences that later led me to write "The Devil Doll."

I went out to South Africa shortly after the end of World War II and, while working in my brother-in-law's business, got the bug to write. My first ventures were supernatural stories, and an English magazine called *London Mystery Magazine* began to publish them. In all, they took 12 or more over a period of four years and one of them, entitled "Twelve Peaks to the Sky," was chosen for an anthology called *Mystery*. Another one was "The Devil Doll."

I've been asked if the 1945 movie *Dead of Night* — a marvelous movie — was an inspiration for "The Devil Doll" because I used the same name, Hugo, for the dummy as was used in that film. I don't remember copying this name (although one can never be sure one's subconscious didn't do so). It was just that Hugo seemed a good, creepy name for the dummy.

"The Devil Doll" appeared in issue #23 of *London Mystery Magazine*. I don't recall any immediate reaction to it after publication but as there were approximately 15 stories in each magazine, one seldom got individual reactions. *London Mystery Magazine* paid me £10 for the rights to publish. Moreover, the magazine's checks were so designed that when they were cashed, one lost all rights in everything else, which was the reason why I lost the film rights in the story and never found out the magazine had *sold* those rights because they never told me. (They didn't have a bad deal going at that time, did they?) I've no doubt that the producers of *Devil Doll* had to pay *London Mystery Magazine* much more for the story than my single £10. It was only later, when I heard the rumor they had sold the film rights to other stories, that I got wise and kept those rights for myself.

I didn't know "The Devil Doll" had been filmed until one afternoon years later, when my son Peter came back from school and asked me, "Dad, didn't you once write a short story called 'The Devil Doll'?" When I told him I had, he said there was a film showing in Bournemouth (where we now lived) but it was the last evening showing of the week. So Peter and I dashed into town and found it *was* a film based on my story. As can be imagined, I wasn't pleased at the time at being kept ignorant about it although I now realize it wasn't the fault of the film's producers, who would naturally think that the news had been passed on to me.

I haven't seen *Devil Doll* since that day many years ago in Bournemouth but I do remember thinking at the time how creepy it was and how well it was handled. In fact, I thought it one of the best things of its genre that I had ever seen.

[*Editor's note: A fuller version of this interview appears in Tom Weaver's book* A Sci-Fi Swarm and Horror Horde *(McFarland & Co., 2010).*]

ISLAND OF TERROR
1966

CREDITS

Executive Producers	**Richard Gordon** & *Gerald A. Fernback*
Produced by	*Tom Blakeley*
Directed by	*Terence Fisher*
Original Story & Screenplay	*Edward Andrew Mann & Alan Ramsen*
Photography	*Reg Wyer (Color)*
Music Composed & Directed by	*Malcolm Lockyer*
Electronic Effects	*Barry Gray*
Editor	*Thelma Connell*
Art Director – Special Effects	*John St. John Earl*
Assistant Art Director	*Fred Hole*
Makeup	*Bunty Phillips*
Hair Stylist	*Stella Rivers*
Special Effects Makeup	*Billy Partleton*
Special Effects Assistant	*Michael Albrechtson*
Production Manager	*Roy Baird*
Assistant Director	*Don Weeks*
Camera Operator	*Frank Drake*
Continuity	*Kay Mander*
Sound Recordist – Dubbing Mixer	*Bob McPhee*
Wardrobe Mistress	*Rosemary Burrows*

90 minutes

CAST

Peter Cushing	*Dr. Brian Stanley*
Edward Judd	*Dr. David West*
Carole Gray	*Toni Merrill*
Eddie Byrne	*Dr. Reginald Landers*
Sam Kydd	*Constable John Harris*
Niall MacGinnis	*Roger Campbell*
James Caffrey	*Peter Argyle*
Liam Gaffney	*Ian Bellows*
Roger Heathcote	*Dunley*
Keith Bell	*Halsey*
Shay Gorman	*Morton*
Peter Forbes-Robertson	*Dr. Lawrence Phillips*
Richard Bidlake	*Carson*
Joyce Hemson	*Mrs. Bellows*
Edward Ogden	*Helicopter Pilot*

SYNOPSIS

One foggy night, on an island off Ireland's east coast, a farmer is lured into a cave by mysterious sounds — and doesn't come out. Harris, the bike-riding local constable, later finds what's left of him: a pile of flesh inside his clothes. Via autopsy, the small island's one physician, Dr. Landers, determines that the body has no bones. Stumped, he goes to London to enlist the help of pathologist Dr. Stanley and bone disease specialist Dr. West. Stanley, West and West's girlfriend Toni accompany Landers back to the island to investigate.

The three doctors decide to pay a call on Dr. Phillips, a reclusive cancer researcher doing experimental work in the cellar of his island home. Phillips and his assistants are in the same jelly-fied condition. Phillips' papers reveal that he was working to create a form of living matter that would counteract cancer cells; apparently the creatures he produced are on the loose and on the lookout for prey whose bones they can dissolve and ingest. The island is cut off from the world — there are no phones, and a boat comes just once a week.

Constable Harris disappears, prompting the doctors and Toni to look for him at Phillips' place. In the cellar they find his body, and also two of the creatures: turtle-like "Silicates," each with a single, fast-moving, snake-like "tentacle." Dr. Landers is seized and killed, but then both the creatures stop and begin to messily divide in half; the humans take advantage of this opportunity to make a getaway. In the town's meeting hall, West explains to the locals that there are 64 Silicates now, there'll be 128 six hours from now, then 256 — and a million by the end of the week.

The Silicates are impervious to bullets, petrol bombs and dynamite — but they can be killed by radiation, so a plan is hatched to contaminate all the island's cattle with Strontium 90 and then put them in the path of the oncoming army of creatures. Returning yet again to Phillips' house to get the Strontium

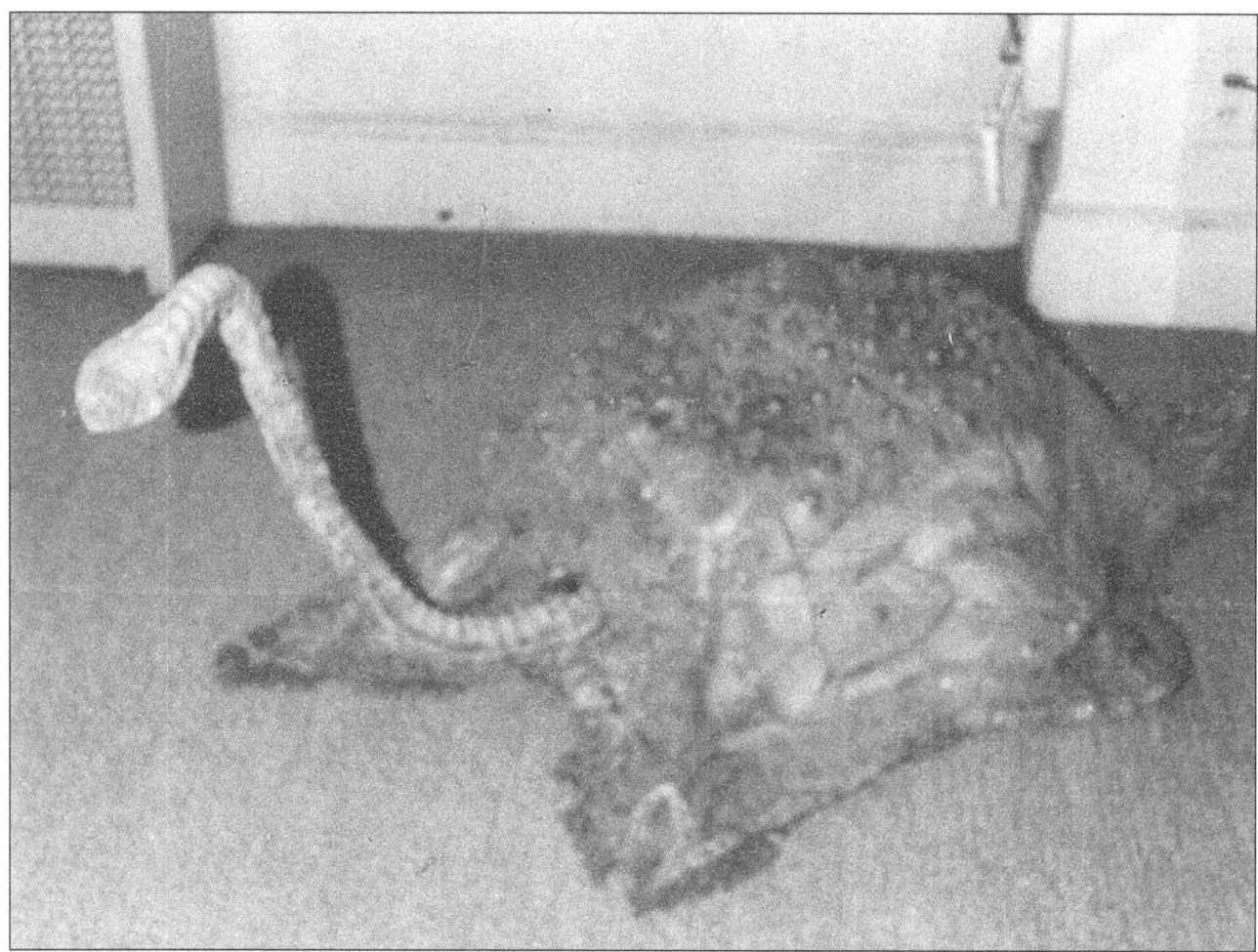

Rare behind-the-scenes shot of an *Island of Terror* Silicate on the floor of a Pinewood Studios office.

90, Stanley is grabbed by the wrist by a Silicate, and West must use an axe to cut off Stanley's hand in order to free him.

The meeting hall is packed with men, women and children on the night the Silicates make a meal out of the cattle and then continue to advance. The monsters shatter windows, drop in through a skylight and begin to bash open the doors; all seems lost, as West prepares a lethal injection and advances on the unsuspecting Toni, planning to spare her the pain of becoming Silicate chow. But in the nick of time, the Strontium 90 does its work and the monsters drop in their tracks.

Universal ad for their 1967 double-bill. *Variety*'s "Paul" liked both pictures and predicted they'd put Gordon's company "into the same league as Hammer and Amicus."

THE PROJECTED MAN
1966

CREDITS

Executive Producers	Richard Gordon & Gerald A. Fernback
Associate Producer	Pat Green
Produced by	John Croydon & Maurice Foster
Directed by	Ian Curteis
Screenplay	John C. Cooper [John Croydon] & Peter Bryan
Story	Frank Quattrocchi
Photography	Stanley Pavey (Color)
Editor	Derek Holding
Music Composed & Conducted by	Kenneth V. Jones

Music Played by the Sinfonia Orchestra of London

Art Director	Peter Mullins
Special Effects	Flo Nordhoff, Robert Hedges & Mike Hope
Second Unit Photography	Brian Rhodes
Assistant Directors	Derek Whitehurst & Tom Sachs
Camera Operator	Cece Cooney
Sound	S. G. Rider & Red Law
Continuity	Olga Brook
Dubbing Editor	Brian Blamey
Makeup	Eric Carter
Hairdresser	Joan Carpenter
Wardrobe	Kathleen Moore

86 minutes

CAST

Mary Peach	Dr. Pat Hill
Bryant Haliday	Prof. Paul Steiner
Norman Wooland	Dr. Blanchard
Ronald Allen	Dr. Chris Mitchel
Derek Farr	Insp. Davis
Tracey Crisp	Sheila Anderson
Derrick de Marney	Dr. Latham
Gerard Heinz	Prof. Lembach
Sam Kydd	Harry
Terry Scully	Steve
Norma West	Gloria King
Frank Gatliff	Dr. Wilson
John Watson	Sgt. Martin
Alfred Joint	Security Man
Rosemary Donnelly	Girl
David Scheuer	Boy

SYNOPSIS

Working on behalf of the Ministry, Prof. Paul Steiner and his assistant, laser expert Chris Mitchel, are developing a matter-transmitting device at a scientific foundation run by the high-handed Dr. Blanchard. Steiner and Mitchel can convert solid objects into pure energy and then re-materialize them in a different location, but living creatures (like a lab rat) that undergo the process soon die. Steiner brings in a colleague, pathologist Pat Hill, and she makes a suggestion that results in some modifications — and the successful disintegration-reintegration of a small monkey. The Ministry asks Prof. Lembach of the Geneva Institute to attend a projection demonstration.

Dr. Blanchard and his confederate Dr. Latham are determined to discredit Steiner and then steal his scientific secrets. Blanchard succeeds in sabotaging the demonstration, and refuses to give Steiner a second opportunity. Furious, Steiner cooks up a spectacular plan: to transmit *himself* from his lab to Blanchard's home with the intention of materializing right in front of Blanchard and his dinner guest Prof. Lembach. With Sheila, a timid young secretary, operating the controls, Steiner lies down in the transmission cradle and awaits projection. When a mishap ensues, Steiner materializes amidst rubble in a nearby building site, half his face and one hand hideously disfigured. He encounters three crooks in the process of breaking into a shop, and discovers that his touch results in an energy discharge that is lethal to them.

Back at the foundation, Latham is in the process of trying to steal Steiner's records when Steiner finds and electrocutes him. Steiner later gets megavolt vengeance on Blanchard. The half-crazed monster shows up at

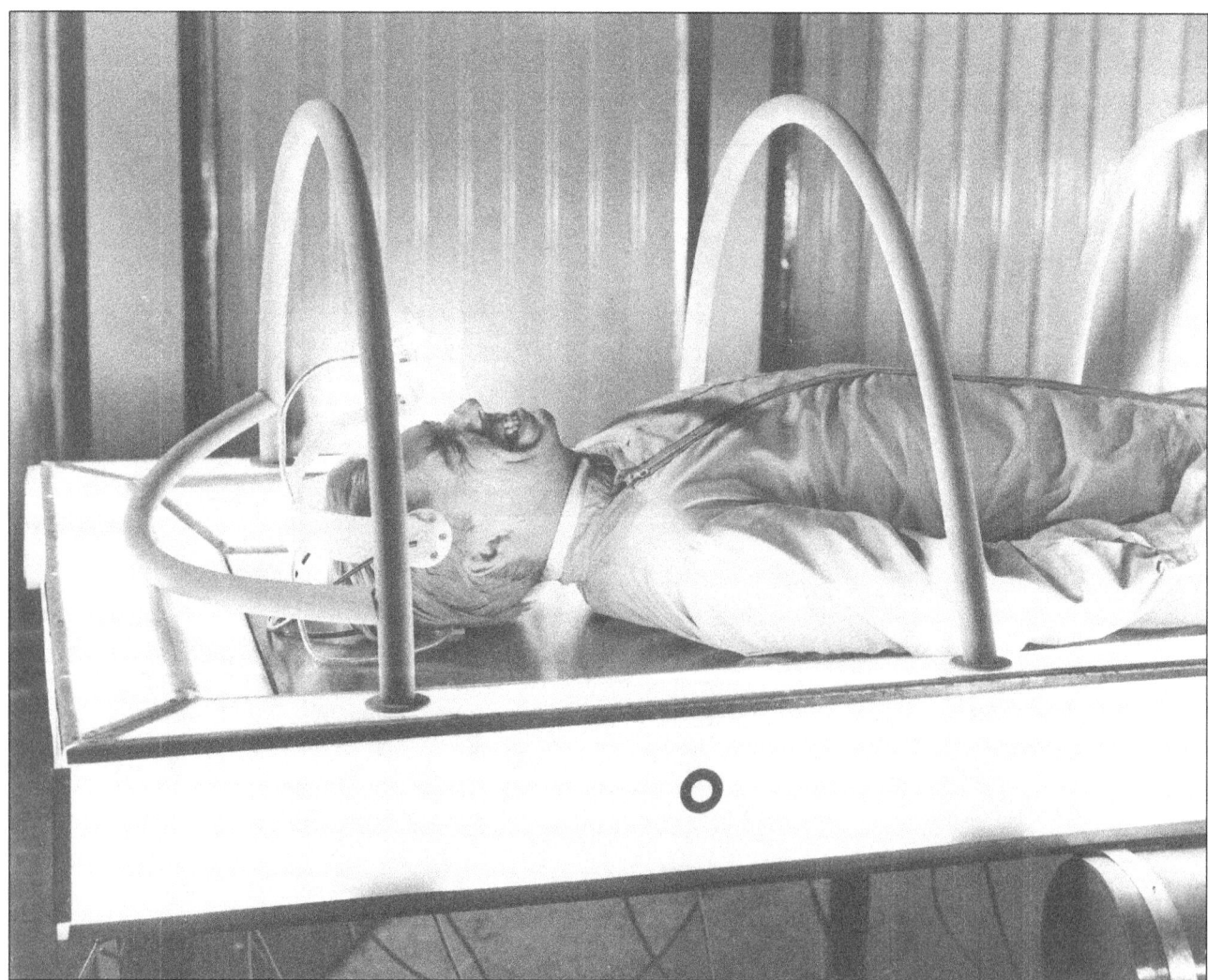

Prof. Steiner (Bryant Haliday) sings...*howls*...the teleportation blues in the malfunctioning transmission cradle in *The Projected Man*.

Pat's apartment where she and Mitchel are making love, jealously threatening their lives before changing his mind and proceeding to a nearby power station for a "recharge." Police find he is impervious to their bullets. Pat enters the power station alone and tries to convince Steiner to return to the foundation, where Mitchel intends to try to reverse the process and de-energize him. Steiner pretends to want to cooperate, but actually he no longer wants to live in such a deformed condition. Once the matter transmitter is fully revved up, Steiner takes the controls, using the laser projector to destroy much of the lab equipment, and then turning the deadly beam on himself. As Pat and Mitchel watch, the monstrous-looking Steiner vanishes from sight.

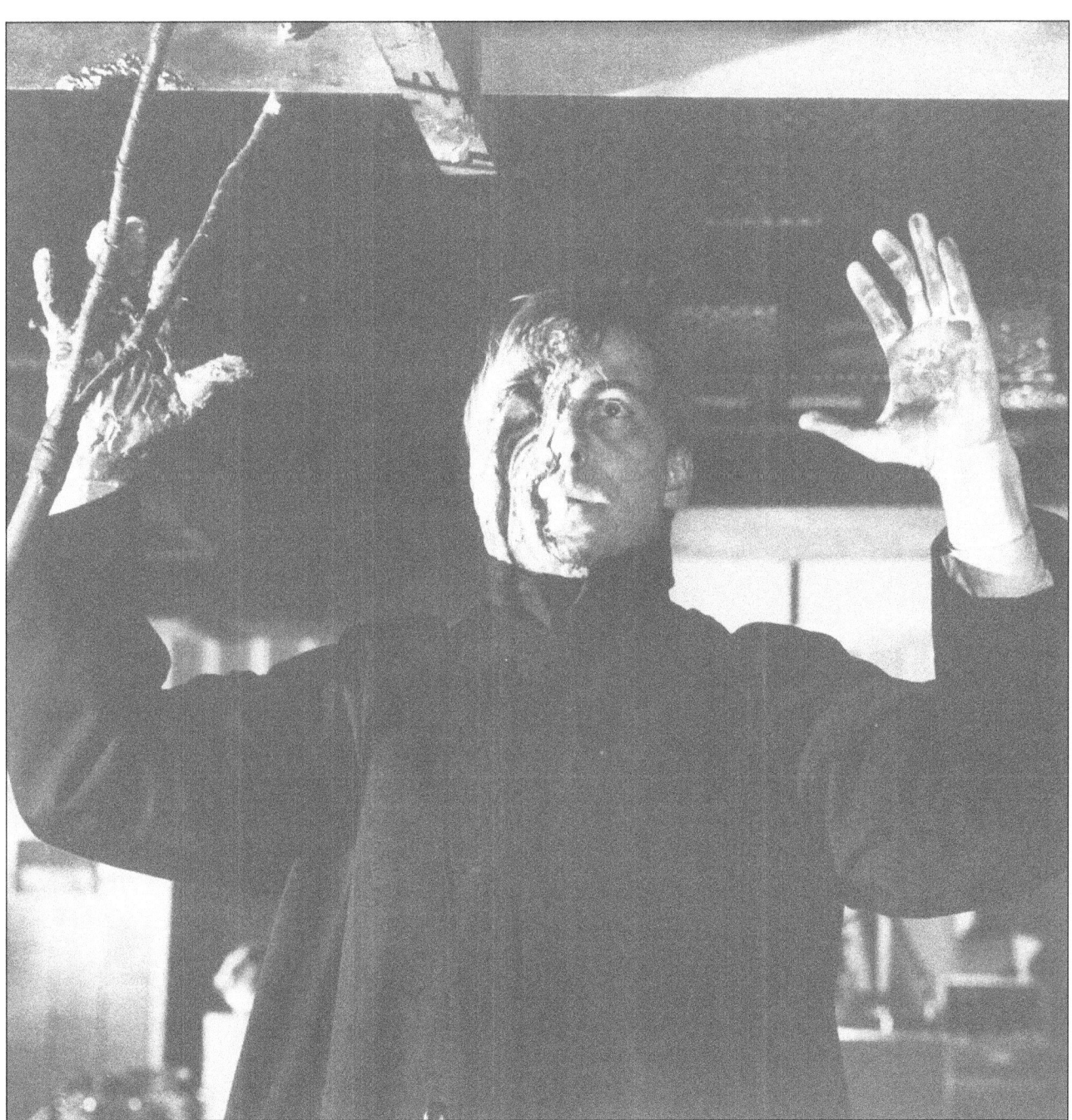

The Projected Man became fodder for TV's *Mystery Science Theater 3000* comics in a 1998 episode; once Steiner (Haliday) is burned, the comments include, "[He] just needs a dab of Dermablend..."

NAKED EVIL
1966

CREDITS

Co-Producers	**Richard Gordon** & Gerald A. Fernback
Executive Producer	Steven Pallos
Produced by	M.F. Johnson
Written & Directed by	Stanley Goulder

Based on the Play "The Obi" by Jon Manchip White

Photography	Geoffrey Faithfull
Editor	Peter Musgrave
Music Composed & Conducted by	Bernard Ebbinghouse
Art Directors	George Provis & Denys Pavitt
Production Manager	Denis Johnson Jr.
Assistant Director	Malcolm M. Johnson
Camera Operator	Len Harris
Sound Recordist	Clive Winter
Makeup	Stella Morris
Hairdresser	Mervyn Medalie
Continuity	Lorna Selwyn

85 minutes

CAST

Basil Dignam	Jim Benson
Anthony Ainley	Dick Alderson
Suzanne Neve	Janet Tuttle
Richard Coleman	Insp. Hollis
Olaf Pooley	Father J.W. Goodman
George A. Saunders [John Ashley Hamilton]	Danny
Carmen Munroe	Beverley
Brylo Forde	Amizan
Dan Jackson	Lloyd
Ronald Bridges	Wilkins

Bari Jonson, Oscar James

SYNOPSIS

In Jamaican black magic, an obi is a bottle filled with grave dirt, egg shells and rum, with feathers tied to the top; smash it and you unleash a devil. And in a black area of London, one drug-dealing gang has begun sending obis to members of another, with psychological results that are always fatal.

Police Insp. Hollis visits the churchyard that is being desecrated for its grave dirt and talks with Father Goodman, an expert on these death charms after having lived for 15 years in Jamaica and written a 300-page book on the subject. Father Goodman takes Hollis to see another expert, Jim Benson, who runs a nearby hostel for university students — a number of them Jamaican. Hollis also meets Benson's assistant Dick Alderson and secretary Janet. Shuffling around the place is creepy janitor Amizan, who lives in the basement in a shack near the boiler.

Benson is the recipient of a death obi, and then a second, and is wracked by fear ("When you've lived in the tropics as long as I have, you come to know the feel of sheer, outright evil!"). Many slaughtered cockerels are found in the woods around the property. Janet finds Benson on the floor of his office, dead after having been repeatedly stabbed. Suspicion falls on physics student Danny, who is half-hysterical in his room with the murder weapon, a spear, on the floor. The dead body of Amizan, found in his shack, is laid on a nearby table and covered with a sheet.

When Alderson slips into a coma-like trance, Father Goodman realizes that an exorcism is in order. Accompanied by Danny and another student, he goes to the basement and performs the rite while burning all of Amizan's voodoo paraphernalia. Lightning flashes,

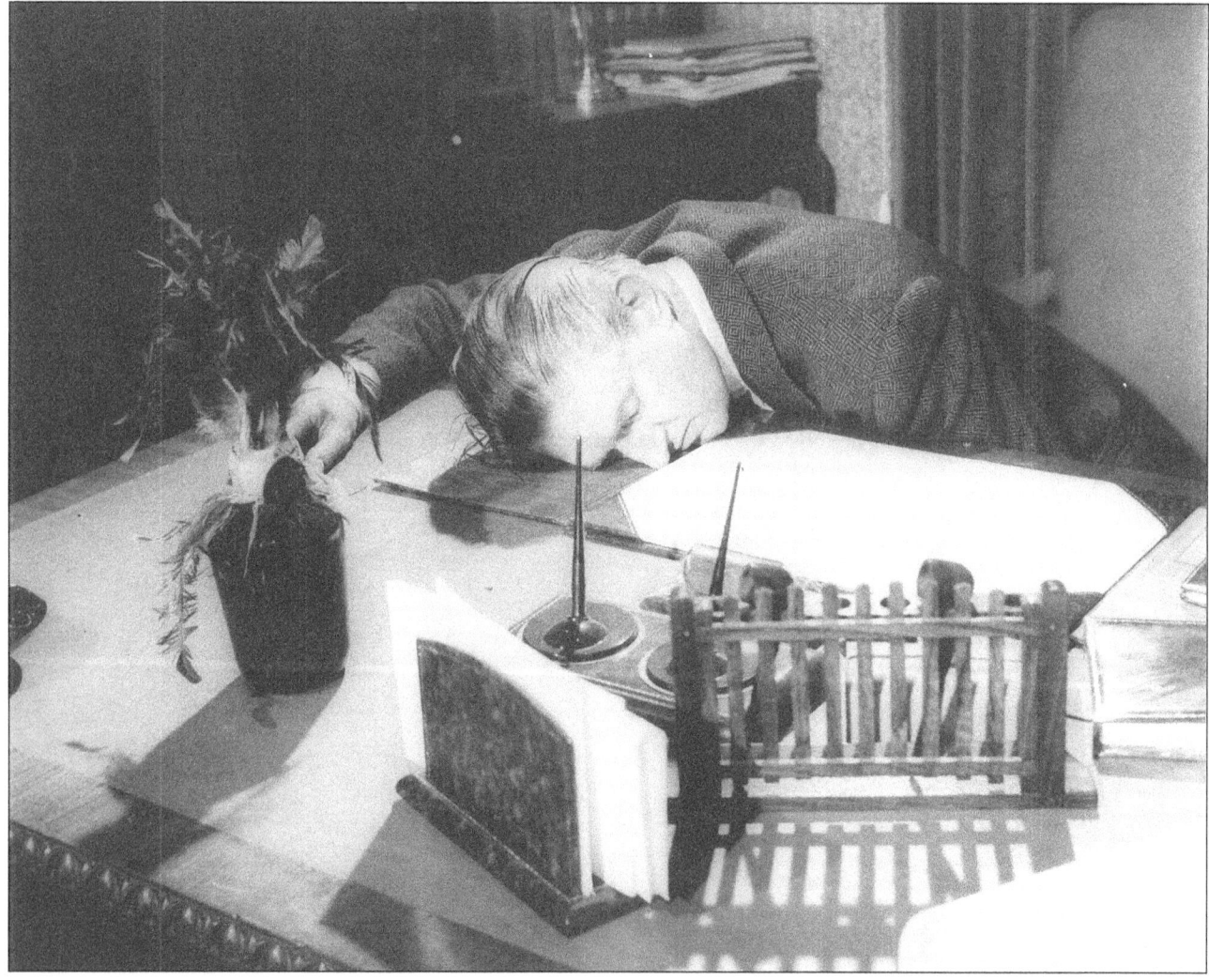

Has the Jamaican death obi (the bottle on the desk) worked its black magic on Benson (Basil Dignam)? Tension mounts in *Naked Evil*.

thunder booms and a great wind blows through the entire building. Amizan's body disappears from the table, and his wandering soul takes control of the body of Alderson. Brandishing a cross, Father Goodman is able to cast it out. Alderson reveals that Amizan killed Benson and tried to frame Danny — and then he, Alderson, possessed by the spirit of Benson, killed Amizan. As Hollis tries to think of a rational explanation for all these fantastic goings-on, Father Goodman declares that the evil of Amizan has left the hostel — and that Amizan's soul will now surely be dragged down to Hell.

RICHARD GORDON ON *ISLAND OF TERROR*, *THE PROJECTED MAN* AND *NAKED EVIL*

Q: You were partnered with Gerald A. Fernback on the production of your next three pictures. How did you first link up with him?

RICHARD GORDON: During the 1950s, I was making a series of B-movie co-productions for which I also negotiated the American distribution deals. Gerry Fernback was the head of Republic Pictures in England. When I screened him a print of my film *The Fighting Wildcats* [1957] which Keefe Brasselle starred in and also directed, Gerry liked it and, on behalf of Republic, bought it for distribution in America. We became friends and shortly thereafter he left Republic to go into business on his own: He bought a travel agency called Embassy Travel and was very successful in that field. We remained in contact, and in 1961 he suggested to me that we form a company to supply American films to British television which, at that time, consisted only of the BBC and one commercial channel, Granada Television. The Hollywood major studios had all agreed *not* to release their films to television in England, and British films were also restricted. For the company we formed, Gerry came up with the name Protelco Productions; I don't remember from where it derived. Protelco became the leading supplier of independent product to the networks.

Q: Then Fernback had a hand in your *Devil Doll* [1964], with no on-screen credit.

GORDON: When I was getting ready to make *Devil Doll* in association with the U.K. distributor Gala Films, Gerry offered to participate in the financing and become a partner in my production plans. *Devil Doll* was very successful, both in England and in the United States. Meanwhile Gerry and I continued our television business in the U.K., and Gerry expanded his travel agency into the freight business, specializing in providing the facilities for film companies that were going overseas on location.

Around this time, there was an independent British production-distribution company called Planet Films which was owned by Tom Blakeley and Bill Chalmers, whom I knew well. Blakeley had been producing low-budget movies in Manchester for several years and Chalmers was running the distribution company Butcher's Films. I was selling their films in America and finding product for them to distribute in the U.K. Planet had just finished a vampire movie, *Devils of Darkness* [1965], which I sold on their behalf to 20th Century-Fox for distribution in America. Blakeley had a script called *The Night the Silicates Came* [later retitled *Island of Terror*] which was sent to him by its two writers who were then living in Spain, Edward Andrew Mann and Allan Ramsen. Ramsen was an American expatriate who had tried to become an actor at Universal in Hollywood with no success. Blakeley wanted to film *The Night the Silicates Came* as his next production but it was a much more expensive project than his usual films and he needed a partner. He brought the script to Gerry and me and asked if we would like to participate in it. The idea was that Planet would distribute the film in England and we could have the rest of the world rights.

When I read the screenplay, I thought it was exactly the kind of thing that we were looking for, and as close to being "ready to go" as any script I had ever read. However, I was hesitant to say yes because, as I explained to Gerry, programming in the U.K. and America, and most of the rest of the world, was still double feature and if we did not have a second film to go with it, we would end up as someone *else's* second feature and get the short end of the deal. We would have to have another film to make up our own double program, especially for the American market where I had done a deal like that with MGM for *The Haunted Strangler* and *Fiend Without a Face* [both 1958]. Gerry agreed.

Q: And that's how *The Projected Man* came about.

GORDON: My brother Alex was then working in Hollywood and very much involved with Jim Nicholson and Sam Arkoff at American International. He used to send me scripts and story ideas that Nicholson and Arkoff had turned down for one reason or another, in case I could use them in England. One such script was already in my possession, called *The Projected Man*, by a Hollywood writer named Frank Quattrocchi. Of course it had an American setting, I believe it was Los Angeles, and Gerry and I decided that it could just as well take place in London or anywhere else. I asked John Croydon [Gordon's collaborator on *Fiend, Haunted Strangler* et al.] to take a look at it and he agreed and said that he could easily supervise a quick rewrite to change the location and have it ready in time to shoot simultaneously with *The Night the Silicates Came* (the title of which I wanted to change to *The Night the Creatures Came* as I felt that no one would know what the word "silicates" meant and therefore it was meaningless). With Alex's help I acquired the *Projected Man* film rights directly from Quattrocchi, who agreed to accept a story credit. John Croydon, who was also a professional writer for which he used the *nom de plume* John C. Cooper, then rewrote the script in collaboration with Peter Bryan to give it an English setting.

It would not have been possible for Tom Blakeley to produce two pictures at the same time, and I would not have been keen on that anyway. So I talked about *The Projected Man* with several other people in London, including Michael Klinger and Tony Tenser of Compton Films, with whom I was on friendly terms. They showed an immediate interest and said yes, provided we kept to a minimum budget, and I made a deal with them very quickly.

Q: So *Island of Terror* and *Projected Man* were scheduled to go into production at more or less the same time?

Constable Harris (Sam Kydd) gets unexpectedly grabbed from above in one of *Island*'s many scare moments.

GORDON: That's correct. Gerry and I agreed to supervise both projects, *The Night the Silicates Came* [hereafter called *Island of Terror*] at Pinewood Studios and *The Projected Man* at Merton Park Studios. Pinewood, which was about 30 miles outside London, belonged to the Rank Organisation and was England's largest studio. Merton Park, much smaller and less expensive than Pinewood, was in a suburb of London. I knew it well because several of my co-productions were shot there.

Q: For the leading role in *Island of Terror*, you got yet another "blue-chip" horror star, Peter Cushing.

GORDON: I was friendly with Jimmy Carreras, the head of Hammer Films. The industry wasn't as big then as it is now, especially in London, and most of the independents knew each other well and always helped one another. We met socially and all belonged to organizations like the Variety Club, frequented the same restaurants and shared information. The idea was that we had to work together in order to compete with the major Hollywood studios and their London subsidiaries as well as the British studios like Rank, Associated British and British Lion.

When I told Jimmy that Gerry and I were about to start on two new productions on our own and that we had a great script [*Island of Terror*] that I particularly liked, he told me that if we were ready to go, he could make available to us on loan two people whom Hammer had under contract but who were at that moment not working on any projects: Terence Fisher and Peter Cushing. Gerry and I jumped at the chance. Tom Blakeley was delighted; he would never have dreamed of going after them on his own, and probably would not have spent that kind of money anyway without our

Dr. Stanley (Peter Cushing) is seized by the wrist by a Silicate in the build-up to *Island*'s most shocking scenes, the hacking-off of his hand. For many fans, it's the high point of the picture; Gordon scoffs, "It looked amateurish."

partnership. On our own, we also got Edward Judd for *Island of Terror*. As far as I was concerned, he was a very good leading man who had already been in some successful pictures like Val Guest's *The Day the Earth Caught Fire* [1961] and Ray Harryhausen's *First Men in the Moon* [1964]. I was happy to have him. In later years one heard stories that he had been difficult on other movies but we did not have *any* problems with him on our picture. I already knew Carole Gray from *Devils of Darkness* and I was aware that she had some other good credits including *Curse of the Fly* [1965] and I thought she would be very good as Judd's girlfriend in our film.

Eddie Byrne [as the island's doctor] and Niall MacGinnis [as its leading citizen] were good value for money and could be kept within the limitations of our budget by scheduling their scenes to be shot together on fixed days so that we did not have to employ them for the entire shooting schedule. The same applied to several other supporting players. The film went ahead under the expert guidance of Terence Fisher, who insured that it would come in on budget and on schedule.

Q: About when did the shooting start?

GORDON: Production on *Island of Terror* was scheduled to commence on November 22, 1965, for five weeks of principal photography. It was shot in its entirety at Pinewood, using their very large back lot that stood in for most of the film's outdoor settings and also their "lake" which appears in the pre-credits sequence. Exteriors like the cancer research team's building, described in the film by Peter Cushing's character as resembling Wuthering Heights, were shot around the studio's permanent buildings.

Q: This was your second time working with Terence Fisher.

GORDON: I had met him casually in 1957 when he directed one of my co-productions called *Kill Me Tomorrow* for which I had brought Pat O'Brien to England. It had been a difficult picture to make because Pat O'Brien had a drinking problem but Fisher handled it very well. He was directing all kinds of independent pictures and was in great demand when Hammer signed him to an exclusive contract. I found him great to work with but he was reclusive. He didn't like to mix socially with anyone when he was working, and during the filming of *Island of Terror*, at midday when most of us went to lunch, he would lock himself in his office with a sandwich and work on the afternoon's and next day's shooting. I never had much opportunity to spend time with him alone — no opportunity at all, really — and I was also preoccupied with *The Projected Man*. I simply saw him whenever I visited Pinewood during the production to see how it was going.

Q: Was this your first time working with Peter Cushing?

GORDON: I first met Cushing when I went to Pinewood to see what was going on with *Island of Terror*. He was very pleasant, very low-key. The character he played had a sense of humor about him, but I honestly can't recall whether or not the character was written that way in the original script. My guess would be that the humor was added after it was decided that Cushing was going to play the role, because that's not the kind of thing that just *any* actor could do. For instance, it wouldn't have worked if we'd hired Christopher Lee [*laughs*]!

After *Island of Terror*, I never met with Cushing again, but some years later, a newcomer named Ken Wiederhorn was trying to put together his first movie *Shock Waves* [1977] and was looking for some actor he could get at a reasonable price to come to Florida and play in it. I suggested Cushing as a possibility, but Ken never could get through to him because Cushing's agent in London, John Redway, wasn't interested in having some independent young American who'd never made a movie, come along and try to get one of his actors on the cheap. I told Ken that I could probably put him in touch with Cushing personally, and I did get hold of Cushing on the telephone and he said he'd be happy to talk to Ken. Ken then contacted him directly, and the outcome of it was that, despite the agent's unwillingness to cooperate and the fact that there was very little money involved, Cushing thought it would be a nice idea because he could have a holiday in Florida at the same time. Ken very much enjoyed working with him — as did I on *Island of Terror*. When I think back on Peter today, he was very much in the Boris Karloff class: Very quiet, very conservative, great sense of humor, not pushing himself into the limelight, and quite content to be there and do what he had to do without making a big fuss about it. And, acting-wise, impeccable. Whatever he was asked to do on *Island of Terror*, he either did it *or*, if he thought it wasn't reasonable or if he felt that he had a better idea, he discussed it. Of course, he *was* working with his old friend Terence Fisher.

Q: Who made the *Island of Terror* Silicates?

GORDON: The Silicates were made by the special effects department at Pinewood and I was quite satisfied with what I saw when their scenes were shot. They were moved around by wires that were so carefully placed that you could not see them on the screen. It was my idea for them to make a slurping sound very much like that of the Fiends in *Fiend Without a Face*; I thought that sound was effective in *Fiend* and that it would give the Silicates more menace. The props representing the corpses of their victims were, in my opinion, well done. Although Hammer was pushing the envelope all the time with censorship in that era, you must remember that it was a very different time then than now and *Island of Terror* was considered quite gruesome in its day. Likewise, there was a topless girl [Norma West] on a morgue table in *The Projected Man*; this was done at Compton's insistence because it would help sales overseas. Then there was the scene in *Island of Terror* where Edward Judd has to cut Peter Cushing's hand off with an axe to save him from a Silicate that has him by the wrist.

The first time I saw the insert shot of the hand coming off and the arm spurting blood was when we screened a finished print at Pinewood Studios. Gerry, Fisher and I all agreed that it didn't work and was badly done. It was an obvious fake, it looked amateurish. Tom Blakeley was the only one who disagreed because he didn't want to spend the money to re-shoot it. I had to get up and say that I didn't want that shot in the film, especially when we screened it for the major distributors in America because it would spoil the mood and make it look like a low-budget movie. I felt an audience would start laughing.

Meanwhile, *The Projected Man*, based at Merton Park Studios, was under the supervision of John Croydon as I could not go tearing back and forth all the time between Pinewood and Merton Park. Croydon had introduced Gerry and me to a young writer who was new in the business and was enjoying considerable success in television. His name was Ian Curteis and he was obviously going to go places although he had not yet attempted a feature film. Croydon was so confident of his success that he persuaded Gerry and me to sign Curteis to direct *The Projected Man*. It turned out to be an unfortunate choice.

Q: Your *Devil Doll-Curse of the Voodoo* star Bryant Haliday returned for *The Projected Man*.

GORDON: To play the title role, I did not want a British actor and frankly we didn't have the money to import a Hollywood star because of our limited budget. It was not a situation like *Witchfinder General* [1968] which Compton made with American International who furnished the services of Vincent Price and paid his salary and expenses. The logical conclusion for me was to sign Bryant Haliday, whom I had already used in *Devil Doll* and *Curse of the Voodoo* and had achieved a certain success in America because *Devil Doll* did so well there. Bryant, [an American] living in Europe, was a big fan of horror movies, and he loved doing *Projected Man*. I thought he was particularly good in it once he became the "monster on the loose" with the heavy burn makeup.

Q: Mary Peach played the female lead in *Projected Man*.

GORDON: Compton got Mary Peach for the female lead. She was a stage actress who had also been in some successful British films and they regarded her as good value for England and insisted that she must have top billing. Norman Wooland, the villain, was a well-known character actor, and also a Shakespearean actor on the stage. Wooland, Derek Farr, Derrick de Marney — as I mentioned earlier, these were the kind of people that we could get for pictures, and even though their names may not have meant anything in the United States or elsewhere, they gave the pictures a lot of extra weight in the U.K.

Unfortunately, *Projected Man* got into trouble early in the filming. Because of his lack of feature film experience, combined with the tight schedule and limited financing, our young director Ian Curteis wasn't able to handle it, it all became too much for him. The picture started falling behind schedule and going over budget, and I found myself spending most days at Merton Park with John Croydon by my side while *Island of Terror* was running smoothly at Pinewood. There came a moment when Michael Klinger and Tony Tenser, who were looking over our shoulders, threatened to step in to take over the production as they were not prepared to increase their financing. Croydon and I decided that there was really only one thing to do: fire Ian Curteis and replace him for the completion of the film. As Croydon had hired him for us, it fell on him to fire Curteis and step in personally as a replacement to finish the last week's shooting. I don't remember any big drama at the studio [when Curteis was notified] and I think Curteis was relieved to step out because he simply didn't know any longer what to do. I would say that Ian Curteis directed 90 percent of *The Projected Man* and Croydon finished it. Croydon's work as director was not reflected in the on-screen credits which list only Curteis as director. One tries not to publicize such incidents.

Q: I wasn't aware that Croydon had ever directed. That might have been the only time.

GORDON: He was one of England's most experienced production supervisors and was capable of doing *any*thing: He could write, he could produce, he could direct, and it became his responsibility to direct the balance of the picture. Croydon later retired from active production — in fact, *The Projected Man* was his "swan song," as he himself called it. But he continued to work as a consultant to a company of guarantors of completion, Film Finances Limited, until ill health forced him into retirement. He was working on his autobiography at the time of his death in 1994.

Soon it was time for me to take over the responsibility of selling both *Island of Terror* and *The Projected Man* in America. In those days, all the major companies had distribution headquarters in New York. I had a pretty good relationship with most of them, having sold them films that I represented over the years. Universal, which occupied a building on the corner of 57th Street and Park Avenue, was my first choice because I was on very good terms with "Hi" Martin, their executive in charge. He had bought several films from me previously which had been quite

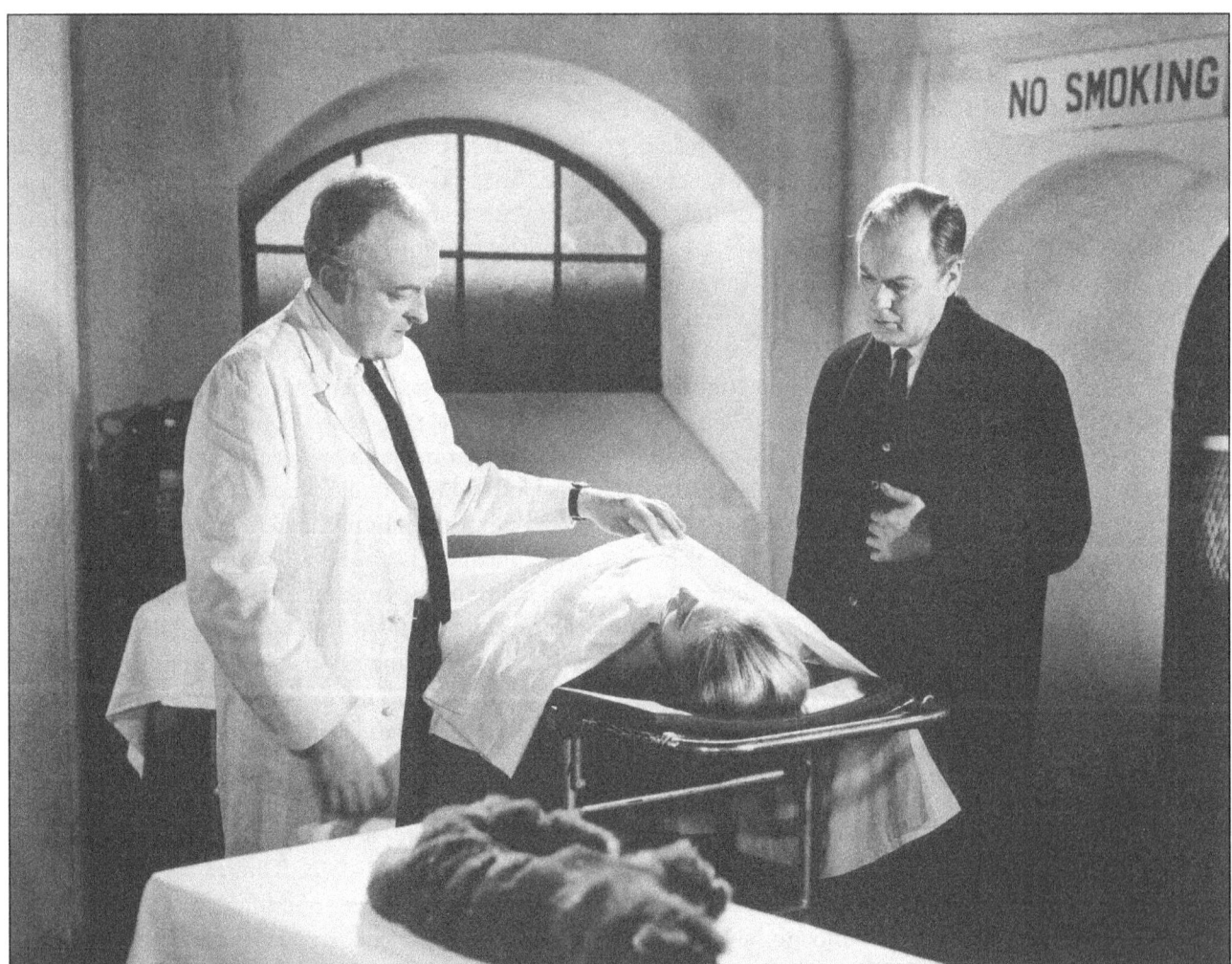

In *The Projected Man*'s English cut, a mortuary doctor (Frank Gatliff) lifts the sheet covering the body of a woman victim (Norma West) and we see that she is topless. In the American cut, he only pulls the sheet down far enough for viewers to see her head and shoulders.

successful for them and he seemed to like me. *The Projected Man* was not yet ready because they were still finishing the special effects in London so I ran *Island of Terror* for him in Universal's screening room. He liked it and expressed an interest in acquiring the rights for Universal. I decided to stall for time because, as I mentioned earlier, if it went out alone, it would end up as a second feature with one of Universal's own productions and we would end up being the bottom half of the bill which would be no good for us financially. I told Hi about *The Projected Man* and that it was nearly ready to be shown and I wanted to withhold from making a decision until I could show him the first print of *The Projected Man* for a possible two-picture deal. He went along with that. To speed up matters, I brought over a work print of *The Projected Man* and ran it for him so that he would know what was happening (and I did not want him to go cold on us!). I don't remember now which scenes were unfinished but the end of this story is that he liked it well enough to say yes and we made a deal for Universal to release the double bill. The price that Universal paid us for the Western Hemisphere rights covered our production costs for the two films; *Island of Terror* was budgeted at £70,000 which would not have included the fees of Protelco, Gerry Fernback and myself. I don't exactly remember the budget of *Projected Man* but it was substantially less.

Now, a funny thing happened involving the hand-chopping scene in *Island of Terror* which was not in the film when I screened it for Hi Martin. I had previously given Universal a copy of the shooting script to keep their interest high and because they wanted to be sure they would have no censorship problems. At the end of the screening, Martin asked me what happened to that shot. I wasn't going to lie about it, I said, "Frankly, I

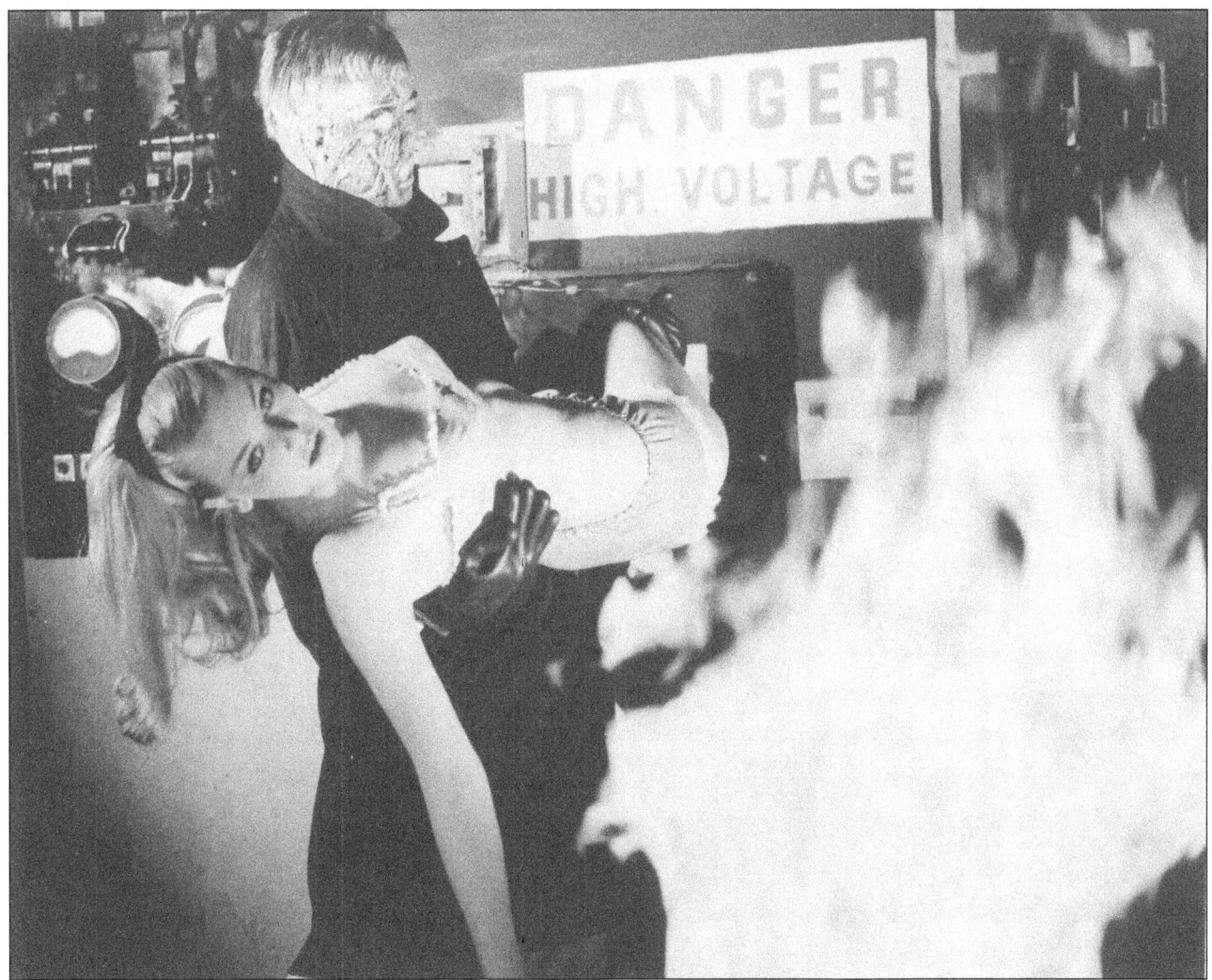

Secretary Sheila (Tracey Crisp) has her choice of things to worry about: fire, high voltage and the hate-maddened Projected Man (Haliday)!

wasn't happy with it. I didn't think it would matter if we left it out; in fact, I thought it would look more horrific if you don't actually see it." He asked, "If we *want* it, can we get it?" I said, "Well, you're certainly entitled to it if you buy the picture for the United States and you want that shot included." He said, "Have it sent over from England, and let the people at the studio in California look at it." Well, they looked at it and they said, "Yes, we want it"! At that time, it was actually surprising that Universal got that shot past the MPAA, that Universal was not forced to cut it. So that's how it came to be in the film. I still think it spoils the mood. When I see the film today with an audience, somebody usually lets out a laugh when they see that shot, because it's so obviously phony. In horror films, sometimes if something's happening off-screen, and you know it's happening but you don't see it, it's actually more horrifying than if it's put on the screen in front of you. Especially if what's put on the screen in front of you looks amateurish and doesn't work properly!

Q: You saw both movies again recently, in preparation for this interview. What were your thoughts?

GORDON: The pre-credits sequence in *Island of Terror* was, I thought, a little bit too long and slow, but *everybody* was doing pictures with pre-credits sequences at that time. I thought the first killing, the Silicate attacking the farmer [Liam Gaffney] off-camera in the cave, was very effective; Terence Fisher handled that particularly well. Also the first visit to the cancer researchers' laboratory, where more bodies are found. The "worst" thing about the movie was the day-for-night shots, particularly the lift-off of the helicopter; one minute it looked like day and the next minute it was dark. But that was a matter of budget.

Q: And *The Projected Man*?

GORDON: It started off a bit slow, and in fact Universal cut it because they felt that it took too long to

The Projected Man just wants revenge. Is that so wrong? (Pictured: Haliday, Norman Wooland.)

get going. Uncut, the picture opens with the scientists teleporting a guinea pig, and then after the arrival of Mary Peach there's *another* experiment with the teleportation machine; Universal cut the guinea pig experiment. Also, I could have done with less of the scantily clad secretary [Tracey Crisp] and the so-called nudity, but that was a necessary ingredient at the time. I thought Bryant was very effective and handled his role extremely well. Towards the end, he was actually able to arouse the sympathy of the audience and did not come across as just a monster on a killing spree. It reminded me of so many films in which Boris Karloff had played a scientist who becomes a monster through no fault of his own, as opposed to Bela Lugosi who was usually an outright villain. In fact, you might say that Bryant paid tribute to the memory of Bela in *Devil Doll* and Karloff in *The Projected Man*! As for the female lead, Mary Peach became Mrs. Jimmy Sangster in the 1990s, and the last time I saw her was with Sangster at one of the FANEX conventions in Baltimore [July 1997]. When I mentioned *The Projected Man*, she said, "Oh, I don't want to talk about that film!" — I think she didn't want to appear to have been a horror film leading lady and become a part of that "clan" alongside actresses like Ingrid Pitt [*laughs*]. So I stayed away from saying anything more about it!

Q: Planet Films quickly went on to make a sci-fi film called *Night of the Big Heat* [1967] but you were not involved.

GORDON: Tom Blakeley was so struck by the success of *Island of Terror* and the deal with Universal that he wanted to rush immediately into a follow-up project, using Terence Fisher and Peter Cushing again while they were still available, and adding Christopher Lee. He hurriedly bought the film rights to a novel called *Night of the Big Heat* which he felt he could make on a very low budget and he thought would interest Gerry Fernback and me. Neither Gerry nor I liked the script. It was too long, too talky, with not enough action, and the budget was much too low to allow for really good special effects. Protelco withdrew from the production and Planet went ahead on its own. No one liked the finished film. I tried to help Planet make an American sale but every studio where I screened it, including Universal, turned it down. Eventually [1971] I sold it off to an American independent distributor who retitled it *Island of the Burning Damned* and paired it with a Japanese Godzilla picture [*Godzilla's Revenge*]. The program was a total failure and helped to lead Planet into bankruptcy.

Q: While you and Gerald Fernback went on to make *Naked Evil*.

GORDON: Gerry and I wanted to get another picture going quickly with Protelco but we didn't have anything of our own that was ready. Allan Ramsen [co-writer of *Island of Terror*] continued to write genre screenplays on spec and submit them to us but neither Gerry nor I liked any of them. At that point, we were approached by Steven Pallos, a producer of some importance in England. He originally came from Hungary along with Alexander Korda to form London Film Productions, and for many years he was Korda's partner. When they split up amicably, Steve formed his own company, Britannia Film Distributors, and also a production company called Gibraltar Films. I sold a number of their films in the U.S. including two titles to Hi Martin for Universal distribution in the Western Hemisphere, *Nearly a Nasty Accident* [1961] and *Mystery Submarine* [1963].

Steve approached Gerry and me because he had been offered a property called *The Obi*, a play about voodoo witchcraft that Jon Manchip White had written for the BBC. Steve thought that [a movie version] would make a very good second feature for distribution both in England and overseas. He talked to Gerry about the possibility of Protelco helping to finance it, and Gerry referred him to me. Steve and I discussed it, and I thought it was quite a good idea. Even though I had done a previous picture of that type [*Curse of the Voodoo*] which hadn't been too successful, I thought that *this* had a chance to be something better and that it was worth doing.

Steve already had a deal in place with Columbia Pictures, which was prepared to participate in the financing and to distribute the film in the United Kingdom and some European countries. However, Columbia envisaged the film [released as *Naked Evil*] as a low-budget second feature that would be useful for them for British quota purposes and wanted it to be made in black-and-white on a budget not exceeding £60,000. Since the industry was switching almost entirely to color except for second features, we tried to persuade Columbia to let us do the film on a higher budget, in color, to increase its potential internationally, but Columbia refused to consider it. Color was then still much more expensive than black-and-white, particularly the cost of release prints, and Columbia saw this proposed picture as nothing more than a second feature for their quota.

In order to keep Protelco active, Gerry and I agreed to do it the way Columbia wanted. However, Gerry was very busy with his other business activities at that time, and I could not see myself going to England to supervise the production since Pallos, an experienced filmmaker with a very good reputation, was already on board. Actually, this is the only film in my career as a producer in which I took no part in the physical activities and was not even in England during any phase of the production. We left it all up to Steve, which in retrospect was a mistake. He assembled the unit, did the casting, supervised the script and generally took charge of the whole production.

Q: The director of *Naked Evil* was Stanley Goulder, who'd worked behind the scenes on some of your '50s films as assistant director and location manager.

GORDON: Stanley Goulder was Steve's choice to finalize the screenplay and to direct the film. Goulder had made a picture for Steve called *Silent Playground* [1963] that had been very well received by critics although it was not a great commercial success because of its subject matter. Goulder had worked on several films of mine in earlier years although I had no recollection of meeting him in person before *Naked Evil*. Shooting took place at various locations in greater London and at Rayant Studios in Bushey, Herts. *Naked Evil* was a considerable improvement over *Curse of the Voodoo* but not enough to create any excitement in the U.S.

Q: On May 4, 1966, Protelco took a double-page ad in *Variety* listing the titles of all the properties you had available for immediate production, among them *Who?*, *Creatures from Beneath the Sea*, *The Brainsnatchers* and *Invasion of the Apes*.

GORDON: *Who?* was based on a novel by the popular science fiction writer Algys Budrys, from whom I originally acquired the film rights. I had a script written by Val Guest but we were unable to raise the financing for its production. Barry Levinson was a New York City writer-producer who did most of his feature films in Europe; when he expressed the interest to buy the film rights, I sold them to him but he did not want, nor purchase, the Val Guest script, which was a very suspenseful science fiction-horror story. The resulting [1973] film concentrated on the philosophical aspects of the novel and therefore had very little appeal to movie audiences.

Yet another property of ours was *The Crooked Cross*, an original screenplay by Peter Myers which was a story of witchcraft and devil worship among students in an old German university town. Bryant Haliday was envisioned to star, and we considered Michael Reeves to direct it. Unfortunately, the project never came to fruition.

Q: Did you ever meet Reeves?

GORDON: He was referred to me when he visited New York City with a print of a film he had made in Italy, *The She-Beast* [1965] with Barbara Steele. He screened it for me and I was quite impressed by it. He was interested to know if I would consider helping to finance other projects that he had in mind or possibly employing him as a director for projects of my own. I remember him as very intelligent, very likable, and someone I felt would achieve success. Incidentally, Boris Karloff spoke to me about Michael several times when I saw him subsequent to the making of Reeves' *The Sorcerers* [1967]. He had a very high opinion of Michael's talent but felt that he was "a very disturbed young man" who needed to sort out his private demons.

When Gerry Fernback decided to give up his film activities and concentrate on his other business interests, that was the end of Protelco as far as we were concerned. In 1999 I was very sad to hear the news that Gerry had died quite unexpectedly; he and I had had a close relationship since the early '60s.

I produced my subsequent pictures under other auspices. Steven Pallos continued his own production and distribution interests for a number of years and then decided to retire when Raymond Rohauer agreed to buy his film library. He moved to Spain and, as far as I know, withdrew from the business altogether. He was a very fine gentleman whom I greatly respected. I would have welcomed a closer partnership in production under other circumstances.

As well as *Island of Terror* and *The Projected Man* did in American distribution, even getting a review in *Variety* that described us as joining the Hammer and Amicus league, Universal has never released either film on DVD; in fact, they've never released *The Projected Man* on home video at *all*. I have no say in the matter so there is nothing I can do about it although I've suggested it several times when talking with their studio executives. Both films have been released independently on DVD overseas. Protelco closed its doors on film production after only the three films *Island of Terror*, *The Projected Man* and *Naked Evil*.

Q: Before we wrap up on the Protelcos... Throughout so many of our interviews, James Carreras' name keeps coming up as someone who helped you, and now on *Island of Terror* you tell me that he got you Cushing and Terence Fisher. I'm getting the idea he was rather an important figure in your career.

GORDON: James Carreras and his father Enrique Carreras, *both*, were important to me in my career. In 1946, when my brother Alex and I came out of the service after the Second World War, both of us were determined to get jobs in the movie business. Alex ended up joining an independent distribution company called Renown Pictures. As I looked for a job, one of the companies I approached was an independent distribution company called Exclusive Films Ltd. that had been formed by Enrique Carreras. Enrique came from Spain, and still had a very strong accent. I went to see him and applied for a job, which he unfortunately couldn't give me; it was a small company and at that moment, he didn't really need anybody. But he gave me a lot of information and a lot of advice that was very, very helpful to me. I was 20.

Q: What kind of job were you hoping to get?

GORDON: I thought that a job in the publicity department would be a good way to learn more about the business. Enrique suggested that I go to some of the bigger companies like Associated British, one of the leading British companies; their distribution outlet was called Pathe Pictures. To help me, he gave me a letter of introduction to William Moffat, the managing director of Pathe Pictures, in which he very kindly said that he'd been impressed with his meeting with me; that unfortunately he had nothing to offer me; but he thought that Pathe Pictures might find me very useful.

Q: Sounds like a real "above and beyond" gesture on his part!

GORDON: It was! But in those days, the industry wasn't so big or so competitive. It was the kind of thing that could happen in those days but I don't think would happen today. Today, nobody seems to be interested in helping anybody else if they can avoid it [*laughs*]!

Q: Today the mindset seems to be, "It's not enough that I succeed. My friends must fail."

GORDON: Yes, it's a cutthroat business now. Anyway, I did get an interview with Pathe's managing director as a result of Enrique Carreras' letter, and I'm glad to say that I got a job in the publicity department which was very educational and very interesting. Pathe at the time was, among other things, the English distributor for Monogram and PRC, two independent Hollywood studios, and my first job was to prepare the necessary publicity materials for the English distribution of Monogram and PRC product.

Q: By hook or by crook, I'm sure you would have eventually gotten into the movie business anyway; but it was a Carreras that helped you get your foot in the door.

GORDON: Yes, I have to credit Enrique Carreras for getting me this job. At the end of 1947, I came to the United States and in 1949 I arranged to form Gordon Films Inc. as a distribution entity for representing producers in England and other European countries, and placing their pictures here in the U.S. One of the people I solicited for product was Enrique's son James, who by that time had taken over the distribution of Exclusive Films and also formed, together with Will Hammer, the company that became known as Hammer Films. *Jimmy* Carreras, as he was known to everybody, gave me an opportunity by sending me three pictures from the Exclusive Films library that he wanted me to sell in the United States. Interestingly enough, one of them was a little picture called *Room to Let* [1950], which was a variation of the Jack the Ripper story, and featured the well-known radio and stage actor Valentine Dyall as the character who is exposed as Jack the Ripper. I was able to place the three pictures for distribution in the United States with Eliot Hyman, who later became a partner with Carreras in the production of their horror and science fiction films starting with *The Curse of Frankenstein* [1957].

Q: Hammer started getting into the business of making horror movies about the same time you did.

GORDON: In England, I established a company, Producers Associates, to go into production. And naturally, as the independent business in England wasn't so big at that time, I came to see quite a lot of the Carreras family who were so active in it, and Jimmy and I became very good friends. Once again, like his father, he tried to be very helpful to me and gave me advice and information. He even tipped me off to certain actors that he thought would be useful for me to have, one of whom was Christopher Lee, whom I put in my *Corridors of Blood* in 1958.

Q: At a time when Hammer was grooming Lee for horror stardom, James Carreras thought *you'd* be helped by Lee's presence in one of your pictures and he handed him over to you.

GORDON: This was the way the Carreras family *was*. Jimmy did not regard me as a competitor, and over the years he directed me towards *several* actors whom he was using in his films, whom he thought I should meet and perhaps use in *my* films. He was just a *very* nice guy, that's the only way I could describe him. *Always* ready to be helpful. I have only the happiest memories of him. If I had to give a list of five people who contributed to my success, Jimmy Carreras would certainly be one of them.

Q: Would you put Boris Karloff on that list?

GORDON: Well, I wasn't thinking of actors at this moment, but now that you mention it, I *would* put Boris Karloff first on the list, because it was Karloff who actually was responsible for my getting into full-scale production on my own [see the *Haunted Strangler* chapter]. But, getting back to the Carrerases — as far as my relationship with them is concerned, I will always be grateful to Enrique and Jimmy for the help they gave me.

So many caption possibilities, but let's just say…Carole Gray in *Island of Terror*.

FUN FACTS

For its U.S. release, Universal shortened the 86-minute *Projected Man* to 77 minutes. Landing on the cutting room floor were an opening-reel matter transmitter experiment that results in the death of a lab rat; a scene of Pat and Mitchel finishing dinner at her apartment; and footage of the burned Steiner prowling dark streets, trying to keep from being seen by various people, including a smooching couple (Rosemary Donnelly, David Scheuer).

Naked Evil was not seen in the U.S. until 1973, when Saxton Films released it in a "multicolor" (tinted) version. Circa 1980, Sam Sherman of Independent-International "enhanced" this tinted version for inclusion in a TV package by shooting 11 minutes of new framing sequences with Lawrence Tierney, Catharine Erhardt and veteran cowboy star Bob Allen as doctors. Retitled *Exorcism at Midnight*, it began showing up on TV in 1981.

SECRETS OF SEX
1970

CREDITS

Executive Producer .... *Richard Gordon*
Produced and Directed by .... *Antony Balch*
Screenplay .... *Martin Locke, John Eliot, Maureen Owen, Elliott Stein & Antony Balch*
"The Story of Lindy Leigh" by *Alfred Mazure*
Photography .... *David McDonald (Color)*
Editor .... *John Rushton*
Music .... *De Wolfe*
Production Manager .... *John Kelly*
Assistant Director .... *Tay Stormett*
Makeup .... *Peter Armston*
Sound Recordist .... *John Jordan*
Sound Supervisor .... *Richard King*
Sound Editor .... *Roderick Hay*
Special Sound Recording .... *Cine-Lingual*
Camera Operators .... *Bill Glass & Vernon Layton*
Focus .... *Jeremy Dunkley*
Clapper Loader .... *Timothy Ross*
Special Consultant .... *Ron Hawkes*

92 minutes

CAST

Richard Schulman .... The Judge
Janet Spearman .... The Judge's Wife
Dorothy Grumbar .... The Photographer
Anthony Rowlands .... The Model
Norma Eden .... Norma — The Photographer's Assistant
George Herbert .... The Steward
Kenneth Benda .... Sacha Seremona
Yvonne Quenet .... Mary-Clare
Reid Anderson .... Dr. Rilke
Sylvia Delamere .... The Nurse
Cathy Howard .... The Cat Burglar
Mike Briton .... The Burgled Man
Maria Frost .... Lindy Leigh
Peter Carlisle .... Col. X
Steve Preston .... Philpott
Graham Burrows .... The Military Attaché
Mike Patten, Raymond George .... Flicker Flashback Boys
Karrie Lambert, Joyce Leigh Crossley .... Flicker Flashback Ladies
Nicola Austine .... The Flicker Flashback Girl
Elliott Stein .... The Strange Young Man/The Mummy
Sue Bond .... The Call Girl
Laurelle Streeter .... The Lady in the Greenhouse
Bob E. Raymond .... The Lady in the Greenhouse's New Valet
Valentine Dyall .... Voice of the Mummy
John Hale, Marilyn Head, Ken Norris

Uncredited

Antony Balch .... *Orgy Participant*
Delta Balch .... *Old Lady with Lizard*

SYNOPSIS

Secrets of Sex is an anthology of outrageous sexploitation tales, some tinged with horror elements. In a pre-credits sequence, a tenth-century Arabian judge returning to his ornate seaside summer house discovers that his young wife has locked a trunk — and a servant believes someone is hidden inside. What is in the trunk? A thief? Another man? Another woman? Nothing at all? The judge considers the problem all night, and then at dawn has a few of his strongest household staff members take the trunk into a field and bury it unopened.

After the credits, a mummy joins the cast; the one-time occupant of the trunk, he tells us that he has observed the struggle of the sexes for the last 1000 years, and narrates footage of young guys and girls romping in the altogether (and a series of other strange sights). He also introduces each of the remaining six stories.

In the next episode, a photographer snaps pictures of a chained-up model for her upcoming art book on medieval tortures. She and her assistant set up a fiendish device called "The Spanish Horse" — a sawhorse-like contraption capped with a long, upward-pointing, razor-sharp blade. They chain the model over it, his legs straddling the blade — and then go to lunch as the panicked model struggles to keep from descending onto it…

Wealthy Sacha Seremona would give anything — *everything* — to have a son but despairs that he's now too old. His young lover, scientist Mary-Clare, tells him that 68 is *not* too old and encourages him, and soon she is pregnant. It is only now that she learns that she may be predisposed by heredity to have a malformed baby…

A man catches a cat burglar in his house; the black-rubber clad crook is such a beauty that calling the constabulary is the last thing on his mind. But after a romp in the shower and then another in the sack, the cat burglar turns the tables on her hapless host…

In a story based on a comic strip character from the men's magazine *Mayfair*, secret agent Lindy Leigh is given her first assignment by Colonel X of the Home Office; all the previous agents sent out on this mission have vanished. Infiltrating a foreign embassy, Lindy puts her sex allure to patriotic purpose…

A nerdy young man's get-together with a call girl goes sour when she discovers that his fetish is having his pet lizard, "Pangy" the pangolin, on the bed with them as they make out. ("I just want him around, because I like him and I feel comfy when he's here.") Brushing aside his claims that this is fashionable, the horrified gal beats a hasty retreat — and on the street, sees an old woman carrying and baby-talking to *her* pangolin…

An eccentric woman brings her new valet Jeremy into her greenhouse, explaining that the human soul can enter trees and flowers — and boasting that she has trapped the souls of 17 lovers in her greenhouse plants. Jeremy turns out to be the one man who has ever escaped her; he strangles her while angrily raving about her "misappropriation of men's souls"…

RICHARD GORDON ON *SECRETS OF SEX*

RICHARD GORDON: I first met Antony Balch during the 1960s at the Cannes Film Festival. I had just produced two pictures in England, *Island of Terror* and *The Projected Man* [both 1966], so I was attending the Cannes Festival to promote them, and also in connection with my distribution business. Antony was a U.K. film distributor, an independent who specialized in importing films from France, Italy and other countries and preparing them for distribution in England. He was very good at what he was doing. He had also leased two cinemas as first-run outlets for the distribution business.

Q: He must have started at a very young age. He was born in 1938, so he was distributing films in his… twenties?

GORDON: He started very young with a great deal of enthusiasm and quickly made a success of his business. One of his accomplishments, for which distributors in England will always remember him: He was able to get Tod Browning's film *Freaks* [1932], which had been banned in England since 1932, through the

British censors. I had tried to do this myself in 1947, and failed completely. At that time, I was representing a company in New York called Excelsior Pictures, the foreign distributors for Dwain Esper who owned *Freaks*. They asked me to try to get it through the British censors so that we could arrange distribution for it in England. I remember very clearly that I called up the British Board of Film Censors, told them I had a film I

Out of the (G)ordinary: Workaholic producer Richard in a relaxed pose on the beach at a mid-1960s Cannes Film Festival. Around this time, at one of these international get-togethers, he met Antony Balch.

needed to discuss with them, and asked if I could come and see them, to talk about it. They were very polite and very cooperative on the telephone. On the day of the appointment, I showed up at their office and was received by three rather elderly ladies who seemed to be running the Board's everyday activities. They were very cordial until I told them that the film I wanted to talk about was Dwain Esper's *Freaks*. At that moment, the temperature in the British Board of Film Censors office dropped something like 20 degrees [*laughs*]. One of the ladies stood up, walked over to the door, held it open and said, "Mr. Gordon, we have nothing to discuss with you." And I was promptly — what *I* would call — thrown out of their office.

Antony was more successful, probably because he had more charm and was a better salesman than I was. And of course, also, times had changed since 1947, and a lot of things were getting through the censors that had never been allowed before.

Q: Reading up on Balch, I see that the first thing he ever did was a 30-second black-and-white TV cat food commercial in the 1950s — when he was probably not much more than a teenager. He must never have had any doubt what he wanted to do with his life.

GORDON: I think he was set on his course very early on, as indeed my brother Alex and I were. We never had any doubts from the time we first started getting interested in movies, in the early '30s, as to what we wanted to do. Alex and I tried to pursue that career, although in our case of course we were interrupted by the war.

Q: What did you like about Balch that you became friendly with him right away?

GORDON: Well, first of all, I discovered that his tastes were very similar to mine — the kind of films that he liked. And then he told me that his favorite actor of all time was Bela Lugosi, whom he had met backstage in Brighton during the rather ill-fated 1951 revival tour of *Dracula*. Antony's father took him to the theater, and Antony even went backstage and met Bela and received an autographed photo, which Bela signed with a pen that wrote in blood-red ink. Of course Antony was very surprised when I told him that I got Bela the deal to *do* that *Dracula* stage tour. Antony further told me that he had his own 16mm print of Bela's film *The Devil Bat* [1940], which he regularly screened for his friends at home. At that moment, I knew that we were going to become lifelong friends!

Q: In an interview, Balch said that Bela was quite hard of hearing. Balch told him how much he liked *The Raven* [1935], especially the scene with the room where the walls come together, and Bela wasn't picking up on what he was saying. Balch repeated, "**Where the walls come together.**" And Bela replied, very enthusiastically, "That's right, my boy! Keep the wolf from the door! Always keep the wolves from the door!"

GORDON: [*laughs*] Well, Lugosi *was* hard of hearing, and that was one of the problems with the stage tour of *Dracula*. Unfortunately, the cast of the touring company was very unprofessional, I would say almost semi-amateur, and they were constantly forgetting their lines, and Bela had of course memorized his role as Dracula and used to speak his lines in reply to what was said by other characters by timing how long it should take them to ask their question or make their statement. So when they blundered, then it threw his reply off-balance, and it caused a lot of audience laughter. That was one of the problems throughout the tour.

Q: What kind of a film programmer was Balch?

GORDON: He was programming mostly French and Italian films, and from other European countries, specializing in films that he could exploit either for their sex or horror angles, because that was about the only way one could compete with the big companies. And he specialized in changing the titles of the pictures to make them more commercial for English audiences, and also in preparing what at that time were considered rather lurid advertising campaigns for which he was well-known.

Q: Can you give me a for-instance?

GORDON: Antony acquired a picture from France starring Alain Delon, *Traitement de choc* [1973], which means "Shock Treatment." He changed the title to *The Doctor in the Nude*, and with a lot of fanfare he opened it in the West End of London, in one of the so-called art houses. The next thing that happened was that the theater received a letter from Delon's lawyers in Paris, threatening to sue them for misleading the public by giving the picture this title. Well, there *was* a quick shot in the movie where Alain Delon runs bare-assed into the ocean for a swim, and Antony turned around and said to them, "Well, there he is. He played a doctor and he's in the nude." [*Laughs*] And that was the end of that threat! When Antony was challenged, if he thought he was in the right, he would not give up.

Q: So in addition to retitling these movies, he had to get a lab to do some work and make new titles and —

GORDON: He did *every*thing, yes. He was a one-man operation, as in fact I suppose I was at that time, with my distribution in the United States. We had to do everything ourselves. He did have a salesman who helped to take the bookings outside London. And as I mentioned earlier, he himself had leased two cinemas in London from a theater chain called Jacey Cinemas. Antony used those theaters as his first-run outlets.

Q: I've read that he exhibited a lot of movies that hadn't gotten much distribution and maybe some that *shouldn't* have gotten much distribution [*laughs*]. Did it ever bother him to be playing movies to half- and quarter-full houses?

GORDON: No, Antony could be very obstinate about that. If he saw a film that he thought the public should see, and he thought it was a challenge to get them to come in and see it, he would acquire it and he would play it in his own theaters, even at the risk of no one showing up.

Q: And, in the case of at least one movie, no one *did*.

GORDON: Exactly, there was a film he put out where on opening day, not a single person showed up at the theater. And Antony was rather *proud* of that, because he felt that that was something of a record [*laughs*]. No one had ever succeeded at doing that before!

Q: He once showed an Asian movie that sounded very bizarre and *not* very appealing, and the last line of his program write-up was, "We are showing this film because no one else will."

GORDON: That was typical of him. He had that kind of a sense of humor. And in those days, things weren't as expensive as they are now, and he was able to indulge himself a little bit with things like that, which offset some of the great successes he had. I'll always remember that he got a-hold of a film which had a lot of sex in it [*Juliette de Sade*, 1969] and he decided to retitle it *Heterosexual*. I said, "Well, that really isn't much of a title. Who's going to know what that means without looking it up?" — in those days, most people would *not* have known. Antony said, "That's exactly the point. If they don't know what it means, they're going to think it's something dirty." [*Laughs*]

Q: At the point when you met him, he'd already made a couple of shorts.

GORDON: He'd made some shorts in association with William Burroughs, the author of the novel *Naked Lunch*. Burroughs was a friend of his and lived in the same London apartment building as Antony.

Also involved in those shorts was a well-known writer at that time, Brion Gysin, who was part of the Beat Generation and lived in France. They had made two experimental shorts, one called *Towers Open Fire* [1963] and the other called *The Cut Ups* [1966]. These films had led to Antony's decision that it was time he started to make his first feature film. We got into a conversation, and I decided that it would interest *me* very much to work with him. I had a tremendous *liking* for him, because he was so enthusiastic about everything, and I also respected him greatly, and so we decided to go together and try to set up a feature film.

Q: Before we get into that…what was William Burroughs like?

GORDON: I met Burroughs casually at Antony's home in London, because as I said Burroughs lived in the same building and they used to socialize. Burroughs was an American, he came from the Midwest somewhere, from a very wealthy family. I must say that he was completely different from what I expected: Both in appearance and in the way he spoke, he reminded me of a Chicago gangster in an old Warner Brothers movie like *Little Caesar* or *The Public Enemy*! But he had a great sense of humor, provided you were able to laugh at his type of jokes, and he was very pleasant.

Q: In addition to appearing in those shorts that Balch made, Burroughs also narrated Balch's re-release of the silent film *Häxan* [aka *Witchcraft Through the Ages*, 1922].

GORDON: That's correct, Antony acquired the U.K. distribution rights to *Witchcraft Through the Ages* and prepared a new version that was narrated by Burroughs. It had considerable success in England. I believe that there is presently in existence a video release of *Witchcraft Through the Ages* with Burroughs' narration and with the picture edited the way Antony prepared it.

Q: What were the names of the theaters he leased and programmed for?

GORDON: One was the Jacey Piccadilly, which was right off Piccadilly Circus in the center of London; it couldn't have been a better location for exploitation films. It was like having a theater in the middle of Times Square. The other was the Times Theatre in Baker Street, a location where *nobody* had ever made a success playing films. At one time it was a newsreel theater, at another time it played only shorts and cartoons; then Antony turned it into a feature film theater. It was a labor of love, because it was too offbeat a location ever to be really commercially successful.

Q: How did *Secrets of Sex* come about?

Describing the history of the battle of the sexes, a mummy appears in *Secrets of Sex*'s framing sequences. Peculiar? Not in one of the strangest sexploitation films ever. Besides, who better than a mummy to do…*wrap-arounds*?

GORDON: We spent some time during the Cannes Festival discussing what kind of a picture it would be fun to do together on a reasonable budget. Antony's feeling was that, as his first feature film, he would like to make a film which would consist of a series of vignettes that could be linked by narration, which would be easier for him than doing a film with a continuous (let's say) 90-minute scenario. So he came up with the idea for a film which at that time he called *Multiplication*, and the idea was that some of the vignettes would be sexy and some of them would be in the horror vein. To give it an extra frisson, there would be narration which would link all of these stories together, and that narration would be a sort of voice from beyond the grave. Eventually, when we were doing the final script, we came up with a talking mummy.

Q: According to the book *Keeping the British End Up: Four Decades of Saucy Cinema*, Balch's original plan was for the movie to be 65 minutes and cost £15,000.

GORDON: Yes, the idea was that it would be a picture running just over an hour, which would make it suitable to be double-billed if necessary with one of the French or Italian films that he was continually importing. And we would not spend more than £15,000 on the total budget. That seemed to be a very reasonable figure; Antony was willing to put up part of the money himself, and I was willing to put up the rest. It seemed that there was nothing to stop us from going ahead because we would not be responsible to any other persons, or have to be concerned with anybody else.

However, six months later, and after we had made extensive revisions in the script and budget, we ended up with a film that in fact ran 90 minutes and had a budget of £32,000, which at that time, compared with the £15,000 we had originally anticipated, was a rather daunting sum for us to put up between ourselves. But we managed, with deferments and all kinds of negotiations, and we did in fact make the picture without any interference from any other persons, and we did bring it in on the budget of £32,000.

From a 1970s newspaper interview with Balch:

I find I operate best when I'm doing it all myself. It's a matter of temperament. I decided long ago that the only way I'd be able to carry this [moviemaking] out was to be my own distributor, cinema exhibitor, businessman and everything else. I hate being turned down, as it were, and so I'd rather turn myself down than go around saying "I'd like to do this" and have all these people say no. In getting backing for moviemaking, people even today still categorize you; either you've made a movie or you haven't. I hadn't made a movie. I'd only made short movies. And in the eyes of the movie world, either you make features or you don't. So the thing was to find, without committing myself to some terrible system, a way of making a feature. Richard Gordon [arranged] to finance half of Secrets of Sex *and I came in with the other half. It was an interesting experiment in that I hadn't handled anything of that length in 35mm before, with actors and all the rest of it. It was useful to me, because it allowed me to make all sorts of mistakes in a relatively unimportant area.*

Q: According to [the above quote from] Balch, he apparently looked back on *Secrets of Sex* as good early training.

GORDON: Yes, he regarded it as a training film. He wanted to convince himself that he was able to do it. The idea was that if it worked out successfully, we would go on to do bigger and better things. What Antony had in the back of his mind, and which I supported, was that this was the type of anthology film that Amicus Films had popularized. As I mentioned previously, it was easier for Antony, as a first-time director, *not* to have to deal with one continuous story that had to be put on the screen for 65 minutes or more; he could concentrate on making each one of the vignettes as polished as possible, which was somewhat akin to when he was making his shorts, and then after that the only thing that had to be done was to use the linking narration to tie it all together.

Q: Sex films, softcore films…in 1960s England, where were these things shown?

GORDON: They usually got their first run in independent cinemas, like the ones that Antony was operating, which were not part of the major theater circuits. The major theater circuits were pretty much controlled and dominated by the Hollywood studios and the big British companies like the Rank Organisation and Associated British. For a film of the type that we're speaking about to get a circuit booking, it first had to prove itself to be very successful in independent halls, and then sometimes you could get either a complete circuit release or certain circuit theaters where they would play it as a second feature. You have to remember that in those days, everything except the big first-run houses was double features, and all theaters needed two pictures to put on a program at all times.

Q: And the production of *Secrets of Sex* — I'm guessing 1969?

GORDON: *Secrets of Sex* went into pre-production towards the end of 1968, and was filmed in 1969.

Q: The most recognizable name in the cast is someone who's not even *in* the movie except for his voice: Valentine Dyall.

GORDON: Yes, the well-known English radio, stage and screen actor Valentine Dyall was the voice from beyond the grave that I mentioned earlier, emanating from a mummy that periodically appeared on the screen. This was the link that was needed to combine all the vignettes into one basic idea. We were able to get him at a price that we could afford, but he added the proviso that he wouldn't have to dress himself up as the mummy [*laughs*] — that the mummy would be played on screen by another actor, which we will get into later. Dyall was known on radio as "The Man in Black" and had a successful radio series going back to the war years, and a very, very distinctive voice, so we were very happy to get him. He was unquestionably the most experienced and best-known actor *in* the cast and that we could afford, and we had a very good experience with him.

Q: It's implied in the movie that the lover who hides in the trunk in the first story becomes the mummy. But how does a guy who hides in a trunk become a mummy? Or is this not the kind of question I'm supposed to be asking?

GORDON: You can ask the question, but let me counter it with another question: How did Bela Lugosi as Dracula always manage to come out of his coffin wearing the latest in fashions, with a tuxedo or an opera cloak or whatever was necessary? And I think the answer is the same [*laughs*]!

Q: Was Valentine Dyall aware that this was a softcore sex film?

GORDON: Oh, yes, he was quite aware of everything that was going on. He thought it was all a big lark, and he was very happy to do it. I think one of the reasons was that he, like almost anybody who got to know Antony Balch, had great respect for him. For his integrity, his enthusiasm, his honesty. I don't think that Valentine Dyall, or some of the other people we worked with later, for instance Michael Gough in *Horror Hospital* [1973], would have agreed to do this kind of thing if it had been in the hands of someone less responsible than Antony Balch.

Q: According to the on-screen credits, *Secrets of Sex* was "shot at Studio Filmcraft, London." Where were you?

GORDON: During the actual shooting, I was back in the United States tending to my distribution business and preparing for other films that I wanted to do in the future. I was in London for the preparations before *Secrets of Sex* started, and I went back to London immediately after the principal photography was completed in order to look at the footage with Antony. And I was then around for the editing and putting the film into its final form. There were a few pickup shots that we needed, that we agreed on, and things like that, but I was not there during the actual filming of the individual episodes.

Q: Looking at the cast list, I've never heard of most — nearly all — of these people. Even the stars.

GORDON: I had nothing to do with the casting, and I have to admit that three-quarters of the people *I'd* never heard of either [*laughs*]. I did know Valentine Dyall, or at least I knew who he *was*, and I was very impressed that he had agreed to work with Antony. And I knew Richard Schulman, who in the opening segment played the Arabian judge, because Richard was an exhibitor in England who also had some theaters that played exploitation pictures and art house product. We all knew each other through the distribution business. I think Richard always was a sort of frustrated actor who never was able to pursue that career. Antony offered Richard that role because Richard looked the part and Antony felt he could play it very well; and as you know from the film, there was not any direct dialogue involved for him because it was all narrated. He agreed to do it, and he enjoyed the experience very much.

Q: That first segment also had George Herbert playing the steward who tells the judge about the locked trunk. He was later in *Horror Hospital*, in a flashback as Michael Gough's laboratory assistant, so I assume he was a friend of Balch's.

GORDON: Yes, he was. Kenneth Benda was in the episode about the wealthy man who becomes the father of the monster baby. Benda was well-known in England as a supporting player in films and also on the stage, and he was very happy also for the opportunity to work with Antony. I have to give full credit to Antony for *all* of these things. If *Secrets of Sex* was any kind of success, if it *remains* any kind of success, or will be remembered in the future, the credit goes 100 percent to Antony Balch.

Antony Balch on the episode "The Spanish Horse":

The boy in that sequence was never ever supposed to be dead at the end. The problem was with the makeup. [The photographer and her assistant] come back from their lunch, she takes her photograph, and then comes up to the boy, taking the chains off, saying, "That's just how I like it, old man." As his head falls down, his hair has turned sparkling white. You know how some people have a terrible shock in their lives, and their hair turns white or yellow? This is what happened: The makeup man was unable to produce the required effect in the given time, and so it's just not visible on the screen that his hair has turned white. So when his head falls forward, everybody assumes that he's dead. Which I thought made it terribly melodramatic. All they've done is to cut his leg a bit, and his hair turned white from the shock. In the English version, where the scene has been completely ruined by the censor, you think he's been cut in half, you have no idea what happened. That's much nastier than the original intention.

Q: Balch had his battles with the English censors over the years. What was his opinion of censors and censorship?

GORDON: Like so many other filmmakers, Antony greatly resented the censorship of films, and felt that the British Board of Film Censors never had any respect for the intentions of producers and directors in the making of their films, and were far too hidebound in what they would approve and not approve. However, John Trevelyan, the head of the British Board of Film Censors at the time when we made *Secrets of Sex* and for some time after that, was an exception to the rule. He was very enthusiastic about giving independent filmmakers a chance to show what they could do, and he would be very helpful and very cooperative if he felt that somebody was sincere in what they were doing and was just not trying to take advantage of him. He did, however, insist on making a number of cuts in *Secrets of Sex* because he felt that Antony had gone too far, and there were nine minutes of the picture cut out in the British release version. Of course, for the 2005 DVD release of *Secrets of Sex*, we put all that footage back into the picture.

Q: Did Balch overshoot at all? When you finished editing, was there much footage left over?

GORDON: Very little, and the main reason was that we couldn't afford that much raw stock. In most cases, the first take had to be the take that was used. Also, quite frankly, a lot of the young actors and actresses appearing in the film came from model agencies and sources other than the British equivalent of the SAG, and their delivery would not have improved on a second take [*laughs*]. What they did was about all they were capable of doing, and it would have been a waste of time and a waste of our money to try to make improvements.

Q: The opening credits make a big thing out of the fact that the movie includes "The Story of Lindy Leigh" and I'm afraid I don't know what the heck that *is*.

GORDON: "Lindy Leigh" was a comic strip in a magazine called *Mayfair*, which was a sort of English version of *Playboy* magazine. She had become a very popular comic strip character, and Antony was able to get permission to use that character in an episode of *Secrets of Sex* [and played by in-demand 1960s pin-up Maria Frost].

Q: Sue Bond, who was in the episode about the Strange Young Man, has a long résumé.

GORDON: Yes, Sue Bond was in a lot of British films. I thought she was very, very good in *Secrets of Sex*. She appeared in that episode opposite Elliott Stein, who was a great friend of Antony's and mine. Elliott was a writer who more recently has been a film critic and a programmer here in the United States. Elliott wrote that episode as well as acting the leading role in it. At the end of that episode, uncredited, the old lady with the lizard is Antony Balch's mother, whom I knew quite well. Her name was Delta Balch and she was a wonderful lady who had a long career in British films as what we used to call "a dress extra." She was a sort of English equivalent to Bess Flowers — if that means anything to you [*laughs*]! For quite a long time in her life, Delta was also a stand-in for Dame Edith Evans. Edith Evans did not make very many films, but whenever she did, she insisted that Delta should be employed as her stand-in. Delta often talked of Edith Evans and what a great personality she was.

Q: Balch's mother is in the movie, but is *he* in it?

GORDON: Antony *is* in the movie but, unless he was pointed out to you, you would never know it. He was one of the young men in the final fireworks sequence. You don't see him in closeup, you wouldn't be able to identify him unless you were told exactly what he does in that scene. The main reason he did it was because we didn't have enough people on the payroll to make the orgy look big enough, so everybody who was physically suitable was rounded up to participate in it. Later, on *Horror Hospital*, he took a couple of bit parts, but that was more for the fun of it than anything else. In *Horror Hospital* I was an extra, because we were in a situation where we had a nightclub scene and we wanted the nightclub to look rather crowded, and there weren't enough people on the payroll to *do* that. So I took part in it, and various other people that we roped in also. But I should say, in case that's giving you the wrong idea, that both *Secrets of Sex* and *Horror Hospital* were union pictures, because you could not in England at that time make a non-union picture and get it played in any cinema theaters. Everybody who was on the payroll was a member of one union or another.

Q: On the subject of the Greenhouse Lady episode, Balch once said that he wrote it the night before he shot it.

GORDON: He did say that, yes.

Q: For years you'd made movies with known stars where everything was "by the book," and now you were producing one where the script is being written the night before things are shot. Were you entirely confident throughout the whole process that Balch would carry it off and that your money was well-invested?

GORDON: I was *completely* confident that Antony would carry it off. And, to be honest with you also, the sum of money was not that great; I knew it could not end up being a total fiasco, and that there was very little possibility that we would not recoup our investment.

Q: Who played the mummy in *Secrets of Sex*? You said Valentine Dyall didn't, so who *did*?

Antony Balch rarely let himself be photographed, because he believed that every time your picture is taken, a bit of your soul is removed from your body. This is one of the (probably very few) photos of Balch in existence.

GORDON: The mummy was played by Elliott Stein, who also played the Strange Young Man. As I mentioned a moment ago, the way we got Valentine Dyall to agree to do the voice was by making it a condition of his employment that he wouldn't have to be made up as the mummy. Elliott enjoyed doing it, and I think it works perfectly well, because the way the mummy speaks, with the bandages partly obscuring his mouth, there were no sync problems or anything like that.

Q: Do you have a favorite among the episodes?

GORDON: Despite what Antony said about the ending of the Spanish Horse episode, I think that one worked the best and was the most commercial. I also think it was very well-placed, being the second of the vignettes, to hold the audience interest and get them to want to see what else was going to happen in the rest of the picture.

Q: My complaint with the picture is that so many of the stories just poop out rather than have a climactic twist. One reviewer said the buildups were always better than the denouements.

GORDON: The denouement is always the most expensive part of making such a picture; and we were very limited with our finances, and also with the abilities of the actors who were playing in the film. So we tried to make the best of it, and this was what we came up with. I do think that audiences were quite satisfied with what they saw.

Q: De Wolfe gets credit for the music.

GORDON: De Wolfe was actually the name of a music library, although the owner of the library *was* named De Wolfe. We couldn't afford an original music score to be composed for the picture, and so we made a deal with De Wolfe. Antony and I both, together, were very much involved in selecting the musical segments from De Wolfe's library, that punctuate the various stories in the movie.

Q: A *Dark Side* magazine article about Balch said that *Secrets of Sex*'s "attitude to women is a little saddening."

GORDON: The people who go to see this kind of movie are more interested in seeing the women as either victims or villains than as heroines, as they might be in bigger pictures.

Q: The movie had me scratching my head sometimes. Some of the nudity is very gratuitous, just like you'd expect, and then at other times, people take showers with their pants on, they make love with their knickers on. Why the back-and-forth with the nudity?

GORDON: If you examine the picture carefully, you'll see that we only put the nudity in scenes where there was no obvious physical contact between two persons. Wherever there was a scene of actual lovemaking in a bed or something like that, we didn't feel it was appropriate. And in those days we would not have been able to get it through the censor board anyway.

Q: When you released the movie, what kind of reception did it get?

GORDON: By that time, of course, the title had been changed to *Secrets of Sex*. When it opened in London at the Jacey Piccadilly, the theater leased by Antony, it received on the whole very good reviews. I give, again, full credit for that to Antony Balch, who was so respected in the industry as a serious young man trying to make a career for himself, that I think the critics, either knowingly or perhaps even unknowingly, leaned in his direction to try to support *Secrets of Sex* as his first venture. The movie was an enormous success at the Jacey Piccadilly, and in fact it played there for more than six months. During its run at the Jacey Piccadilly, it recouped its entire production cost, including of course the government subsidy, which was known as the Eady Fund, which was given to any legitimately British film that played in British cinemas. Between the two, the admissions at the theater and the eventual additional money derived from the Eady Fund, we recovered the entire cost of production. That helped a great deal in our decision to make another film together on a somewhat more ambitious level, which became *Horror Hospital*.

Q: Did you ever see *Secrets of Sex* with an audience?

GORDON: Yes, but not in England; here in the United States. When I first brought the picture to the United States in its complete and uncut form rather than the version approved by the British Board of Film Critics, I had some problems. First of all, U.S. Customs detained the 35mm print while they deliberated whether or not they should allow this film to be imported into the United States, because at that time there were still very strict laws about bringing in films that had any kind of (what they would have considered) pornographic content. Eventually they decided that there was really nothing in the film they could seriously object to, and they did let it go. The next thing was that we applied for a seal from the Motion Picture Association of America and we were unable to get it because they wouldn't approve of the film without cuts.

At that time, I was already quite friendly with Bob Shaye of New Line Cinema, whom I had also met in

Cannes, and with whom I had done some business; I'd licensed him a couple of films for U.S. distribution. It was the very early days of New Line Cinema when they were still distributing mostly experimental and very offbeat kinds of pictures. Bob Shaye, who also knew Antony Balch, took a liking to this film and *again* I think because of Antony's involvement decided that he would release it for us. He did, however, suggest that we change the title to *Bizarre*, which had been the working title at one time, because *Secrets of Sex* would create the impression that it was a pornographic movie. He released it as part of a New Line Cinema series of films called "Art or Pornography?," in which they tried to show that artistic films that were sometimes labeled by the press as having pornographic content, should not be judged the same way as pictures that were made purely as exploitation films, and had no other reason for their existence.

Q: And did it do well for New Line?

GORDON: It was a limited distribution, but it did well enough. Then some time later, after I had produced the film *Tower of Evil* [1972] which was released in America by Fanfare Films through the exchanges of American International Pictures, I took *Secrets of Sex*, re-edited it into a much shorter version stressing the horror element over the sex element, called it *Tales of the Bizarre*, and used it as a second feature with *Tower of Evil*, which did extremely well for us. After that, the film was not seen until its 2005 DVD release. Of course it's never played on television, neither in England nor in the United States.

Q: I know you've got other stories about releasing and promoting the picture, both here and overseas.

GORDON: Well, after the film opened in London, I decided to take out a double-page advertisement in *Variety* magazine in order to promote the distribution of the film in the United States. In the ad, I quoted from reviews from *The Guardian*, *The Financial Times*, *The London Times* and other newspapers whose reputations were beyond reproach. After I had booked this two-page space in *Variety* and sent my copy for the ad down to their office, I received a telephone call from the editor of *Variety* thanking me for taking out the advertising space — but asking me in somewhat guarded tones whether I would have any objection to bringing the reviews down to his office, because he'd be interested in seeing them himself. The real motivation of course was that he was afraid I was faking reviews from very respectable newspapers — newspapers that might lodge a complaint if they found themselves quoted, and the quote hadn't actually appeared in their pages. The *Variety* people just wanted to convince themselves that these were legitimate quotes. I went down there and brought all the reviews with me and they looked them over and, I have to give them credit, they apologized for doubting our copy and of course they ran the ad without any further ado [in the March 4, 1970, *Variety*].

The next thing that happened was that I got a surprising telephone call from Al Goldstein of *Screw*, a magazine we had not included in our screening list, or otherwise had any previous dealings with. He had apparently heard of the film, and he asked if he could have a screening of it for *Screw* magazine; he said he would then like to write an article on it, because by that time it had proved to be a phenomenal success at the Jacey Piccadilly. I arranged a screening, which in those days meant showing a 35mm print in a projection theater, and the next thing that happened was that Al Goldstein ran an article and a review in *Screw* magazine with the headline **THE SUN JUST SET ON THE BRITISH EMPIRE**, which I thought was rather a marvelous quote that we then proceeded to use in advertising the film at the Cannes Festival and elsewhere.

Q: The *Screw* review is excellent, praising the photography, the production, everything *about* it.

GORDON: They were very pleased with the picture when they saw it, and we were very pleased to get the writeup that we did.

Q: Your second and last movie with Antony Balch, which you've mentioned already, was *Horror Hospital*.

GORDON: After I had arranged distribution for *Secrets of Sex* in Germany and France and other countries, Antony and I felt it was time that we should think about making another film, and making it on a somewhat bigger scale, and in more conventional terms… although I think that nothing Antony Balch was ever likely to do would be considered *strictly* conventional! We talked about doing an out-and-out horror film of the type that Hammer Films and such companies were doing. So, rather like Mickey Rooney and Judy

Garland when they decided "Let's put on a show!," Antony and I decided, "Let's do a horror picture."

Q: *Secrets of Sex* makes me think of *Glen or Glenda* [1953], with a mummy [instead of Lugosi as "The Scientist"] narrating and linking a couple of sex-related tales. And *Horror Hospital* makes me think of the Lugosi Monograms: Dr. Storm brings people to his house to use them as experimental subjects as Lugosi does in *The Corpse Vanishes* [1942] and *Voodoo Man* [1944], he's got a dwarf sidekick as Lugosi does in several of his pictures, he's even got an accomplice [Kenneth Benda as a train station master] sending people to his house the way George Zucco did in *Voodoo Man*. All these "Lugosian" plot elements!

GORDON: Antony and I decided that we both wanted to include a sort of tribute to the old horror films. Antony would have been more responsible for taking things from the horror films of the '40s, I was more inclined to include things from the horror films of the '30s.

Horror Hospital turned out well, and Antony and I were going to continue to make additional films together. Antony had a particular desire to make a film of William Burroughs' *Naked Lunch*. Through his friendship with Burroughs, and having shown Burroughs *Secrets of Sex* and *Horror Hospital*, both of which Burroughs heartily endorsed, Burroughs was persuaded to give Antony an option on the film rights for *Naked Lunch*, and Antony started work on a screenplay. I read the first draft and it was brilliant, but it was so akin to the novel *Naked Lunch* and so explicit in the same way as the novel was, that I said to Antony, "There is no censor anywhere in the world who would permit this picture to be shown. And it's totally un-commercial and not feasible to go ahead." The script as proposed by Antony would have cost at least £150,000, which would have been more than three times the cost of *Horror Hospital*, and there was no way that we could set it up.

We then talked about doing a different kind of picture together; Antony said he would either set aside *Naked Lunch* or try to set it up on his own without me,

"Unisex Explodes in the Film They Tried to Stop!" said one ad when the absurdist *Secrets of Sex* made its bow in 1970.

because I really didn't feel comfortable with it. But unfortunately at that point, Antony became ill, and it turned out that he had cancer. He went through a terrible time. I don't want to go into it now, it's too painful to remember. He fought it in every possible way, but eventually it overcame him, and in 1980 he died at the age of 42 or 43.

Q: Did you have any ideas in mind for future films with Balch? Or just the desire to make more?

GORDON: We were thinking of making another horror picture, but on a more elaborate level than *Horror Hospital*. It seemed logical to make at least one more horror picture on a bigger budget before embarking on other kinds of films. I'm absolutely convinced, and I think almost everybody who met Antony and got to know him were also convinced, that had he lived, he would have become one of the outstanding young film-makers of the British film industry, somewhat akin to [director] Michael Reeves who died at an even *younger* age shortly after completing *Witchfinder General* [1968], which is considered a classic horror film. There's no one who misses him more than I do. His mother survived him, and I remained in contact with her for a number of years until eventually she passed away from old age.

Q: What prompted you to restore *Secrets of Sex* for DVD release?

GORDON: What brought it on was the opportunity to show the early work of Antony Balch in a medium which didn't exist before, namely the DVD, where on the audio commentary track I could also discuss things about Antony and about the film. *Secrets of Sex* deserves to be seen again. I was fortunate to be able to obtain also copies of Antony's two shorts *Towers Open Fire* and *The Cut Ups* to include on the DVD. For the first time, *Secrets of Sex* was seen in England in the form in which Antony originally intended, without the censor cuts that were imposed upon it in 1970.

TOWER OF EVIL
1972

CREDITS

Produced by	*Richard Gordon*
Associate Producer	*John Pellatt*
Executive Producer	*Joe Solomon*
Screenplay & Directed by	*Jim O'Connolly*
Original Story	*George Baxt*
Photography	*Desmond Dickinson (Color)*
Editor	*Henry Richardson*
Music Composed & Conducted by	*Kenneth V. Jones*
Production Supervisor	*Ted Lloyd*
Production Designer	*Disley Jones*
Assistant Director	*Peter Price*
Makeup	*Jimmy Evans*
Hairdresser	*Gordon Bond*
Sound Recordists	*Ken Ritchie & Nolan Roberts*
Camera Operator	*Norman Jones*
Continuity	*Kay Rawlings*
Wardrobe	*Jackie Cummins*
Production Secretary	*Midge Warnes*
Casting	*Rose Tobias Shaw*
Still Photographer	*Harry Gillard*

90 minutes

CAST

Bryant Haliday	*Evan Brent*
Jill Haworth	*Rose Mason*
Mark Edwards	*Adam Masters*
Jack Watson	*Hamp Gurney*
Anna Palk	*Nora Winthrop*
Derek Fowlds	*Dan Winthrop*
Dennis Price	*Laurence Bakewell*
Anthony Valentine	*Dr. Simpson*
Gary Hamilton	*Brom*
George Coulouris	*John Gurney*
William Lucas	*Detective Superintendent Hawk*
John Hamill	*Gary*
Candace Glendenning	*Penny Read*
Robin Askwith	*Des*
Serretta Wilson	*Mae Harvey*
Fredric Abbot	*Saul Gurney*
Mark McBride	*Michael Gurney*
Marianne Stone	*Nurse*

SYNOPSIS

Sailing from the Cornish village of Portray, fishermen John Gurney and his son Hamp make a nocturnal crossing on their boat the *Sea Ghost* to rocky, fog-shrouded Snape Island. Ashore, they discover a mutilated corpse among the rocks, then another in an abandoned lighthouse. In an adjacent shed, a third body is pinned to a wall with a gold spear. A young girl, hysterical, nude and blood-spattered, appears suddenly, fatally stabbing John before she is knocked out by Hamp.

The girl, 18-year-old American tourist Penny, is brought to a London hospital in a catatonic stupor. When Dr. Simpson injects her with a drug that jolts her back into semi-consciousness, she replays in her mind (as we see in flashback) her arrival on the island with her three American friends Gary, Des and Mae. It appears to the police that the horny group went to Snape to party, and then Penny lost her mind and murdered the others.

When the gold spear turns out to be an ancient Phoenician relic, an archaeological expedition is formed to search Snape Island and determine whether a high-ranking Phoenician's tomb — and treasure — is hidden there. Rose Mason, Adam Masters and husband-and-wife Dan and Nora Winthrop comprise the group; the quarrelsome foursome have a complicated history of love triangles. Evan Brent, an American private detective hired by Penny's parents, accompanies them. They are ferried to the island by Hamp and his nephew Brom. The sight of bloodstains and police chalk outlines await them. According to Hamp, Snape's last inhabitants were his brother Saul and Saul's wife Martha; Hamp says that the couple were lost at sea six months earlier. A 20-year-old photo of Saul, Martha and their baby Michael, who Hamp says died in infancy, stands framed on a table in the lighthouse.

Back in London, again under the influence of Dr. Simpson's drug, the screaming Penny mentally envisions the gory deaths of her friends at the hands of a cackling, hairy madman.

As night falls on Snape Island, action (of various kinds) is hot'n'heavy: The promiscuous Nora goes to bed with Brom, the *Sea Ghost* inexplicably explodes and burns, and the corpse of a woman is found in a rocking chair. Hamp admits that it is the body of Martha; his new version of past events is that his brother Saul was mad, and that he was cared for by Martha until her recent death. It is presumed that Saul is the killer and that he hides in subterranean caves.

Saul, now a caveman-like brute, follows Nora to the top of the lighthouse, and the panicked woman falls over a parapet to her death. In the caves, the treasure, a statue of the Phoenician god Baal and an ancient altar are located in a grotto. Brom is killed by an unseen fiend. Dan gets into a losing fight with Saul and has

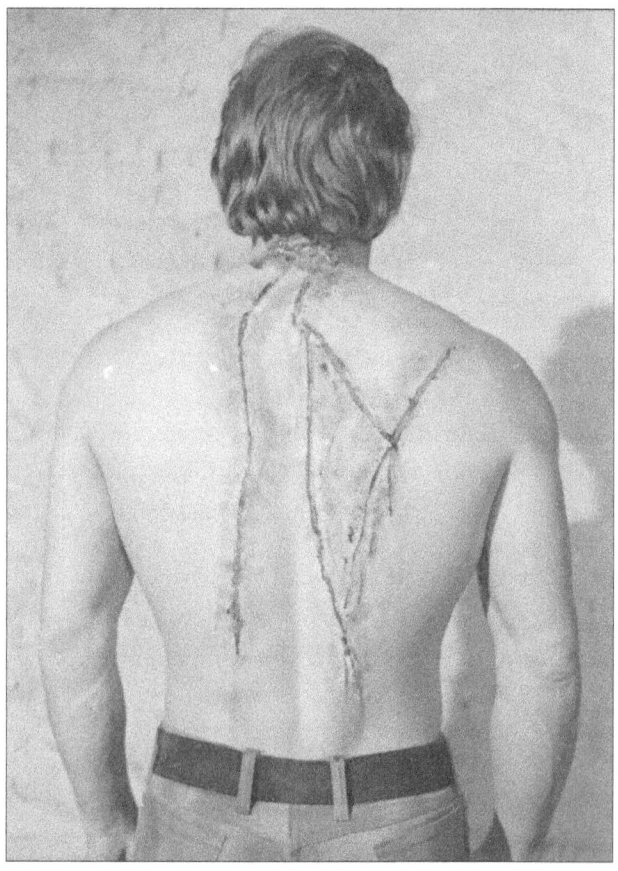

Makeup Dept. "slashes" on the back of actor John Hamill added a grisly touch to the scene where his naked body is found on the beach.

his neck broken. Brent arrives on the scene, shooting and killing Saul.

Hamp and Nora return to the lighthouse, where Hamp is bloodily slain by a *second* hairy horror: Saul and Martha's supposedly dead, hideously deformed son Michael. Nora throws a kerosene lamp at the cackling madman, setting him on fire. Even though ablaze, he continues to stalk her, while the kerosene fire sets off an inferno in the paraffin-filled caves below. Michael at last collapses and is consumed. Nora escapes to the outside, where she is joined by Brent and Adam, and they watch as the burning lighthouse explodes thunderously.

RICHARD GORDON ON *TOWER OF EVIL*

RICHARD GORDON: At the beginning of 1971, I was looking around for a suitable project for a film to be made in England, which Joe Solomon of Fanfare Films in Hollywood wanted to co-finance and set up with me. Max Rosenberg of Amicus Productions introduced me to a writer by the name of George Baxt, an American who was living in England but was visiting New York. For some time George had been a very successful writer of crime novels and screenplays. I first met him at the Monkey Bar of the Hotel Elysée on East 54th Street where we sat and talked for a while — or, I should say, where we sat and *George Baxt* talked for a while [*laughs*], because it was very hard to get a word in edge-wise when one was dealing with George. He was quite enthusiastic about the idea of our doing a film together. He had an idea for a script which he called *Tower of Evil* and he wanted to interest me in it. Out of that discussion came a story outline that George wrote very quickly and submitted to me. I looked at it and then sent it to Hollywood for Joe Solomon to look at. Joe and I thought this would be a good project for us.

I signed a contract with George that he would write a screenplay for a fee of $5000. Six months later, George presented me with a finished screenplay which I read and then immediately sent on to Joe Solomon for his comments. Unfortunately, we did not like the script at all. Not only didn't it live up to the story outline, it had far too much humor of the kind that George was known for, which we didn't want to use.

Q: Bitchy humor?

GORDON: Yes, and the kind of sarcasm that he specialized in. Joe and I decided that we could not use the script, and Joe authorized me to go ahead and have a new script written in England.

By that time, I was already looking for a director. The first director I interviewed for the job was Sidney Hayers, who had made a number of films for Hammer and American International Pictures. Hayers was a great personal friend of George Baxt's; George had introduced me to him. Well, this proved to be useless, because Hayers took one look at the script and, I suppose because of his relationship with George, said, "Oh, this is wonderful, I can shoot it for you. I'm ready to go whenever you want." Well [*laughs*], this was exactly what I did *not* want to hear. I wasn't looking for somebody who *liked* the script, I was looking for somebody who would criticize it, so we could put it in good order. I interviewed several other people, and I couldn't come up with anybody who had the same line of thinking as I did. Then Herman Cohen, who

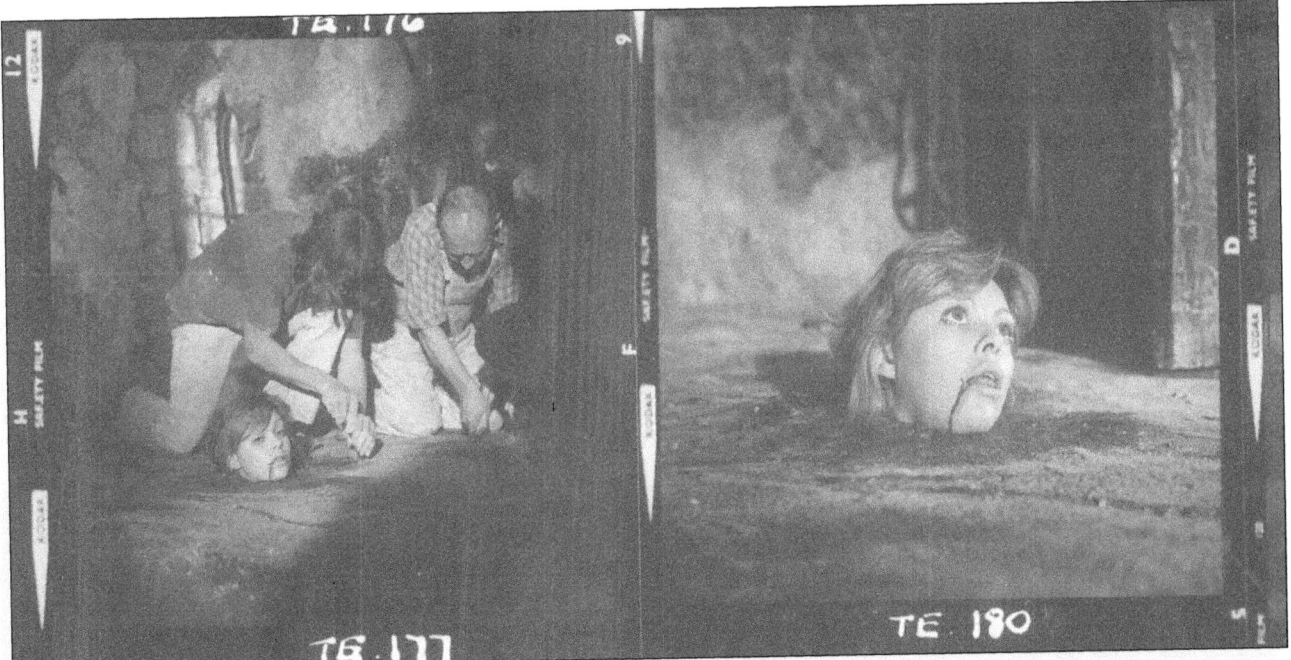

Left: Crew members "bury" Serretta Wilson in a staircase landing. Right: The result: a couldn't-be-more-realistic (because it's *her!*) disembodied head.

was then working in England, put me together with Jim O'Connolly, who had directed for Herman a Joan Crawford film, *Berserk* [1967]. I met with Jim and I was immediately very impressed when the first thing he said to me was, "This script is a load of rubbish!" [*Laughs*] I thought, "For a director to say that when he's looking for a job, he must be a straight shooter." I asked, "Jim, do you think that if you and I work together, we can make this into something that would appeal to us?" and Jim said, "Give me a little time. I will work on this script and I will come back to you." Jim soon came back with a script that had *very* little resemblance to what George Baxt had written. I liked it immediately, and I rushed it off to Joe Solomon in Hollywood who liked it as well as I did. So I made a deal with Jim O'Connolly.

Q: When Baxt eventually found out that his script had been rewritten, what was his reaction?

GORDON: The problem was that I had not yet told Baxt that we weren't going to use his script and that I was having it rewritten. I was of course going to notify him in due course. But he heard about it from other sources and he felt that I had double-crossed him, and he went into a great rage; his ego just couldn't take it.

Q: Did he express his rage to you over the phone or —

GORDON: Face to face. From that day onwards, he never spoke to me again, and our relationship was completely severed.

Q: And you were both New Yorkers, so I'm sure you had to put up with seeing each other on the street occasionally.

GORDON: Once in a while I used to run into him and he would ignore me completely, so I did the same. We never had any connection together after that.

While I was waiting to get a script that we could go forward with, I had already made an association with John Pellatt, who became my associate producer on the film. John had done some work for American International in England for "Deke" Heyward, who highly recommended him to me. With John's assistance, I set up the production at Shepperton Studios, where he was used to shooting some of the AIP product. John felt that, with the facilities they had available, we could shoot it at the studio, and would not have to go on any expensive location trips.

Q: Even though a good bit of *Tower of Evil* is set outdoors, 99 percent was shot on soundstages.

GORDON: Yes, it was almost entirely shot in the studio. John at the time was finishing off an American International picture with Shelley Winters, *Who Slew Auntie Roo?* [1972], and so I scheduled the production to start almost immediately after he finished that.

Q: If he could handle a Shelley Winters movie, he could handle *any*thing!

GORDON: Yes, that's absolutely true. In fact, there *was* a near-crisis towards the end of the shooting of *Who Slew Auntie Roo?*, when Shelley Winters suddenly announced that she had to have a couple of days off to fly to New York where her daughter was getting married. (We found out later that it was what they used to call a "shotgun wedding.") She promised to come back immediately after the weekend, but in the end she stayed for almost another whole week, and by the time she got back to England, "Deke" Heyward and John Pellatt and everybody else were climbing the walls!

Q: Talk about the various *Tower of Evil* sets you had to build at Shepperton.

GORDON: Nothing was pre-existing, we had to build every set that was necessary. I had a very, very good production designer, Disley Jones, build all the sets. We only went on location for one day during the entire shooting of the film, and that was to a small town in the south of England where we had to shoot some exterior footage for the sequence where the characters go to Snape Island.

Q: Did you tag along?

GORDON: No, I was busy with the shooting of other scenes at Shepperton Studios. I spent the whole of my time at Shepperton during the making of this film.

Q: The sets built at Shepperton would include Snape Island's rocky beach. And even the footage of people on the deck of the boat at sea were shot there.

GORDON: Yes, they were shot against back projection of the ocean. There was one particularly large stage at Shepperton that could be used for sequences where there was no direct dialogue, and that was where we did the scenes of the boat — the opening sequence when Jack Watson and George Coulouris arrive at the island, and later the sequence where Watson and Coulouris make the trip again with the rest of the characters. Those scenes were all dubbed later.

Q: You'd already worked with Coulouris in your *Kill Me Tomorrow* [1957] with Pat O'Brien.

GORDON: Yes, where Coulouris was the chief villain. On *Kill Me Tomorrow* we only met briefly, not enough even that he remembered when it came to *Tower of Evil*. When [casting director] Rose Shaw told me that Coulouris would be available, I jumped at the idea because, after all, he was a well-known actor in America; he was in *Citizen Kane* [1941]! He was living in England, making pictures there, and I was very pleased to have him.

Q: He was also in so many of those great old Warners pictures that are right up your alley, alongside Claude Rains and Charles Boyer and Lorre and Greenstreet—

GORDON: — and Bette Davis and Paul Lukas in *Watch on the Rhine* [1943] and so on, yes! On *Tower of Evil* we only had him for a couple of days' shooting, and on the days when he was at the studio, I tried to spend as much time as possible with him, to get him to tell me some interesting stories about his career in Hollywood. But the only thing he wanted to talk about was Orson Welles and his involvement with Welles in the Mercury Theatre, and I just couldn't get him to talk about anything else! He had an extraordinary memory: He would sit there with me on the set, waiting to be called, and start telling a story about Welles, and Jim would come over and say, "We're ready now, George, for your scene." Coulouris would stop speaking, go and do the scene, and then he would come back and he would pick up *exactly where he left off* and tell me the rest of his story! He was a wonderful man, I respected him enormously.

Q: *Tower of Evil* is "A Grenadier Film." Did you come up with that name?

GORDON: I needed a British company to set up *Tower of Evil* so that there would be no problems about British quota, British nationality and so on. At the time, there was a restaurant not far from where I was living in Manhattan, called the Grenadier, on First Avenue and 48th Street. It prided itself on its "very British" décor, and appealed to British people. I thought, "This is a good name for a company," and I formed Grenadier Film Ltd. in England. I used Grenadier again subsequently when Radley Metzger and I made *The Cat and the Canary* [1978].

Wilson poses with her own prop head, made for a shock shot where it rolls down stairs. Wilson once said that when she saw that scene in the rushes, it was so horrible she had to close her eyes.

Q: As always, I'd like you to talk about the casting process.

GORDON: During the period that I was on friendly terms with George Baxt, when we were preparing the production, he introduced me to a friend of his, Rose Tobias Shaw, one of the most successful casting directors in England at the time. She had lived for many years in the United States, where she had quite a successful career working for David Susskind —

Q: Right here in New York.

GORDON: Here in New York, yes, but I didn't know her at that time. But then she moved to England and established herself there. She and George were very friendly, and he introduced me to her, and she agreed to act as the casting director for me on this film, even though she was usually engaged on much bigger and more expensive films for major Hollywood companies that were making films abroad. So Rose helped me with the casting other than [top-billed] Bryant Haliday, whom I had starred in several films before. I was determined to use him as one of the leading players in *Tower of Evil*.

Q: You had no trouble getting Haliday into your earlier pictures, but you've told me that *this* time things didn't go smoothly.

GORDON: I'd used Bryant three times before in England, on *Devil Doll* [1964], *Curse of the Voodoo* [1965] and *The Projected Man* [1966], which were no problem. But when it came to the casting of *Tower of Evil*, all of a sudden the British union raised an objection to my casting an American actor: They said the role could just as easily be played by any English actor, and the economic situation being what it was, they did not want to issue permits to American actors that would put English actors "out of work," so to speak.

Q: If you wanted a non-English actor, you had to have a darn good reason.

GORDON: You had to have a darn good reason before that actor would be issued a labor permit, yes. When I started to run into trouble over this, Jim O'Connolly said, "While you're straightening out the situation, why don't we put someone 'on hold' who could step in if, at the last minute, you can't get the permission to use Bryant Haliday?" He suggested the actor Lee Patterson, whom I knew because he had played a supporting role in one of the Zachary Scott films I had made some years earlier, *The Counterfeit Plan* [1957]. Under ordinary circumstances, Lee would have been perfectly acceptable —

Q: Oh sure, he was a good name. He'd been on the TV series *Surfside 6* and even the soap opera *One Life to Live*.

GORDON: That's right, and he'd also played opposite Joan Crawford in *The Story of Esther Costello* [1957]. He had a good career going. But I wasn't about to be pushed into doing something I didn't want to do, so I went to see both the Labour Exchange and the Union, and I said, "I am making this film, I am financing this film from the United States, and I want an American actor in the lead who will give it some added value

Taking time out from playing a corpse impaled to a wall, Robin Askwith chats with George Coulouris.

when it is released in the United States." I told them how I had established Bryant Haliday in *Devil Doll*, *Curse of the Voodoo* and *Projected Man*, and I saw no reason why they couldn't accept him for *Tower of Evil*. Well, they continued to give me a hard time, so finally I said, "Look, if we don't have Bryant Haliday, we lose our American financing. If we lose our American financing, 50 people will be out of a job instead of just Bryant Haliday. If that's what you want, then go ahead, and we have nothing further to talk about."

Q: And this was a bluff, yes? You were willing, and in fact ready, to have Lee Patterson play the part if the Labour Exchange continued to play hardball.

GORDON: That's correct. But they did give way, and I got the permit for Bryant.

Q: What was Lee Patterson's reaction to being on standby for Bryant Haliday, an actor he probably never even heard of?

GORDON: Lee of course was very disappointed not to get the part. He did it as a favor to Jim O'Connolly and me because he was a very close friend of O'Connolly's. He would not have done it under other circumstances.

Q: And as for the rest of the casting?

GORDON: The procedure we followed was that Rose Tobias Shaw would give me a list of names of people she recommended; she would then set up interviews with these people for Jim and me; and Jim and I would decide (and we very rarely disagreed) on whom we wanted to use. We were looking for people who were either American or Canadian but lived in England and could "speak the language" the way we wanted, so that the film would be more acceptable in the American market. I must say that I think, with Rose's help, we put together a very strong cast of British actors and actresses who had a great deal of experience. Thanks to Rose, a few years later for *The Cat and the Canary* we were able to get wonderful names like Wendy Hiller, Edward Fox, Daniel Massey, Michael Callan, Carol Lynley, Wilfrid Hyde-White, Honor Blackman — Rose helped us to put together one of the best casts for a British low-budget movie that's ever been assembled.

Q: The four archaeologists who come to the island — Rose, Adam, Nora and Dan — all have a lot of "back story." Who came up with that, Baxt or Jim O'Connolly?

GORDON: That was Jim O'Connolly. I should make it clear that in the script by Jim and in the final production, there was almost nothing left of George Baxt's screenplay except the original concept of people coming to the island and so on.

Q: The four characters have *such* a complicated history of hook-ups and break-ups and infidelity — it'd take a TV soap opera a month to establish what *Tower of Evil* does in five minutes!

GORDON: I have to give the credit to Jim for that. He wrote such a tight script that he got all this background information into the film without slowing it up, and kept the horror and killing scenes going all at the same time. Jim did a wonderful job of directing *Tower of Evil*, and if I could have used him again at a later date, I would have been delighted. He had an apartment not far from the hotel where I was staying during the making of *Tower of Evil*. Every morning a driver came and picked me up, then we drove to Jim's apartment and picked *him* up, and as we were driven to the studio — an hour's drive in the morning, with heavy traffic — we'd discuss the shooting for the day. I found that in almost every respect, he was on top of it, and I had nothing to worry about while I had him as the director.

Q: Jill Haworth was another good name for your movie. She'd been in big pictures like *Exodus* [1960] and *In Harm's Way* [1965].

GORDON: She was absolutely cooperative in any and every respect. A few years earlier, I saw her on the stage in New York in the original production of *Cabaret* and I was very grateful to Rose Shaw that she was able to get Jill Haworth to agree to do this film. I was shocked and saddened when I heard that she had passed away a few months ago [in January 2011].

I was still of course on very friendly terms with Jimmy Carreras of Hammer Films, and he used to tell me about people he was working with in his pictures, actors whom he thought might be suitable for me. At the time when Rose was casting *Tower of Evil*, Jimmy had just made a film called *Blood from the Mummy's Tomb* [1971] and he called me up and told me that he had a young actor in it, Mark Edwards, that he thought was going to have a considerable career in movies; and he said that if I was still casting my picture, it would be a good idea if I would take a look at it because I might want to employ him in *Tower of Evil*. I went to see a rough cut of *Blood from the Mummy's Tomb* at Hammer's offices and I was very impressed with Mark and I thought he was ideal for the role in *Tower of Evil*. I signed him up without any further question. I always got a lot of help and cooperation from the Carreras family and Hammer.

Jack Watson, who played Hamp, was a well-established stage, screen and television character actor in England. He was one of the persons that Rose Shaw recommended to me, and both Jim O'Connolly and I immediately accepted, after we met him and had a chance to discuss the role with him. Jack had a face that any and every filmgoer in England would recognize at once, from the number of films he made.

Incidentally, one of the people that Rose Shaw brought in for an interview for the part of Adam was a young actor called Shane Briant, who was making pictures for Hammer at the time. He was up for the role of Adam that was eventually played by Mark Edwards. Now flash-forward to many months later, after *Tower of Evil* was completed, and I decided to go to see it in a theater in England where it was playing on a double-bill with Hammer's *Demons of the Mind* [1972], just to see the audience reaction. Well, throughout the showing of *Tower of Evil* I was annoyed by two guys sitting right behind me, laughing at everything and making various comments; I'd have *liked* to turn around and say, "I'm the producer of this picture, shut the hell up!" but of course I wasn't about to do that. And after *Tower of Evil* was over and I got up to leave, I saw that it was Shane Briant, who'd apparently come to see his own film *Demons of the Mind*.

Q: [*laughs*] I'm glad the little squirt didn't get the part, then!

GORDON: You and me both!

Q: Gary Hamilton, who played Brom in *Tower of Evil*, was a young musician who had moved to England from America with his parents as a kid; he gets special "And Introducing" billing.

GORDON: At the time, Gary was appearing on the London stage in *Hair*, and was very successful with it. Jim O'Connolly had seen him in *Hair* and predicted the possibility of a very substantial career in the movies for Gary if he could get a break. Jim went all-out to persuade me, first of all to see Gary in *Hair*, and then to use him in the key role of Brom in *Tower of Evil*. So I saw *Hair* and I was very impressed with Gary, and when I met him offstage, I thought he had a lot of possibilities. His parents were living in England at the time as well; and I thought, as an American "type," he was just perfect for Brom. Incidentally, one of the other people we interviewed for the part was Nicky Henson, the son of the noted British stage and

Gordon appears to be keeping score as Jill Haworth, Anna Palk and Gary Hamilton play ring toss with the spear in Robin Askwith's gut.

screen actor Leslie Henson. As an actor, Nicky Henson's credits included such titles as *Witchfinder General* [aka *Conqueror Worm*, 1968] with Vincent Price and *Psychomania* [1973] with George Sanders.

Q: I know you have a great story about Anna Palk, who plays the promiscuous Nora.

GORDON: Anna was a very lovely young lady with whom I was very impressed; I thought she would have a great career. Unfortunately, some time after *Tower of Evil*, she contracted cancer and died at a relatively young age. On *Tower of Evil* we had no problems with her *except*…there was one sequence, rather risqué at the time, where her character, Nora, goes to bed with Brom [Hamilton]. When it came time to shoot that sequence, and she was expected to do it in the nude, she started to raise objections.

Q: When she accepted the job and signed the contract, did she know it involved nudity?

GORDON: The script didn't specify clearly that her character would be completely nude, so I don't think she realized it. When we got to the sequence and Jim told her that she would have to play it in the nude, she didn't want to do it. I finally persuaded her, promising her that we'd shoot that sequence on a closed set with only the minimum number of people present, people who *had* to be there. Gary Hamilton, as you can imagine, having appeared in *Hair*, had no inhibitions about undressing on stage or screen [*laughs*]!

Well, when she came out to do this sequence on the closed set, she appeared with little pasties which she had stuck on the nipples of her breasts, which of course was absolutely out of line with the story and with the character. Then it came time to start to shoot the footage of her and Gary making love. As she was lying on the bed, she suddenly pulled out a bottle of some kind of perfume and sprayed it on Gary, which led *almost* to disaster! Gary was so taken aback, so offended, that he was going to get up and walk out — except he was nude [*laughs*], so he couldn't make a quick and easy exit! We finally persuaded her that this was after all for a scene in a certain type of movie, and there really should be no objection.

Q: There *is* a lot of nudity in *Tower of Evil*. Besides this incident, did this present any other challenges?

GORDON: As far as shooting the scenes, everything went smoothly, with that one exception. I was aware, of course, that some of these scenes would eventually be cut by censors. When the film was first released in England, the nude scenes were somewhat cut short, and in the United States also. Joe Solomon, who was going to distribute the film through American International Pictures, made some cuts in the picture in order

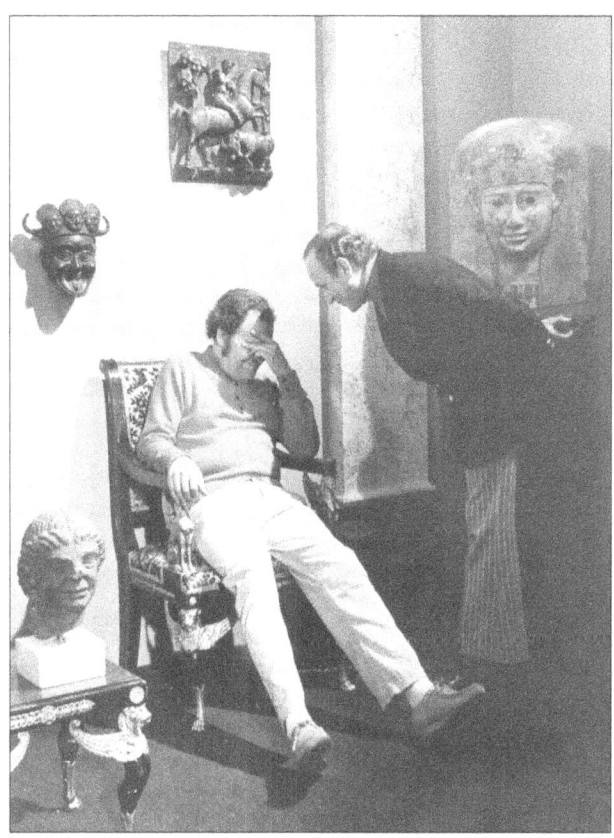

Producer Gordon gets director Jim O'Connolly laughing on *Tower of Evil*'s British Museum set.

to get a Code seal. By present-day standards there's absolutely nothing objectionable there whatsoever. The film, in recent years, even on television, has been shown in its original uncut version, which is the only version that I would approve these days.

Q: *Tower of Evil* is ahead of its time; plot-wise it's like the "teenagers have sex and die" horror movies of the '80s, but it predates them by a decade.

GORDON: Hammer was pushing the envelope, as they say, continually getting more nudity and violence into their films, and I felt that we had to keep up with them; otherwise we would get left behind when it came to the distribution of the picture. Jim O'Connolly assured me that he could shoot the scenes in such a way that they would not be considered objectionable, but that they would provide us the kind of thrills and excitement that we wanted. I relied on him completely to do that because I felt that, if he went overboard, I could always cut and re-edit the picture after it was finished. But he was so enthusiastic about the various aspects of the script — which of course he had written himself [*laughs*] — that I didn't want to discourage him. I told him to go forward and do everything he wanted to do, and then we'd deal with the rest in post-production. But it didn't become necessary, because he shot everything in such an intelligent way that we never had a serious problem.

Q: When making *Tower of Evil*, did you not keep eventual TV sales in mind? When it played on local channels "way back when," so much had to be cut that the story couldn't be followed.

GORDON: At that time, the only thing we were interested in was that it would play theatrically both in England and the United States — and, for that matter, all over the world. It was shot in such a way that if we had to make cuts here and there for specific countries, we could do it. I was very pleased with it when it finally was released.

Q: I remember trying to make sense out of it, watching it on New York's Channel 9 as a teenager. Every time characters were about to get romantic — or get killed! — there'd be a splice and the action would jump way ahead. And there were *lots* of splices!

GORDON: Well, that enabled you to use your imagination [*laughs*]! In those days, television wasn't important enough to make any concessions to it. The important thing was to get a picture that would play theatrically, and would be accepted everywhere. TV was a secondary consideration; if it wasn't going to be acceptable for TV, that was just too bad. We were competing not only with Hammer but also with American International Pictures — Jim Nicholson and Sam Arkoff, who pioneered making this kind of film for the American market. As long as we're talking about TV, I'll also mention that when the film was finished and we started screening it within the industry, Joe Solomon was approached by MGM, who bought the television rights for the United States and Canada, and accepted it in the form in which we submitted it. They've owned the television rights ever since; in fact, it has most recently been shown on Turner Classic Movies. Admittedly, at about two o'clock in the morning [*laughs*]!

Q: Just to finish up on the cast, I wanted to ask about Dennis Price, making his second movie with you [after *Curse of the Voodoo*].

Tower of Evil's rocky-beach-and-lighthouse set at Shepperton Studios, lit for day and night.

GORDON: Rose Shaw said, after studying the script, that she had a suggestion for the role of the museum administrator: She thought she could get Dennis to come and do it, because it could all be shot in one day, and that it would be very useful in the credits to have him listed as one of the guest stars. I thought this was a terrific idea, but I was a bit worried because at the time he was living on Sark Island in the Channel Islands —

Q: It coulda been worse, he coulda been living on *Snape* Island!

GORDON: [*laughs*] That's right! Rose said, "You don't have to worry about that, he'll come to London to do his scenes." So I accepted the idea immediately. I was very impressed with the way he played the role. He did it all in less than a day, and it was a very happy association. Later, when Antony Balch and I were casting *Horror Hospital* [1973], we decided that we would try to get him for an important role in that film, which we did.

Q: Price gets guest star billing, and so does a guy I never heard of, Anthony Valentine, who plays Penny's doctor-hypnotist.

GORDON: He was somebody I didn't know until Rose Shaw introduced him to me at a casting session, but he was obviously very well-known in England, and it was very good that we got him. I'm told that he's still around and still working, most recently on *Coronation Street*, one of the longest-running and most successful soap operas on British television.

Anthony Valentine's nurse in those hospital scenes was played by Marianne Stone, who was married to Peter Noble, quite a well-known journalist in the English film industry; he was at one time the editor of *Today's Cinema*, the British equivalent of *Variety*. She played a lot of supporting roles in films, sometimes bit parts, sometimes larger roles. Rose Shaw thought it would be a good idea if we employed Marianne because this might help us get some extra publicity from the husband [*laughs*]! So I said yes, by all means. Incidentally, some years earlier when Marshall Thompson was starring in my *First Man Into Space* [1959], Marianne and Peter invited me to their home for a dinner party, and asked me to bring Marshall along, which I was delighted to do. (I'm sure they were more interested in Marshall than in me!) Marshall and I went to their home, and there were only two other guests to whom I was introduced. One was introduced to me as Sean Connery, whom I'd never heard of [*laughs*] — I had no idea who he was! — and the other was Diane Cilento, his future wife. At the time I paid no particular attention; I thought, "Well, maybe Peter thinks this is an actor I could use in one of my pictures," but I couldn't see myself doing it, so I shrugged it all off! But I remembered meeting him, and some time after that came *Dr. No* [1962], and the rest is history.

Q: You even got some good people to play the American kids in the flashback scenes.

GORDON: John Hamill [who played Gary] had a career as a model before he became an actor, and at that time he was building up to a successful career in movies. Jim O'Connolly recommended him to me; perhaps, because of Jim's association with [producer] Herman Cohen, he had seen Hamill in Herman's film *Trog* [1970] with Joan Crawford. When I met Hamill, I felt that he was absolutely right for the role. The unfortunate thing was that when we called him for a casting session, he thought he was being interviewed to play the role of Brom; he had, after all, played some co-starring parts by that time, including *The Beast in the Cellar* and *No Blade of Grass* [both 1970]. When I told him that Brom had already been assigned to Gary Hamilton, and that the role I wanted him for was one of the American kids, he was very disappointed, because by comparison it *was* a very small and very limited role. But he accepted it, and we were very satisfied with him. He had no compunction about doing the nude scene, there was no problem there.

Q: Serretta Wilson — the only one of the four who *was* American — played the girl whose head rolls down the stairs.

GORDON: I remember her very well, because she was very cooperative and a lot of fun. She thought it was all a big lark and did exactly what we asked. When you see her head roll down the stairs, that was a prop — of course [*laughs*] — but when you see it sitting in the middle of the floor, that actually was her head; the rest of her was beneath the floor. Candace Glendenning [who played Penny] was in *Nicholas and Alexandra* [1971], which was her debut. Rose Shaw recommended that I see the film, because she thought Candace would be good for the role in *Tower of Evil*. I did go and see it, and as a result of that, she got the part.

Robin Askwith played the fourth American teenager, Des. It was the first time that I had the experience of dealing with him. At first we considered him for the role of Brom; we felt that he wasn't quite right for that, but that he was exactly what we needed for the role of Des. He had had a bit of a career already in films, starting with the famous film *If....* [1968]. He worked very well for *Tower of Evil*. A few years later, he had the leading role in *Horror Hospital*. By the way, Askwith's voice was dubbed for the American market because Joe Solomon felt, since they made a point in the story of saying that he was an American kid, that his voice wasn't acceptable. John Hamill was also dubbed.

Q: I wish the credits of *Tower of Evil* included the names of the special effects people. There are some terrific effects in the movie.

GORDON: The Shepperton special effects team was part of the studio's contribution to the film. Just like the Rank Studios at Pinewood had a special unit for special effects, Shepperton had such a unit, and made it available to us. Part of what they did were the shots of the island: The island didn't exist in reality; when you see it, you're actually seeing a glass shot. All the sequences *on* the island, including the landing of the boat, were all shot in the studio, on sets built by Disley Jones our art director. Framed on the wall of the office of Gordon Films Inc. in New York, I have a rendering of the exterior of the Tower of Evil set that was sent to me by Disley, which I value greatly.

Q: Also in the movie, courtesy of the special effects and prop departments, are a severed hand, a severed head and a headless body, you've got the lighthouse blowing up at the end like something out of a Republic serial — and you've got that fabulous fire scene that I'd love for you to talk about.

GORDON: I was very worried about that fire sequence, because I couldn't quite see how it was going to work, especially in the confines of a studio. But Jim O'Connolly had the situation well in hand: He'd worked it all out with the special effects unit, and when it came to the shooting of that sequence, it worked perfectly. Of course, the apparent size and ferocity of the fire had a lot to do with how it was photographed, the way the cameras were placed to create that effect. But it *was* an extraordinary sequence, and I was very proud of it at the time.

Q: And hats off, too, to a stuntman named Mark McBride, who played Michael and wades right through the fire.

GORDON: That worried me more than anything else, because he was going to have to do the sequence of the character being set on fire and thrashing about while being burned alive, on a set that was burning around

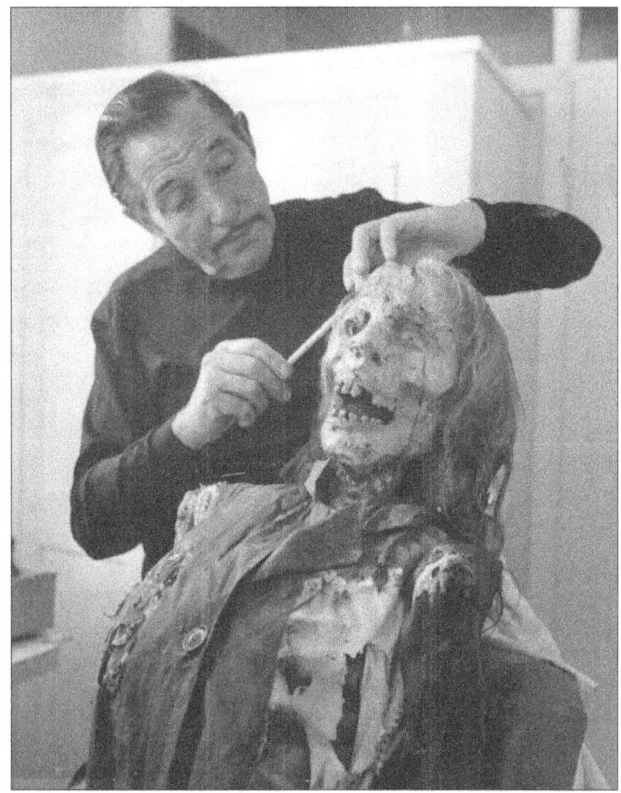

Doing the *opposite* of the usual makeup job, this fellow is making sure the corpse of lighthouse-keeper's wife Martha looks her *worst* in this behind-the-scenes shot.

him. The main consideration was that he could only stay in that protective clothing, with that fire all around him, for a limited period of time. There was absolutely no question of a rehearsal, no second chance; it was either going to work or it wasn't. But he shrugged it all off; he had done this before, knew exactly what to do, and he wasn't the least bit worried about it. He said, "Don't worry about it. I know exactly what you want me to do, and I'll do it. You don't have to be concerned." Again, I have to give credit to Rose Shaw, who found him to play that role.

Q: Fire scenes in old movies are so much more exciting than today's. Now they have protective clothing where the guy could practically walk on the sun, the fire might just be CG — what a bore. In the old pictures, you knew the guy was risking his neck.

GORDON: In the old days, the fire sequences were exactly what you saw on the screen. Today with the CG, you know it's fake practically from the word go, and the camera has to cut away constantly because you can't look at a CG shot too long without noticing all the fake elements that go into it. So it doesn't have the same excitement as it did in the old days. We knew on *Tower of Evil* that it had to be okay on the first take, and Jim O'Connolly was able to do that. I was very thrilled with it.

Another interesting thing about Shepperton Studios was that there were always other people working there at the same time, whom one could meet. Milton Subotsky, who was Max Rosenberg's partner in Amicus, had a permanent office at Shepperton, where they shot most of their pictures. I got to know him and we got to be quite good friends. At the time when I was shooting *Tower of Evil*, Milton was shooting one of those omnibus pictures that Amicus was very successful with. One day Milton came to see what we were doing and he was impressed with our cave sets, and he asked if it was possible for me to let him shoot a scene for a film *he* was making, using our set; and if so, if I wanted to use one of *his* sets for anything that *I* was doing, he would reciprocate.

Q: I love the stories of everybody "scratching each others' backs" on these little independent pictures.

GORDON: In those days, particularly in England, independent filmmakers were all trying to help each other, because we were all competing with Hollywood; and we could do it more easily if we cooperated with one another in the production of our films. I had a *lot* of help from the Carreras family at Hammer Films with suggestions and recommendations, and wherever I could do something that I thought might be useful for *them*, I made it available to *them*. We had very good relationships.

Q: The *Tower of Evil* plot [two bickering couples stranded in a lonely house are terrorized by the weird people who live there] makes me think of *The Old Dark House* [1932]. Especially once I spotted what I think might have been an intentional nod to that movie.

GORDON: I wanted in *Tower of Evil* a couple of scenes that people who had seen some of the great Hollywood horror classics would recognize. So at the end, when Michael [McBride] is about to come down the stairs, the first thing you see of him is his hand on the wall at the top of the stairs, before he appears. That shot was a tribute to James Whale's picture *The Old Dark House* in which a shot of the hand of Saul

Gordon poses with the statue of Baal in a...dare we say it?...*idol* moment.

[Brember Wills], on the banister at the top of the stairs, is one of the most memorable moments in the picture.

Q: One of the two "monsters" in the movie also had the *name* Saul. Even if touches like that went over the heads of most of the audience members, *you* knew they were in there.

GORDON: I knew they were in there, and I figured there would be enough people who would recognize them and appreciate them.

Q: I didn't "get" the *Old Dark House* tribute moment the first time I saw *Tower of Evil*, because I hadn't yet seen *Old Dark House*. But I certainly "got" it when the rocking chair pivoted around to show the mother's rotted corpse sitting in it.

GORDON: Obviously that was from *Psycho* [1960]. I tried also, in other horror and science fiction films that I made, to pay tribute to some of those great horror stars, directors and studios and the films they made in the '30s.

Q: Seeing *Tower of Evil* in a nice print after years of seeing chopped-up versions on local TV, I was very impressed with Desmond Dickinson's photography.

GORDON: Desmond Dickinson I was very lucky to get. That was arranged by John Pellatt, who knew him. Desmond was one of the earliest cinematographers in England, going back to the silents. I of course knew all about him and his history, and when Pellatt said to me that Desmond would be available to shoot *Tower of Evil*, and that he was in very good health and still very active, I jumped at the opportunity. When I met Desmond, not only to discuss the shooting of *Tower of Evil* but to talk about his history in filmmaking, I was even more impressed. He photographed the only serial ever made in England, *Lloyd of the C.I.D.* [1932], which was a serial in the tradition of Mascot and other producers of serials in America. I thought it was just wonderful to get a guy with that background and that ability to shoot our film, and I was thrilled to meet him and talk to him. I think he did a brilliant job of photographing *Tower of Evil* considering that *everything* — exteriors and interiors — was shot in a very short space of time.

Q: Joe Solomon having been part of the picture from Day One, he was all set to release it in the United States, correct?

GORDON: At that time, Joe was doing his physical distribution through American International Pictures. He was persuaded by American International to retitle the picture *Horror on Snape Island*, a title I didn't care for. But this was Joe's territory and, after all, he was the principal financier of the picture, so there wasn't much I could say about it. *Tower of Evil* did very well in England; it was released there by Anglo Amalgamated, which was one of England's leading independent film distributors, and had a full circuit booking. I distributed it throughout the rest of the world. And as soon as the rights of American International Pictures expired, I made a reissue deal with Sam Sherman of Independent International Pictures, and he retitled the picture *Beyond the Fog* because there had just been a picture directed by John Carpenter, *The Fog* [1980], and Sam wanted to cash in on that. My attitude was, "Anything is better than *Horror on Snape Island*!" [*Laughs*]

Gordon watches as Martha's corpse (a dummy) is installed on the set for its *Psycho*-like moment in the movie. His *Tower of Evil* is an ahead-of-its-time bridge between vintage fright films (the fogbound Gothic setting) and the coming wave of "horny young people have sex and die horribly" slasheramas.

Q: AIP's "tips for exhibitors" were the usual thing: a "challenge" midnight screening for a brave female; have a menacing stranger dressed in black walk through your main streets. (Today he'd probably get arrested!) When you were a kid going to see horror movies in England, did this kind of stuff go on?

GORDON: Oh yes, absolutely. When some of the bigger pictures, like *Bride of Frankenstein* [1935], opened, particularly in the West End of London, they would have nurses in attendance, an ambulance waiting in front of the theater in case somebody fainted or had a heart attack, etc. That was a standard part of exploitation. I must say that in those days, exhibitors had much more imagination than today.

I was completely satisfied with *Tower of Evil*. For myself, I think it's one of the two or three best pictures I produced, taking into account what we set out to do and what the aim of the picture was. Even when I look at it again now, I feel that there's nothing in it that I would like to change if I had the opportunity to do it over again.

Great posed shots of Rose (Jill Haworth) and the caveman-like Saul (Fredric Abbot). Genre specialist "The Phantom of the Movies" wrote of *Tower of Evil*, "Dripping with creepy atmosphere, [it's] a thrilling stalkathon..."

HORROR HOSPITAL
1973

CREDITS

Produced by	*Richard Gordon*
Associate Producer	*Ray Corbett*
Directed by	*Antony Balch*
Screenplay	*Antony Balch & Alan Watson*
Photography	*David McDonald (Color)*
Music	*De Wolfe*

Song "Mark of Death" Composed by Jason De Havilland

Editor	*Robert Dearberg*
Casting Director	*Thelma Graves*
Art Director	*David Bill*
Assistant Director	*John Hansen*
Makeup Supervisor	*Colin Arthur*
Post-Production Supervisor	*Matt McCarthy*
Property Master	*Charles Burgess*
Property Buyer	*Liz Richards*
Construction Coordinator	*Peter Richardson*
Sound Recordists	*Paul Le Mare & Tony Anscombe*
Sound Editor	*Michael Hopkins*
Boom Operator	*Don Wortham*
Stunt Supervisor	*Martin Grace*
Camera Operator	*John Crawford*
Focus	*Bob Jordan*
Clapper Loader	*Peter Biddle*
Grip	*Jim Gomm*
Assistant Editor	*Rod Howick*
Publicist	*Dennison Thornton*
Production Secretary	*Midge Warnes*
Story Idea (Uncredited)	*Antony Balch &* ***Richard Gordon***

90 minutes

CAST

Michael Gough	*Dr. Christian Storm*
Robin Askwith	*Jason Jones*
Vanessa Shaw	*Judy Peters*
Ellen Pollock	*Aunt Harris*
Dennis Price	*Pollack*
Skip Martin	*Frederick*
Kurt Christian	*Abraham Warren*
Barbara Wendy	*Millie*
Kenneth Benda	*Carter*
Martin Grace, Colin Skeaping	*Bike Boys*
George Herbert	*Laboratory Assistant*
James IV Boris, Allan "The River" Hudson, Simon Lust	*"Mystic" Rock Group Members*

Uncredited

Antony Balch	*Bearded Man in Nightclub/Bike Boy*
Ray Corbett	*Hunter*
Alan Watson	*Transvestite in Nightclub*
Richard Gordon	*Nightclub Patron*

SYNOPSIS

Young pop song writer Jason loses a nightclub fistfight with the performer who stole one of his songs, the latest in a series of setbacks that make the angry young man realize he needs a vacation. At the offices of "Hairy Holidays," shady travel agent Pollack recommends a trip to Brittlehurst Manor, the "health hotel" of a Dr. Storm. En route via train, Jason meets Judy Peters, who is going to the Manor to visit an aunt she never met.

At Brittlehurst, Judy's Aunt Harris lays out the un-welcome mat for her, insisting that she'd written Judy *not* to come. Dr. Storm's "health hotel" is a spooky old castle where Jason and Judy encounter sardonic dwarf servant Frederick, see a bed soaked in blood and are horrified at the sight of Dr. Storm's other "guests" — zombie-like young men and women with lurid forehead scars (suggesting lobotomies) and waxy white faces. Dr. Storm is just as creepy, a wheelchair-bound knuckle-cracker who abuses little Frederick. Leather-clad, crash-helmeted "Bike Boys" mutely obey Dr. Storm's every command.

Pollack shows up demanding more money for directing unsuspecting young people to this horror hotel, where Dr. Storm uses them as experimental surgery subjects. Dr. Storm orders that Pollack be paid, but then dispatches his "guillotine car" — a limousine with a long blade protruding from the side. As the departing Pollack walks along the road outside the Manor, the car roars past him and his head is neatly severed, landing in a cloth sack suspended behind the blade.

Captives Jason and Judy are joined by a third prisoner, Abraham, a young chap who arrived at the Manor in search of a missing girlfriend. Worried about the authorities closing in on the place, Aunt Harris announces to Dr. Storm that she intends to leave — but as she is in her room packing, she is seized and killed by a faceless, hideously burned monster.

In Dr. Storm-narrated flashbacks, the mad surgeon tells his captives that he began his Pavlovian experiments in the 1920s, working with animals and graduating to human guinea pigs when Harris (then a whorehouse madam) began providing him with some of "her girls." His laboratory was destroyed by fire when a trespassing hunter saw some of Dr. Storm's corpse-like surgical victims and dropped his lantern in horror.

Jason and Abraham are freed from a locked bedroom by Frederick, who pays with his life at the hands of a Bike Boy. They rescue Judy and wreck Dr. Storm's laboratory, setting fire to the house. Dr. Storm and the monster are one and the same; he received his horrific burns in that long-ago lab fire and for years he has worn a mask to conceal them. When the monster escapes from the house on foot, Jason, Judy and Abraham give chase in the guillotine car. His head is lopped off and his body topples off the road into quicksand.

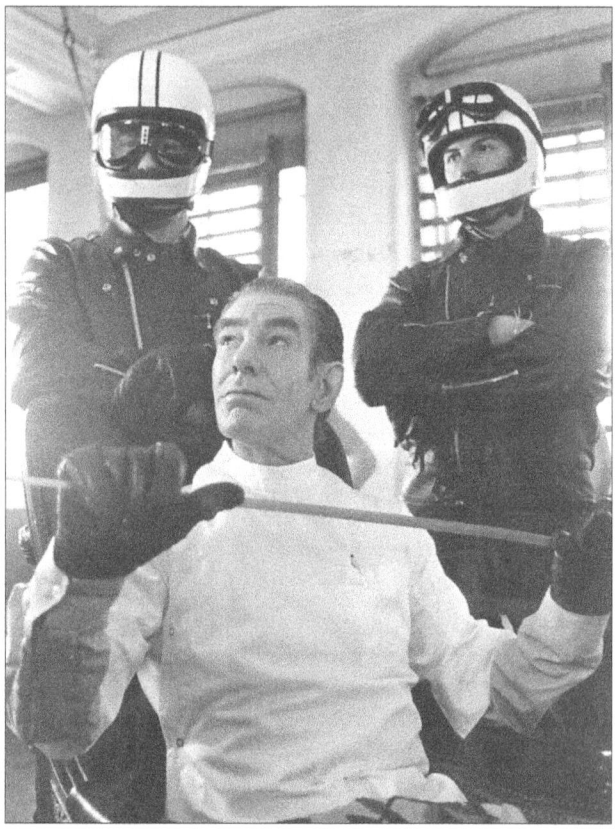

In the black-comic *Horror Hospital*, Dr. Storm (Michael Gough) describes his "patients" and Biker Boys as "just like puppets — and I'm the puppet master."

RICHARD GORDON ON *HORROR HOSPITAL*

RICHARD GORDON: I first met [*Horror Hospital* writer-director] Antony Balch at a Cannes Film Festival in the 1960s, when I used to go there every year in the pursuit of my other business as a distributor and importer and exporter of films. Antony had also came to Cannes looking for product; he had a distribution company, Noteworthy Films, and was importing foreign films, and he also operated two first-run theaters in London. We hit it off right away because we found we had very similar interests, in particular with regard to our liking for horror films and for the great actors of horror films like Boris Karloff and Bela Lugosi. In fact, Antony's favorite actor *was* Bela Lugosi, and he had his own 16mm prints of some of Lugosi's films which he used to run at his London apartment for friends and for anyone *else* interested in seeing them.

I found out that Antony was very much interested in getting into production himself. After we had various conversations about it, we decided to do a film together, *Secrets of Sex*, which materialized in 1969, came out in 1970 and was enormously successful. Extremely satisfied with the results, we then talked about doing something *else* together. We decided that we would do a horror picture by first designing a title and a theme, and then having a script written to suit ourselves.

Q: Which was the way AIP, including your brother Alex, did it back in the 1950s.

GORDON: Yes, that's how Jim Nicholson and Sam Arkoff at American International used to do it; in fact, they even went so far as to produce posters for the theaters before they started making the films.

After a number of discussions at one of the Cannes Festivals, Antony and I decided on a title, *Horror Hospital*, and then set about devising a story idea that would be suitable for it. We worked on it together and put our ideas down on paper. Also present in Cannes at the festival was a friend of Antony's, Alan Watson, a young Englishman who had done some scriptwriting and was also a great fan of horror pictures and that type of product. We made a deal with him to write the screenplay after Antony and I had plotted out a synopsis and made a list of the things that we would want to have included in the film.

Q: As you cooked up this story, did you have any actors in mind for particular parts?

GORDON: We immediately had in mind that we would write the leading character for the English actor Robin Askwith, who was then quite popular, and with whom I had worked previously: He had had a supporting role in *Tower of Evil* [1972] and I was very impressed with him at the time. Then Antony and I discussed the prospect of getting the right actor to play the leading villain, and Antony was very keen on getting Michael Gough, who had made a number of horror films at Hammer Films, and also other independent pictures —

Q: A number of Herman Cohen's movies, for example.

GORDON: That's right. We thought he would be eminently suitable for it, so the script was written with those two actors in mind. Antony approached Michael Gough directly, by arrangement with our casting director Thelma Graves, and asked Michael if he would be interested in playing the leading role. Antony also said that he would like to screen his, Antony's, favorite Bela Lugosi film, *The Devil Bat* [1940], *for* Michael, and show Michael the kind of personality and acting [Lugosi's] that he envisaged for the leading role of Dr. Storm in *Horror Hospital*. I wasn't present that evening because, first of all, we felt that Antony as the director, rather than me as the producer, should be the one to discuss this with Michael, and I would enter into the situation later when it came to arranging the terms if Michael agreed to do the film. I thought it would be best left to them, together, to do this. Apparently it worked very well: Michael came to Antony's apartment in London and they screened *The Devil Bat* and Michael thoroughly enjoyed the film, which he had never seen. Antony said to me later, "Michael turned to me and said, 'If that [a Lugosi-type performance] is what you *want*, that's what you'll *get*.'" [*Laughs*] From there on, the rest is history, as they say!

We were able to start production on *Horror Hospital* in October 1972. The film was designed to be shot mostly on locations, but also with some studio work, and we had a four-week shooting schedule which came off without a hitch. Then there was the usual business of getting pick-up shots and other things that were needed, to fill in.

Q: Where did you shoot?

GORDON: Part of the production took place at one of the so-called "stately homes of England," Knebworth Castle in Hertfordshire, which was just outside London. It had once been the home of the author of the novel *The Last Days of Pompeii*, [Edward] Bulwer-Lytton. In *Horror Hospital*, when you see Dr. Storm's clinic from the outside, you're seeing the home of Bulwer-Lytton and his family. At the time [1972], the grounds of that place was also used quite often for outdoor music festivals — somewhat along the lines, but not on such a big scale, as the Woodstock Festival in the United States.

Q: You shot only exteriors there?

GORDON: We couldn't afford to shoot interiors at Knebworth Castle; it would have required too much insurance coverage because of the risk of damaging any of the rooms. So, yes, only the exteriors were shot there. We shot the *interiors* of Dr. Storm's hospital in a vacated town hall in Battersea, a suburb of London. When you see the interior of Dr. Storm's Brittlehurst Manor, the interior set was shot at Battersea Town Hall.

Q: Was this comparable to the situation you had on *Devil Doll* [1964], which was shot in a theater that was about to be torn down, so you could make as much of a mess as you wanted?

GORDON: Yes, we were free to use the town hall as we saw fit, because it was just standing there, disused; they had not yet started to pull it down. When we see Robin Askwith in the street outside Dennis Price's travel agency, that was in the West End of London, one of the back streets in the Soho area. We went very early in the morning and tried to shoot without attracting any attention as we did not have a permit. When you see Robin running to catch the train, that is Waterloo Station in London. The train interiors were shot on an actual train. We arranged with British Railways to let us shoot on a train that was in use on their tracks.

Q: You added one car to a train that was making its regular run, and shot in it.

GORDON: That's right. The public was kept out of that one car and we could do anything we wanted in there. Then when Robin and [female lead] Vanessa

Abraham (Kurt Christian) discovers that his missing girlfriend Millie (Barbara Wendy) has become one of Dr. Storm's victims.

Shaw arrive at their stop and get off the train, that was a railway station near Merton Park — in fact, it was called Merton Station when it was in use. It had been taken out of service by British Rail, it was no longer being used, so it was very convenient for us to shoot there.

Q: Vanessa Shaw — how did you find her?

GORDON: Our casting director Thelma Graves sent us various actors and actresses to interview for the different roles in *Horror Hospital*. I had taken an apartment in London for the entire shooting and post-production period, and we conducted our interviews there. Vanessa Shaw, who arrived using the name *Phoebe* Shaw, was one of those we interviewed. We had Robin present, because we wanted to be sure that we got a girl who was also acceptable to him, for the scenes they were going to play together. We all agreed that she would be very good for this. But I did not want to use the name *Phoebe* Shaw because I thought it sounded too old-fashioned and wouldn't look well on the screen. So we rechristened her Vanessa Shaw, and to the best of my knowledge she kept that name for her use later in her career.

Q: At least one of the *Horror Hospital* reviewers didn't think much of her acting but it's such a daffy movie that her performance fits right in with the rest of the craziness.

GORDON: I felt that too. I didn't want some girl who was so experienced in making films that she would try to create another character of her own. I thought she worked very well with Robin in the scenes that they did together. I never heard about Vanessa Shaw much again after *Horror Hospital*, I never came across her again, so I assume she gave up her acting career. [*Editor's note: In a article on* Horror Hospital *in the magazine* The Dark Side, *Robin Askwith is quoted as saying, "[She and I] became great friends and even went out together for a while. She ran off to France with a Frenchman in 1972 and was never seen again!"*]

Q: Skip Martin, the dwarf, who plays Frederick?

GORDON: He was one of three or four "little people" — in those days, we simply referred to them as dwarves — whom our casting director sent when we had our casting sessions. One of the others who came was one of the stars of *Willy Wonka and the Chocolate Factory* [1971], I don't remember his name. But as soon as Antony and I interviewed Skip, and listened to him, and watched him, we decided that he was the ideal person for this part and we signed him at once. He was wonderful to work with. During the shooting, he immediately became everybody's favorite on the set, because of his enthusiasm, because he never said *no* to

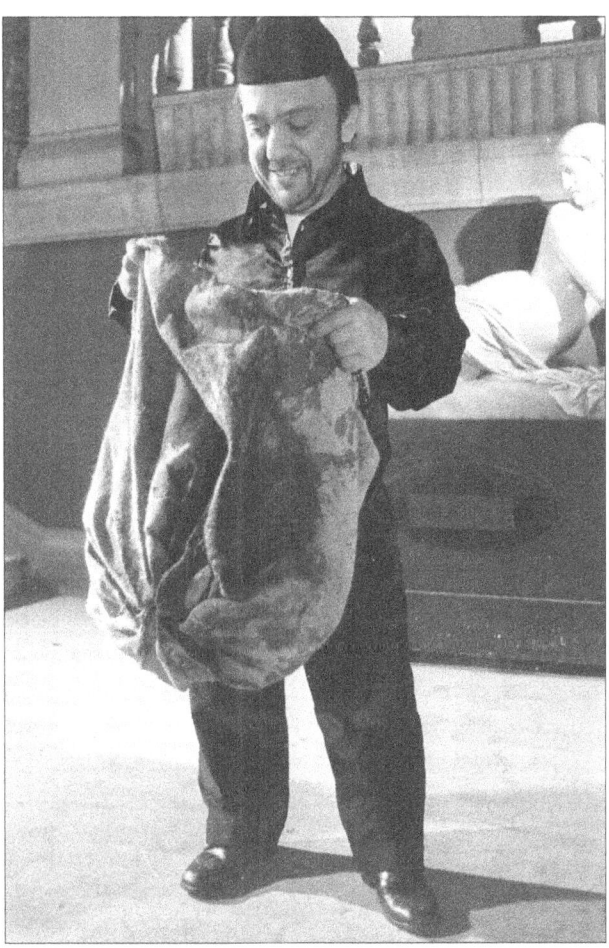

During *Horror Hospital* production, says Gordon, pint-sized performer Skip Martin "immediately became everybody's favorite." Martin's other genre credits include Vincent Price's *The Masque of the Red Death*, Hammer's *Vampire Circus* and Gordon's *Corridors of Blood*.

anything that was suggested he do, and because he had such a great sense of humor. Outside the camera range, especially together with Robin, he kept everybody in a great mood, and was constantly making everybody laugh. The whole film, because of Skip's involvement, along with Robin and the others, became one of my favorite pictures because of the way that everybody collaborated and everybody was having such a good time.

Q: My favorite "Skip Martin Moments" in the movie are both "physical comedy bits": where he's struggling to dig a grave, and trying to pile up two unconscious Bike Boys so he can stand on them and reach a doorknob.

GORDON: That whole sequence [piling up the Bike Boys] was of course scripted, but with the advice and help of Skip himself, who knew just what he could do and what he couldn't do. Obviously there was no double available for him [*laughs*]. As I watch that scene, I think that for a little man, particularly one who wasn't a kid any more [he was 44 years old], to be able to do all that was quite extraordinary. He had such determination, and he never minded if anybody laughed *at* him or laughed *about* him. He had no hang-ups, and he was willing to *try* anything and to *do* anything, in order to comply with our requests and also in order to give the picture that little extra touch that you don't see in too many films of this type.

Q: You told me once that this was the most fun you ever had making a movie.

GORDON: Yes, and I think it shows up on the screen as well. Skip was a great guy and he was a very good learner. He was actually a very good *actor*. He'd already appeared in one of my films, *Corridors of Blood* [1962] with Boris Karloff, but only in a minor role, uncredited, in crowd scenes in a tavern. Of course, Skip didn't always have enough acting roles, so in between he ran a tobacconist shop for a living, somewhere in the suburb of London where he lived.

The other person with whom I was already familiar, and who impressed Antony greatly, was Ellen Pollock, who played Aunt Harris. She had started her career on the stage in England in the 1930s as a Shakespearean actress, and she was seen on one occasion by George Bernard Shaw, who persuaded her that she should join his company and appear in some of the plays that he wrote and that were being put on in England. This was, of course, a little before my time [*laughs*].

Q: According to *Horror Hospital*'s publicity kit, she and Shaw met in 1932.

GORDON: That was not within my era. But in the mid-1940s and towards the end of the 1940s, Ellen Pollock co-produced a series of Grand Guignol horror plays on the London stage in which she co-starred with Tod Slaughter, the very successful stage and screen actor who specialized in Victorian horror melodramas, mostly always period pieces. These included, for instance, an English version of the Wilkie Collins novel *The Woman in White*. I remembered seeing Ellen Pollock in these Grand Guignol plays on the London stage, which would have been around 1947 or '48. I did not meet her at that time. When our *Horror Hospital* casting director Thelma Graves suggested Ellen as a possibility for Aunt Harris, I was immediately very impressed and asked that Ellen come to my apartment so I could introduce her to Antony and see how he felt about it. Well, Ellen arrived at our casting flat in a striking costume with a jeweled "bat" pin and red turban and very exotic clothes — clothes which, in fact, she later incorporated into scenes in *Horror Hospital*. Antony took one look at her and turned to me and signaled, "*Yes, that's it!*" [*Laughs*] We signed her up immediately, on the spot.

Q: She knew what kind of part she was being offered, and dressed appropriately.

GORDON: Oh, yes. All of the actors and actresses we interviewed were given descriptions of what *Horror Hospital* was all about and the part that they would be expected to play, so that they could prepare one or another scene and read it for us if we needed it.

Q: Robin Askwith looks a lot like Mick Jagger. Was that a help in his career, having a Mick Jagger look?

GORDON: Well [*laughs*], I think at that time in England, *all* the young people who were very "with it" patterned themselves a little bit after the appearance of Mick Jagger, one of the big heroes of rock music in that era. The best thing about working with Robin Askwith was his enthusiasm for taking part in such a venture, and his ability to add little bits and pieces to his performance and his characterization, to make it more appealing. One bit of business in *Horror Hospital* that I particular enjoyed was an idea of Robin's: At the end, when Brittlehurst Manor is burning and Robin and Vanessa Shaw and Kurt Christian run through the kitchen to get out of the house, Robin sees a pie on a counter and stops dead in his tracks and starts eating it, and Kurt Christian has to come back for him to get him out of there! Robin thought that up, and Antony and I thought it was a great idea. Robin was just the kind of person who would *do* that, so we put it into in the film.

So, yes, Robin was very cooperative, he was a very likable guy, he had a tremendous sense of humor, and I felt that he was going to have a major career in British cinema. I had seen him, and Antony had too, in a serious romantic drama called *Cool It Carol!* [1970]; and he had been in several other films after he made his screen debut in Lindsay Anderson's film *If....* [1968]. It was on my *Tower of Evil* where I first met him in person. I was very impressed with him but had no opportunity on *Tower of Evil* to give him a bigger role than he had, which what was not much more than a cameo appearance.

Q: Askwith was about 20 at the time, I would think.

GORDON: He was 21 when we made *Tower of Evil*, so he would have been 22 or 23 when we shot *Horror Hospital*.

Q: The makeups on Dr. Storm's "advanced students" — their waxy faces and forehead scars — look as good as the makeups in George Romero's later, bigger-budgeted *Living Dead* movies.

GORDON: Credit for that goes to Colin Arthur, who was in charge of makeup and special horror effects for *Horror Hospital*. He did such a great job, not only with the zombies, but also with the burned version of Dr. Storm and the mask of Michael Gough that you see towards the end of the movie. Colin had worked on *2001: A Space Odyssey* [1968] and other major films, he designed some of the masks for the *Star Wars* series, he was really a top-flight guy and we were lucky to get him. He enjoyed the whole idea of doing our film. The great thing about the script of *Horror Hospital* was that almost everybody who read it thought it would be so much fun to do, that they were willing to play in it without too much regard as to whether it made any sense or not [*laughs*].

Q: Throughout the movie there are moments that make me flash back to older movies: the shower scene in *Psycho*, blood coming out a faucet in *The Tingler* and so on. Mainly, however, I'm reminded of *Mystery of the Wax Museum* [1933]. I'm thinking these were conscious homages.

GORDON: That was very much the case. In all of the horror movies I made, I always tried to pay tribute to some of the earlier Hollywood classics, to famous scenes from those classics, to remind people of what this sort of thing was all about.

Q: Never more brilliantly than the cackling madman's claw-like hand on the wall at the top of the stairs, recalling *The Old Dark House* [1932], in your *Tower of Evil*, in my opinion.

GORDON: Thank you very much. I *was* very proud of that hand-on-the-wall scene. But I have to admit that, at the time, there was no one on the set of *Tower of Evil* who had the slightest idea what I was talking about —

Q: [*laughs*] And possibly not in the audience either!

GORDON: — when I insisted that I wanted that scene played the way it is, with the hand that appears on the wall. That was always one of my favorite moments in James Whale's picture *The Old Dark House*. I tried to do the same thing in *Horror Hospital* with *Mystery of the Wax Museum*, and there are other touches here and there where the idea was to pay homage and tribute to great horror classics of the '30s.

Q: And Balch of course would be in your corner on all these decisions, because he was as much of a fan as you were.

GORDON: Antony was absolutely enthused about it and was always urging me to think of other scenes that we might pay tribute to. But I said, "We don't want to overdo it. The whole thing will look like a hodge-podge to audiences who remember the old films." But he and I really disagreed very little on the creation of the script and the filming of *Horror Hospital*. That's another reason why it was one of my favorite films: There was never any discord between me as producer and him as director in the making of this film.

Q: Well, you once told me that you and he disagreed about the way he wanted to come to work every day.

GORDON: Antony never learned how to drive a car — nor did I, for that matter, and to this day I don't know how to drive a car. But he had a motorcycle on which he used to travel around London, and as we were preparing to do *Horror Hospital* it was his idea that he would come by motorcycle every day to wherever we were doing the shooting. I said, "Antony, absolutely not. There is too much of a risk in having you roaring around on a motorcycle in and out of London." And I knew that the insurance company, without whose help we could not make such a film, would never allow it. I said, "That's one thing you have to give up for the time being." We hired a limousine with a chauffeur which picked him and me up every day and took us to wherever we happened to be shooting, whether it was in the studio or outdoors or anywhere else. I used to have the car pick me up and then drive to Antony's apartment which was not too far away from the apartment that I had rented, and he would join me. Then during the ride to work, he and I would discuss the day's shooting and try to iron out any problems that we thought might arise or had already arisen. We had a great relationship.

Q: The first time I saw *Horror Hospital*, the crossdressers and the beefcake and just the general vibe made me think of movies like *The Rocky Horror Picture Show* [1975] and *Phantom of the Paradise* [1974], and I assumed that it was just part of that mid-1970s cycle. But now I realize that it *predates* those more-famous movies, that it led the whole pack.

GORDON: The idea came from Antony and me together; I can't really say that it was either my idea or his. Somehow we seemed to agree on everything, and that's another reason I think it was such a happy set. Michael Gough and Robin and all the others were enthusiastic about doing this, and felt that the fun of making the film would communicate itself to the audience, because it was never intended for this film to be taken seriously as a horror picture.

Q: What do you think about comedy relief in horror movies in general? Your movies up to this time had very little, almost no comic relief, and suddenly here this rat's nest of outrageous horror nonsense.

GORDON: I never liked the idea of too much comic relief in horror movies. They used to say that it was necessary, to give the audience a chance to breathe in between scenes that would terrify them, but I think it almost always ended up spoiling the mood of the film. On the great horror films of the '30s and '40s, there was much too much comic relief put in, usually with one particular actor or actress doing the comic scenes. I was not in favor of it. There's very little humor in the other horror films I've made, as you know. The reason that it appears here is because this whole project started out to be a horror comedy from the word go. Therefore I don't look upon it as having comic scenes inserted into it, but as being a tongue-in-cheek horror movie from the start.

Q: Stuntmen Martin Grace and Colin Speaking played two Bike Boys. They later became *top* stuntmen, working in James Bond movies and Indiana Jones movies and so on.

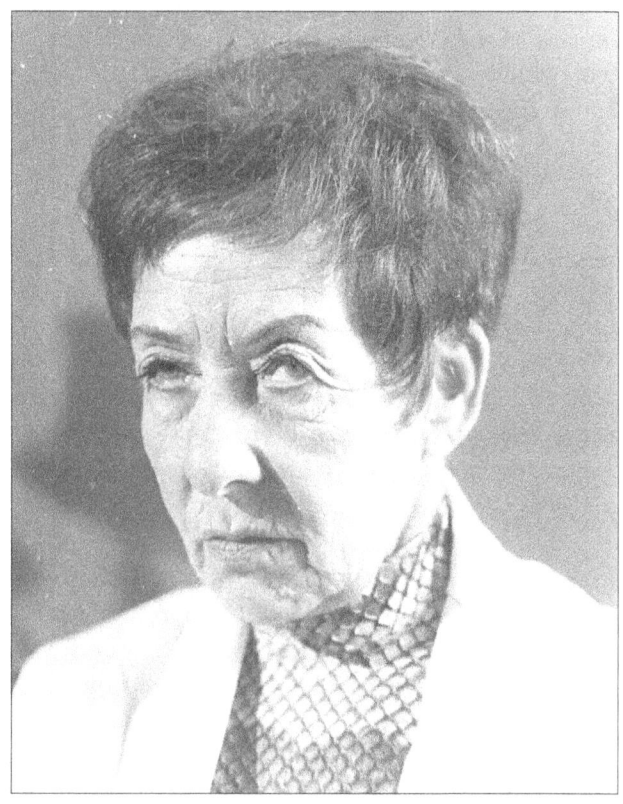

Decades after seeing Ellen Pollock on the stage in horror plays with Tod Slaughter, Gordon signed her as *Horror Hospital*'s ominous Aunt Harris.

GORDON: Martin Grace was a stunt supervisor who managed a small group of stuntmen and made their services available when needed for various films. In *Horror Hospital*, Grace also acted as a stuntman himself. But there were one or two scenes that we had to do when they were otherwise occupied and weren't available when we needed them. So, because of the way the Bike Boys were dressed and masked, other people replaced them, and *those* guys did a great job as well. In fact, in one scene *Antony Balch* is one of the Bike Boys, but only because we needed an extra close-up or something like that at a time when the two guys were not available. It didn't involve any kind of stunt.

Q: Robin Askwith really throws himself into his fight scenes with the Bike Boys. Was there ever a stuntman for Askwith, or was it all him?

GORDON: It was all him. Robin was the most amazing person in that regard: He said, "Whatever the character has to do in this film, I want to do it. And if I can't do it or if it doesn't work and you want to replace me with a double, then you can go ahead and do that. But I want the chance to do it myself." And he really was quite heavily beaten up in the outdoor fight scene with the Bike Boys. There are not many actors, especially young men of the age that he was when we made this film, who would agree to do scenes like that without a double. He was the absolute professional in that regard.

Q: Except for *Horror Hospital* I'm not familiar with Robin Askwith but I know he's some kind of star in England. What makes him so famous over there but not here?

GORDON: Because most of the pictures he made were made strictly for the British market. Very shortly after *Horror Hospital*, he was signed by Columbia Pictures in England to make a sex comedy called *Confessions of a Window Cleaner* [1974], which was directed by Val Guest, and was a huge success in England. In fact, it was one of the top-grossing British films in England that year, and was so successful that they made three more films along the same lines, using him to play the same character over and over. He also was in a lot of other films in which he did extremely well. He was very versatile, Robin; in fact, there was a television special called *Hans Brinker* [1969] with people like Eleanor Parker appearing in it, a network show, and he played the title role of Hans Brinker! Robin could play *any*thing, just as long as you didn't try to cast him as a character that was so foreign to him that he couldn't get under the skin of that character. He did a lot of West End London stage appearances, he toured in Australia and South Africa in various sex comedies, and he really made a great career for himself. On several occasions after the making of *Horror Hospital*, when I went to England to do other films, he'd be appearing in the West End of London, I'd go to see him and we'd have a great time together. And he also passed through New York several times on his way to exotic locations where he was appearing, and we maintained a wonderful relationship.

In 2005 I was invited to the Festival of Fantastic Films in Manchester, England, where they were going to honor me for some of the work that I've done, and I was able to persuade them to invite Robin as well. Robin is living now on the island of Malta and he has a very good life there, but he did agree to come to Manchester and we had a reunion, and we spent a whole evening together having a meal and talking about the old days. He's a wonderful guy and I love him and I'm very grateful for his contributions to my success with his appearance in the two films he made with me.

Q: Is his hair shorter now?

GORDON: Well [*laughs*], I haven't seen it lately, but it wasn't shorter yet when we reunited in Manchester. I think it's a sort of a trademark with him.

Q: I once saw Michael Gough in a Broadway play called *Breaking the Code* and afterwards, backstage, met him and tried to get him to agree to do an interview with me, about his horror and sci-fi credits, some time down the line. He was nice about it but he wouldn't say yes — and I knew that was going to happen, because I'd heard that he *never* said yes!

GORDON: He just didn't want to be characterized as a horror star, to be remembered for his horror roles in movies rather than some of the other, more serious things that he did on the stage and the screen. I approached him myself at the time of the release of *Horror Hospital*, to see if he would consent to do some interviews [in order to help publicize the movie], and as you said, he couldn't have been nicer about it, but he more or less said, "Look, I did everything you wanted me to do when I made the movie, I lived up to my obligations, but — I don't want to make a career out of it." I also once went to see him backstage when he was in New York — *not* in the play that you referred to, but in Alan Ayckbourn's comedy *Bedroom Farce* [1979], and he was very nice, he said he was glad to see me again and so on and so forth, but he was adamant about the fact that he didn't want to do any promotion for his horror films. He passed away just a short time ago [in March 2011].

Q: What was Balch like on the set of this movie, dealing with all the day-to-day stuff that a director has to deal with? Since *Secrets of Sex* was more or less

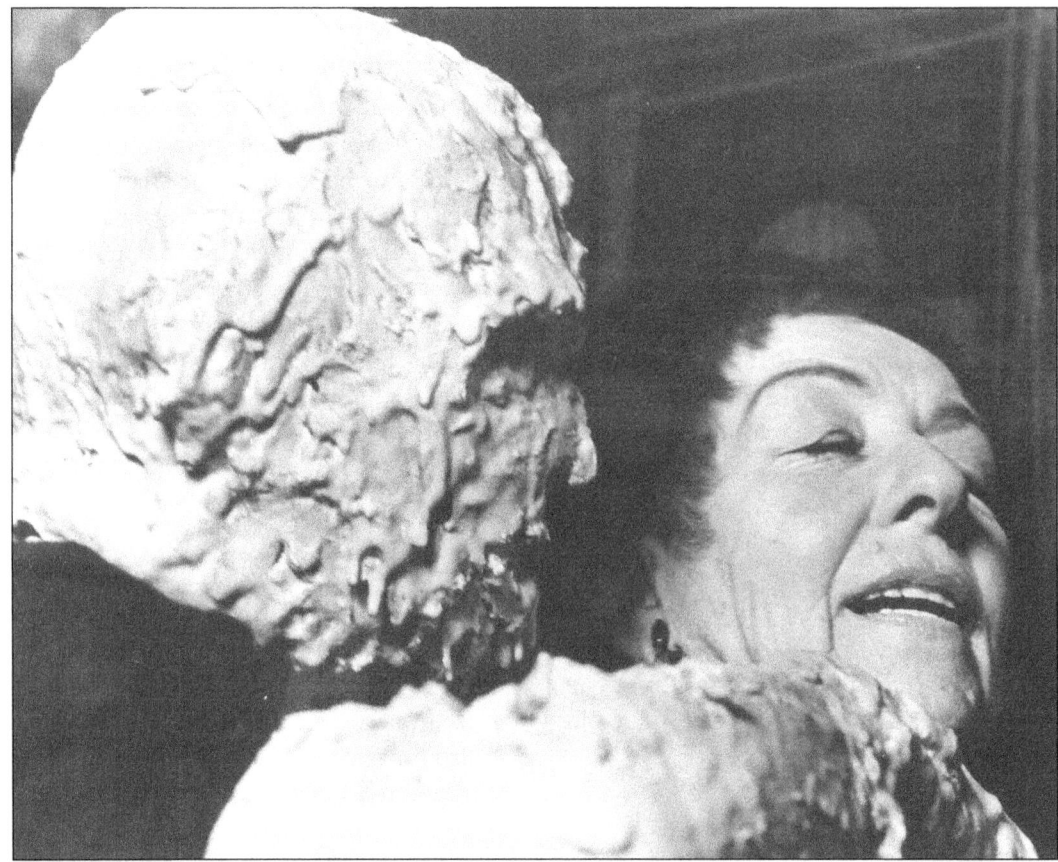
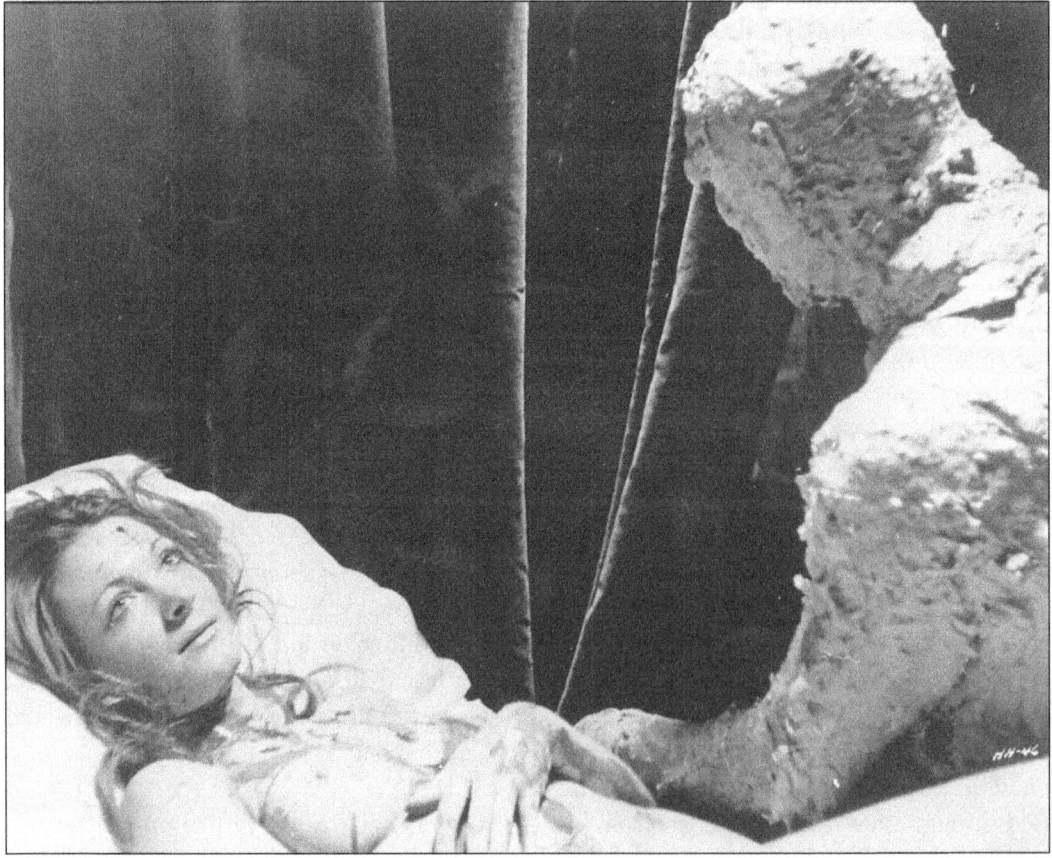
Brittlehurst Manor's resident lumpy-bumpy monster dispatches Aunt Harris (Pollock) and Millie (Wendy).

a series of shorts strung together, in a way *Horror Hospital* was the only *feature* he ever did.

GORDON: He was completely composed, thoroughly prepared. Always arrived in the morning with everything for the whole day planned. There were really never any problems. Fortunately, we were not dealing with any actors who would create problems for a director, particularly a director who was almost a first-time director, because as you say, *Secrets of Sex* with its episodic nature doesn't really count. The actors all took a tremendous liking to him and decided that they would do everything possible to make him as comfortable and relaxed as possible, and to do what he asked without causing any problems. That's something very rare among many actors. I've had many bad experiences in that respect on other films.

Q: The last actor I wanted to ask you about was Kurt Christian, who plays the latecomer prisoner Abraham.

GORDON: I must admit that I'd never heard of Kurt Christian when [casting director] Thelma Graves sent him along with some other fellows, although in fact he *had* had stage experience and made some other films. What I liked about him immediately was that both physically and as a personality, he was in such tremendous contrast with Robin Askwith. I thought the two of them would play together and against each other extremely well, and I was very happy with him. He seemed to be absolutely right for it, he had the enthusiasm, he and Robin hit it off immediately, and I felt that he did a very good job. He had a background of appearing on the stage, he was on Broadway in New York in a small part in *The Royal Hunt of the Sun* [1965-66], he had done other plays, I think he was in some television series, and he was also in a couple of other movies.

Q: The burned Dr. Storm looks a little like the First Man Into Space. Who was inside the costume?

GORDON: Oh, it was just one of the extras.

Q: For a tongue-in-cheek movie, *Horror Hospital* has a pretty ominous horror movie score.

GORDON: We got the music from De Wolfe, the music library in London that supplied soundtracks for independent and major studio filmmakers who did not want to go to the expense, or could not afford the expense, of having special music composed for their films. They were very nice people. I first met them when Antony and I made *Secrets of Sex* because we needed background music for various episodes, and we went to the De Wolfe library and listened to recordings and picked out the music that we wanted. Antony and I decided when we made *Horror Hospital* that there was so much music available from De Wolfe that we would do the same thing again. With the exception of the opening sequence of *Horror Hospital* that takes place in the nightclub with the rock band playing, all the rest of the music came from the De Wolfe library. A lot of the credit [for the music cue selections] goes to Antony, who spent hours and days listening to music at De Wolfe and picking out various themes that he thought could be suitable, and then calling me in. We ran his choices and picked out the ones we wanted. One waltz piece that we'd already used in *Secrets of Sex*, we used again in *Horror Hospital* in the flashback sequence where we see Aunt Harris in her brothel with the various girls who were being displayed there.

I want to tell you about a very funny incident that happened at the end of shooting *Horror Hospital*. There was, as is usual with independent pictures as well as major studio pictures, an end-of-picture party, and we set it up at a pub near the location of Knebworth Castle, and among the people I invited were a very important American friend of mine, who was considering investing in some future films of mine; he'd come to England and arrived in time to see the last couple of days of *Horror Hospital* shooting. I arranged that after the party was over, I would take him and an associate of his to a very luxurious dinner at one of London's swankiest restaurants, the Mirabelle in Curzon Street, where we would have a late supper and talk about everything. Well, the end-of-picture party included friends of various actors and actresses; Robin at the time had a girlfriend whom he said he would like to bring, and I said, "Of course, you bring anybody you want." She arrived with an assortment of cookies that she said she was contributing to the party. What I didn't know was that she had baked the cookies with hash. Everybody who started to eat them became slightly...well, the equivalent of being drunk. I was the only exception, because I was on a diet at the time and didn't eat anything in particular. By the time I took my American guest and his associate to the Mirabelle, they'd had a few cookies, and the result was that when we sat down at the table, the associate placed his order for food and then fell asleep, and slept through the entire meal. And my friend was in pretty bad shape also, and I had to take him back to his hotel and take care of him 'til the next day. It's something I will never forget.

Q: When the smoke cleared and they woke up, how did they feel about what had happened?

GORDON: They just said, "Let's not even talk about it!" [*Laughs*]

Q: How did *Horror Hospital* do theatrically?

GORDON: Now, you have to bear in mind that in England at that time, as in the United States, everything was double-feature; *Horror Hospital had* to be put on a program with something else. Antony and I discussed what was the best way to handle this situation, and decided that in order to protect our investment, the only way to do it was for us to acquire a second film which would play as the support to *Horror Hospital* and therefore not take away any of the film rental or the government subsidy to which we were entitled.

Q: You didn't want to just throw it out there and let it end up on the bottom of a double-bill with a Hammer movie or something.

GORDON: Right exactly. Antony had seen, I think at the Cannes Festival, a film called *The Corpse Grinders* [1971], made by the producer-director Ted Mikels; Antony thought it was an outrageous film that also could be taken as a spoof rather than be taken seriously. And with that title, it would make a very good support for *Horror Hospital*. So I made it my business to go to Hollywood and meet Ted Mikels and acquire the rights for the U.K. distribution of *The Corpse Grinders*, and we put the two together, and that's how the program was released throughout England. In England it opened at a big London theater called the New Victoria, opposite Victoria Railway Station. That was a theater with over a thousand seats, and *Horror Hospital*

The guillotine car rushes at the duplicitous Pollack, played by Dennis Price in his third and last Gordon production.

did extremely well in its first week, and was held over. Of course it eventually got a full circuit release.

Q: Did it play in Balch's theaters also?

GORDON: No, it didn't, because Antony's theaters were more specialized, and didn't go in for double-billing, and usually had open-end runs. *Horror Hospital* went out like any normal Hammer or AIP production, or any film of that type. We were very satisfied with the results.

In America, I made a deal for the distribution of the film with a New England-based company called Hallmark, which had had an enormous success a year earlier with the 1970 German horror film *Mark of the Devil*. Hallmark were looking for something to follow *Mark of the Devil* so I screened them this film, and they immediately liked it and went for it, and we made a very advantageous deal. They released it not only as *Horror Hospital* but also tried it out in different kinds of theaters under the title *Computer Killers*, which I didn't think much of, and which didn't prove to be any success. So that idea was dropped very shortly after it started.

The film was also released, of course, all over the rest of the world, we got many good deals on it. It was released in Germany under the title of *Frankenstein's Horror Clinic* and in the dubbing, the Germans changed Michael Gough's character name from Dr. Storm to Dr. Frankenstein — which I thought was a little farfetched, but it seemed to work for them!

Q: So it did very well around the world on a budget of…

GORDON: The film was budgeted at £50,000, which at that time would be about $125,000, and it didn't go over budget.

Q: And it's also the only movie in which you appear.

GORDON: *Four* people involved in the making of the movie make "Hitchcock-type" appearances. Alan Watson, who co-wrote the script with Antony, played the transvestite in the opening scene in the nightclub and fights with Robin Askwith. Then when Robin stumbles away and rejoins his friends who are sitting at a table, Antony Balch is one of them. He has a beard and glasses, he says to Robin "Snorting coke again?," and he suggests that it's time for Robin to take a holiday in the country for a few days.

Q: You told me once that Balch didn't like to be photographed. How did you get him to do that?

GORDON: He felt it was different: Because he had the fake beard and all, he wasn't being photographed as Antony Balch, he was being photographed as a character in the movie. Antony didn't like to be photographed in real life because he believed in a tradition that orig-

In *Horror Hospital*'s action-filled finale, Robin Askwith battles his way out of the burning "health hotel."

inated in Morocco or somewhere, where the Arabs believe that every time you have a picture taken, a little bit of your soul is removed from your body. Therefore, there are very few photographs of Antony in existence.

Incidentally, as we were preparing to shoot the long shot of the nightclub at the beginning of the movie, we realized that we didn't have enough extras, and the place looked half-empty. So Antony rounded up one or two other people from the studio payroll at Merton Park, and even the tea lady [*laughs*] — and I also agreed to do it, so I appear in that shot myself. I'm one of the people standing in the foreground, moving to the music.

Q: Your one and only "cameo" in 20-whatever movies.

GORDON: My only Alfred Hitchcock-type appearance, and only in long shot where unless I drew your attention to it, you would never notice it. The other person making an appearance was Ray Corbett, our production manager. He was a wonderful guy who did a tremendous job on the film, so much so that we credited him as associate producer in the screen credits. He appeared as the hunter in a flashback sequence, dropping his lantern and setting fire to Dr. Storm's early laboratory in Finland, and was later "dead" on the ground with the spike through his body. Ray was later my production manager and associate producer on other films I made, like *The Cat and the Canary* [1978] and *Inseminoid* [1981].

Q: Shooting *Horror Hospital* at Merton Park marked your return to that lot for the first time since the start of your career, when you made *The Counterfeit Plan* [1957] with Zachary Scott there.

GORDON: And my *other* Zachary Scott movie *Man in the Shadow* [U.S. title: *Violent Stranger*, 1957].

Q: How did the critics react to *Horror Hospital*?

GORDON: The critics were divided. Either they were absolutely appalled, because they didn't really "get it," or they were enthusiastic about Antony's talent and about the cleverness of making a horror spoof as entertaining as it was. I would say that on the whole, because Antony was very popular with critics as well as people within the industry, that they tried to support us as much as possible. Antony was invited to come to Paris for a premiere showing of the French-dubbed version, and the French publication, *Cinema D'Aujourd'Hui*, which means "Cinema Today," published a review that became one of my favorites.

Jean-Claude Michel's *Cinema D'Aujourd'Hui* review of *Horror Hospital*:

The deliriously crazy film for which we have been waiting has arrived! Made by an old familiar, Antony Balch, a fanatic collector of Karloff and Lugosi movies, who here has directed his second

Richard Gordon makes his one and only cameo ("My 'Hitchcock,'" he jokes) in *Horror Hospital* — clearly visible in this photo, but in the movie itself, nothing but a shadowy figure in a long shot.

full-length feature, Horror Hospital *is not one of the greatest masterpieces but why let it spoil our pleasure? One is carried away into the world of a castle of horrors presided over by Michael Gough, in better form than ever before…[E]verybody seems to have been delighted to participate in the making of the film, which is understandable. For once, however, the fight scenes are really realistic and the young blond who has the unenviable role of hero looks as though he gets half-killed by the henchmen of Dr. Storm when they set upon him. All this is very convincing and even disturbing. Antony Balch, who came to present his picture, is even more disturbing! So we hasten to affirm that we think only the best of his film. Yes, Yes!*

Q: Some of the English reviews did make mention of the fact that it was reminiscent of *Mystery of the Wax Museum* and other famous horror pictures.

GORDON: Those English reviews were very gratifying, and some were in the leading newspapers in England. These were serious newspapers and their reviewers respected Antony Balch: They respected him as a human being, they respected him for his ambitions and they respected him for his talent. One of the great tragedies in my career is how after we had such a success with *Secrets of Sex* and *Horror Hospital* and we were planning to make more films together, he suddenly became ill and it completely destroyed him. It was horrific to see.

Q: Were you able to visit him in England during his illness?

GORDON: Yes, several times, because I was over there preparing *Inseminoid*. But I did not realize that it had reached the terminal stage until I got a telegram from the salesman who handled his distribution, informing me that Antony had passed away.

Q: Where were you when you got the telegram?

GORDON: Here in New York, on the point of leaving for London to start pre-production on *Inseminoid*. If I'd known how serious Antony's illness was, I would have gone over sooner. My thought was, "Well, I'll be in London soon, I'll be able to visit him once more" — but it was too late. It was a tremendous loss…

SCRIPT TO SCREEN CHANGES

In *Horror Hospital*'s pre-credits sequence, a bandaged and blood-spattered young couple runs alongside a road until Dr. Storm's "guillotine car" comes along and decapitates them. In the movie, they drop to the ground instantly, but the script called for a shot of their headless bodies "staggering about in the road for a brief instant before collapsing into the ditch."

The script describes Jason boarding the train and walking down a corridor; "past Delta Balch" is handwritten (no doubt by Antony Balch) alongside this text. But Delta, Antony's mother, does not appear in the scene.

The last scene in *Horror Hospital* finds Jason, Judy and Abraham on a train; the last scene in the *script* has them on a commercial airplane. After the stewardess asks all passengers to put on their seat belts, we see in the back row of the plane "two leather-gloved pairs of hands fastening their seat belts. The CAMERA PULLS back to reveal two BIKE BOYS sitting there…" With a description of a shot of the plane takeoff, the script ends.

THE CAT AND THE CANARY
1978

CREDITS

Produced by .... **Richard Gordon**
Associate Producer .... Ray Corbett
Screenplay and Directed by .... Radley Metzger
    Based on the Play by John Willard (by Arrangement with Raymond Rohauer)
Photography .... Alex Thomson (Color)
Music Composed & Conducted by .... Steven Cagan
Editor .... Roger Harrison
Art Directors .... Anthony Pratt & John Hoesli
Casting Director .... Rose Tobias Shaw
Makeup .... Mary Hillman & Tommy Manderson
Hairdresser .... Sarah Monzani
Assistant Director .... Alan Carpenter
Second Assistant Director .... Brian Bilgorri
Wardrobe .... Monica Howe & Lorna Hillyard
Camera Operator .... Michael David Fox
Focus .... John Golding
Clapper/Loader .... Martin Hume
Stills .... Frank Connor
Sound Recordist .... Clive Winter
Sound Assistant .... David Sutton
Boom Operator .... Ken Weston
Continuity .... Angela Allen
Production Buyer .... Dennis Maddison
Property Man .... Derek Creedon
Construction Manager .... Tony Neale
Electrical Supervisor .... David Clark
Post-Production .... Roger Cherrill Ltd.
Dubbing Mixer .... Paul Carr
Dubbing Editor .... Anthony Sloman
Assistant to the Director .... Tamasin Day-Lewis
Production Assistant .... Jo Gregory
Production Secretary .... Jane Oscroft
Publicist .... Allen Burry

    90 minutes (original release)
102 minutes ("Uncut Director's Edition" home video release)

CAST

Honor Blackman .... Susan Sillsby
Michael Callan .... Paul Jones
Edward Fox .... Hendricks
Wendy Hiller .... Allison Crosby
Olivia Hussey .... Cicily Young
Beatrix Lehmann .... Mrs. Pleasant
Carol Lynley .... Annabelle West
Daniel Massey .... Harry Blythe
Peter McEnery .... Charlie Wilder
Wilfrid Hyde-White .... Cyrus West)

SYNOPSIS OF THE PLAY

"The Cat and the Canary" by John Willard (1922)

ACT I (Library. Eleven-thirty. Night.)

In September 1921, on the 20th anniversary of the death of eccentric millionaire Cyrus Canby West, distant relatives gather at Glencliff Manor, his spooky Hudson River home, for the reading of his will. In the library, Roger Crosby, executor of the will, takes it from a wall safe under the watchful eye of the guardian of the house, West Indian "voodoo woman" Mammy Pleasant, the house's sole occupant since Cyrus' death. Also appearing out of the night are Annabelle West ("a vigorous, beautiful girl, frank and fearless and very modern"), comically indecisive Paul Jones ("I have felt better — but on the other hand, I *have* felt worse"), Harry Blythe ("[a] quiet, cynical, bored man, but dangerous…the gentleman heavy type"), Charlie Wilder ("a tall, handsome, leading man type…full of charm"), Susan Sillsby ("a female with an acid temper") and Cicily Young ("a pretty blond girl").

At midnight, Crosby commences by saying that West hated all his living relatives, then opens the envelope and reads the will. It leaves everything to the descendant "who bears the surname of West" — which makes Annabelle the beneficiary. But Cyrus makes one stipulation: If the heir is subsequently found to be of unsound mind, then Crosby is to open an envelope containing a different will and name the replacement heir. Mammy Pleasant produces a letter which the dying Cyrus instructed her to hand to the heir; Crosby speculates that it may pertain to a West family heirloom, a valuable sapphire-and-ruby necklace.

Making a middle-of-the-night entrance is a man who introduces himself as Hendricks, head guard at a nearby asylum. Carrying a straitjacket, he says he's searching for an escaped patient: a homicidal maniac with sharp teeth and claw-like fingernails who crawls on all fours like a cat.

Crosby is in the library privately consulting with Annabelle when a wall panel opens and a hand reaches out, grabbing Crosby by the throat and pulling him into the secret passage. When Annabelle tells the others of Crosby's disappearance, several treat her as though she was crazy — which perhaps some of them hope she *is*, because then they will have a second crack at Cyrus' fortune.

ACT II (The next room. A few minutes later.)

In her bedroom, Annabelle opens the letter and reads a cryptic verse that directs her to a secret recess in the mantel. It contains the West necklace, which she wears to bed. After she's fallen asleep, another wall panel opens and a claw-like arm reaches for her throat, snatching the necklace and waking her. Her description of the terrifying scene again fuels speculation that Annabelle is mad — until she finds and opens the wall panel. As it slides open, the dead body of Crosby tumbles into the room.

ACT III (Library. A few minutes later.)

It is discovered that the phone lines have been cut, so after much arguing, Harry agrees to take Susan and Cicily to the train station, Charlie says he'll go to the police station and Mammy heads off to get a doctor for Annabelle, who is one shock away from either insanity or death-by-fright. A drink of whiskey has an immediate effect on Paul, turning the blithering dolt into a keen thinker who realizes that a plot against Annabelle may be afoot, and that perhaps "the next heir" is responsible. After more strange goings-on, the Cat creeps into the library where Annabelle is alone. Hendricks rushes in, prevents Annabelle from shooting the Cat, and begins leading the Cat out of the library. Annabelle darts forward and pulls the mask from the head of the monster, revealing Charlie Wilder. Suddenly Charlie *and Hendricks* seize Annabelle and pin her to the couch: Hendricks, not really an asylum guard, is actually an accomplice in Charlie's scheme to drive the girl mad. But Hendricks doesn't approve of the fact that Charlie killed Crosby during one of his "crazy spells" — Charlie is obviously quite insane — and soon the two villains are fighting. Harry and Paul arrive on the scene and get the upper hand, with a gun-wielding Harry declaring that he's taking Charlie and Hendricks to the police. Alone with Annabelle, the dithering Paul tells her that he thought she'd be less nervous if she had him as her husband, and sent Mammy to fetch a minister. They embrace as the curtain closes.

SYNOPSIS OF THE FILM

In 1924, on the 20th anniversary of the death of eccentric millionaire Cyrus West, members of his family converge at England's Glencliff Manor for the reading of his will. His lawyer Allison Crosby, the first to arrive, is greeted by the housekeeper Mrs. Pleasant, the Manor's sole occupant since Cyrus' death. Also appearing out of the dark and stormy night are the relatives: fashion designer Annabelle West, American songwriter Paul Jones, surgeon turned pharmacist Harry Blythe, ex-flying ace Charlie Wilder, big-game hunter Susan Sillsby and Susan's roommate Cicily Young.

Mrs. Crosby reveals that the will is to be read by none other than Cyrus West, who before his death

A poster for the 1927 film adaptation with Laura La Plante.

had himself photographed on film with a synchronized sound recording. At midnight when the film is shown, the sardonic West names Annabelle as the sole inheritor of his vast fortune (including a priceless necklace). West also informs his relatives that a *second* filmed will names another beneficiary, but it may only be shown if Annabelle dies or proves to be insane.

Making a dramatic entrance at the house is Hendricks, who introduces himself as the chief psychologist at a nearby asylum for the criminally insane; he says he's searching for an escaped patient who believes himself to be a cat, and uses his sharp teeth and claw-like fingers to rip his victims apart — slowly. Mrs. Crosby is in the library privately consulting with Annabelle when a bookcase swings open like a door behind her, revealing a secret passage and the terrifying "Cat" who pulls Mrs. Crosby into the darkness of the passage. When Annabelle tells the others of Mrs. Crosby's disappearance, several treat her as though she's crazy — which perhaps they hope she *is*, because then they will have a second crack at Cyrus' fortune. Paul seems to be Annabelle's only true friend, and romance blossoms.

The Cat next appears in Annabelle's room, reaching for the West necklace around her pretty throat. Her screams scare the intruder away. A cupboard in her room swings open like a door, revealing the body of Mrs. Crosby, a bloody cloth bag around her head. Susan later becomes the Cat's second victim.

Annabelle is kidnapped by the Cat and dragged to a secret chamber where the struggling girl pulls off her attacker's mask and reveals Charlie, who has hatched this murderous scheme with the intention of becoming the new heir. Hendricks is not really a psychologist but an old army buddy of Charlie's and now his partner in crime. Annabelle is secured to a chair and Hendricks is preparing to spend the next several hours toying with her with a variety of surgical knives. But instead it's the two madmen who lose their lives — Charlie shot by Mrs. Pleasant and Hendricks shot by Paul. A bright future looms for Annabelle and Paul.

RICHARD GORDON ON *THE CAT AND THE CANARY*

Q: What attracted you to the idea of making a new version of *Cat and the Canary*?

RICHARD GORDON: After looking for some time for another project, because I hadn't made a film in a couple of years, I was impressed with the revival of interest in Agatha Christie's stories and the success of films like *Murder on the Orient Express* [1974] and *Death on the Nile* [1978] [both based on Christie novels]. I thought it would be a good idea to do something along those lines. Of course I was already quite aware of *The Cat and the Canary* because it had been part of the history of the theater and the cinema for many decades, and I began to think that a remake with an all-star cast like the Agatha Christie pictures would appeal to the same kind of audience.

Q: And of course you'd seen both the silent *Cat and the Canary* [1927] and the Bob Hope version [1939].

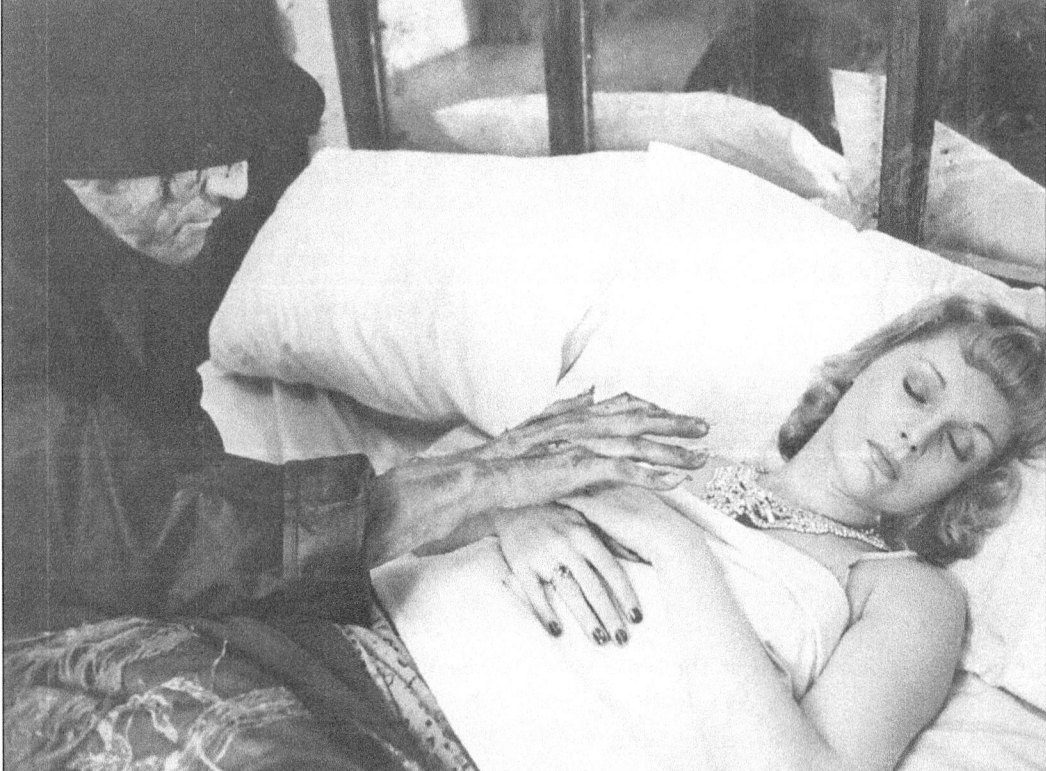

Above: The 1939 version of *The Cat and the Canary* with Paulette Goddard. Below: Gordon's 1978 version with Carol Lynley.

GORDON: I had seen the silent *Cat and the Canary* a number of times because it was one of the great classics of the silent screen; I was also familiar with the Bob Hope picture; and I knew the history of *The Cat and the Canary* in the theater. It seemed to me that this was a good time to make a new version, and try to go back a little more to the original play than the other film versions had done.

The author of *The Cat and the Canary*, John Willard, had been an actor and a newspaperman, and also listed among his occupations aviator, miner and cowboy. He had acted in films and acted in the theater, and in 1921 he wrote *The Cat and the Canary* for the stage as a one-act thriller. His wife who was an actress, Gladys Caldwell, persuaded him to turn it into a full evening's entertainment. The first production of *The Cat and the Canary* was presented by Kilbourn Gordon — no relative of mine [*laughs*] — in February 1922 at the National Theatre in New York City, and starred Florence Eldridge and Henry Hull. Florence Eldridge was the wife of Fredric March, and Henry Hull of course later became best-known for playing the title role in *WereWolf of London* [1935].

Q: One old article about Willard says he dreamed up the story for *Cat and the Canary* during World War I while he was in an airplane, flying a mission. Then he forgot about it, but three years later it came back to him and he started writing it as a play.

GORDON: When it opened on Broadway, it was such a huge success that they had to make the traffic in the area of the theater one-way, because of the crowds flocking to get seats. Alexander Woollcott, in his review in *The New York Times*, warned that *The Cat and the Canary* would "unsettle the innocent playgoing bystander who may be expected, from time to time, to bite the nearest usher and run bleating up the aisle."

The international cast of Gordon's *The Cat and the Canary*: standing, Daniel Massey, Michael Callan and Peter McEnery; seated, Olivia Hussey, Wendy Hiller, Carol Lynley, Beatrix Lehmann and Honor Blackman.

The critic of the *Evening Journal* advised his readers to get a hairnet before going to see the play [because it was hair-raising]. The element of fear and surprise was promoted in all the early productions of the play, and a standard program note was the following advice: "If you like this play, please tell your friends. But do not pray inform them how it ends."

The first film version of *The Cat and the Canary*, the classic Universal silent one, was produced in 1927 by Carl Laemmle and directed by Paul Leni, the famous German director, making his American film debut. The stars were Laura La Plante, who was then a big name, Creighton Hale and Arthur Edmund Carewe. It was described by *The New York Times* as "the first time that a mysterious melodrama has been lifted into the realm of art." In 1930, Universal produced a talkie version entitled *The Cat Creeps*, which was directed by Rupert Julian, who had directed Lon Chaney in *The Phantom of the Opera* [1925]. *The Cat Creeps* starred Helen Twelvetrees, Neil Hamilton and Raymond Hackett, and followed the silent screenplay closely. At the same time, Universal also produced a Spanish-language version entitled *La voluntad del muerto*, which literally translated means "The Death Will." This was directed by George Melford, with Lupita Tovar and Antonio Moreno. *The Cat Creeps* and its Spanish equivalent now seem to be lost movies, no one has been able to rediscover any prints of these pictures. We have to assume that they will never be seen again.*

Q: But we can *hear* the English-language version.

GORDON: That's right, [film collector-distributor] Raymond Rohauer had a soundtrack of *The Cat Creeps* which was taken off the original sound discs. Radley Metzger and I once listened to a tape of it. It simply proved that the sound version had followed very closely the silent Paul Leni version.

Q: People complain about today's Hollywood being remake-crazy but in 1937 Universal announced they were going to make *Cat and the Canary again*, which would have been the third version in ten years. Well, the *fourth*, counting the Spanish-language one!

GORDON: Paramount eventually acquired the remake rights from Universal and made the production with Bob Hope. It was directed by Elliott Nugent, who earlier in his career had several times played the leading role himself on the stage. The screenplay of the Bob Hope version was substantially altered in order to make it a vehicle for Hope, who was just then becoming a very popular Hollywood star. Paulette Goddard co-starred with him in this version. *The New York Times* described it as "more hare-brained and more hair-raising than ever."

Q: Unlike the play and earlier movies, the Bob Hope one was set in the bayou near New Orleans.

GORDON: The silent *Cat and the Canary* is a far more artistic venture than the Bob Hope version, it really is a great classic. The Bob Hope one is wonderful entertainment because of Hope and because of the rest of the cast but it's not a very literal translation of the original play. When we decided in 1976 to make a new version, the first one in color, and to produce it in England, we tried to go back more to the original play, rather than to think of it in terms of a remake of any of the earlier film versions.

In addition to its run on Broadway, *Cat and the Canary* was performed on the stage *many*, many times, and was always a great success. It was revived several times during the '30s and '40s; as late as 1965 it was on an off-Broadway stage called Stage Three where I saw it for the first time in the theater. In England it had played since 1922; in 1959, there was even an English live television production with Bob Monkhouse. And so, one way or another, *The Cat and the Canary* has lived for all these years and remained a classic standby of that kind of entertainment.

Q: To me, yours *does* feel more like a play than the silent version and the Bob Hope. Mostly it's the acting that makes me think that.

GORDON: We were going after that, thinking it would give it a sort of "historical importance." And we cast it accordingly. I think it works. Incidentally, Margot Grahame was once in a stage production of *Cat and the Canary*. She was an actress who was very successful in England in the theater and in the cinema; I remember her best from *The Soldier and the Lady* [1937] and *Crime Over London* [1936]. When we were shooting our *Cat and the Canary*, I got in touch

---

* *Boo* (Universal, 1932), a *Fractured Flickers*-like comedy short, features clips from *Nosferatu* (1922), *Frankenstein* (1931) and, yes, *The Cat Creeps*. The approximately 1m:40s of *The Cat Creeps* seen in *Boo* is presumably all the footage still in existence.

with her by telephone and asked her if she would like to one day come down to our location and watch us shooting our version, and perhaps pose for some publicity photographs with our actors. It was all arranged, but the day before she was supposed to visit, she called back to say she was in bed with the flu and couldn't make it. So I never actually got to meet her.

Q: Radley Metzger, an American, was your director.

GORDON: Radley and I had been friends for many years. I first met him in the early '60s when he was, among other things, directing a lot of English-dubbed versions of foreign-language films. I had imported a 1959 German film, *Verbrechen nach Schulschluß* [Crime After School], from the Berlin Film Festival and wanted to dub it into English, and Radley signed on to direct the English-dubbed version [*The Young Go Wild*]. We became good friends, and I used to talk to him often about the possibility that one day we might do something together. When I decided that I would like to make *The Cat and the Canary*, I mentioned it to him and he reacted very enthusiastically, and so we came to the conclusion that this was a good time to do something together, especially as he was interested also in writing the screenplay as well as directing.

Q: Radley is a big fan of old movies and, I *assume*, a fan of horror pictures.

GORDON: Yes, horror movies and "old" movies, and he certainly was familiar with the whole history of *The Cat and the Canary*, both on the stage and on the screen. We took a look at the silent version and the Bob Hope version — not so much from the standpoint of copying anything from them, but just to get an idea of how it was treated at that time. But of course, as we were going to make our picture in England, it wasn't really applicable to what we were doing.

Q: You moved the setting of the story to England. I guess you *had* to, because you were going to shoot it there and have a lot of English actors in it.

Gordon (right) consults with director Radley Metzger in this candid shot.

GORDON: Yes. The type of story that it was, it could take place anywhere in the world — it didn't necessarily have to have a New York setting. The Bob Hope version had already proved that, by moving the setting to the Louisiana bayou.

Q: An old-fashioned, practically bloodless "reading of the will" horror movie…you had faith that this would go over in the late '70s?

GORDON: I thought it would go over very well, as I was influenced by the success of the Agatha Christie pictures. I felt that if we also put together an interesting cast, for which certainly there was plenty of room in the type of script that it was, it would interest the public *and* it would be something different that would appeal to horror fans as well as to mystery fans, and have a wider appeal than some of the other horror or science fiction pictures that I've been involved in.

Q: I assume you got a copy of the original play and went through that.

GORDON: Radley certainly got a copy of it because we did in fact acquire the property on the basis of planning a film version of the original play.

Q: Getting the rights to an old property can often be a very tangled procedure. How well — or how badly — did it go for you?

GORDON: When I found out that the rights were controlled by Raymond Rohauer, it was not a complicated thing, because I knew Raymond, I had made some overseas distribution deals for him on some of the pictures he owned when I was concentrating on my Gordon Films Inc. activities. He was delighted with the idea that we were interested, and was very cooperative in arranging the deal.

Q: As I mentioned earlier, many fans nowadays talk about "the good old days" when Hollywood wasn't so remake-happy. But I look at three *Cat and the Canary*s in 13 years [1927-39], and you and I could think of dozens of other examples, and I wonder if there ever really *were* any such days!

GORDON: Hollywood in the early and mid-30s remade a lot of films that had been great silent pictures, or even *not*-so-great silent pictures [*laughs*], simply because the new medium of sound gave them a whole new lease on life. Also, the older titles very often were well-known in the public's mind and that gave them an added selling factor.

Q: How many times, apart from *Cat and the Canary*, did you ever consider remaking an oldie?

GORDON: *Cat and the Canary* was *not* the only time I ever thought of remaking an older picture. For instance, in the 1950s when I made my two pictures with Boris Karloff, I was very much interested in the possibility of remaking a Karloff film which at that time was considered a lost movie, *The Ghoul* [1933]. But the rights were not available at the time. And while Karloff and I were making *The Haunted Strangler* [1958] we had discussed the possibility of doing what I suppose *could* be called a remake, but actually a new version of Bram Stoker's *Dracula*, with Karloff in the leading role. That's something that he would have been very keen on, and that MGM was very interested in. But it turned out that the rights were not yet available because the property was not in the public domain; it was still controlled by Universal, who were about to make a deal with Hammer Films to remake it in England as *Horror of Dracula* [1958].

Another occasion when I was contemplating a remake was when I was working with Bryant Haliday, with whom I made *Devil Doll* [1964] and *Curse of the Voodoo* [1965]. Bryant had shown particular interest in the possibility of remaking *The Most Dangerous Game*, which he thought would be an ideal vehicle for himself. He wanted to play the count, the role played by Leslie Banks in the original 1932 movie. I liked that idea very much and I spent some time researching the remake rights, but it turned out they were so complicated, between various parties who owned certain rights and not other rights, that it was almost impossible to unscramble the whole thing. So we could never move ahead with that idea.

Q: *Cat and the Canary* presented none of those problems.

GORDON: *The Cat and the Canary* presented no problems at *all*, because Raymond Rohauer clearly had the rights and in fact was even in a position to guarantee that during the first three years of the distribution of our film, the Bob Hope version would not be reissued or play on television. He co-owned that version, and it couldn't be re-released without his approval.

Q: Carol Lynley and Michael Callan, both Americans, are in the cast of your *Cat and the Canary*. Were either of them in England at the time, or did you have to bring them over from the U.S.?

GORDON: We brought them both over from the United States. Carol Lynley had been in England a number of times; she was in Otto Preminger's film *Bunny Lake Is Missing* [1965] with Laurence Olivier, and she had also made a low-budget horror film in England, *The Shuttered Room* [1967]. She was popular in England and she liked working there, and she enjoyed the idea of going back to London to do this film.

Q: Bringing in two Americans to play the top parts — was that with the American market in mind?

GORDON: It was partly for the American market, and partly to give the cast an international feel, as had been done with the Agatha Christie films, where various actors from different countries all came together. We thought it would make an interesting film. We were in fact going to have a third player from Hollywood because we had decided that the role of Charlie Wilder could very well be played by Horst Buchholz, a popular international actor of German origin. I'd met him in the 1950s, at a Berlin film festival, when he was being touted as Germany's answer to James Dean. Buchholz was now living in Hollywood, and we thought he'd be very good in the Charlie Wilder role.

Q: His name comes up in early announcements of the movie in the various trade papers.

GORDON: We had a very unhappy experience with that: I worked out a deal with Buchholz and his agent, and it was all set, and Radley and I were already in England working on pre-production of the film, and the other cast members were standing by. Buchholz

Crosby (Hiller) and Mrs. Pleasant (Lehmann) retrieve the filmed reading-of-the-will from cold storage. The discovery of the living moth inside the long-sealed crate is the one moment in the '78 *Cat* "borrowed" from the silent version.

was scheduled to fly in from Hollywood more or less at the last minute, just in time for the start of production. Suddenly he reneged on the contract we had made, claiming that he had forgotten about an option that had been granted to a German theatrical producer who wanted to utilize his services in a play in Germany. I don't know what the *real* reason for his backing-out was —

Q: But you don't think a play was the real reason.

GORDON: No, I don't believe it, and I don't find that there was ever any evidence that he went to Germany to do a play at that time.

Q: How did you find out he was reneging? Did "his people" call "your people" or did he tell you himself?

GORDON: He called me on the phone and I talked to him personally and he gave me this excuse about the German play. I didn't get into an argument with him or anything, and I never spoke to him again. By backing out at the last moment, he left us in a very difficult situation, and my attorneys in London advised us that we had every right to file a suit against him, sue him for damages. We decided, however, that it wasn't worth the time and effort. We felt that it would be easier — even though it was very difficult! — to replace him. However, there wasn't time to get another actor from Hollywood. We had already signed Peter McEnery for one of the roles in the film, and we switched McEnery to the part that Horst Buchholz would have played because McEnery was quite well-suited for it. Then my casting director came up with Daniel Massey to take over McEnery's original role, and that put everything back on track.

Q: Your casting director was Rose Tobias Shaw, who had worked with you a couple of times in the past.

GORDON: Rose Tobias Shaw was a wonderful casting director. She had worked in New York for many years for David Susskind, and then she went to London where she married an English actor, Maxwell Shaw, and established herself as a casting director. I had met her quite early on in my career and we became close friends and she did several pictures for me. When we came to the casting of *The Cat and the Canary*, I immediately turned to her and asked for her help. She was very happy to go along with it.

Q: Was she American or English?

GORDON: She was American. Well, actually, she was from Europe, but she had grown up and lived in America for a great deal of her life and was, I believe, an American citizen.

Q: What was your "dream cast" for this movie? At the outset, who all did you have your sights set on?

GORDON: We had difficulty, actually, deciding which way to go, because the problem in *The Cat and the Canary* is that there is no single starring role that would necessarily attract an actor who wasn't interested in doing anything *except* being the lead in his own film. So we cast it like the Agatha Christie films, with what were (to some extent) cameo roles that actors would be happy to play. The first problem of casting was to get someone to play the lawyer, Crosby, who for a while is really the focal point of the story. In the original play and all the previous films, it was a man's role.

Q: Tully Marshall in '27, Lawrence Grant in '30, George Zucco in '39.

GORDON: We tried for several people; for instance, we approached James Mason to play Crosby and he wasn't really interested unless he could rewrite the whole screenplay. Our immediate reaction was that we were not interested in any such situation. Then we approached several other people, with whom we had different problems. At that point Rose Shaw came up with the idea, "Since you're modernizing the story to some extent anyway, to give it a new approach, why not make Crosby a woman's role?" She said that she had somebody in mind if we would consider doing that, someone she thought would be eminently suitable for it. And the person she had in mind was Wendy Hiller, the wonderful actress —

Q: *Dame* Wendy Hiller. *Please*!

GORDON: [*laughs*] *Dame* Wendy Hiller, whom I had admired ever since I originally saw her in *Pygmalion* [1938] with Leslie Howard. She was a wonderful choice for the part. We agreed to that very quickly and Rose was able to arrange a deal with Wendy Hiller's agent.

We then had the problem of casting the role of Cyrus West, which is of course *truly* a cameo role; we would only need the actor for one or two days. We approached Robert Morley, who was not interested in doing it. We also approached Alastair Sim, who probably *would* have been willing to do it but unfortunately was quite ill at the time. In fact, he died [in August 1976] even before the film was finished and released.

I have to give Rose Shaw credit for the fact that she came up with the suggestion of Wilfrid Hyde-White, who turned out to be a perfect choice to play the role. Wilfrid had been in a lot of films and a lot of stage plays and, at the time when we were planning our movie, was touring in a revival of an Oscar Wilde play; it was going around England and eventually was to come to London's West End. Rose got in touch with his agent and it was arranged for Radley and myself to meet him at the theater in Guildford, in Surrey, where he was currently appearing in the play. We went to see him and immediately took a great liking to him; I mean, you couldn't help but like him, he was such a wonderful personality. We talked with him before the play, during the intermission and after the end of the performance, in his dressing room. He had read the *Cat and the Canary* script — in fact, he had read the *whole* script, not just his role — and he was quite enthusiastic about doing it.

But there were a few problems that had to be worked out. For one thing, we could really only rely on using Wilfrid for one day, because of his theatrical commitments. The day could not be one on which he had a matinee performance because certainly he was not going to miss a performance of his play in order to make the film. We also had to guarantee that we would get him back to the theater in time for him to do the evening performance. But we were able to schedule all of those things, and it worked out extremely well.

Q: And he had a lot of dialogue in *Cat and the Canary*.

GORDON: It *was* a lot of dialogue for one day, and when we were with him backstage at the theater in Guildford, as we were talking about it and he was looking at the script, he said to us, "This is an awful lot of dialogue. You surely don't expect me to learn it all by heart and do it in one day. I presume that you're going to have cue cards on the set for me to read." I was a little taken aback, because cue cards were really the province of television rather than theatrical movies, and I had never even contemplated it. (I suppose I hadn't thought it out properly.) But on the spur of the moment, both Radley and I agreed that we would have cue cards available. We did have cue cards made, but when he came for his one day's shooting, he never asked for them; he had learned his whole role and he was word-perfect. He not only sailed through it absolutely smoothly with no problem whatsoever, but he finished *ahead* of time, and there was no problem about getting him back to the theater where he was doing his play. He even brought his own lunch with

No way to treat a lady — not even a lady lawyer (Hiller).

him [*laughs*], which wasn't necessary, because naturally we had catering facilities for all of the actors. But he brought his own lunch and he was just an absolute pleasure to work with.

I remember particularly, when we were speaking backstage at the Guildford theater, that Wilfrid said his film career had really started when he was given a very small role in the Charles Laughton film *Rembrandt* [1936]. He had been on the stage up to that time and he considered *Rembrandt* the beginning of his film career…until I reminded him that that same year he had in fact already made a sort of British quota second feature called *The Scarab Murder Case* [1936] in which he played Philo Vance the detective, and that *that* should really count as his first film rather than *Rembrandt*. He was very taken aback when he heard me say that, and he then looked at me and made a remark which I discovered later was a sort of trademark saying of his: He looked at me and he said, "*You're a very dangerous man, Mr. Gordon.*" [*Laughs*] And that was not the *last* time he said that to me! But we got along very well, and of course on the day he came to the set he bonded immediately with Wendy Hiller, because they had known each other for many years through their stage work. He also knew Beatrix Lehmann. They were three "deans" of the British stage, and got along very well together.

Q: Lehmann is in his *Cat and the Canary* scene with him, playing the housekeeper Mrs. Pleasant.

GORDON: Beatrix Lehmann came to the role rather late in our casting. We had first thought of a number of other people, because Beatrix Lehmann was not really considered a movie actress as much as a stage actress. She had been in the theater for many years and was quite a big star on the London stage. One idea for which Radley Metzger certainly deserves the credit was to try and get Elisabeth Bergner to play the role of Mrs. Pleasant. Rose Shaw arranged for Radley and me to visit with her at her apartment, and we had a very nice meeting with her, but she declined to do it. After reading the script and discussing it with us, she felt that it was not something that she could handle, that it was not in her style.

Q: Well, at least you got to meet her.

GORDON: Elisabeth Bergner was absolutely charming and, yes, for me it *was* a very nice experience to meet her in person after having seen her in so many films over so many years. She was such an important star, not only in England but all over the world.

Getting back to filling the role of Mrs. Pleasant: I had the idea that we might use Flora Robson, who I thought would be extremely good casting. She had, at one time or another, played Mrs. Danvers in *Rebecca* on the stage, so she could conjure up the kind of personality that we needed. But unfortunately she was not in good health. The same thing happened when we approached Cathleen Nesbitt, whom you'll remember from *So Long at the Fair* [1950]. I think the problem was that the role, by necessity, had to be played by someone who was quite old, and the actresses whom we approached were all at a stage in their lives where they either weren't really interested, or they…

Q: And/or they had all the problems *associated* with being that old.

GORDON: Exactly. But when we went to see Beatrix Lehmann, which was also arranged by Rose Shaw, she rather liked the idea, because she had not done very much film work and she thought it would make a *pleasant* (if you'll pardon the pun) change. She, however,

A stunt double took Hiller's place for the shot where Crosby's body falls out of the cupboard.

imposed one condition upon us: She had a dog that had to come to the location with her. When I saw the dog on the day that we went to visit her at her apartment, the first thing that came into my mind was, "My God, here's the Hound of the Baskervilles!" [*Laughs*] It was *that* kind of an animal. She said she would be happy to do the film but she had to have the right to bring this huge dog down to the location with her, and take care of it, because she was not going to leave it alone for a whole day at a time at her apartment.

Q: *You* guys had to take care of the dog.

GORDON: *We* had to take care of it, or give *her* time to take care of it. In the end, she went for long walks with it, around the location, when she wasn't working on the set. It all worked out very well, and I thought she was extremely effective in the role.

Q: Being one of the oldest people in the cast, she was the first to pass away afterwards.

GORDON: Yes, she died a year or two after. Again, she and Wendy Hiller and Wilfrid Hyde-White got along very well, and that helped to create a friendly atmosphere on the set.

Q: Who came up with the idea of having the late Cyrus West read aloud his own will via recorded film and sound?

GORDON: Radley and I probably came up with it together; if it was *one* of us, then I would say he should have the credit for it. We wanted to give our *Cat and the Canary* a few modern touches, to make the story more accessible to younger audiences, and we thought this would be an interesting gimmick. To my knowledge it had only ever been used once before on the screen, and that was in the George Arliss film *The Last Gentleman* [1934], in which he had himself photographed reading his will to his heirs after his death. I remembered that, I think Radley remembered it also, and we thought it would be a good idea to incorporate it into our story.

Q: I like the way Beatrix Lehmann is in the reading-of-the-will film-within-a-film with Wilfrid Hyde-White and then also walking behind the screen when the film is projected for the heirs. That must have taken some split-second timing.

GORDON: That was entirely Radley's idea, I give him full credit for it, and I think he staged it brilliantly. It's really one of the highlights of the movie.

Q: Did it require a lot of takes?

GORDON: No it didn't, as a matter of fact. It took a number of *rehearsals*, but it didn't require a lot of takes.

Q: Where was *Cat and the Canary* shot?

GORDON: Our associate producer Ray Corbett also acted as a sort of production manager, and as we were getting ready, he scouted around for a suitable location where we could shoot the entire film. We had decided that we didn't want to do it in a studio, we wanted to find a country house somewhere in England that could be used as a base of operations as well as for the actual shooting. Ray came up with the location that we eventually used, Pyrford Court, the ancestral home of Lord Iveagh of the Guinness Trust. It had been used once before for filming certain sequences in *The Omen* [1976] with Gregory Peck. We went down and took a look at it, and immediately decided that it was ideal for our purposes. It was a *huge*, rambling house, with all kinds of rooms of different shapes and sizes, on more than one level, including rooms underground and strange passageways — I don't know *what* kind of an existence the previous owner lived there [*laughs*]! It was large enough also to accommodate dressing rooms and all the other facilities that we needed; and outside on the grounds, there were formal gardens and acres of woodland. So we based the entire production there. It was in Surrey, which is not far from London, and was within the required 30-mile limit of London that enabled all of the actors, and in fact *all* the personnel connected with the film, to go home at night, and we did not have to put them up in hotels.

Q: Where did you stay during the making of the picture?

GORDON: I stayed at an apartment in London, and I went to the location every day. Because Radley was very busy at night preparing the next day's shooting and so on, he opted, for a while at least, to stay at a hotel nearer to the location. Everybody else went home at night. On several occasions, my driver and I picked up people like Edward Fox and Olivia Hussey and drove them out to the location.

Q: So actor-wise you only got stuck with hotel bills for Michael Callan and Carol Lynley.

GORDON: Yes, they of course had to be accommodated. That was always a part of any contract for artists coming from America or anywhere else overseas.

Q: So the house we see from the outside is Pyrford Court and the interiors were shot there too.

GORDON: Yes. It's one of the rare occasions in my life when I shot films on location where the outside and the inside were one and the same place. All credit for finding that place to Ray Corbett. I had worked with Ray on several pictures before. He was a very, very experienced man who had been a production manager, also a first assistant director, and graduated to associate producer, and he was very helpful with the whole thing.

Q: Was the house furnished and "good to go" when you got there, or did you have to set-decorate it?

GORDON: The furnishings had been sold at public auction several years earlier, so yes, we had to set-decorate it. The house itself was in fairly good shape because at the time the owners' solicitors were trying to sell it.

Q: What time of year were you working there?

GORDON: We were shooting in the winter, and it was very cold. Everybody was sort of huddling around space heaters in the library and trying to keep warm in between shooting.

Q: Even *in* the house, it was cold?

GORDON: Yes, because it wasn't properly heated. Of course, the lights from the filming helped to warm it up, but it was not the most comfortable location in the world.

Q: Between all the white walls in the house, and all the light, this has to be one of the *brightest* horror movies I've seen. Especially compared to the silent *Cat and the Canary* which is so dark you'd think it was made for an audience of bats!

GORDON: That was Radley's concept and I think it worked well. We didn't want it to be yet another "spooky old country house horror film" where everything takes place in the middle of the night. That was too old-fashioned, I think that idea had sort of rather gone out of style by then.

Q: I'm assuming, with this cast, that *Cat and the Canary* had to be one of your bigger-budgeted pictures.

GORDON: It *was* a bigger-budgeted picture than most of my films, yes. The shooting schedule was actually four to five weeks, but because of the nature of the story and the casting, not everybody had to work for

It's the ultimate "bad heir day" as Annabelle struggles in the grip of the Cat.

the entire period. Wilfrid Hyde-White of course did his entire role in one day; Wendy Hiller was with us for two weeks; Edward Fox was with us for several days, spread out over the period of four weeks, and so on. It was all very carefully planned, and it came in on schedule and on budget.

Q: More days in the schedule and more money in the budget — does that mean bigger or smaller headaches for the producer?

GORDON: Usually it means bigger headaches, and I would say that was true also in this case.

Q: Let's go down the castlist, alphabetically, as they're listed in the on-screen credits: Honor Blackman as Susan Sillsby?

GORDON: She was very pleasant to work with, she was a lot of fun. She had a great sense of humor, and she helped in many instances to lighten the atmosphere when things were getting kind of heavy.

Q: Her character keeps referring to herself and Cicily [Olivia Hussey] as "roommates" in a way that makes you think they're *more* than roommates. Where did that come from?

GORDON: It came from the script, it was something that Radley wrote into the script. It wasn't meant to be overt, it was just something that could add a little extra frisson to the story.

Q: Michael Callan as Paul Jones?

GORDON: Michael was very, very nice, I had no criticism of him. I remember seeing him on the Broadway stage in the original production of *West Side Story* [in the late 1950s]. With all of the different kinds of movies he'd made, and all the different Hollywood studios he'd worked in, he was certainly experienced enough to be able to handle any situation. He and Carol Lynley got along very well together. He was a delightful star with charm to spare. I remained in touch with him after *Cat and the Canary* and visited with him and his wife in Hollywood. It was nice to read in a recent magazine article that he still remains active. Unfortunately, I never had another project that would have suited him.

Q: The male leads in other movie versions of *Cat and the Canary* were very un-heroic heroes. Callan's is more conventional. Did Radley think the comic "brave coward" was also a thing of the past?

GORDON: Our picture did show Paul [Callan's character] as being rather comic at the beginning, and then as he warmed up to the Carol Lynley character, he took on more heroic proportions.

Q: Edward Fox as Hendricks?

GORDON: He was also very cooperative and very helpful. I think he fitted in with everybody else extremely well. He rather enjoyed doing the role, and I think it comes through on the screen. He was a good name to add to the picture.

Q: Wendy Hiller as Lawyer Crosby?

GORDON: It was very enjoyable working with her for two weeks. At the beginning I was a little bit worried: First of all, at that point in her career, she hadn't made so many films, she was more of a stage actress. She was also used to being in major studio productions. In short, when I considered her background and the fact that she was Dame Wendy Hiller, I thought that the experience of working on an independent production, under what by her standards had to be considered rather primitive conditions, might create problems for us. But, as so often happens when you're dealing with *real* professionals as opposed to newcomers, she turned out to be one of the most cooperative and helpful of all the people in the cast, and she was a real joy. She got on extremely well with Radley. It was really a pleasure to work with her.

Q: Olivia Hussey as Cicily Young?

GORDON: She was full of fun. She and Honor Blackman got along very well together, they very much helped to lighten up the atmosphere at times.

Q: Why did the atmosphere need lightening up? Just the sheer amount of work that had to be done in x-number of weeks?

GORDON: Yes, the sheer amount, and the difficult conditions of the temperature, and the facilities not always being exactly what one might have hoped for.

People having to double-up with dressing rooms, and share bathroom facilities, and —

Q: Walking Beatrix Lehmann's dog [*laughs*]. Did *you* end up walking the dog?

GORDON: No, I never did. But I think Ray Corbett did, on several occasions. But it wasn't an easy picture to shoot because of the conditions under which it was made.

Q: Beatrix Lehmann as Mrs. Pleasant?

GORDON: She was well-known as a stage actress. She kept very much to herself; I think she may have felt a little bit out of place in such a situation. But she and Wendy Hiller of course got along very well together and had known each other for many years.

Q: Carol Lynley as Annabelle West?

GORDON: Carol was very cooperative, and had had experience in making low-budget movies as well as major studio pictures. She'd had experience working in England and she enjoyed the whole thing. We had no problems with her whatsoever.

Q: And Wilfrid Hyde-White you liked also. Well, that's great, you had no problems with anybody in the whole cast….No, wait, I've got two more: Daniel Massey and Peter McEnery.

GORDON: The experience that I had with Daniel Massey and Peter McEnery was, shall we say, not as happy as with the other players in the film.

Q: Or even the dog!

GORDON: [*laughs*] As I mentioned earlier, we had signed Peter McEnery to play the part of Harry Blythe, the part that was eventually played by Daniel Massey. Peter McEnery instead played Charlie Wilder. McEnery was a very fine actor and he had done some wonderful things on the stage in England. I think the problem with him was that he had had at one time the expectation of becoming a sort of young matinee idol in British films, and it never quite worked out that way, he never achieved the kind of "romantic young leading man" roles that he hoped for. At the time when we made *The Cat and the Canary*, he was already past the age when he could have any expectations of having that kind of a career, and so he was a little bit bitter about his experiences in the past with films. I felt that he took an attitude that he was doing us a favor by appearing in our kind of film, and we didn't really appreciate that. He also didn't get along well with some of the other people in the cast.

There was one incident where we were shooting the dining room scene, which required practically every

Daniel Massey's sour look is unchanged by the cheeriness of Gordon and writer-director Metzger.

member of the cast to be on the set at the same time. It was a very difficult scene to shoot, Radley was handling it beautifully, and we were just about ready with the lighting of a particularly important shot. A few more minutes were needed to get things in place, and as everybody was waiting on the set for the word *go*, Peter McEnery suddenly looked at his watch and announced in a very loud voice, "It's lunchtime. I'll be back after lunch," and walked off the set. I will always remember the look of amazement on the face of Wendy Hiller, because if ever there was a trouper, Wendy Hiller was one. And she said in an equally loud voice, "I think that is one of the most obscene gestures I've encountered in my career." And I must say, I agreed with her, and I think so did everybody else.

Q: Did McEnery hear her say that?

GORDON: McEnery *must* have heard her make that statement.

Q: And Daniel Massey?

GORDON: Daniel Massey, who came from a very notable stage and screen family, was the other one who sort of took an attitude that he was doing us a favor by appearing in this film, and always made us feel as though he didn't take it seriously, because he thought it was something that was really sort of beneath him. Just like Wendy Hiller, Wilfrid Hyde-White and Beatrix Lehmann bonded so beautifully, *he* decided to bond with Peter McEnery and between the two of them, they did give us some troublesome moments. Also I suspected, and later found out it was true, that Massey was drinking rather heavily at times, and that didn't help the situation.

Q: I haven't seen a lot of Daniel Massey in movies, but I've never seen one where he looks and sounds more like his father than *Cat and the Canary*.

GORDON: Yes, as he got older, he more and more resembled Raymond Massey. Of course he had one big success in Hollywood when he played the role of Noël Coward in the Julie Andrews film *Star!* [1968].

Q: In real life he was the godson of Noël Coward. And he made his film debut playing Coward's son in *In Which We Serve* [1942].

GORDON: *Star!* was a failure at the box office, but he was nominated for a Best Supporting Actor Oscar.

Q: The guy who plays the Cat does a good job, with makeup by Tommy Manderson.

GORDON: Except for the scene where he's unmasked, the Cat was played by one of the standby extras we had

Daniel Massey does to Peter McEnery what Richard Gordon (and others) might have *liked* to have done to Peter McEnery. And then done to Daniel Massey!

on the set. We thought the makeup was very effective. We didn't want to go overboard; I mean, look at the Cat in the silent *Cat and the Canary*, it's really so overdone that it has a comical effect. It didn't really work. We thought that the makeup that was devised for our *Cat and the Canary* was far more realistic, and didn't look like a mask until the denouement when it's revealed who is underneath.

Q: Did you *ever* feel any temptation to include more bloodshed in order to "keep up with the Joneses" — the other horror moviemakers of the time?

GORDON: No, we didn't want to do that, we didn't want to make it look like a Hammer picture — and I don't mean to insult Hammer by that statement [*laughs*]. We wanted it to be more like *Murder on the Orient Express* or *Death on the Nile*, a picture that would appeal to people who don't normally go to see horror films. We didn't want anybody to be put off from going to see it by having it labeled as a gruesome horror film.

Q: I guess the most gruesome scene in your *Cat* is when Crosby the lawyer falls out of the secret passage with the blood-spattered bag over her head, and as the bag is removed you see a little of the mutilated face. Was that Wendy Hiller in the makeup?

GORDON: No. I did not feel that I could ask Wendy Hiller to come crashing to the floor, with her face all mutilated. That is a scene for a stunt person to do, rather than the actor or actress.

Q: Not until the end of the movie, when you find out who the Cat is, does the pre-credits sequence make sense. The pre-credits sequence improves on your second viewing of *Cat*, because now you know what it's all about. Why did you start the picture with a scene of violence like that?

GORDON: I felt that we needed something to grab the audience in the beginning because by the nature of the story, once you get underway, there has to be quite a lot of dialogue and exposition before you come to any action. In order to sort of "reassure" audiences that they were going to see something that would be in the nature of a thriller, we wanted an opening sequence that would grab everybody's attention and make them wonder, "What's all this about? We don't really understand it. What's happening?" They would keep that thought in the backs of their minds, and eventually it would all tie up together.

Q: Am I allowed to say that that's an awfully realistic-looking dead cat hanging from the tree, Mr. Gordon…?

GORDON: [*laughs*] Yes, you can certainly say it, and I'll take that as a compliment, because it *wasn't* a real cat. It was a prop cat.

Q: The *Cat and the Canary* ads don't reflect the fact that it was done with a light touch, you get the impression it's a straight mystery-horror thriller. Did you just assume, in that era of stylish Agatha Christie-type mysteries, that people would know what they were getting into?

GORDON: Yes, we felt that between the cast and the fame of the property and everything else, people would know what kind of a picture they were going to see. The picture got some very, very good reviews when it opened. *Films in Review*, which was a prestigious publication, described it as being infinitely superior to *Death on the Nile*; and there were reviews in other publications that also lauded it very highly.

Q: How would you describe the comedy in your *Cat and the Canary*? One review called it "tongue in cheek," another called it "camp."

GORDON: Well, I certainly don't think it falls into the category of camp. I think it had some rather sophisticated humor in it, which was injected by Radley when he wrote the screenplay, and I thought it was very appropriate to the personalities of the characters. I would describe it as a sophisticated comedy-thriller.

Q: And Radley was a good director for comedy in your opinion?

GORDON: Yes, I think he did a good job. He had previously not made this kind of a picture; it was his first experience at directing a picture of that scope, and with a traditional studio-type shooting and a great cast and a large unit.

Q: How well did he get along with the actors? Maybe in particular the troublemaking actors?

GORDON: He left the troublemaking actors to *me*, because he didn't have time to deal with them. I learned over the years that there's a way of dealing with all these situations. Between the two of us, we managed all right.

Q: Of all the people in *Cat and the Canary*, if you had to get stuck in an elevator with one of 'em for an hour and talk show-biz experiences, which one would it be?

GORDON: Well, if I were stuck in an elevator for an hour —

Q: I know, I know — the elevator repairman!

GORDON: [*laughs*] No, no, I was thinking that, with a feeling of mounting hysteria about *being* stuck in an elevator, I would have liked Wilfrid Hyde-White to be there, because I think he would have kept me so amused that I wouldn't have worried about what was going on around me. And also I thought Wendy Hiller was a wonderful person to be with.

Q: Did you notice Radley gravitating to anybody?

GORDON: No, Radley — rightly so, as the director — gave equal attention to everybody, in order not to create any problems. So that nobody would feel that there was favoritism involved somewhere.

Q: Your d.p., Alex Thomson, went on to bigger-budgeted pictures and a lot of award nominations. As did art director Anthony Pratt.

GORDON: Radley and I were very impressed with Alex Thomson's professionalism, and with the way he handled himself. We were very lucky to get him, because shortly after that, he moved up into a much higher echelon of filmmaking. I didn't have too much contact with Anthony Pratt. But certainly, considering the budget and the circumstances, I think he gave us a very well-designed picture.

Q: Talk about the release of *Cat and the Canary*.

GORDON: In England, the picture was handled by Gala Film Distributors, which was an independent distributor. The head of Gala was Kenneth Rive, who had been my production partner on *Devil Doll*. It opened at a theater in London, the Odeon Theatre in Kensington, and it had a very good release in England. In the United States, I discussed the possibility of distribution with several major studios, but they didn't seem to be particularly enthusiastic or want to guarantee me the kind of distribution that I would have expected from them. So Radley and I then decided to go with an independent company called Cinema Shares. We got some very nice reviews, and also a very nice spread in *Life* magazine — a full-page reproduction of the scene where the creature snatches the diamond necklace from around Annabelle's [Carol Lynley] throat. Of course, in the rest of the world *I* distributed the picture, because I had my international distribution setup through Gordon Films Inc.

Actually, the first country where *The Cat and the Canary* was released was *not* England or the United States, but Italy. I had made a deal with a distribution company in Italy, a very well-respected one, and the picture opened. And without my having been informed of this in advance, or my even knowing about it, the Italian distributor decided to sell it like an Agatha Christie film — which was fine, because we were trying to capitalize on the success of *Death on the Nile* and *Murder on the Orient Express*. But in their great enthusiasm, the Italian distributor advertised it as *being* "Agatha Christie's *The Cat and the Canary*" [*laughs*]. I still have the newspaper clippings from Rome and Milan and other cities where it was so advertised. The immediate result was that the Agatha Christie estate got in touch with the Italian company and threatened to sue them, and there was a big brouhaha about it. The Italian distributor's somewhat disingenuous defense was that our publicity material called it "infinitely superior to *Death on the Nile*," which was actually the quote about it from *Films in Review* I mentioned earlier. The resultant publicity, of course, only added to the value of the picture; I was able to cash in on the Italian newspaper stories while making my deals elsewhere. *The Cat and the Canary* became one of the top-grossing pictures of that year in Italy; in fact, I think the only picture that year which out-grossed it in Italy was *Superman* [1978].

Q: It also beat *The Deer Hunter* [1978] — and *Death on the Nile*!

GORDON: Yes! So that got it off to a very good start, and immediately created tremendous interest in France and Germany and elsewhere. I got the picture very, very widely released, all over the world. I would say that, in terms of distribution, it was by far the most successful of all of my pictures — not counting perhaps the ones that went through a major studio like MGM worldwide. When it later went to TV, the BBC telecast it a number of times, and it became a perennial favorite all over Europe.

Q: Did its success get you to thinking about other old properties?

GORDON: The success of it immediately gave me the idea that Radley and I should follow up with something else, perhaps along similar lines, while the publicity and the success of *The Cat and the Canary* was still on everybody's mind. At that time, Raymond Rohauer, from whom we'd acquired the *Cat and the Canary* remake rights, also owned the remake rights to *The Old Dark House* [1932]. That film was actually based on a J.B. Priestley novel called *Benighted*; but what everybody remembers, of course, is the great classic that James Whale directed for Universal with Boris Karloff and such a wonderful cast.

Q: Including Raymond Massey!

GORDON: Exactly. Rohauer thought that he could interest Radley and me in doing a remake of *The Old Dark House* next. But both Radley and I agreed that, while it was a very tempting proposal, and a pre-sold, famous title, the quality of the original picture was such that it would be absolutely foolish to try to attempt to copy something like that. It could only end in disaster, just as William Castle's unfortunate remake [released in 1963] ended in disaster. So we declined that offer. Then, gradually, Radley got interested in other things, and I felt it was time for me to make an up-to-date science fiction picture rather than horror and I got involved with *Inseminoid* [1981]. And so Radley and I never got around to the idea of doing another film together.

Q: It's sort of funny that you went from the old-fashioned, practically bloodless *Cat and the Canary* to your blood-and-gutsiest movie, *Inseminoid*.

GORDON: Well, that just shows you my versatility [*laughs*]!

Q: *Inseminoid* had all the gore that was expected at that time, and also a good bit of nudity.

GORDON: That's right. So all of those things combined, and the fact that I didn't want to go to work as a producer for hire for some major studio, made me decide it was time for me to give it up.

Q: In 2004, First Run Features released an "Uncut Director's Edition" DVD of *Cat and the Canary* with a good bit of extra footage.

GORDON: At the time when we finished the shooting of the film and it was being edited, we felt that there were moments when it was perhaps a little on the slow side and needed tightening up. So some footage was eliminated, and now that footage [approximately 12 minutes] has been reinstated.

Q: Was it just whittled a few seconds here and there, or can you point to any entire scenes that we haven't seen 'til now?

GORDON: No, it was mostly "a little here," "a little there." For example, there is one passage of dialogue in the reading-of-the-will scene where Wendy Hiller and Daniel Massey get involved in a discussion about a quote from Kipling, which I think you'll find very funny when you see it now.

Incidentally, in 2009, at the Walter Reade Theater at Lincoln Center here in New York, there was a series called "30 Years of First Run Features" and *The Cat and the Canary* was one of the movies they ran. It was a gorgeous print, it looked like a never-run Technicolor print — I never saw the picture look so good! After the movie, Radley Metzger went up in front of the audience and did a ten-minute Q&A.

Q: You once said that *Horror Hospital* was the most fun you ever had on a movie set. How did *Cat and the Canary* score on your "Fun to Make" scale?

GORDON: Well, it depends what you mean by "fun on a movie set." *Horror Hospital* was a tongue-in-cheek horror film to begin with, and then with people like Robin Askwith who was forever keeping everybody in stitches, it was a lot of fun making it. It was of course also a very low-budget picture, and didn't have all the heavy baggage that accompanies a bigger budget. But I would say that *Cat and the Canary* also was a fun picture to do because of the opportunity to work with such a wonderful cast.

Q: You know what just jumped into my mind? The way your brother Alex used to stock his movies with actors he admired, all the way down to bit parts and even extras. To have a lot of your favorites all around you on your own movie set must have been a thrill.

GORDON: Oh, it was wonderful. I mean, I think back to when I was perhaps 12 years old and I first saw *Pygmalion* with Wendy Hiller, and to think that I would actually get to meet her and talk to her and *be* with her…it was a marvelous experience.

INSEMINOID
1981

CREDITS

Produced by	*Richard Gordon* & *David Speechley*
Executive Producer	Peter M. Schlesinger
Presented by	Sir Run Run Shaw
Directed by	Norman J. Warren
Screenplay	Nick Maley & Gloria Maley
Photography	John Metcalfe (Color)
Editor	Peter Boyle
Assistant Editor	Chris Blunden
Music	John Scott
In Charge of Production	Ray Corbett
Casting Director	Rose Tobias Shaw
Production Designer	Hayden Pearce
Assistant Art Director	Ian Watson
Special Makeup Effects/Makeup Supervisor	Nick Maley
Makeup Chief	Sheila Thomas
Hairdresser	Ross Carver
Makeup Assistant	Derry Haws
Assistant Director	Gary White
Second Assistant Director	Adrian Rawle
Third Assistant Director	Derek Harrington
Construction Manager	Alan Board
Props Master	Brian Wells
Props Buyer	Brian Winterborn
Prop Man	Chris Jefferies
Sound Recordist	Simon Okin
Sound Editor	Jim Elderton
Boom Operator	Paul Botham
Footsteps Editor	Roy Burge
Assistant Sound Editor	Chris Reed
Sound Maintenance	John Scarlett-Davis
Dubbing Mixer	Colin Martin
Stunts Arranger	Peter Brayham
Camera Operator	Dick Pope
Focus Puller	John Simmons
Clapper Loader	Mike Metcalfe
Camera Grip	Dennis Lewis
Gaffer	George Boner
Still Photographer	Barry Peake
Video Services Supplied by	Martin Denning
Titles & Special Optical Effects	Geoff Axtell Associates
Costumes	Olinkha
Wardrobe Mistress	Veronica McAuliffe
Music Mixer	Otto Snel
Production Assistant	Lorraine Goodman
Production Accountant	Patrick Isherwood
Continuity	Alison Thorne
Lab Assistants	Robert Keen & Jez Harris

93 minutes

CAST

Robin Clarke	Mark
Jennifer Ashley	Commander Holly Mackey
Judy Geeson	Sandy
Stephanie Beacham	Kate
Stephen Grives	Gary
Barry Houghton	Karl
Rosalind Lloyd	Gail
Victoria Tennant	Barbra
Trevor Thomas	Mitch
Heather Wright	Sharon
David Baxt	Ricky
Dominic Jephcott	Dean
John Segal	Jeff
Kevin O'Shea	Corin
Robert Pugh	Roy

SYNOPSIS

The Earth spaceship *Xeno* deposits a team of archaeologists (Commander Holly Mackey, sub-commander Mark, doctor-biologist Karl, Sandy, Mitch, Gary, Sharon, Dean, Ricky, Kate, Barbra and Gail) on an inhospitable alien planet to investigate the origins — and the extinction — of a past civilization. Once an air-filled, habitable headquarters has been set up underground, the spacesuited Dean and Ricky proceed to explore vast tomb chambers complete with hieroglyphic-like wall carvings. Also in the caves are glowing crystals surrounded by an "energy force." When some of them unexpectedly explode, Dean is killed and Ricky injured.

Ricky receives medical attention but later inexplicably runs amok, donning a spacesuit and attacking everyone who stands in his way. In the caves, he knocks down Gail, damaging her spacesuit's thermal unit. Gail dies a horrible death. When Ricky menaces Kate, she shoots and kills him. There is speculation that Ricky's exposure to the crystals caused him to go wild.

In a tomb chamber, Sandy and Mitch are attacked by a fast-moving alien creature that bloodily tears Mitch apart. Sandy soon finds herself naked and supine, with the alien approaching her. As the presskit puts it, "Helpless and half-conscious she is artificially inseminated with the seed of the alien civilization."

Unaware of what has happened to Sandy, her colleagues take her to Sick Bay where Karl sedates her — and determines that she is pregnant. Sandy later goes into the same sort of trance that Ricky did; she viciously attacks and kills Barbra. As the others mobilize against Sandy, she gathers explosives and sets off a blast. Now showing her pregnancy, and abnormally strong, she fights Karl, Sharon and Holly all at once. Karl and Holly are killed. During a later skirmish with Sandy, a spacesuited Gary takes refuge in an airlock — but Sandy, who is becoming more and more inhuman and can now breathe the planet's air, enters and attacks him. She then feeds on the dying man's body. Amidst many screams, Sandy gives birth to two alien babies. Mark later finds the twin monsters and takes them to Sharon. Kate falls victim to Sandy.

Mark and Sandy have a fight to the death in a storage room, with Mark managing to wrap a length of electrical wire around her neck and strangle her. But the succession of horrors is not yet over: Mark returns to Sharon's hiding place and sees that she has been killed by one of the alien babies. He falls victim to the other.

The crew of a Space Explorer arrives to pick up the archaeological party, and finds only carnage. As they prepare to leave the planet, we see that the two babies have stowed away aboard.

RICHARD GORDON ON *INSEMINOID*

Q: For you, the story of *Inseminoid* begins with your acquaintance with director Norman J. Warren, yes?

RICHARD GORDON: In the 1970s, Norman Warren was well-known in London as a maker of low-budget movies. He had done some sex exploitation pictures and a couple of horror pictures. Naturally he and Antony Balch and I, and others like us, always got together at different functions, and Norman and I talked about the possibility that one day we would make a film together. Then one day, at my office in New York, I got a letter from him telling me that he'd come across a project which he thought was particularly interesting, which turned out to be *Inseminoid*, and that he had a potential backer in a man called Peter Schlesinger. Peter, who was in the financial and banking business, came from a family that had been living in South Africa and emigrated to the U.K. He was very much intrigued by the prospect of doing some filmmaking, and he and Norman had become very close friends. Peter was interested in helping to back *Inseminoid* if I was willing to join.

Q: The Shaw Brothers also came in on the project.

GORDON: From the late 1950s until the year 2000, it was my practice to take part in most of the film festivals and marketplaces around the world where distributors came from all over to buy and sell films from one country to another. Consequently I was on very good terms with people like the Shaw Brothers and we maintained good relationships while trading back and forth. The famous Shaw Brothers were Run Run Shaw, the head of the company, who not so long ago celebrated his hundredth birthday, and his brother Runme Shaw, who has since passed away. They were the most important producers, distributors and exhibitors in the Far East, with headquarters in Hong Kong and Singapore, and from time to time they invested in the production of independent films that were being made elsewhere, in addition to their own studio product. The Shaw Brothers and I had just generally talked about the fact that if they or I ever came across something that seemed suitable for production in England, why not try to do it together? They had just had a good success with a [Hollywood] horror picture called *Blood Beach* [1980], which Sidney Beckerman produced.

When Norman Warren came to me with the script of *Inseminoid*, I suggested that we submit the idea to the Shaw Brothers and proposed that we would share the financing and distribution 50-50. Peter Schlesinger was also keen to bring in the Shaws as partners. I proposed that I would try to get the Shaws to put up 50 percent of the production cost if Peter would arrange the rest. In addition to several long

Plans for an archaeological examination of an alien planet go way off-corpse in the sci-fi shocker *Inseminoid*, brought to us by Robin Clarke, Gordon, Jennifer Ashley, Peter Schlesinger, Norman J. Warren (standing), Stephanie Beacham and Judy Geeson (seated). To this day, Beacham calls the movie *Insecticide*.

telephone conversations with Hong Kong which (on my end) took place mostly in the middle of the night due to the different time zones, I made a few trips there to work out all the details of production, distribution and exhibition between the partners. The Shaw Brothers' studio was outside the city, probably an hour's drive by car up into the more mountainous area. It was a very large studio where they did all their production, both for theatrical distribution and for television. They took me up there and showed me the whole place and treated me very nicely. Although the

Shaws reserved the right to be present during filming and to be consulted on all important matters, they did not in fact take any active role once we started shooting. I simply kept them informed, almost on a daily basis, by telex and telephone with details of how we were proceeding.

Q: The screenwriters, Nick Maley and his wife, actress Gloria Walker, had met on one of Warren's pictures, *Satan's Slave* [1976], and subsequently married.

GORDON: The script was originally titled *Doom Seeds* and, yes, it was written by Nick and Gloria, who subsequently did the special effects for the movie. For the Maleys, *Doom Seeds* was intended to show their ability at making that kind of a picture — the special effects, the monsters and all of that. Nick had already worked in that capacity on major motion pictures such as *Star Wars* [1977], *The Empire Strikes Back* [1980] and *Superman* [1978]. When I first read their script, I thought it was perhaps a little more bloody than the movies I had done in the past, but it seemed like a good project.

Q: You've mentioned in past interviews that Ken Wiederhorn also worked on the script.

GORDON: I felt that, in various places, the dialogue in the *Doom Seeds* script sounded too British. I was on very friendly terms with Ken, who was then active in the television business in New York, and I gave the script to Ken to take a look at. He agreed that there *were* a number of places where the dialogue was too British, and that the script could be improved by Americanization of the dialogue. After consulting with the Shaws and with Peter Schlesinger, I made a deal with Ken to rewrite portions of the dialogue and Americanize it. Just the dialogue — nothing to do with the situations.

Q: One of the most interesting things about *Inseminoid* is *where* it was shot.

The mating of horror and heroine (Geeson), one of the more shocking scenes of its type since *Rosemary's Baby* (1968).

The shooting of the insemination scene with production designer Hayden Pearce (pointing), clapper loader Mike Metcalfe (holding cut-out), Judy Geeson (on floor), camera operator Dick Pope and focus puller John Simmons.

GORDON: After the first step of lining up the financial arrangements between the Shaw Brothers and Peter, which was not too difficult, the second step was to determine where and how to shoot the film. Ray Corbett, with whom I had worked on a couple of other films [*Horror Hospital*, 1973, and *The Cat and the Canary*, 1978], was very well known in England as a production manager and location scout for these sort of pictures, and he came up with the idea of doing it in Chislehurst Caves — 22 miles of caves that ran under the Kent countryside. A few TV episodes and commercials had been shot there in the past, ours was the first motion picture to be completed there.

Q: Shooting a movie in a cave…how did that idea sound to you, when it was first broached?

GORDON: When it was first broached, I didn't realize how complicated it was going to be. I was communicating with them from New York, getting information, and I thought shooting in the caves sounded like a very good idea; I liked the fact that we wouldn't have to go into a major studio. Working at a studio would have been *much* more expensive than renting facilities…[*laughs*]…underground!

I wanted to come to England and take a look at the caves, and discuss the situation, and it was arranged for Harold Shaw, the son of Runme Shaw, to be there at the same time. We all met in London, and from there we went to the caves. Ray Corbett showed us exactly how he visualized sets being built in the caves, and told us he felt that the whole picture could be shot there, minus a few studio shots that could be added later. Ray said he thought shooting in the caves would be something unusual and very "different," and he recommended it highly.

Q: Was this place a tourist attraction?

GORDON: It had been a tourist attraction for *years*, yes, although I myself had never been there before. They weren't caves, actually, but mines, dating back *many* centuries. I went down into the caves with Harold Shaw, Norman, Ray Corbett and Peter Schlesinger, we all made an "expedition" down there [*laughs*], and after seeing the place, it seemed like a perfectly logical way to make our picture at a reasonable cost by shooting it almost in its entirety there. We naturally had to arrange with the people who were in charge of the caves, that there would be a period of four or five weeks, while we were shooting, when the public would not be allowed to enter.

Q: Once you walked through the cave entrance, how long before you got to the area where you'd be shooting? Was it right inside the entrance, or did you have to walk a ways?

GORDON: We had to walk *quite* a ways, perhaps half a mile. We needed larger areas where sets could be built, the dolly rails laid for the little train and everything. Most of the production work of that kind was undertaken by Ray Corbett and Peter Schlesinger; Peter was very much a hands-on guy who wanted to participate in everything. By the time I came to London and ready to take charge of the production itself, everything was pretty much in place. Toilet facilities were installed, and the makeup people and the girls' dressing room were set up in caravans [trailers] outside the cave entrance. I must tell you that I wish I had known in advance what the difficulties were going to be. I very much thought later, "It was crazy to do this!" [*Laughs*]

Q: Talk a little about the casting process.

GORDON: On the budget we had, we couldn't afford any big stars. Harold Shaw said, "We ought to have at least one or two American names in the picture, so that when it's distributed in the United States there's some recognition. You have connections with casting agents in Hollywood. Let's see if you can come up with some suggestions." Well, I was on very friendly terms with the Robert G. Hussong Agency, a talent agency for actors and actresses in…I suppose you might say B-movies. When I told Hussong what I was planning to do, he said he had several artists under contract who might be suitable, and he thought I should come out to Hollywood and meet with him and meet with them. So that's what we did: I went out there and took a room at a hotel, and he brought various people there to meet with me, including Jennifer Ashley and Robin Clarke and maybe half a dozen others, I don't remember their names now.

Jennifer Ashley had been in a number of Hollywood exploitation pictures, including *The Pom Pom Girls* [1976], and Robin Clarke was considered an up-and-coming…[*Pause*] If I had only known! [*Laughs*] He was considered an up-and-coming actor. Hussong was particularly anxious to be involved in production overseas, so he made very fair terms for the two of them. Some of the problems that arose later were not apparent at that time. Then my dear friend Rose Tobias Shaw came to the rescue with casting some other roles.

Q: Rose Shaw — no relation to the Shaw Brothers.

GORDON: [*laughs*] None whatsoever! Rose for instance arranged for Victoria Tennant to join the cast, and Victoria was quite pleased to do it. She was given, of course, a copy of the script in advance, and she made no comment on it whatsoever except that, yes, she was willing to do it, the money was agreed upon, and so on. But, to jump ahead for just a moment, when it came to the shooting of the scene that takes place in a toilet area, with Victoria sitting on a toilet, she refused to do it.

Q: But the scene was in the script, yes?

GORDON: Yes. I think she probably read the script and read that scene and didn't like it, and thought to herself, "I'll take care of this when the time comes" — I've experienced this with actors before. So we had some problems with that, she was difficult.

Q: What became of the Maleys' original title *Doom Seeds*?

GORDON: Talking to Norman Warren, I said, "*Doom Seeds* is hardly a title that's going to attract anybody," and Norman said that Peter Schlesinger had had a great idea for a title that he would like to submit to us. That title was *Inseminoid*. I asked, "Well, what does it *mean*?" and Norman said, "I don't *know* what it means." [*Laughs*] But it sounded good and it sounded appropriate, and the Shaw Brothers also liked the sound of it.

Q: Did the Shaws visit the set once things got underway?

If *Alien* (1979) was the first rip-roarin' outer space action picture with an actress (Sigourney Weaver) as the heroine, *Inseminoid* was the first to feature an actress (Geeson, who got special "And" billing) as the *monster*.

GORDON: Harold Shaw did come over to London a couple of times during the preparations, because he was always coming to that part of the world for the Cannes Film Festival and the MIFED Film Market in Milan, Italy, and so on. He traveled a great deal, it wasn't unusual for him. In fact, the Shaw Brothers maintained a permanent apartment in the Mayfair in London where they stayed whenever they came. The Shaws didn't give us any trouble; their attitude about the whole thing was, "We like the idea of this, it's unusual, it's different, and the budget is right. We leave the whole thing to you."

Q: Was it Norman Warren's biggest picture to date?

GORDON: I think it *was* the biggest and most important picture that he made, yes. Well, the budget was around £1,000,000, so it was also the most expensive that *I* had been involved in. And I don't think Norman had ever before worked with financiers of the scope of the Shaw Brothers. For me, it was different, I was used to dealing with those kinds of executives, so I kind of breached the middle between Norman and the Shaws. As far as I was concerned, the Shaws' main requirement was that I keep them informed almost from day to day on what was going on, by telex. We also sent the Shaw Brothers some footage, and their main comment was, "Let's have more blood." They wanted the picture to be as bloodthirsty as it could be, which in the end it turned out to *be*.

Q: Everybody who's been interviewed about *Inseminoid* talks about how damp the caves were.

GORDON: Yes, a feeling of dampness and discomfort. I must say, it was the most *un*comfortable location of any film I ever made. There was water seeping through the caves, and the dampness even affected the sets; the wood used in set-building would quickly absorb moisture and swell up. Therefore we had to get in and out of all the sets just as quickly as we could. It wasn't a healthy atmosphere. It affected everybody in the cast.

Q: It affected their health, or their attitudes?

GORDON: Their attitudes — but to some degree, their health as well. In addition to the dampness, it was cold down there, the air wasn't very good, *and*, it really was difficult for people to work down there without getting claustrophobic, and become somewhat neurotic about being buried under the ground! Nobody could work for more than a couple hours without needing to go outside to get some fresh air and daylight. Things didn't go well from the start, and that was a problem caused by being in the caves; I don't think we realized what the complications and the difficulties were going to be, and how it would get on everybody's nerves. People were arguing with each other about this and that, and it was a very difficult shoot, probably the most difficult I ever engaged in on a day-to-day basis. The Chislehurst Caves were only about 12 miles from London, so obviously we didn't have to stay in hotels there at the location, we could just go back and forth. I had a room in a hotel in the center of London, and Norman lived not far from where I was staying, so he used to pick me up every morning, and as we would ride out to the location together, we'd discuss what was going to go on that day, how to deal with problems, etc.

Q: Judy Geeson had the most demanding part in the whole picture, obviously. Did she mind doing any of the nudity or any of the gore scenes or any of the *any*thing?

GORDON: No, she was 100 percent with it. She was a particular favorite of Norman's, and of course she was well-known in England, a star name. I was very thrilled when Norman said he could get her to play the leading role. She was very happy to do it.

Q: You rolled your eyes earlier, when you first started talking about Robin Clarke.

GORDON: Robin Clarke turned out to be very difficult. I don't think he really was expecting what was required of him, and he didn't get along too well with some of the English cast members. He was argumentative, and he wanted to do things his way when Norman Warren wanted them done a different way. There were some quarrels and there were some fights. It was not altogether a happy set all the time.

Q: You mention "quarrels" *and* "fights." Are you talking about hitting-each-other fights?

GORDON: No, but Peter Schlesinger and Robin were threatening to beat each other up at one point. Peter said, "If you don't do what Richard Gordon wants you to do, I'm going to come after you" — it was *that* kind of a thing. The only reason it *didn't* escalate into a fistfight was the fact that it was broken up by Ray Corbett, our production manager. A certain amount of this tension, of course, was caused by the circumstances under which we were shooting, in the caves.

Q: There are two producers listed in the on-screen credits, you and someone named David Speechley.

GORDON: On my first trip to London in connection with *Inseminoid*, Peter Schlesinger brought along Speechley, an employee of his, whom he more or less kept on salary so that whenever he, Peter, was involved in the making of a film, Speechley would work on it on a day-to-day basis and report to Peter. I wasn't crazy about the idea of having a co-producer's name on the screen with me, but I saw no reason to object to it. So I agreed that Speechley could have co-producer credit with me, but I added, "There has to be an understanding that he's not going to interfere in my activities, and that I'm the one who's really producing this picture." So Speechley was there more or less on behalf of Peter, to keep an eye on things, and report to Peter anything and everything that was going on.

Q: How often was Peter on the set?

GORDON: Every day.

Q: So why did he need a guy to tell him what was happening on the set, if *he* was on the set?

GORDON: Well, because Peter wasn't that knowledgeable about the film business.

Q: And the Maleys? What did you think of their special effects?

GORDON: Nick and Gloria Maley were good to have on the set and they did a superb job. But we couldn't allow them to have *too* much leeway, because they wanted things done their way, I wanted things done

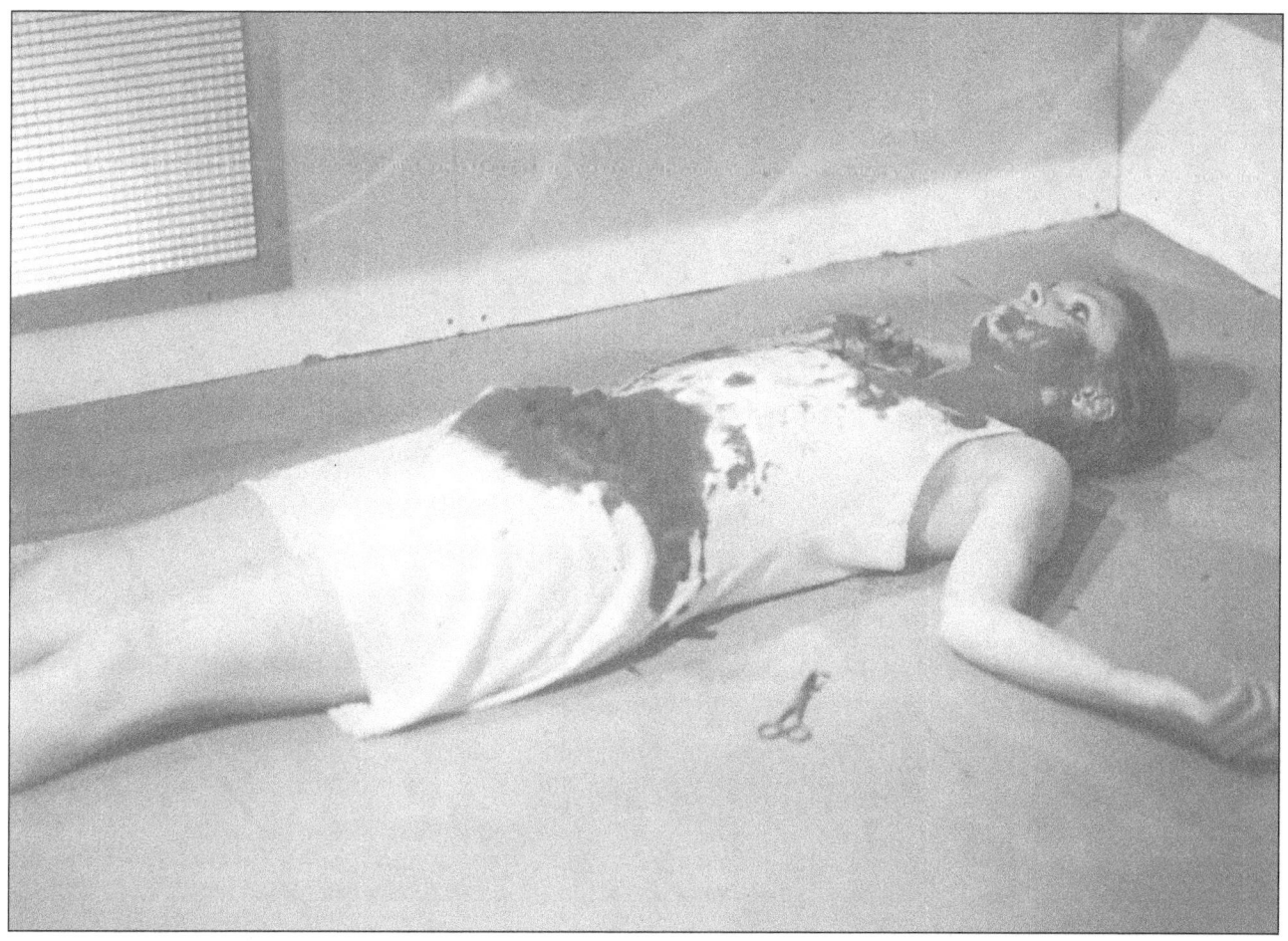

Every time the Shaw Brothers got to see rushes, their only comment was "More blood." The filmmakers complied, as in this scene with Victoria Tennant.

my way — and the Shaw Brothers wanted things done their way [*laughs*].

Q: I get the feeling, from the way you're talking, that they were the type to fiddle and fine-tune, and that if it was up to them, you'd *still* be in that cave shooting!

GORDON: [*laughs*] Oh, absolutely! But they were all right; to them, *Inseminoid* was a showcase for the kind of special effects that they could do, and they hoped that this picture would lead them to other films.

Once we were done with all the scenes that had to be shot in Chislehurst, we went into Lee International Film Studios in Wembley, a suburb of London, to shoot one or two scenes that couldn't be shot in the caves. Lee Studios was not like Shepperton or Pinewood, it was one of the smaller studios, for B-movies and so on.

Q: There's a bit of footage of spacesuited characters outdoors, walking on the planet's desolate surface.

GORDON: We sent a special unit to Malta to shoot those exteriors — Norman Warren and four others [d.p. John Metcalfe; his brother, camera operator Mike Metcalfe; second assistant director Adrian Rawle; and third assistant director-runner Derek Harrington]. I didn't go along because there was too much to do in England. They arrived in Malta late one evening, and early the following morning they took the ferry out to Gozo, a small island a few miles off the coast of Malta. After a quick drive round the island to check out possible locations, they settled on a salt quarry and started shooting. Crowd artistes [extras] from Malta played the film's characters. As the spacesuits had been made to measure to fit Judy Geeson, Stephanie Beacham, etc., the crowd artiste got the job if they fitted the spacesuit [*laughs*]. It was just a day or two's worth of shooting.

Q: When *Inseminoid* came out, there were a few reviews that compared it to 20th Century-Fox's *Alien* [1979].

Victim Holly (Jennifer Ashley) hung on a Chislehurst wall. Still a tourist attraction today, these labyrinthine caves of antiquity are supposedly haunted; the sounds of footsteps and crying children have never been satisfactorily explained.

GORDON: Yes, there were some comments made that we had "obviously" copied some things from *Alien*. There was really nothing in *Alien* that we took or used, or *wanted* to incorporate into *Inseminoid*.

Q: The idea of movie characters trapped with a monster on another planet, or in a spaceship, goes back to the 1950s — including your pal Marshall Thompson's *It! The Terror from Beyond Space* [1958].

GORDON: Of course! But at one point the Shaw Brothers were a little bit concerned that 20th Century-Fox might claim that some of **Inseminoid** was copied from their film — the Shaw Brothers were, after all, the leading theatrical distributors in the Far East, and very much clients of Fox. So at the request of Harold Shaw I arranged for one of the Fox executives, I don't remember now who it was, to screen **Inseminoid**. After he screened it, he wrote a very nice letter saying that he saw no objectionable connections between **Alien** and **Inseminoid**, and in fact wished us well with our picture.

Q: After a point in *Inseminoid*, there's no plot any more, it's just Judy Geeson killing one person after another after another — like *Friday the 13th* [1980] on another planet! How much satisfaction did you get out of making this kind of a movie?

GORDON: I got satisfaction out of making the movie and seeing that it was completed, and that it got out on its way in distribution. But it was not the sort of movie that I would have chosen for myself, if I had continued with production of pictures. I felt that *Inseminoid* went overboard on the blood, at the request of the Shaws. But we delivered to the Shaw Brothers what they wanted. And I enjoyed working with Norman Warren, and would have liked making *more* pictures with him. He's still a friend to this day.

Incidentally, when the Shaw Brothers and I were setting up the production, they wrote into the contract that I would be responsible for producing some of the *Inseminoid* publicity material that they could use both in the Far East and in the rest of the world. Harold Shaw kept telling me, "Make a very strong, very graphic poster that's really going to hit everybody right between the eyes." The Shaw Brothers' New York representative was a man called Wolfe Cohen, and when the time came, I told him I'd submit the poster to him before sending it to the Shaw Brothers. I arranged for the making of the poster, and when I presented it to Wolfe, he looked at it and he said, "This is obscene! You can't *do* this." I said, "Well, this is what Harold kept talking about, he *wanted* something that hits you in the face." Wolfe said, "I'm very much against it, and I don't think you should use it in the United States. But we'll send it out to the Shaw Brothers and we'll see what they have to say." Well, Harold Shaw was *very*

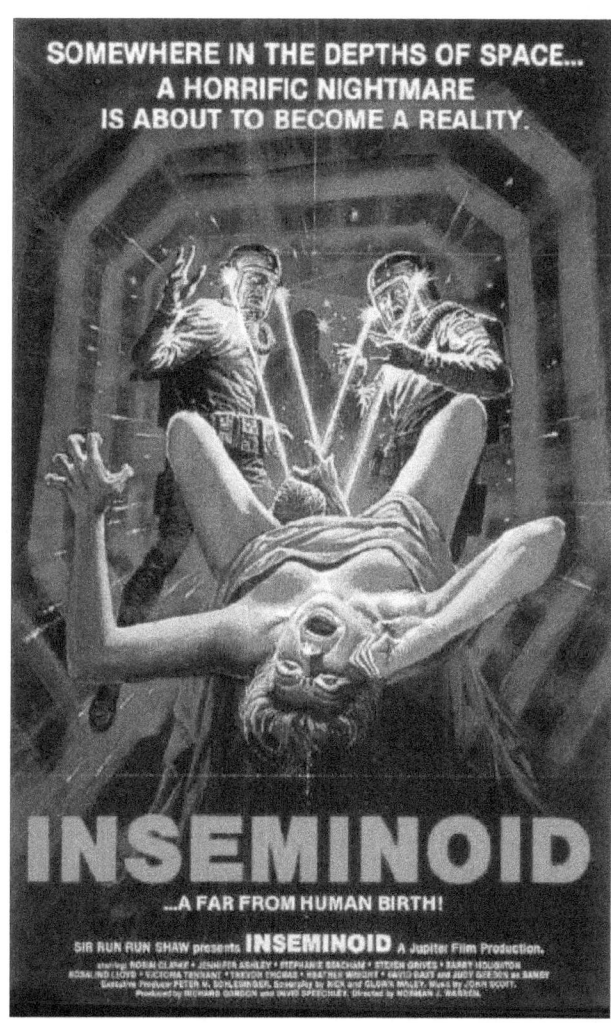

Gordon's attempt to fill the Shaw Brothers' request for a poster that would "hit everybody right between the eyes" (among other places!). Even the Shaws' representative was a bit shocked!

pleased with it [*laughs*], and they used it in different countries overseas.

Peter and Norman set up the distribution in the United Kingdom. Distribution in the United States was through independent distributors, the logical people for this kind of picture. It wasn't a picture that you could submit to a major studio and expect them to take on. The Shaws and I also jointly handled the foreign sales, and I must say we did extremely well. We showed the picture to people in the film business for the first time at the MIFED Film Market in Milan; Harold Shaw and I took an office there and set ourselves up to make deals. We sold more than 80 percent of the world territories outside of the U.S. and the U.K. *at just that one convention*. Overall — taking into account the production costs and the difficulties of making the film, and everything else — I think we turned out a very satisfactory subject.

Q: In the U.S., it was called *Horror Planet*.

GORDON: That title came in when Almi Pictures, the American distributor, had reservations about the title *Inseminoid*. First of all, they felt that it sounded too suggestive, and secondly, the word didn't really have a proper meaning. They wanted something that was more commercial to attract the public. I don't remember now whether it was Peter Schlesinger or Wolfe Cohen or I who came up with it, but somehow we came up with the title *Horror Planet* and decided that that would be a good title for the American distribution.

Q: *Inseminoid*, which is now 30 years old, is still your last picture to date.

GORDON: By the early '80s, the whole business of independent film production had changed. First of all, budgets started to go sky-high. Secondly, marketing costs began to become a major factor; the amount of money that was being spent on promoting pictures, and the new methods of distribution where pictures would open in hundreds (and eventually thousands) of theaters at the same time, made it almost impossible for an independent to compete unless he was tied up with a major studio. I was not interested in doing that. The other thing that happened was that the whole business of horror pictures changed, as what we now call the slasher movie came into prominence. Films like *Halloween* [1978] and *Friday the 13th* set the pace and

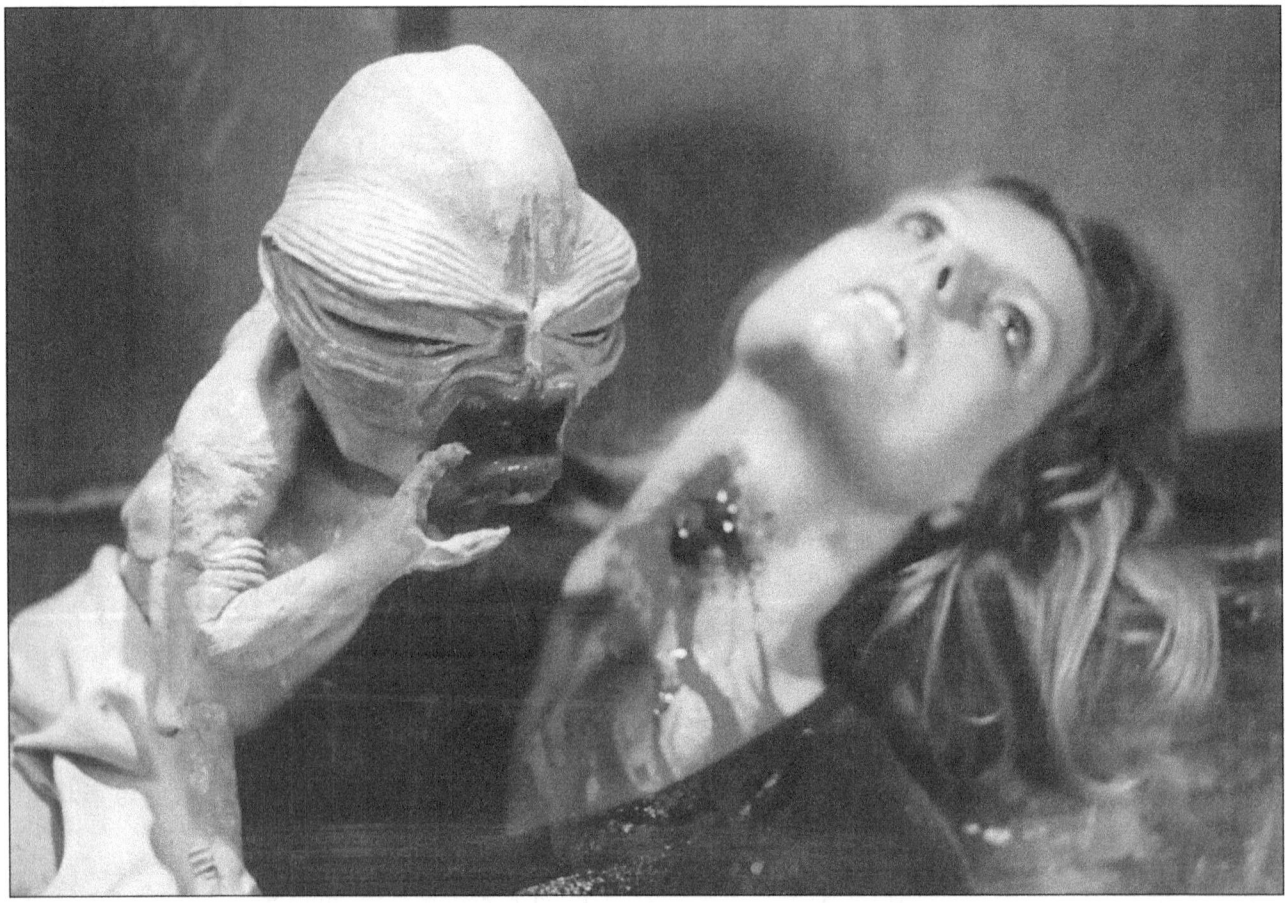

Sharon (Heather Wright) falls victim to one of the nasty newborns. In the U.S. theatrical version *Horror Planet,* the scene in which Sharon and Mark are killed was the end of the movie, the subsequent footage of the arrival of the Space Explorer having been deleted.

horror pictures became increasingly violent. It seemed like every picture tried to out-gross the last one. Not *box office* out-gross, but in *taste* out-gross every previous picture. And for me, the fun went out of it. I didn't enjoy the making of *Inseminoid* the way I should have, because it had to be overdone in order to appeal to the audiences of its time.

Q: You haven't produced any more movies since *Inseminoid* but of course Gordon Films Inc. is still chugging along, doing what it's done since 1947.

GORDON: Yes, in the distribution business. And there've been some rather special projects in the years since, like for instance my rediscovery of the short film *Return to Glennascaul* [1953].

Q: A ghost story featuring Orson Welles, made in Ireland. Prior to you re-distributing it, had it been a lost film?

GORDON: Even though it had been nominated for an Academy Award in the Best Short Subject category, it had become a *forgotten* film, something that no one had bothered with since the 1950s when Rank released it as a supporting featurette in the U.K. In 1992 I was doing business with an Irish television network, and one of the people there told me they had a print of *Return to Glennascaul* and had shown it on TV and asked me if I'd ever seen it. I said, "No, but it sounds very interesting and I'd like to take a look at it." They arranged for me to see it, and because of Welles' presence in the cast I thought this was something that would be good to show in the American market. I was then introduced to the solicitor who was handling the estate of the late Hilton Edwards, the producer of *Return to Glennascaul*, and I bought the film lock, stock and barrel from the solicitor — the negative and the world rights.

Then I contacted Peter Bogdanovich, who had been a great friend of Orson Welles, and asked him if he would be interested in looking at it. Yes, he said, he

Once a fan, always a fan: For the sheer fun of it, Gordon regularly attends classic-themed movie conventions, from the Festival of Fantastic Films in England to Syracuse's Cinefest and Pennsylvania's Monster Bash. He's seen here in Baltimore at the 1991 FANEX with lifelong friend William K. Everson, John Agar and Yvette Vickers.

was *very* interested; he'd heard about it, but he'd never seen it. I arranged to show it to him, and we talked about it, and I asked, "Peter, would you consider doing an on-camera introduction to the film? You could talk about the fact that it was made while Welles was shooting *Othello* [1952], explain the circumstances under which it was made, and so on." Peter, very generous, said, "Yes, by all means, I'd be happy to do it as a tribute to Orson Welles. In fact, you can come and shoot it in my home in California." So I went to his house with a small crew, ten people, and in 35mm I shot what you now see as the prologue for *Return to Glennascaul*. Peter couldn't have been nicer that day; he just said to the crew guys, "Be careful in my house. Don't bust up anything!" [*laughs*], and he said to me, "You're an experienced filmmaker, you know what to do. I will do it the way you want it."

Because I thought that the title *Return to Glennascaul* would be meaningless, I changed it to *Orson Welles' Ghost Story*. Its first public showing took place at the 1994 International Mystery Film Festival in Cattolica, Italy, where on opening night I introduced it from the stage. Simultaneously it was shown at several other Italian film festivals. I subsequently distributed it for a great many years.

Q: Do you *ever* intend to retire?

GORDON: In a word, no [*laughs*]. I am continuing to exploit my own pictures; I also represent certain other companies and help them with their international sales; and I'm representing companies placing *their* films here in the United States. I work with home video distributors Criterion Collection, Kino International and First Run Features, and with the cable television networks Turner Classic movies, the Sundance Channel and others.

So I have no desire to retire, and for as long as I'm able to do so, I want to continue running my business. It's something that I've always enjoyed, something I *still* enjoy, and [*laughs*]…I can see no good reason to stop!

INSEMINOID DIRECTOR NORMAN J. WARREN SALUTES RICHARD GORDON

I first met Richard Gordon in 1968 when he visited Isleworth Studios in London, where I was directing

Inseminoid director Norman J. Warren in a recent pose.

my second feature film *Loving Feeling*. Our second meeting was when Richard was in London to produce *Horror Hospital* [1973] with the uniquely talented Antony Balch. However, the most significant meeting for me was to take place several years later. Two fellows who ran a small production company in London, asked if I would consider directing a horror film entitled *Gargoyles* and went on to say that they had approached Richard about the project and that he said that if they could get me as director, he would produce the film with them. I liked the script and thought it was a subject I could do well, so we came to New York and met with Richard at his office in Columbus Circle. I must confess to pinching myself several times during the meeting, just to be sure it wasn't a dream. Here I was in the office of the man who had produced some of my all-time favorite films, including the classic *Fiend Without a Face* [1958], and we were discussing a new film which I would direct! It was a magical moment for me, and one I will never forget. Back in London, I was doing some additional work on the script, when suddenly the two fellows who ran the production company disappeared. They just vanished, and in fact I've not seen or heard anything from them to this day. So that was the end of *Gargoyles*!

Richard was still keen to do a production, so I started looking for a suitable script. Special effects makeup man Nick Maley and his wife, actress Gloria Walker, invited me to their first wedding anniversary celebration, and in a general conversation I mentioned that I was looking for a new script. A few weeks later they presented me with a first draft script that was to become *Inseminoid*. I liked the basic story very much and immediately sent the script to Richard. He also liked the story and came to London in order to secure the script and start the production process.

Working with Richard is a joy. He's a truly professional producer, and with his many years of experience in production and distribution he is able to guide a film from script to screen. I will always be grateful to him for making *Inseminoid* a reality and for giving me the opportunity to direct it.

I'm pleased to say our association has continued until the present time and over the years there have been numerous occasions when I've had the pleasure of being with Richard at various film festivals and special events where he is always warmly welcomed. Not only is he one of the nicest people you could ever wish to know, Richard Gordon is also a Cinema Legend and I'm pleased and proud to be able to call him my friend.

Norman J. Warren

INDEX

Ackerman, Forrest 48, 54
The Adventures of Sadie (1953) 27
Alexander, Ruth *20*
Alien (1979) 222-23
Allan, Elizabeth 33, *33*
Allen, Bob 142
The Amazing Exploits of the Clutching Hand (1936) 76
Anouilh, Jean 26
Arkoff, Samuel Z. 16, 48, 70, 112, 132, 168, 177
Arlen, Richard 19, 26
Arliss, George 25, 203
Arthur, Colin 181
Ashley, Jennifer *215*, 218, *222*
Askwith, Robin 11-12, *11*, *164*, *166*, 170, 177, 178, 179, 180-81, 182, 183, 185, 187, *187*, 210
Assignment Redhead see *Million Dollar Manhunt*
Autry, Gene 74
Ayres, Robert 77
Balch, Antony 11, 146-50, 151-53, *153*, 154, 155-57, 169, 176-77, 180, 181-82, 183-85, 186, 187, 188-89, 215, 226
Balch, Delta 152-53, 157, 189
Banks, Leslie 116, 198
Barclay, George *see* Kinnoch, Ronald
Battle Beneath the Earth (1967) 20, 103
Baxt, George 161, 162, 163, 165
Beacham, Stephanie *215*
The Beast in the Cellar (1970) 169
The Bells (1926) 111
Benda, Kenneth 152, 156
Bendix, William 27
Benighted (novel) 26, 210
Bergner, Elisabeth 202
Berserk (1967) 162
Beyond the Blue Horizon (1942) 17
Beyond the Fog see *Tower of Evil*
Bierce, Ambrose 114
Bizarre see *Secrets of Sex*
The Black Castle (1952) 33
The Black Cat (1934) 26, 88
The Black Klansman (1966) 112
Blackman, Honor *195*, 205
Blakeley, Tom 131, 132, 133, 135, 139
Blood Beach (1980) 215
Blood from the Mummy's Tomb (1971) 165
Blue Denim (stage) 88-89
Bluebeard (stage) 106
The Body Snatcher (1945) 95
Bogdanovich, Peter 225-26
Bond, Sue 152
Boo (1932) 196

Booth, Karin 17
The Bounty Killer (1965) 19
Boyd, William 26
The Boys (1962) 104
Bracken, Eddie 20
Brasselle, Keefe 8, 18-19, 131
Briant, Shane 166
Bride of Frankenstein (1935) 32, 172
Browning, Tod 146
Bryan, Peter 132
Buchholz, Horst 199-200
Buck Rogers (1939) 49
Budrys, Algys 140
Burroughs, William 148-49, 156
Busman's Honeymoon (1940) 75
Byrne, Eddie 134
Cabaret (stage) 165
The Cabinet of Dr. Caligari (1919) 111
Caldwell, Gladys 195
Callan, Michael *195*, 199, 203, 205
Cameron, Rod 19
Canton, Arthur 38, 39
Carpenter, John *78*, 79
Carpenter, Paul 51
Carreras, Enrique 141, 142
Carreras, James 73, 86-87, 133, 141, 142, 165
Castle, William 210
Castle, Peggie 19
The Cat and the Canary (stage) 192, 193, 195-96, 197, 198
The Cat and the Canary (1927) 193-95, *193*, 196, 208
The Cat and the Canary (1939) 193, *194*, 195, 196, 198
The Cat and the Canary (1978) 163, 165, 188, 190-211, *194*, *195*, *197*, *199*, *201*, *202*, *204*, *206*, *207*
The Cat Creeps (1930) 196
Cavalcanti 110
Cave of the Living Dead (1964) 27
Chalmers, William G. *17*, 131
Champagne Charlie (1944) 107
Chaney, Lon 110
The Chinese Bungalow (stage) 106
Christian, Kurt *178*, 180, 185
Christie, Agatha 193, 198, 199, 200, 209
Christmas Carol A (1951) *15*, 27
Cilento, Diane 169
Cinema D'Aujourd'Hui (magazine) 188
Clarke, Robin *215*, 218, 220-21
Clemens, Brian 54, 67, 115
Cohen, Wolfe 223
Cohen, Herman 54, 161-62, 169, 177
Cohen, Nat 19

Colleano, Bonar 72, 79
Computer Killers see *Horror Hospital*
Confessions of a Window Cleaner (1974) 183
Connery, Sean 169
Conqueror Worm see *Witchfinder General*
Cool It Carol! (1970) 181
Cooper, John C. *see* Croydon, John
Corbett, Ray 188, 203-04, 206, 218, 221
Corman, Roger 17
The Corpse Grinders (1971) 186
The Corpse Vanishes (1942) 156
Corre, Sadie *106*, 109, 110, *111*, *114*
Corridors of Blood (1962) 20, 30-31, 33, 35, 61, 73, 77, 80-95, *83*, *85*, *86*, *87*, *89*, *92*, *94*, 103, 104, 142, 180
Coulouris, George 18, 20, 163, *164*
The Counterfeit Plan (1957) 19, 68, 92, 164, 188
Coward, Noël 207
Crabbe, Buster 49
Crabtree, Arthur 19, 54
Crawford, Joan 162, 164, 169
Crisp, Tracey *137*, 139
The Crooked Cross (proposed Gordon movie) 140
The Crooked Sky (1957) 17, 54
Croydon, John *28*, 29-30, 36-37, 38, 40, 53-54, 58, 70, 72, 84, 85, 86, 87, 90, 91, 103, 107, 110, 132, 135, 135-36
Currie, Finlay *86*, 87
The Curse of Frankenstein (1957) 86, 87, 141
The Curse of Simba see *Curse of the Voodoo*
Curse of the Fly (1965) 134
Curse of the Voodoo (1965) 54, 100-03, *102*, 104, 109, 114-18, *115*, *116*, *117*, 135, 139, 140, 164, 168
Curteis, Ian 135-36
Cushing, Peter 95, 133, *133*, 134-35, 139, 141
The Cut Ups (1966) 149, 157
Daktari (TV) 50
Dallas, Trixie 108
Daniely, Lisa *117*
Dante, Joe 47
Davis, Stratford *see* Sharman, Maisie
Dawson, Anthony 33, *34*
Day the World Ended (1956) 17
Day, Robert 35, 55, 70, 73, 90, 91
Day, Vera 20, 35
de Marney, Derrick 135
De Wolfe 154, 185
De Wolff, Francis 104, 109
Dead of Night (1945) 40, 86, 103, 109, 110, 111, 118
Death on the Nile (1978) 193, 208
Death Over My Shoulder (1958) 19
Delgado, Roger 79
Delon, Alain 148
Demons of the Mind (1972) 166
Denning, Richard 8, 17, *17*
The Desert Fox (1951) 27
The Devil Bat (1940) 147, 177
Devil Doll (1964) 54, 86, 94, 96-99, *99*, 103-14, *105*, *106*, *108*, *109*, *111*, *113*, *114*, 115, 116, 117, 118-19, 131, 135, 139, 164, 178, 209
"The Devil Doll " (story) 98-99, 103, 110, 111, 118-19
Devils of Darkness (1965) 131, 134
Dial M for Murder (stage) 33-34
Dickinson, Desmond 172
Diffring, Anton 17

Dignam, Basil 87, *130*
Doctor Blood's Coffin (1961) 104
Dr. No (1962) 34, 169
Domergue, Faith 19
Dorne, Sandra 108
Dracula (novel) 83, 84
Dracula (stage) 147-48
Dracula (1931) 25, 84
Dracula (1958) see *Horror of Dracula*
Dracula's Revenge (proposed Gordon-Karloff movie) 83-84, 198
Dummy (proposed Gordon movie) 114
The Dummy Talks (1943) 110
During One Night (1960) 104
Dyall, Valentine 141, 151, 153
The Dynamiters (1956) 17, 47
Eastwood, James 19
Ed Wood (1994) 90
Edwards, Hilton 225
Edwards, Bill *69*, 71-72, 73
Edwards, Mark 165, 166
Edwards, Meredith 19
Eldridge, Florence 195
The Electronic Monster (1958) 19-20, 35
Erhardt, Catharine 142
Escapement (novel) 19
Escapement (movie) see *The Electronic Monster*
Esper, Dwain 147
Evans, Edith 153
Evans, Maurice 33, 34
Evel Knievel (1972) 112
Exorcism at Midnight see *Naked Evil*
"The Facts in the Case of M. Valdemar" 84
Faithfull, Geoffrey 73
Famous Monsters of Filmland (magazine) 48
Fangoria (magazine) 32, 58, 69, 86, 90
Farr, Derek 135
Fernback, Gerald A. 19, 131, 133, 135, 137, 139, 140
Fiend Without a Face (1958) 20, 29, 30, 35-36, 38-39, *39*, 40, 42-62, *46*, *47*, *49*, *50*, *52*, *53*, *59*, *60*, 67, 68, 69, 70, 71, 72, 77, 83, 85, 91, 95, 108, 135, 227
The Fighting Wildcats (1957) 19, 54, 131
First Man Into Space (1959) 20, 30, 35, 47, 50, 51, 54, 61, 64-79, *68*, *69*, *71*, *72*, *73*, *74*, *75*, *76*, *77*, 83, 85, 91, 92, 95, 169
Fisher, Terence 17, 133, 134, 135, 138, 139, 141
Flash Gordon (1936) 49
The Fog (1980) 172
Ford, Ruth 19, 88
Fox, Edward 203, 205
Francis, Kay 26
Frankenstein (1931) 25-26, 87, 90
Frankenstein 1970 (1958) 88
Frankenstein Meets the Spacemonster (1965) 117
Fraser, Brendan *57*
Freaks (1932) 146-47
Frost, Maria 152
The Frozen Dead (1967) 48
Furie, Sidney 104, 105, 117
Geeson *215*, *216*, *217*, *219*, 220, 223
The Gelignite Gang see *The Dynamiters*
Gélin, Daniel 105
The Ghoul (novel) 86
The Ghoul (1933) 30, 86, 90, 198

The Ghoul (proposed Gordon movie) 86, 198
Gigi (1958) 39
Glen or Glenda (1953) 156
Glendenning, Candace 169
Goddard, Paulette *194*
Goldman, William 114
Goldstein, Al 155
Gone with the Wind (1939) 75
Gordon, Alex 7, *7*, 15, 16, 17, 19, *20*, 25, 26, 33, 48, 50, 67-68, 70, 74, 75, 76, 77, *78*, 79, 86, 95, 131-32, 141, 147, 177, 211
Gough, Michael 151, *176*, 177, 182, 183, 187, 189
Goulder, Stanley 140
Grace, Martin 182
Grahame, Margot 196-97
Graves, Thelma 177, 179, 180, 185
Gray, Carole 134, *142*
The Great Gabbo (1929) 110
The Green Helmet (1961) 20, 103
The Green Man (1956) 73
Green, Nigel 87
Grip of the Strangler see *The Haunted Strangler*
Guest, Val 140, 183
Gysin, Brion 149
Hair (stage) 166, 167
Haliday, Bryant *102*, 104-05, *105*, 107 *108*, 109, *109*, 110, *111*, *113*, 114, 115-16, *116*, 117-18, *126*, *127*, 135, *137*, *138*, 139, 140, 164-65, 198
Hamill, John *160*, 169, 170
Hamilton, Gary 166, 167, 169
Hardy, Lindsay 17
Hargreaves, Lance Z. *see* Vetter, Charles Jr.
Harris, Julie 26
Harvey, Cy 105
The Haunted Strangler (1958) 7, 15, 20, 22-40, *24*, *29*, *31*, *32*, *33*, *35*, *36*, *37*, *38*, *39*, *40*, 47, 48, 49, 51, 54, 55, 59, 69, 72, 73, 77, 83, 85, 88, 90, 91, 93, 95, 108, 198
Haworth, Jill 165, *166*, *173*
Häxan (1922) 149
Hayers, Sidney 161
Heflin, Van 27
Hell's Angels on Wheels (1967) 112
Henson, Leslie 167
Henson, Nicky 166-67
Herbert, George 151-52
Heyward, Louis M. 162
Hiller, Wendy *195*, *199*, 200, *201*, 202, 203, 205, 206-07, 208, 209, 210, 211
Homolka, Oscar 26
Hope, Bob 193, 195, 196, 198
Horror Hospital (1973) 11, 12, 107, 116, 151, 153, 154, 155, 156, 157, 169, 170, 174-89 *176*, *178*, *179*, *182*, *184*, *186*, *187*, *188*, 210, 226
Horror of Dracula (1958) 84, 198
Horror on Snape Island see *Tower of Evil*
Horror Planet see *Inseminoid*
Horrors of the Black Museum (1959) 54
The Hound of the Baskervilles (1959) 73
The House of Rothschild (1934) 25, *25*
Housemaster (1938) 53
Howard, Trevor 27
Hull, Henry 195
Hussey, Olivia *195*, 203, 205
Hussong, Robert G. 218
Hyams, Phil 29
Hyams, Syd 29
Hyde-White, Wilfrid 201-02, 203, 205, 207, 209
Hyman, Eliot 141
If.... (1968) 170, 181
Illing, Peter 19
Inseminoid (1981) 89, 108, 188, 189, 210, 212-227, *215*, *216*, *217*, *219*, *221*, *222*, *223*, *224*
The Invisible Ray (1936) 25, 26
Island of Terror (1966) 57, 95, 120-23, *122*, *123*, 131, 132-35, *132*, *133*, 137-38, 139, 140-41, *142*, 146
Island of the Burning Damned see *Night of the Big Heat*
It Came from Hollywood (1982) 47
It! (1967) 48
Jaffe, Carl 19
Johns, Mervyn 19
Jones, Disley 162, 170
Judd, Edward 134, 135
Juliette de Sade (1969) 148
Jurgens, Curt 27
Jusqu'à plus soif (1962) 105
Just Imagine (1930) 49
Kalmenson, Ben 19
Karloff, Boris 7, 15, *24*, 25-26, *25*, 26, *27*, 28, 29, 30, *31*, 32-34, *32*, *35*, *36*, 37, 39, 40, *40*, 47, 48, 51-52, 55, 61, 68, 73, 77, 83, *83*, 84, 85, 86, 87, 88, 89, *89*, 90, 91, 92, *92*, 93, *94*, 95 111, 139, 140, 142, 198
Karloff, Evelyn 15, 30, 90, 93
Kent, Jean *31*, 34
Kilburn, Terence 50, 51
Kill Me Tomorrow (1957) 17-18, *18*, 73, 134, 163
King, Frank 86
Kinnoch, Ronald 54, *67*, 103
Klinger, Michael 132, 135
Korda, Alexander 139
Landau, Martin 89-90
Landi, Marla *72*, 73, *73*
Lang, Fritz 49, 74
The Lark (stage) 26
The Last Gentleman (1934), 203
Law, Pamela 108
The Lawless Rider (1954) *78*, 79
Leder, Herbert J. 48, 49
Lee, Christopher 84, 86-87, *94*, 95, 139, 142
Lehmann, Beatrix *195*, *199*, 202-03, 206, 207
Leni, Paul 196
Lennon, John 88
Levine, Joseph E. 114
Levinson, Barry 140
The Linden Tree 15, 26
"Lindy Leigh" (comic strip) 152
Lloyd of the C.I.D. (1932) 172
Loder, John 67
The Lodger (1932) 33, 53
London Mystery Magazine (magazine) *98*, 103, 118
Long, Amelia Reynolds 44-45, 54-55
Looney Tunes: Back in Action (2003) 57
Lucan, Arthur *16*
Lucas, Tim 7
Luckwell, Bill 17, 18
Lugosi, Bela 26, 31, 33, 84, 88, 89-90, 109, 139, 147-48, 177
Lycanthropus see *Werewolf in a Girls' Dormitory*
Lynley, Carol 89, *194*, *195*, 199, 203, *204*, 205, 206
MacGinnis, Niall 134

Magic (novel) 114
Magic (1978 movie) 114
Maine, Charles Eric 19
Maley, Nick 216, 221-22, 227
Maley, Gloria *see* Walker, Gloria
The Man and the Snake (1972) 112
Man in the Shadow see Violent Stranger
The Man with Nine Lives (1940) 83
Manderson, Tommy 207
Mann, Edward Andrew 131
Margulies, Irwin 91, 103
Mark of the Vampire (1935) 33, 111
Martin, Skip 179-80
Martin, "Hi" 136-38, 139
Martin, Skip *179*
The Mask of Fu Manchu (1932) 88
Mason, James 200
Massey, Daniel *195*, 200, 206, *206*, 207, *207*, 210
Massey, Raymond 207, 210
Mathews, Carole 17, *17*
Matthews, Francis 85, 86, *89*, *92*
Maugham, Robin 27
Maxwell, Lois 18
McBride, Mark 170, 171
McEnery, Peter *195*, 200, 206-07, *207*
Melniker, Ben 54
Metropolis (1927) 49
Metzger, Radley 163, 196, 197, *197*, 198, 201, 202, 203, 204, 205, 206, *206*, 208-09, 210
Michel, Jean-Claude 188
Mikels, Ted V. 112, 186
Million Dollar Manhunt (1956) 17, *17*
Minter, George 17, 18, 27
Moffat, William 141
Moore, Kieron 104
Morley, Robert 201
Morris, Chester 26
Morris, Wayne 8, 17, 47
The Most Dangerous Game (1932) 116
The Most Dangerous Game (1932) 198
The Most Dangerous Game (proposed Gordon-Bryant Haliday movie) 116
Mother Riley Meets the Vampire (1952) *16*, 31
The Murder in the Red Barn (stage) 106
Murder on the Orient Express (1974) 193
Murphy, Mary 19
My Son, the Vampire see Mother Riley Meets the Vampire
Myers, Peter 140
Mystery of the Wax Museum (1933) 181, 189
Nagy, Bill *74*
Naked Evil (1966) 87, 128-31, *130*, 139-40, 141, 142
Naked Lunch (novel) 148, 156
Napier, Alan 34
Neff, Hildegarde 27
Nesbitt, Cathleen 202
Nicholas and Alexandra (1971) 169
Nicholson, Jack 112
Nicholson, James H. 16, 48, 70, 112, 131-32, 168, 177
Night of the Big Heat (novel) 139
Night of the Big Heat (1967) 139
No Blade of Grass (both 1970) 169
Noble, Peter 169
Nordhoff, Flo 58

Nugent, Elliott 196
The Obi (TV) 139
O'Brien, Pat 8, 17-18, *18*, 134
O'Connolly, Jim 162, 163, 165, 166, 167-68, *167*, 169, 170, 171
O'Grady, Tony *see* Brian Clemens
The Old Dark House (1932) 26, 40, 171-72, 181, 210
The Old Dark House (1963) 210
The Omen (1976) 203
Ordung, Wyott 68, 69, 70, 71
Orr, Buxton 72
Orson Welles' Ghost Story see Return to Glennascaul
Othello (1952) 226
Our Girl Friday see The Adventures of Sadie
Palk, Anna *166*, 167
Pallos, Steven 139, 140
Parker, Kim *49*, 50, 51-52, *52*, 108
Patterson, Lee 19, 164-65
Peach, Mary 135, 139
Pellatt, John 162, 172
Percy, Edward 15
Perrins, Leslie 33
Pettingell, Frank 87, *87*
Phantom of the Paradise (1974) 182
Phillips, Jack *17*
The Playgirls and the Vampire (1960) 27, 112
Poe, Edgar Allan 84
Pollock, Ellen 107, 180, *182*, *184*
Pratt, Anthony 209
Preminger, Otto 27
Price, Dennis 116, *117*, 168-69, 178, *186*
Price, Stanley 114
Price, Vincent 135
Priestley, J.B. 15, 26, 210
The Projected Man (1966) 54, 95, 107, 109, 115, 116, *123*, 124-27, *126*, *127*, 131-33, 134, 135-36, *136*, 137, *137*, *138*, 138-39, 140-41, 142, 146, 164
Psycho (1960) 172, 181
Psycho (1998) 61
Quattrocchi, Frank 132
Ramsen, Allan 131, 139
Rathbone, Basil *15*
The Raven (1935) 26, 147
Read, Jan 15, 28, 30, 33, 37, 85
Reeves, Kynaston 50, 52-53
Reeves, Michael 140, 157
Règlements de comptes (1963) 105
Requiem for a Gunfighter (1965) 19
Requiem for a Redhead (novel) 17
The Return (1973) 114
Return to Glennascaul (1953) 225-26
Richard, Cliff 104
Rive, Kenneth 103-04, 105, 107, 109, 112, 114, 115, 116, 117, *117*, 209
Robson, Flora 202
The Rocky Horror Picture Show (1975) 182
Rogers, Jean Scott 84, 85
Rohauer, Raymond 140, 196, 198, 210
Romain, Yvonne 86, 104
Room to Let (1950) 141
Rosemary's Baby (1968) 88
Rosenberg, Max J. 161, 171
Shaw, Run Run *see* The Shaw Brothers
Shaw, Runme *see* The Shaw Brothers

Ruppel, K.L. 58, 71
Rydman, Sture 112-14
S.O.S. Eisberg (1933) 28
Sangster, Jimmy 139
Schlesinger, Peter 215, *215*, 216, 218, 219, 220-21, 223
Schulman, Richard 151
Schwartz, Fred 93
Scott, Zachary 8, 19, 55, 68, 88, 188
Scrooge see *A Christmas Carol*
The Secret Man (1958) 7, 20, 50, 54, 67, *67*, 73, 78-79
Secrets of Sex (1970) 144-57, 149, 156, 177, 183-85, 189
Sharman, Maisie 19
The Shaw Brothers 215-16, 218, 219-20, 223, 224
Shaw, Harold 218, 220, 223, 224
Shaw, George Bernard 180
Shaw, Phoebe *see* Shaw, Vanessa
Shaw, Rose Tobias 163-64, 165, 166, 169, 200, 201, 202, 219
Shaw, Vanessa 178-79, 180
Shaye, Bob 154-55
The She-Beast (1965) 140
Sherman, Sam 142, 172
Shock Waves (1977) 134
Shonteff, Lindsay 104, 105, 115, 117, *117*
The Shop at Sly Corner (stage) 15, 26
Silent Playground (1963) 140
Sim, Alastair 201
Simba (1928) 74
Siodmak, Robert 27
Slaughter, Tod 106-07, 180
Small Soldiers (1998) 47
Smith, Frederick E. 98, 103, 110, 111, 112, 118-19
The Snake Woman (1961) 104
Solomon, Joe 112, 116, 161, 162, 167, 168, 172
Solway, Jerry 112
The Sorcerers (1967) 140
Speaking, Colin 182
Speechley, David 221
Star! (1968) 207
Steele, Tommy 18
Stein, Elliott 152, 153
Stepanek, Karel 104, 109
Stone, Marianne 169
The Story of Esther Costello (1957) 164
The Strange Door (1951) 33
Subotsky, Milton 171
Susskind, David 163
Sutro, John 27
Svengali (1954) 27
Sweeney Todd, the Demon Barber of Fleet Street (stage) 106
Sylvester, William 104, 109
Tales of the Bizarre see *Secrets of Sex*
Tennant, Victoria 219, *221*
Tenser, Tony 132, 135
The Testament of Dr. Mabuse (1933) 74
Des Teufels General (1955) 27
Des Teufels General (play) 27-28
Thompson, Marshall 30, 50, *50*, 51, 61, 67-68, *67*, *68*, 73, 77, 78, 169
Thomson, Alex 209
"The Thought-Monster" 44-45, 48-49, *54-55*, 58
Tierney, Lawrence 142
The Tingler (1959) 181
Tom Brown's Schooldays (1951) 27

Tomb of Torture (1963) 27
Tower of Evil (1972) 11, 108, 116, 117, 155, 158-73, *160*, *161*, *163*, *164*, *166*, *167*, *168*, *170*, *171*, *172*, *173*, 177, 181
Towers Open Fire (1963) 149, 157
Traitement de choc (1973) 148
Trevelyan, John 152
Trog (1970) 169
Tully, Montgomery 19
Udet, Ernst 27-28
The Unholy Three 1925 110
The Unholy Three 1930 110
Valentine, Anthony 169
Verbrechen nach Schulschluß (1959) 197
Vetter, Charles Jr. 7, 16, 17, *18*, 20, 29, 47, 48, 49, 53, 54, 59, *67*, 70, 71, 77, 91, 103
Video Watchdog (magazine) 7
Vidor, Charles 27
Violent Stranger (1957) 19, 68, 188
La voluntad del muerto (1930) 196
von Stroheim, Erich 110
Voodoo Island (1957) 88
Voodoo Man (1944) 156
Vosper, Frank 28-29
Vosper, Margery 28-29
Walker, Gloria 216, 221-22, 227
The Walking Dead (1936) 26
Warren, Norman J. 215, *215*, 218, 219, 220, 222, 223, *226*, 226-27
Watson, Alan 177, 187
Watson, Jack 163, 165
Weird Tales (magazine) *44*, 44-45, 48, 54
Welles, Orson 163, 225, 226
Wells, Horace *84*
Wendy, Barbara *178*, *184*
Werewolf in a Girls' Dormitory (1963) 93, 94
West of Suez (1957) 18-19, 54
West, Norma 135, *136*
Whale, James 26, 90, 171, 181
What a Carve Up! aka *No Place Like Homicide!*, 1961). 86
White Corridors (1951) 85
White, Jon Manchip 139
Who Slew Auntie Roo? (1972) 162
Who? (1973) 140
Who? (novel) 140
Wiederhorn, Ken 134, 216
Wildcat (1942) 19
Wilder, Billy 27
Willard, John 192, 195
Williams, John 33
Wills, Brember 40, 171
Willy Wonka and the Chocolate Factory (1971) 179
Wilson, Serretta *161*, *163*, 169
Winters, Shelley 162
Winton, Sheree *71*, *74*
Witchcraft Through the Ages see *Häxan*
Witchfinder General (1968) 135, 157, 167
Womaneater (1958) 20, 35
The Woman in Question (1950) 34
The Woman in White (stage) 180
Wood, Edward D. Jr. 79
Wooland, Norman 135, *138*
Zuckmayer, Carl 27

Bear Manor Media

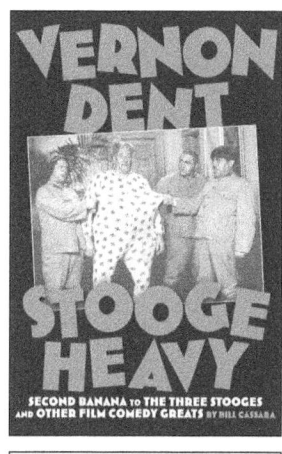
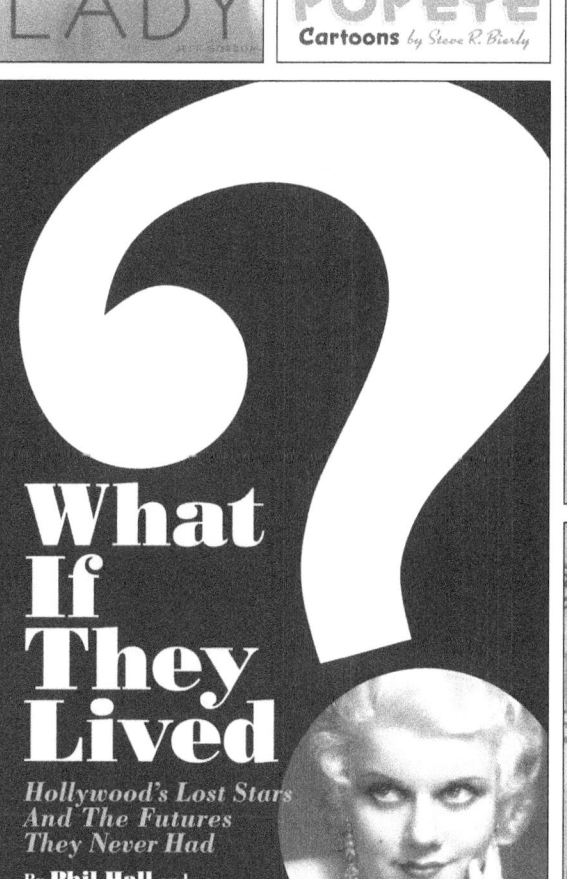

Classic Cinema.
Timeless TV.
Retro Radio.

WWW.BEARMANORMEDIA.COM

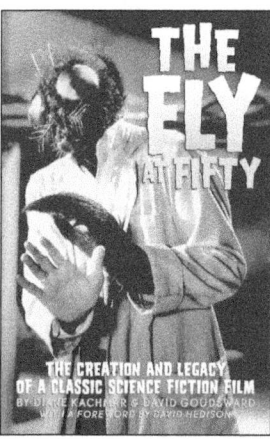

www.ingramcontent.com/pod-product-compliance
Lightning Source LLC
Chambersburg PA
CBHW081147230426
43664CB00018B/2832